Trade Politics

GW00578110

Trade has always been an intensely political activity. Its conduct determines the well-being of entire national communities, and expansion of trade since the Second World War has been one of the major engines of world economic growth.

In this new, fully updated edition of *Trade Politics* leading experts from Europe, North and South America, Africa and the Asia-Pacific region provide a comprehensive overview of the politics of international trade in the twenty-first century. The book explains the changing political environment in which trade policy is shaped, the core political issues, the future trade agenda and the role of the key actors. Subjects covered include:

- transatlantic trade relations;
- regional trading agreements in Asia, Europe, North America and Latin America;
- how trade affects developing countries;
- the politics of the World Trade Organization;
- key policy areas such as agriculture, competition and intellectual property;
- the role of firms and governments in international trade;
- how trade impacts on human rights and the environment.

With more case studies in each chapter, suggestions for further reading, lists of websites and chapter summaries, this is the ideal text for students of trade politics, international political economy and international business.

Brian Hocking is Professor of International Relations at Coventry University.

Steven McGuire is Senior Lecturer in the School of Management at the University of Bath.

Trade Politics

Second edition

Edited by Brian Hocking
and Steven McGuire

Routledge
Taylor & Francis Group

LONDON AND NEW YORK

First published in 1999 by Routledge
Second edition first published in 2004
by Routledge
2 Park Square, Milton Park, Abingdon, Oxon, OX14 4RN

Simultaneously published in the USA and Canada
by Routledge
270 Madison Ave, New York NY 10016

Routledge is an imprint of the Taylor & Francis Group

Transferred to Digital Printing 2007

Typeset in Baskerville by
Taylor & Francis Books Ltd

British Library Cataloguing in Publication Data
A catalogue record for this book is available from the British Library

Library of Congress Cataloging in Publication Data
A catalog record for this title has been requested

ISBN 0–415–31016–4 (hbk)
ISBN 0–415–31017–2 (pbk)

Contents

Illustrations

Tables

Figures

Boxes

Contributors

David N. Balaam is Professor of Politics, Government and International Political Economy at the University of Puget Sound in Tacoma, Washington, USA.

Bijit Bora is a counsellor in the Economic Research and Statistics Division, World Trade Organization, Geneva, Switzerland

Duncan Brack is Head of the Sustainable Development Programme at the Royal Institute of International Affairs, London, UK

Ann Capling is Associate Professor in Political Science, Department of Political Science, University of Melbourne, Australia.

Andrew F. Cooper is Professor, Department of Political Science and Associate Director, Centre for International Governance Innovation, University of Waterloo, Ontario, Canada.

Chad Damro is Lecturer in Politics, School of Social and Political Studies, University of Edinburgh, UK.

Robert Falkner is Lecturer in International Relations at the London School of Economics and Associate Fellow of the Sustainable Development Programme at the Royal Institute of International Affairs, London, UK.

Brian Hocking is Professor of International Relations, Coventry Business School, Coventry University, UK.

Donna Lee is Lecturer in International Organisations and Economic Diplomacy, Department of Political Science and International Studies, University of Birmingham, UK.

Gijsbert van Liemt is a self-employed international economist based in the Netherlands.

Steven McGuire is Senior Lecturer in International Business, School of Management, University of Bath, UK.

Bruce E. Moon is Professor of International Relations, Department of International Relations, Lehigh University, Bethlehem, Pennsylvania, USA.

Amrita Narlikar is Lecturer in International Relations, Department of Politics, University of Exeter, UK.

John Peterson is Jean Monnet Professor of European Politics, Department of Politics, University of Glasgow, UK.

Geoffrey Allen Pigman is Lecturer in International Relations, University of Kent, Brussels School of International Studies, and Fellow, Center for Global Change and Governance, State University of New Jersey – Rutgers (Newark), USA.

John Ravenhill is Professor of Politics, School of Social and Political Studies, University of Edinburgh, UK.

Razeen Sally is Senior Lecturer in International Political Economy at the London School of Economics and Director, Trade Policy, at the Commonwealth Business Council, London.

Jan Aart Scholte is Professor in the Department of Politics and International Studies and Acting Director of the Centre for the Study of Globalisation and Regionalisation at the University of Warwick, UK.

Timothy M. Shaw is Professor of Commonwealth Governance & Development in the School of Advanced Study at the University of London and Director, Institute of Commonwealth Studies, London, UK.

Michael Smith is Jean Monnet Professor of European Politics, Department of European and International Studies, Loughborough University, UK.

Janis van der Westhuizen is Senior Lecturer, Department of Political Science, University of Stellenbosch, South Africa.

Paulo S. Wrobel is Adviser of Science and Technology at the Brazilian Embassy in London.

Preface

Almost five years have elapsed since we put the finishing touches to the manuscript of the first edition of *Trade Politics*. We argued then that trade-related issues appeared to be assuming an increasingly prominent place on both the international and domestic political agendas. In part, this is due to the changing character of international trade as an activity and the impact that 'behind the border' issues pose for societies and their governments. Trade now impacts on people's lives in ways that it did not forty years ago. However, we did not anticipate quite how dramatically international trade and the institutions associated with it, particularly the WTO, would grab the headlines through events such as the riots accompanying the WTO ministerial summit held in Seattle in December 1999 and the apparent triumph of anti-trade non-governmental associations in defeating the Multilateral Agreement on Investment. Since then, free trade and its institutions have become key foci for the activities of anti-globalisation groups. In addition, the traditional dominance of the trade agenda by the USA and EU continues to erode, as emerging players like China and India assert their claim to be taken seriously in matters of international economic governance. But if these events represent a challenge to the consensus after the Second World War in favour of free trade, then an even more dramatic one was to hove into sight in the form of 11 September 2001. A sudden rewriting of the military security script of world politics has brought with it a potential new threat as governments themselves have come to examine the costs as well as the advantages of globalisation. Suddenly, an older set of issues (familiar from the Cold War era), in which the demands of free trade confronted those of security, has appeared. Nevertheless, in December 2001, a new round of trade negotiations was launched in Doha but, significantly, with an avowed 'development' agenda.

But as with the first edition, the aim of this new edition is not simply to focus on dramatic change. Rather, it is to balance the interaction between the forces of change and continuity in this area of the policy agenda. Thus, as five years ago, we see the trade agenda configured by an interaction between the new and the old agendas. As we write, in the run-up to the Cancún summit, traditional issues represented by agriculture mix with the new in the form of intellectual property, specifically the problem of drugs patents and the access by the developing countries to generic drugs. In general terms, we believe that the broad images determining trade politics conveyed in the first edition are relevant five years later, despite the dramatic changes in world politics. These embrace a gradual erosion of boundaries marking off significant aspects of the policy processes as a result of issue-linkage, the growing patterns of interaction between governmental and non-governmental actors, and the visible intermeshing of subnational, national and international political arenas in ways that erode traditional assumptions as to the points of interaction between them. Taken together, these developments have produced a much more intricately textured, multilayered environment for trade politics within which distinctions between domestic and international policy processes have become increasingly eroded.

As before, the core aim of the book remains to explore the parameters of change and continuity in trade politics by bringing together an international group of scholars and policy practitioners. However, following advice gained from contributors, colleagues, reviewers and – most critically – our students, we have restructured the book, partly to reflect developments referred to above and partly to make the book more useful to those teaching and studying what appear to be a growing number of courses focusing on trade. Keen-eyed readers of both editions will see that the WTO now has its own part, reflecting the centrality it has assumed in the emerging debate on trade politics. Apart from this, the three parts on environments, agendas, and actors and processes remain. However, we have restructured them in the light of comments and advice. One of the difficulties in this kind of exercise is to decide what to include and what to omit. And the second edition of a text always presents hard decisions. Some excellent chapters in the first edition are no longer here, either because authors were no longer able to provide updated versions or because we felt that other issues needed to be covered and space prevented us including everything.

As is usually the case with edited volumes, we have confronted a number of problems, but have managed to adhere to our schedule. This would not have been possible without the assistance of various people. Our academic colleagues Donna Lee, Thomas Lawton, John Ravenhill and Routledge's referees offered useful comments on the early outline of the second edition. Several University of Bath students – particularly Jesper Ekelund, Mark Rogers and Mark Sugden – offered valuable thoughts on both content and layout. Ed Watkins designed the cover, skilfully navigating conflicting aesthetic demands in doing so. We also wish to thank members of the Routledge editorial staff, particularly Craig Fowlie and Zoe Botterill, for their advice and support. However, amongst those who helped shape this volume, special thanks go to our editorial assistant, Chris Nicoll, whose contribution in processing the manuscript cannot be exaggerated. Finally, to repeat the final sentence of the preface to the first edition, we owe a great debt of gratitude to our families for their support and understanding in yet another project which impinged on time that is as much theirs as ours.

Brian Hocking and Steven McGuire
July 2003

Abbreviations

ACP	African, Caribbean and Pacific
ADDs	Anti-Dumping Duties
AFTA	ASEAN Free Trade Area
AGOA	African Growth and Opportunity Act
AGP	Agreement on Government Procurement
AIA	Advance Informed Agreement
AIDS	Acquired Immune Deficiency Syndrome
AMS	Aggregate Measurement of Support
AoA	Agreement on Agriculture (Uruguay Round)
APEC	Asia-Pacific Economic Cooperation
APHIS	Animal and Plant Health Inspection Service
ASCM	Agreement on Subsidies and Countervailing Measures
ASEAN	Association of South-East Asian Nations
ASEM	Asia–Europe Meeting
AU	African Union
BEMs	Big Emerging Markets
BGMEA	Bangladesh Garment Manufacturers and Exporters Association
BIT	Bilateral Investment Treaty
BOP	Balance of Payment
CAP	Common Agricultural Policy
CARICOM	Caribbean Community and Common Market
CBD	Convention on Biological Diversity
CBI	Cross-Border Initiative
CEC	Commission for Environmental Cooperation
CEEC	Central and East European Countries
CFCs	Chlorofluorocarbons
CIEL	Centre for International Environmental Law
CKD	Completely Knocked-Down
COCOM	Coordinating Committee
COMESA	Common Market of Eastern and Southern Africa
CSOs	Civil Society Organisations
CTE	Committee on Trade and Environment
CUTS	Consumer Unity and Trust Society (India)
CVD	Countervailing Duty
DDA	Doha Development Agenda
DFAIT	Canadian Department of Foreign Affairs and International Trade
DSB	Dispute Settlement Body (WTO)

DSU	Dispute Settlement Understanding (WTO)
EAI	Enterprise for the Americas Initiative
EC	European Community
ECA	Economic Commission for Africa
ECLAC	Economic Commission for Latin America and the Caribbean
ECOWAS	Economic Community of West African States
ECSC	European Coal and Steel Community
ECU	European Currency Unit
EEC	European Economic Community
EFTA	European Free Trade Area/Agreement
EMIT	Environmental Measures and International Trade
EMU	European Monetary Union
EP	European Parliament
EPA	Environmental Protection Agency
EU	European Union
Euratom	European Atomic Energy Community
FAO	Food and Agricultural Organization
FDA	Food and Drugs Administration
FDI	Foreign Direct Investment
FSC	Foreign Sales Corporations
FTA	Free Trade Agreement/Area/Association
FTAA	Free Trade Area of the Americas
GATS	General Agreement on Trade in Services
GATT	General Agreement on Tariffs and Trade
GCA	Global Coalition for Africa
GCF	Global Competition Forum
GDP	Gross Domestic Product
G-22	Group of Twenty-Two
GM	Genetically Modified
GMOs	Genetically Modified Organisms
GSP	Generalized System of Preferences
HIPC	Heavily Indebted Poor Countries Initiative (now SAP)
HIV	Human Immunodeficiency Virus
HOD	Heads of Delegations (WTO)
IBASE	Brazilian Institute for Social and Economic Analysis (Rio de Janeiro)
ICC	International Chamber of Commerce
ICFTU	International Confederation of Free Trade Unions
ICN	International Competition Network
ICPAC	International Competition Policy Advisory Committee
ICTSD	International Centre for Trade and Sustainable Development
IDB	Inter-American Development Bank
IDC	South African Industrial Development Corporation
IISD	International Institute for Sustainable Development
ILO	International Labour Organization
IMF	International Monetary Fund
IOCU	International Organization of Consumer Unions
IP	Intellectual Property
IPC	Intellectual Property Committee

IPE	International Political Economy
IPEC	International Programme on the Elimination of Child Labour
IPRs	Intellectual Property Rights
ISA	International Strategic Alliance
ISACs	Industry and Sector Advisory Committees
ISO	International Organization for Standardization
ITA	International Trade Administration
ITC	International Trade Commission
ITCB	International Bureau on Textiles and Clothing
ITO	International Trade Organization
ITSs	International Trade Secretariats
IUCN	International Union for Conservation of Nature or World Conservation Union
LDCs	Less Developed Countries
MAI	Multilateral Agreement on Investment
MDGs	Millennium Development Goals
MEAs	Multilateral Environmental Agreements
Mercosur	The Common Market of the South
METI	Japan's Ministry of Economy, Trade and Industry
MFA	Multi-Fibre Arrangement
MFN	Most Favoured Nation
MNC	Multinational Corporation
MNE	Multinational Enterprise
MRA	Mutual Recognition Agreement
MTN	Multilateral Trade Negotiation
MWENGO	Mwelekeo wa NGO (Reflection and Development Centre in Eastern and Southern Africa)
NAFTA	North America Free Trade Agreement
NAOs	National Administrative Offices
NATO	North Atlantic Treaty Organization
NEC	National Economic Council
NEPAD	The New Partnership for Africa's Development
NGLS	UN Non-Governmental Liaison Service
NGO	Non-Governmental Organisation
NICs	Newly Industrialised Countries
NSC	National Security Council
NSI	North–South Institute (Ottawa)
NTA	New Transatlantic Agenda
NTB	Non-Tariff Barrier
OAS	Organization of American States
OAU	Organisation for African Unity
ODA	Official Development Assistance
OECD	Organization for Economic Cooperation and Development
OEEC	Organisation for European Economic Cooperation
PAN	National Action Party
PGA	Peoples' Global Action against 'Free' Trade and the World Trade Organization
PPMs	Process and Production Methods

PRI	Institutional Revolutionary Party (Mexico)
PRSPs	Poverty Reduction Strategy Programmes or Papers
PTAs	Preferential Trade Agreements
QRs	Quantitative Restrictions
RandD	Research and Development
RTAs	Regional Trade Agreements
RTAA	Reciprocal Trade Agreements Act
SAA	South African Airways
SAARC	South Asian Association for Regional Cooperation
SACU	Southern African Customs Union
SADC	South African Development Community
SAL	Structural Adjustment Loan
SAP	Structural Adjustment Policy/Programme
SARS	Severe Acute Respiratory Syndrome
SDT	Special and Differential Treatment
SEA	Single European Act
SEM	Single European Market
SME	Small- and Medium-sized Enterprise
SMP	Single Market Programme
SPS	Sanitary and Phytosanitary (SPS) Agreement
SSA	Sub-Saharan Africa
TABD	Transatlantic Business Dialogue
TAFTA	Transatlantic Free Trade Area
TBT	Technical Barriers to Trade (TBT) Agreement
TICAD	Tokyo International Conference on African Development
TNCs	Transnational Corporations
TPA	Trade Promotion Authority
TPRM	Trade Policies Review Mechanism (of the WTO)
TRIMs	Trade-Related Investment Measures
TRIPs	Trade-Related Aspects of Intellectual Property Rights
TRQ	Tariff-Rate Quota
UCC	Universal Copyright Convention
UK	United Kingdom
UN	United Nations
UNCED	United Nations Conference on Environment and Development
UNCTAD	United Nations Conference on Trade and Development
UNECA	United Nations Economic Commission for Africa
UNEP	United Nations Environment Programme
UNESCO	United Nations Educational, Scientific and Cultural Organisation
UNICEF	United Nations International Children's Emergency Fund
US	United States
USA	United States of America
USAID	United States Agency for International Development
USSR	Union of Soviet Socialist Republics
USTR	Office of the United States Trade Representative
WCL	World Confederation of Labour
WEDO	Women's Environment and Development Organization (New York)
WEF	World Economic Forum

WIDE	Women in Development Europe (Brussels)
WIPO	World Intellectual Property Organization
WTO	World Trade Organization
WWF	World Wide Fund for Nature

Introduction

Trade politics: environments, agendas and processes

Brian Hocking and Steven McGuire

Trade, together with war, constitutes one of the oldest modes of international communication and affects the well-being of an ever-larger segment of the world's population. Because of this, it has always been a central issue in national, regional and international politics, reflecting the fact that policy decisions regarding, for example, levels of tariffs at national borders, have differential effects on groups within and outside national communities. Whilst fashioning trade policy has never been easy, it has become immensely more difficult over the last few years. What we have witnessed since the mid-1990s is the interaction of old and new modes of trade politics reflecting an evolving trade agenda and changing configurations of political forces. Indeed, surprising things have happened to the world inhabited by trade diplomats. From operating in a relatively closed arena characterised by the arcane formulae of tariff negotiations, suddenly, as at the Seattle World Trade Organization ministerial meeting in December 1999, they have been initiated into the world of public protest, tear gas and violence on the streets. Underpinning this, of course, lie the tensions created by globalisation, of which trade constitutes a key component. And here, the debates over the merits and demerits of this contested concept have been further clouded by the consequences of 11 September 2001. Suddenly, assumptions concerning the inevitability of growing international interdependence have been torn asunder by the impact of the 'new' security agenda and the fears that terrorism, and the responses to it, might halt what had hitherto appeared – to some at least – as an irreversible process, with disastrous consequences for world trade. This book seeks to shed light on what are proving to be these increasingly complex and highly significant issues.

When one of the seminal works on trade politics – Schattschneider's study of the passing of the 1930 Smoot–Hawley Tariff by the US Congress – was published in the mid-1930s, its focus was on the ways in which protectionist interests succeeded in capturing Congress (Schattschneider 1935). Since then, however, the sites of political contestation built around the trade agenda have vastly increased. Certainly, the historic free trade–protectionist arguments have lost none of their thrust. But enhanced interdependence and globalisation have reinforced them as across the world, groups of workers find themselves lashed by the storms of economic and social change. The language and context may have changed: 'fair trade' arguments now confront the free trade case but the essential debate about the benefits and disbenefits of opening up versus restricting access to markets remains (Lang and Hines 1993).

Nevertheless, as elsewhere, the US trade agenda has moved on during the half-century since Schattschneider's book was published. Now, the waters of trade politics swirl around new rocks. It is not simply, as various chapters in this book demonstrate, that the nature of what is being traded has changed. Certainly, against the continuing arguments about agriculture, with its own constellation of forces as illustrated in Balaam's chapter (11), the rise of services – telecommunications and financial services, for example – generates new concerns. But understanding the politics surrounding the creation and development of the North American Free Trade Agreement (see Cooper, Chapter 4), to take but one instance, leads us beyond the arguments deployed by various business interests and into the politics of human rights, the environment and the respective powers of federal and state governments in a globalising economy. We only have to look at the current list of trade disputes to see how traditional issues are interwoven with these new concerns as discussed by van Liemt (human rights and labour standards, Chapter 16) and Brack (environmental issues, Chapter 15) to produce a complex political agenda in the trade sphere:

- The increasingly bitter dispute between the USA and the European Union (EU) over the latter's ban on the import of genetically modified foodstuffs.
- The conflict over access by Third World states to drugs protected by patents taken out by the big pharmaceutical companies.
- The long-running argument between Washington, US business interests and governments and firms around the world on federal and state-level sanctions policies directed towards, amongst others, Cuba, Iran, Libya and Burma.
- Opposition to the Bush Administration's introduction of tariffs on steel imported into the USA and the subsidies for farm exports.
- Conflict between India, Malaysia, Pakistan and Thailand on one side and the USA on the other over the latter's ban on the sale in the USA of shrimps caught in nets that do not allow sea turtles to escape.
- Pressures brought to bear on governments and firms on human rights grounds, as with Occidental Petroleum in Colombia and Shell in Nigeria.
- Claims by the EU that South Korea is selling ships at below cost price, supported by state subsidies.

What is noticeable in these and many other cases is how the traditional arguments about free trade and protectionism are interwoven with new issues sponsored by actors, particularly the ever-expanding list of non-governmental organisations (NGOs), whose concerns now firmly impinge on the trade politics agenda. Thus enhanced issue complexity generated by the evolution of the trade agenda beyond its preoccupation with tariff reduction in the early GATT (General Agreement on Tariffs and Trade) negotiating rounds, to embrace the much more complex problems associated with non-tariff barriers (NTBs) and trade in services, meets another form of complexity produced by processes of issue-linkage. Nowhere is this more clearly visible than in the tensions present in transatlantic relations as conflicts on steel, GMOs, agriculture and export subsidies for US firms have meshed with the divisions generated by policy towards Iraq (see Peterson, Chapter 2)

Consequently policy makers now find the conduct of intergovernmental trade policy to be much more testing – not least because the texture of contemporary trade politics is enriched by the emergence of new networks of non-governmental influence on processes that have been regarded as relatively insulated from the attentions of all but a select band of players. However, these developments present problems for the analyst as well as the policy practitioner. How do we describe and explain what is happening in this part of the policy agenda?

Approaching trade politics

As many of the following chapters clearly indicate, the landscape of contemporary trade politics exists uncomfortably alongside realist, state-centred approaches to international relations, for at least two reasons. First, there is a presumption in such approaches that politics and economics inhabit separate worlds and that, in terms of international relations, it is political relationships, informed by the pursuit of power, that are dominant. This has never constituted a compelling argument and, in the light of the growing integration of the global economy, it looks increasingly tenuous. The conflicts that one observes in relation to international trade do not arise simply out of disagreements over specific policies. They are often underpinned by very different conceptions about the appropriate relationship between state and market. Examining this relationship is the essence of political economy. As proponents of 'complex interdependence' pointed out in the 1970s, the notion that there is an automatic hierarchy of issues on the international agenda – 'high' and 'low' politics – with economic issues relegated to the second category, below that represented by the military–security agenda, fails to take account of their significance in determining outcomes in world politics or the inherent fluidity of the categories themselves (Keohane and Nye 1997).

Second, the very nature of trade policy, with its focus on balancing the economic interests of a range of domestic constituencies, undermines the notion of the state as a unitary actor, pursuing a clear and identifiable 'national interest'. Indeed, in many senses, trade politics, concerned as it is with the distribution of resources within and between political communities, is amongst the clearest manifestations of the processes determining who gets what, why and how. And as the trade agenda becomes more complex, explaining how trade policy is formulated and articulated demands that the role and interactions of a range of governmental and non-governmental actors be taken into account. For political economists, markets do not arise automatically; they are created within a society that provides supporting mechanisms, such as an ability to enforce contracts, and cannot be properly understood outside this context. Douglass North was an elegant exponent of this view. In his analysis of the uneven development of market economies throughout the world North reminds us of the importance of supporting institutions and norms of behaviour to the evolution of a market. Successful market economies develop because a society created situations conducive to their development. By contrast, where these supporting institutions were not created, market economies did not evolve (North 1991)

The study of trade politics also suggests that there is little evidence for the argument that the state is in a condition of terminal decline, as some work on globalisation has suggested. As is recognised in much of the literature exploring this contested concept, an increasingly integrated global economy and enhanced communication flows are having more subtle effects on national governments than is often suggested (Jones 1995; Hirst and Thompson 1999; Strange 1996; Clark 1999; Held *et al.*1999; Scholte 2000). The state may be challenged, its functions may be changing, but it is not powerless (Weiss 1998). In this phase of the evolution of the Westphalian system, we are witnessing a dialogue between the forces of interdependence and globalisation on the one hand and territoriality on the other. Far from witnessing the demise of the appeal of the locality in its various, territorially expressed forms, the pressures generated by global economic forces are reinforcing the function and the appeal of national and subnational political communities.

Levels of analysis

The central problem in explaining the complexities of trade politics lies in disentangling the impact of influences at the systemic, state and substate levels, as well as the impact of ideas. The literature of international political economy and foreign economic policy is replete with explanations as to the behaviour of governments in fashioning their international policies (Moon 1987; Mercado 1995). This behaviour does not occur in an intellectual vacuum: it is informed (knowingly or not) by theories shaped by both the political and the economic: liberalism, mercantilism and Marxism (Gilpin 2001). The political economy of liberalism is underpinned by neoclassical economics. In his book, *An Inquiry into the Nature and Causes of the Wealth of Nations* (1776), Adam Smith was the first to suggest that the market mechanism was the most efficient way to allocate resources. '[Smith] pointed out that the very public respon- sibilities of generating and distributing wealth are better accomplished through a free interaction of private economic agents' (Underhill 2000: 130–131). Smith used the famous metaphor of the invisible hand to argue that individuals, pursuing their own interest, could none the less work to the advantage of all. For neoclassical economists, trade arises for a simple reason: comparative advantage. Economic actors come to understand the mutually beneficial gains that arise from specialisation in a liberal, open international economy. Neoclassical economics does not really have a place for history, culture or politics in its world view. To the extent that these are taken on board, they are seen as imperfections, annoyances that distort an otherwise elegant economic theory. Markets arise more or less naturally (though supporting institutions make them function more effectively). Tariffs arise, in this view, because of corporate rent seeking that damages consumer welfare by protecting ineffi- cient firms. The best way to help developing countries is to open up markets and so allow for the most efficient allocation of resources. With the collapse of the Soviet Union, neoclassical economics, contained within a broader liberal framework emphasising democracy, has attained an intellectual ascendancy in political debate.

Though liberalism dominates much contemporary political debate about trade, other theo- ries none the less make their mark. Mercantilism conceives of international trade as a competition between states, waged via national firms. Whereas liberalism sees trade as mutually beneficial, mercantilists see it as a zero-sum competition among states, where the aim is to generate a trade surplus. Mercantilist thought traces its roots back to the 1600s, but modern policy makers, whenever they refer to foreign states as competitors, are unwit- tingly calling back to the thought of Thomas Mun (1571–1641) and Friedrich List (1789–1846). Mun's advice to England's leaders on international trade matters was simply '[England] must ever observe this rule: to sell more to strangers yearly than we consume of theirs in value' (quoted in Hill 2001: 124). Mercantilism enjoyed a renaissance in the 1980s when US observers blamed their country's competitiveness problems on the unfair trade practices of foreign states (Krugman 1986; Tyson 1992). The answer, some argued, was to develop strategic trade policies where government intervened on behalf of domestic firms in high-technology industries. Spectacular economic growth during the 1990s in the USA

Box 0.1 Comparative advantage

First developed by David Ricardo in 1817, the theory of comparative advantage explains how states, by specialising in goods they can produce relatively more effi- ciently than others, can engage in mutually beneficial trade. Increased specialisation allows states to enjoy both higher production of export goods *and* consumption of imports. Trade is not a zero-sum competition – as it is in mercantilist thinking – but a way for all trading partners to increase their wealth.

removed much of the rationale for these policies, but politicians remain willing to see international trade as a competition between states and not firms. The growing salience of regionalism – as outlined in the chapters by Cooper, Ravenhill and Wrobel – may yet herald a return of mercantilist thinking, with trade blocs in Europe, the Americas and perhaps even Asia seeing each other as competitors in a zero-sum economic contest.

Marxist thought has been very influential in international political economy for many years. Like mercantilism, Marxist thought eschews the liberal assumption that trade is mutually beneficial: there are winners and losers. For Marxists, however, the unit of analysis is class, not the state, and the losers in international competition are members of the working class (which can be construed widely to include people who are marginalised on the basis of gender or race). The dominant class – and the important driver for the globalisation of the capitalist system – is a 'transnational capitalist class' of corporate leaders and technocrats in governments and international institutions (Sklair 2001: 3). Modern Marxist thought ascribes the dominance of neoclassical economics not to the supremacy of the theory but to the 'hegemony' that liberalism enjoys in the international political economy. Hegemony refers to the ability of a ruling class to persuade other groups to accept its key organising principles (Gill 2003: 84). Hegemony is not about coercion; it is about constricting political space such that the alternatives to liberalism are no longer viable. This intellectual dominance is buttressed by international institutions such as the WTO, which exist to entrench market liberalism. For Marxists, the WTO is not an objective organisation or an empty political vessel; it exists to promote and enforce a particular world view – market liberalisation.

Moving from the realm of ideas to that of policy making, a similar complexity emerges. Whilst some may veer towards systemic factors, others emphasise the significance of decision-making processes and yet others focus on the nature of national societies, there is a significant consensus that no one level of analysis can, alone, provide a satisfactory account (Ikenberry *et al.* 1988). On the one hand, systemic theories do little more than explain broad policy characteristics. Statist approaches fail to penetrate the complexities of decision-making processes. Societal explanations, whilst providing a far richer tapestry of policy influences and exposing the limitations of an assumed national interest, can easily lead to the belief that policy is simply the expression of conflicting domestic constituencies, with policy makers exercising little or no influence over the shaping of public policy. The problem is highlighted in the trade policy sphere in terms of arguments concerning the relationships between government and multinational business enterprises (MNEs). Here, it has become conventional wisdom, certainly within a certain sector of the globalisation literature, that MNEs, having outgrown the confines of national economies, have relatively little concern with territorial 'place' and the governments that preside over it (Reich 1991; Ohmae 1995). Others, however, sketch more subtle pictures, arguing that business works with state bureaucracies in promoting the interests of both sets of actors, an argument reflected in Cox's depiction of the relationship between the US government and big business:

> The extent to which MNCs [multinational corporations] are successful depends on the depth of their institutional ties to political elites in the United States and elsewhere, and on the resistance to their policies by domestic social actors, including domestic business firms and labor interests.
>
> (Cox 1996)

Recognition of less clear-cut relationships such as this has prompted many analysts to develop 'integrative' approaches giving due weight to domestic influences whilst assigning a clear role to the policy maker at the point of interface between international and domestic negotiating environments (Evans *et al.* 1993).

Certainly, as the contributions to this book make clear, understanding trade politics demands that we adopt broad, 'multiperspectival' approaches to understanding trade politics. Rather than engaging in debates as to whether one actor or another is of primary significance, what is needed is recognition of the linkages and interactions between actors and the arenas in which they operate. A key theme of this book is the importance of linkages, such as those between the domestic and international dimensions of public policy, and the balance of continuity and discontinuity between issues, actors and political arenas.

Environments

Economics and politics in foreign policy

One of the central features of the changing environment of trade politics is the erosion of the boundary demarcating the pursuit of the political in international policy (foreign policy) and the economic (foreign economic policy). As noted above, this distinction has frequently been expressed in terms of the relationship between high and low policy, a distinction which has become far less easy to sustain as economic issues on the international agenda have risen in prominence and economic and political issues have become evermore intertwined.

The setting since the Second World War favoured the intermeshing of security and economic policy. Whilst it was a key objective of governments to avoid what were seen as critical errors in the interwar period marked by the growth of protectionism, the context within which the newly established GATT operated was that configured by the Cold War. Not only did this delimit the range of participants engaged in multilateral trade diplomacy, it helped to ensure that the broader patterns of trade politics would be overlain by the geopolitical imperatives of the developing global conflict.

A manifestation of the emergence of the East–West divide and the use of trade as a foreign policy tool was the US-led strategic embargo symbolised in the US Export Control Act of 1949 and the Coordinating Committee (COCOM) whose aim was to coordinate the embargo amongst the often unwilling US allies. And where trade relationships developed between East and West, as they did during the 1960s when declining agricultural productivity led the USSR to become a net food importer from the West, then their use as a foreign policy tool in situations such as that which arose following the Soviet intervention in Afghanistan in late 1979 proved irresistible.

But by the 1980s, the relationship between foreign policy and trade policy had become far more complex. In part this reflected the lessening of East–West tensions accompanied by the growing significance of the economic dimension of foreign policy underscored by growing Third World economic demands and the emergence of resources diplomacy stimulated by the energy crises of the 1970s.[1] Whatever the realities of military bipolarity, the international economy had become multi-polar, with a USA whose hegemony was challenged, whose confidence appeared to be sapped and which was confronted by rival centres of power in the shape of Japan and Western Europe. On the trade front, these developments manifested themselves in a proliferation of trade conflicts that seemed to strain the resources of diplomacy. These extended to the very heartland of the Western alliance as when, in 1982, European governments, particularly France and the UK, found themselves confronting the Reagan Administration over their agreement with the USSR to import gas from Siberia.

In the vastly changed environment of the post-Cold-War world, such conflicts came to be regarded as characteristic of an era which, in the view of a number of observers, was marked by the dominance of geoeconomics over geopolitics. Here, the traditional image of the relationship between foreign and trade diplomacy was reversed as the major systemic context of world politics was portrayed as one of conflict between rival forms of capitalism based on North America, Western Europe and the Asia–Pacific. Consequently, it was easy to argue, as some came to do, that foreign policy had been subsumed by commercial policy or, to put it slightly differently, that all foreign policy was now foreign economic policy.

By the late 1990s, a decade after the end of the Cold War, things looked rather different. Geopolitical movement in the Asia–Pacific, uncertainty as to the future role and intentions of China, apprehensions regarding Russian foreign policy and the reassertion of nuclear politics combined with the onset of the Asian financial crisis to erode assumptions that the politics in world politics had melted away. This was clearly reflected in the USA where President Clinton's famed emphasis on economics as the central preoccupation of his Administration manifested itself in the attention given to trade negotiations and the creation of jobs through export-oriented programmes such as the Big Emerging Markets strategy. A less hospitable global, political and economic environment, together with domestic pressures – at both Congressional and state/local levels – to wield the economic sanctions stick at a range of countries, reaffirmed the linkages between foreign and commercial policies (Haass 1998)

The events of 11 September 2001 and thereafter have served to reinforce this trend in dramatic fashion. As we will see later, one consequence has been to pose critical questions regarding the nature of the global economy and the degree to which globalisation – and free trade as its key component – might be threatened by responses to another dimension of a globalising world, namely transnational terrorism.

The changing global economy

Many of the major changes in the environment of trade politics are related to the broadening and deepening of the global economy. From what was an *international* economy in, say, the late nineteenth century, when geographically discrete national markets were linked by flows of trade and investment across national boundaries, we have witnessed the evolution of a 'networked world economy' based on electronically integrated networks operating across rather within those boundaries (Kobrin 1997). During the twentieth century, the progressive internationalisation of production has been underpinned by the growth of the MNE, the increasing mobility of capital, the significance of knowledge and information within the global economy, and the revolution in information and communications technology – which has both facilitated economic integration and stimulated even deeper integration (Dicken 2003). As noted earlier, these changes are most often depicted in terms of 'globalisation' whose precise nature and implications for the state as a political and economic actor are the subject of considerable debate.

Thus it appears indisputable that the nature of the trading environment is very different from that of a century ago. The globalisation of production now means that it is virtually impossible to identify in a meaningful sense the origins of a given product. Cars, computers, household electrical goods, each are sourced from components across the world and may be produced in a variety of locations. Central to these processes has been the growing significance of the MNE, now estimated to account for between one-fifth and one-quarter of world production. As a consequence, foreign direct investment has assumed added importance and an increasing volume of trade is intrafirm trade (trade between different parts of the same firm) rather than trade in goods between national economies. Although, as Dicken notes, there are no definitive statistics on intrafirm trade, it is estimated that it makes up around one-third of total world trade (Dicken 2003: 52–53).

At the same time, the location of production has changed. The traditional image of a geographical division of labour between a core of developed, industrialised countries producing manufactured goods and a periphery providing them with natural resources has been fundamentally transformed by the relocation and globalisation of production and the emergence of the newly industrialised countries (NICs). As several of the chapters in Part I make clear, this reflects in part the regionalising dynamics of the post-Cold-War economic order (see Ravenhill, Chapter 3, and Wrobel, Chapter 5). The image confronting us at the international level as we seek to untangle the complexities of contemporary trade politics is one of transformation and uncertainty. Despite the rise of new centres of economic power, particularly in East Asia, it is still the case that a few core economies dominate world trade, with the majority of developing countries experiencing substantial economic difficulties and many marginalised from the benefits of trade liberalisation (Shaw and van der Westhuizen, Chapter 6).

Agendas and processes

Against this background, the nature of the trade agenda has changed in fundamental respects. When the GATT began to function in 1948, its small membership was relatively homogeneous in terms of political and economic characteristics. Furthermore, the central agenda, tariff reduction, if by no means politically uncontentious, was susceptible to negotiation through comparatively simple mechanisms (Sjöstedt 1991). Thus the early GATT negotiating rounds recorded notable successes in reducing tariffs, albeit from very high levels (Ostry 1997; Winham 1992). The shift towards non-tariff barriers (NTBs) was a notable feature of the Tokyo Round of GATT negotiations in the 1970s and reflected success in reducing tariff barriers at national borders as well as the nature of what was being traded. Between 1970 and 1987, trade in the major commercial services such as telecommunications and financial services grew rapidly and by the beginning of the Uruguay Round negotiations in 1986, services were firmly on the agenda of the advanced industrialised states.[2] This reflected the emergence of 'service societies' in the post-industrial countries of the West and the recognition that services should be subject to the same trade 'laws' as those relating to manufactured goods (Dunkley 2000: 174–176). In 1980, manufactured goods accounted for 23 per cent of world production and services 53 per cent. By 1994, the figures were 21 per cent and 63 per cent respectively. In the UK, 8.5 million workers were employed in manufacturing in 1970, a figure that had dropped to 5 million by 1998 (Legrain 2002). By the turn of the millennium, it was estimated that services accounted for 70 per cent of employment in the industrialised countries and for something of the order of half the world's trade and investment (Rugman 2000: 25–26). This development was closely related to the growth of foreign direct investment (FDI) since most services, by their nature, can only be delivered directly rather than traded across national borders as in the case of goods. Hence presence in markets has become as significant as access to those markets.

Alongside these developments, the homogeneity of the trading system was greatly reduced. By the time that the old GATT was replaced by the WTO in 1995, the former's membership had grown to 128; by April 2003, the WTO membership stood at 146 countries and territories. As a result, agendas differ far more markedly than in the early years of the GATT, as illustrated by the priorities of developed and developing countries during the Uruguay Round negotiations. Given the fact that international trade in commercial services constitutes a much smaller proportion of their gross domestic product, Third World countries were far more concerned with gaining enhanced access for their goods to the markets of the developed world. Thus, Africa (see Shaw and van der Westhuizen, Chapter 6), always marginalised in international trade negotiations, became even more so during the Uruguay Round with its inclusion of issues – Trade-Related Aspects of Intellectual Property Rights (TRIPs) and Trade-Related Investment Measures (TRIMs) – far from the core concerns of the countries of the region.

The 'new' trade agenda

Apart from the growing significance of services, as Part II of this book demonstrates, other issues were crowding onto what has come to be regarded as the 'new' trade agenda (Cable 1996; Schott 2000). In the case of intellectual property (see Capling, Chapter 12), these new issues present differing kinds of challenge. On the one hand, they are often inherently more technical than the 'older' issues on the trade agenda. Second, as we shall see below, in adding to the range of issues on the agenda, they increase complexity measured in terms of the potential interaction between issues. Third, since many of these issues reach far more deeply into national communities than the older 'boundary' trade issues as represented by tariffs, they challenge core social values and can easily be presented in terms of challenges to national autonomy and provide a focus for sovereignty-related debates. We shall return to these points shortly, but before doing so, it is important to an understanding of the nature of trade politics that we recognise the boundaries of 'newness'.

One the one hand, as events since 11 September 2001 demonstrate, there is a continuing interface between security concerns and trade, albeit in a new context. But the script was already being rewritten during the 1990s as security challenges became more diverse and complex. The growth of transnational crime and illicit forms of trade, particularly in drugs, is facilitated by globalisation and confronts governments and their societies with profound dilemmas. At the same time, differences of interest between firms who wished to export encryption technology and the intelligence and security community who feared the consequences of doing so, underscored one of the continuing problems confronting the state in fashioning trade policies and in responding to the competing political interests on which these rest.

What has happened since 11 September, however, is the emergence of a twofold challenge to international trade. First, the impact of the terrorist threat, combined with the downturn in the global economy, checked the growth of world trade and precipitated a sharp fall in FDI (Legrain 2002: 116–117). Security measures introduced to meet the terrorist challenge – border controls and the introduction of heightened surveillance of container shipping and air transport, for example – created the prospect of new transaction costs which some feared would have a serious impact on global trade (Lenain *et al.* 2002; Knight 2003). The second, related, challenge focuses on the very nature of globalisation itself and its impact on the international community. Simply put, for some 11 September demonstrated the transience of globalisation. For others, it served to reinforce the fact that whilst it might bring economic prosperity (at least to some), it was also fanning the flames of social fragmentation, racial and religious hatred and violence (Davis 2003).

Beyond the rewriting of the trade–security nexus, continuity in the trade agenda is reflected in the continuing salience of 'traditional' issues. Agriculture, for example, is alive and well and central to an understanding of the politics of the Uruguay Round negotiations and, now, the Doha Round. Here, the problems confronting the EU in reforming the Common Agricultural Policy have proved to be one of the major stumbling blocks to progress in the negotiations. Additionally, in the context of a growing public concern with health, 'food politics' is taking on a new lease of life in the form of disputes such as that between the USA and the EU over hormone-treated beef and genetically modified food-stuffs (see Falkner, Chapter 17). Moreover, returning to issue-linkage, it is important to remember that issues do not exist in isolation from one another. Indeed, the very nature of trade negotiations is rooted in the development of issue interrelationships, as in the case of agriculture and audio-visual issues in the final phases of the Uruguay Round. Even the growing significance of commercial services needs to take account of the fact that this accompanies and feeds off the growth in world trade in goods.

The ethical dimension of trade politics

Much of the current debate about the new trade agenda relates to the evolving multilateral trading system. At one level, issues such as minimum labour standards and the environment, as van Liemt (Chapter 16) and Brack (Chapter 15) respectively demonstrate, present problems with which trade policy makers, both at the national level and within international organisations, principally the WTO, are seeking to grapple. At the same time, they are also issues around which a cluster of actors is gathering in pursuit of political interests and goals which are broader in their focus and raise fundamental questions about the place of societies in a globalising economy and the goals which they should pursue. From one perspective, this is seen as part of a general shift towards a more ethical and humane brand of international politics underpinned by far greater sensitivity towards resource scarcities and the future of the planet. Hence it fits within Pirages' identification of a set of economic, ecological and ethical issues which, he argues, is changing basic perspectives in international politics and which he terms 'ecopolitics' (Pirages 1989). However one regards such a claim, it is certainly the case that alongside the well-established business of conducting trade policy, there is an increasingly densely textured pattern of trade-related politics.

As Cable has noted, a growing ethical agenda impacts on trade politics in two senses (Cable 1996: 240–241). On the one hand, trade is identified as promoting violations of what are portrayed as fundamental and universal values, whether these relate to human rights or respect for the environment. Opponents of the export of live animals, the importing of tuna caught in nets which also trap dolphins, and trading with countries accused of employing children or imposing inhuman conditions on workers, regard trade conducted in such circumstances as inadmissible. On the other hand, trade offers a tool by which deviations from accepted norms can be punished. In one sense there is nothing new in this. Governments have used trade as a tool of statecraft for centuries and the new security climate of the early twenty-first century has served to provide a new twist to an old technique. At the same time, the objectives of sanctions have also acquired a more overt ethical dimension removed from the interplay of traditional power politics.

This has been reinforced by growing differences between governments and societies over these issues. The firm resistance of growers of tropical timber to controls over trade in this product reflects the fact that it is a significant earner of foreign exchange for a country such as Indonesia. And human rights/labour standards issues pose, at one and the same time, problems of differing cultural values and economic interests. The goal of free trade often sits uneasily with national communities' desire to preserve their cultural identity. But the entertainment industry is big business and accounts for a significant and growing proportion of world trade. This fact underscores the significance of intellectual property as a trade politics issue, but the import of foreign films, literature and music poses broader political issues where societies resent the imposition of foreign cultures.

Of course, this manifests itself most clearly in clashes between Western and non-Western societies, but there is considerable resistance in Europe and Canada to the 'Americanisation' of the media which has led to, amongst other measures, the imposition of local content rules for television programmes. And the economic choices are by no means clear cut. It may appear unacceptable to consumers in the advanced industrialised societies that their vegetables and sportswear are produced by child labour or workers whose level of remuneration is vastly lower than that enjoyed by equivalent workers in the West. But the alternatives, in the absence of carefully constructed programmes of support, may be unemployment or far worse. One of the key problems is that concern with the environment and human rights may simply serve as a cloak for protectionist interests and certainly be seen as such by those who come to believe that the developed world's preoccupation with the ethical trade agenda is little more than a plot to deny the Third World legitimate opportunities to enhance its wealth.

The roots of much of the stuff of trade politics, then, are located in the growing integration of the global economy. The pressures that flow from this are balanced by fragmentary responses at both regional and domestic levels – the latter frequently dubbed 'globalisation backlash' which has grown since the riots at the WTO ministerial summit at Seattle. Changes in the world trading patterns as well as in the substance of that trade have created pools of displaced and disaffected workers alienated from processes which they believe favour the interests of others over their own. These beliefs readily embrace a range of issues, notably attitudes to immigration, which lead to the politics of protest as represented by political parties and pressure groups that are able to capitalise on the resentments produced by global economic integration. All these issues have become interwoven with the effects of 11 September noted above, and with the lack of progress in furthering the Doha agenda with its promise of advancing the interests of the developing countries (see Sally, Chapter 7, and Narlikar, Chapter 9). As a result, contemporary trade politics is marked by major differences of approach, both to the desirability of trade liberalisation and to strategies for furthering or opposing it. Even those most opposed to globalisation and the WTO hold differing views as to the way forward, with one consistent critic, George Monbiot, revising his argument for the total abolition of the WTO in favour of a rewriting of its rules to make it a 'Fair Trade Organisation' (Monbiot 2003). This contrasts with the views of another prominent anti-globaliser, Colin Hines, who has argued that the only way to reverse the inequalities produced by globalisation is 'localisation' – that is, for all countries to produce either nationally or regionally the goods and services they consume, with international trade as a last resort (Hines 2000).

Processes

The developments outlined above have created a far more testing environment for trade policy makers and negotiators. As we have seen, not only are the issues themselves technically more complex, but they embrace matters which have traditionally been regarded as falling within the domestic arena and as therefore the preserve of national governments. As McGuire notes in his discussion of business–government relations in Chapter 19, this reflects the growing importance of regulatory issues in world trade. From financial services – as demonstrated only too well in the context of the Asian financial crisis – to the often bitter conflicts generated by the politics of food, the role of state institutions as regulators has become a central concern of trade diplomacy. The dispute between the EU and the USA over the former's reluctance to allow the sale of genetically modified foodstuffs is viewed in Washington as a failure of European regulatory procedures for vetting foodstuffs. How can Brussels take three years to undertake the necessary processes when the USA, Canada and Japan completed them in eight months (de Jonquières *et al.* 2003)? Complicating the European scene is the relationship between Brussels and member states, with the resultant constraints on the EU's ability to develop coherent policy positions (Smith, Chapter 20).

Underpinning such disputes lie deeper pressures for convergence in regulatory proce-dures and standards which pose critical issues for national political leaders who are confronted by external demands to adopt standards which might well be resisted by domestic constituencies for a variety of social, cultural or political reasons. As Vogel has suggested in the context of transatlantic trade relations, domestic politics and international trade diplomacy collide with and feed off one another, stimulated by differences of approach to issues of consumer and environmental protection. Rather than disarming regulatory disputes, the similarities between the USA and the EU in terms of their levels of development and the salience of environmental issues within their respective societies simply serve to enhance pressures for greater regulation on an ever-widening range of issues and to emphasise variations in consumer attitudes on matters such as animal rights and food safety standards (Vogel 1997). Moving beyond the transatlantic arena, it is these pressures that have produced what is referred to as 'system friction' as the very nature of different cultures and the structure of political and social systems becomes a key issue for trade diplomacy. Continuing US attempts to pressure Japan to adopt US policies and prac-tices to facilitate access for US exporters to Japanese markets have received most attention in this context (Ostry 1997).

At one level, this growing interaction between domestic and international environments is not particularly new and can be traced back to the Tokyo Round of GATT negotiations that gave far greater salience to NTBs. But the process has gone much further and deeper as trade negotiators concern themselves with areas and issues traditionally regarded as the province of national jurisdictions. Indeed, a central characteristic of modern trade diplo-macy, with its growing regulatory agenda, is a concern with the nature, role and capacity of jurisdictions. What might be termed 'jurisdictional diplomacy' has grown in importance and assumes a number of forms. The linkage between trade and competition policy has made national regulations concerning such issues as business mergers and acceptable or unacceptable business practices of central importance (Damro, Chapter 13). Alongside this lies the thorny issue of the role of the WTO in such regulatory areas as competition policy, one of the so-called 'Singapore issues' first raised at the WTO ministerial summit in the city-state in 1996. About half of WTO member states have no competition laws and there are huge variations in practice amongst those that do.

A further twist to the jurisdictional dimension of trade diplomacy is provided by what seem at first sight to be contrary trends: the extension of national jurisdictional claims outside national territories and the growing significance of subnational jurisdictions (states, provinces and cities) to trade diplomacy. In the first category, US claims to extraterritorial jurisdiction, as represented by the Helms–Burton Act, intended to punish foreign firms investing in US property expropriated by the Castro regime in Cuba, have been the source of considerable friction between the EU and Washington (Dunne 1998). Somewhat less visibly, so have attempts by Brussels to establish common rules for the export of various forms of personal data that could restrict data flows within companies' global communications network. Such a threat has led the US Administration to refer the matter to the WTO and Congress to pass legislation prohibiting US firms from observing the EU directive.

The growth of subnational authorities' involvement in trade diplomacy reflects the pattern of changes discussed in this and other chapters. Their significance as purchasers of goods and services has ensured that preferences given to local suppliers have become an issue on the trade agenda. Furthermore, many of the policy areas which determine national competitiveness – education, for example – fall under subnational jurisdiction and are thus of central concern to both government and business. Finally, local and regional authorities are increasingly pressured to adopt stances on the range of issues that form the stuff of trade politics. This is clearly demonstrated in the notable tendency for US state and city governments to adopt economic sanctions against a growing range of targets, from companies trading with Burma to Swiss banks and other institutions for failing to produce satisfactory settlements on the Nazi gold issue.

In the broader context of trade politics, jurisdictional diplomacy is also reflected in the growing tendency for individuals and groups to use the courts of other countries in pursuing claims against MNEs where their activities are seen to be in conflict with human rights principles. The upholding of the right of a group of Burmese farmers to sue the US energy firm Unocal of California in US courts on the grounds that the company was aware that the Burmese government was using slave labour to construct a pipeline to transport its natural gas is a case in point and poses new challenges to firms and governments in managing the interface between trade and human rights (Meyer 1998).

We shall return to this issue, but it is important to recognise that the changing trade agenda fundamentally alters the parameters within which negotiators are required to operate – not least , as noted earlier, due to the tensions generated by a much more intrusive global economy. Sustaining a national social consensus for further trade liberalisation rubs up against resistance from those who find their jobs threatened and groups who believe that other values – in such areas as social welfare and the environment – are being sacrificed to the demands of global capital. The refusal of Congress to grant the Clinton Administration renewal of fast-track authority in trade negotiations in late 1997, later to be granted by a very narrow majority (under the new title of Permanent Trade Authority) to the Bush Administration in 2002, is indicative of the potency of renewed protectionist sentiment within Congress (see Pigman, Chapter 21).

A critical feature of this changing policy milieu is the relationships between key actors and the interests which help to determine them, not least the patterns of expectations that condition the relationships between business and government. Despite the decline of national economies and the territorially bound business enterprises on which they were based – epitomised in Reich's now famous question 'who is us?' – it is clear that firms, both MNEs and small- and medium-sized enterprises (SMEs), have expectations of government, albeit redefined to take account of the changing conditions of the global economy (Kapstein 1991/2).

A major reason why this is so is that only government can determine the policies that, in the form of health, education and welfare provision, are a major conditioning factor in business competitiveness. At the same time, the rise of what Rosecrance has termed the 'trading state', whose capacity to perform its essential functions no longer rests on the control of territory and the exercise of force, demands that government opens a dialogue with firms to enhance national wealth through attracting inward investment to jurisdictions and ensuring that this investment remains in place (Rosecrance 1986). What Strange has characterised as 'triangular diplomacy', based on the interactions between firms and government, reflects the nature of mutual needs that bring together the worlds of governments and business (Strange 1992).

Civil society and trade politics

But this image of triangularity fails to explore the full complexities underpinning the nature of the changing environment in which trade policy is shaped. In addition to government–firm interactions, both are increasingly required to engage with representatives of civil society in achieving their policy goals. In the words of one study, 'something is happening in the relationships between governments, NGOs and companies which draws them to engage more closely together to deal with certain issues' (Mitchell 1998). Accounting for this 'something' requires an appreciation of the forces outlined above and in other chapters of this book. As one senior Canadian trade official has noted, trade diplomacy was, until relatively recently, marked by low levels of consultation and public interest:

> In the early years of the General Agreement on Tariffs and Trade, federal ministers and officials rarely consulted with major industries that were directly affected and this seemed to cause little concern across the country. Successive rounds of GATT negotiations were routinely approved by the government with scant public or political debate. Trade disputes were fewer and less contentious than they are today.
>
> (Johnstone 1996–7)

Not only have the pressures associated with globalisation impelled a more diverse range of actors to become involved with both bilateral and multilateral trade negotiations – as Scholte's discussion of the WTO and civil society (Chapter 10) demonstrates – but also they have provided the opportunity for such engagement. The information and communications revolutions, in particular, have enabled Greenpeace to challenge Shell over the dumping of oil rigs in the North Sea and its operations in Nigeria, native groups in Colombia to pressure Occidental Petroleum to re-evaluate its oil exploration activities, and Global Witness to challenge successfully the trade in 'conflict diamonds' fuelling conflict in Africa. However overdrawn the attribution of the problems at the Seattle WTO ministerial summit and those surrounding the negotiations on the Multilateral Agreement on Investment conducted within the Organisation for Economic Cooperation and Development to the activities of various NGOs exploiting the resources of the Internet, it is undoubtedly true that such negotiations have to take account of these new pressures (Henderson 1999; Das 2000; Sampson 2001; Dymond and Hart 2000).

Moreover, consumer groups have become central actors in trade politics as they bring pressure to bear on companies to source their goods from ethically and environmentally sound sources by organising – or threatening to organise – consumer 'buycotts' of their products. It is in such situations that the loop between the shaping of trade policy and the broader patterns of trade-related politics closes. Consumer-led pressures on high-street stores to stock 'fair trade' tea and coffee and source furniture from countries with sustainable forest management policies clearly impact on the issue of 'eco-labelling', or giving official recognition to such goods.

This reflects, once again, the growing significance of regulatory issues in the global economy. Answering his own question as to why regulations governing, for example, food hygiene, should have become such a contentious issue in US–EU relations, Vogel argues that it is due to the activities of NGOs rather than pressures from relevant producer groups (Vogel 1997: 59). The expansion of those involved in trade politics to embrace the agents of civil society, however, serves to reinforce conflict, he suggests. On the one hand, as noted above, this reflects cultural and political differences and different priorities on the part of consumers and the groups that represent them. At the same time, it follows from a strong inclination on the part of NGOs to view each regulatory battle as crucial lest defeat on one issue leads to challenges to other regulations regarded as important on environmental or other grounds.

Trade diplomacy

Because a core characteristic of this changing environment appears to be the enhanced dependency of the key actors – governments, firms and NGOs – on each other and the need for communication between them, diplomatic strategies need to adapt accordingly. Rather than focusing on the pre-eminence of one diplomatic actor, such as governments, over the others, trade diplomacy has become much more of a coalition-building activity depending on the establishment of networks of relationships (Hocking 1998). The trade agenda is by no means unique in this respect for growing complexity is a characteristic of a number of issue-areas with which diplomacy has to deal. However, the diplomatic strategies referred to here reflect two types of complexity: that relating to the inherent characteristics of a set of issues and that resulting from the growing issue-linkage. The interaction of both varieties of complexity, as noted earlier, is one feature of trade politics and the diplomacy which it generates and can be portrayed in terms of diplomatic 'sites' characterised by a growing diversity of actors, embracing a broader agenda of issues and located on varying terrains.

Conventionally, these terrains might be differentiated in terms of 'multilateral' or 'bilateral' diplomacy (always a problematic distinction in practice) and one of their defining qualities regarded as their 'international' as distinct from their 'domestic' qualities. But as several contributors to this book make clear, the erosion of boundaries between these sites and the ways in which they touch upon one another is one of the stark realities that trade diplomats have to confront.

In particular, the growing linkage between the domestic and international components of diplomatic sites has affected the processes of trade policy making as internal bargaining goes hand in hand with international bargaining. A former US Special Trade Representative, Robert S. Strauss, recalled that during the Tokyo Round, 'I spent as much time negotiating with domestic constituents (both industry and labor) and members of the US Congress as I did negotiating with our foreign trading partners' (Twiggs 1987). The need to sustain internal as well as external coalitions means that negotiators need to engage simultaneously in 'two-level games', with both domestic constituencies and international negotiating partners, treating domestic ratification of international agreements as a continuing process and one that cannot safely be left until the ink is dry on the paper. The domestic–international linkage may encourage trade negotiators to use it as part of their negotiating strategy: during the Uruguay Round negotiations, for example, US diplomats cited the existence of protectionist forces at home as a constraint on their freedom to negotiate (Hoekman and Kostecki 2001: 138).

The processes of trade politics also reflect their substance. The focus of the GATT on the reduction of tariffs during the early negotiating rounds (from Geneva in 1947 to the Dillon Round in 1960–1961) meant that it was marked by a relatively low level of complexity, a high degree of transparency and the quantifiable nature of the core issues. Changes in the trade agenda, including the growing importance of NTBs and trade in services, have made the character of negotiation far more complex. Whereas it is fairly easy to quantify gains and losses in tariff negotiations, exchanges of concessions on which the principle of reciprocity is based are far harder to achieve when NTBs come to dominate the agenda (Sjöstedt 1991).

Moreover, the character of the negotiations (as in other areas of the global agenda) demands the generation of new knowledge as issues such as intellectual property assume greater prominence. Contemporary negotiations involve processes of mutual learning and are as much concerned with developing principles and systematising new knowledge as persuasion. This is part of the move to what Winham has termed negotiation as a 'management process', marked by its technical qualities, complexity, uncertainty and bureaucratisation rather than the traditional concept of the trading of concessions in pursuit of a negotiated settlement (Winham 1977). Thus Ryan's account of the negotiation of the Agreement on Trade-Related Aspects of Intellectual Property Rights (TRIPs) – what he refers to as 'knowledge diplomacy' – involved processes of organisational learning at several levels (Ryan 1998). For the Office of the US Trade Representative (USTR), the emergence of intellectual property on the trade negotiating agenda demanded that an organisation whose prime focus prior to the 1980s had been on manufactured goods and agriculture needed to develop new competencies. Similarly, the challenge of the new agenda required that the main functional international agency in the area, the World Intellectual Property Organization (WIPO), enhance its resources and develop a role as a body capable of helping developing countries meet the obligations that TRIPs imposed upon them. In turn, these developments have affected the structure of trade negotiations. Agenda setting during often extensive pre-negotiations (establishing the negotiating agenda of the Uruguay Round took five years) has become a common phenomenon (Preeg 1995). In the case of TRIPs, the content of the negotiations demanded that a 'layered' approach to the negotiations be adopted whereby the trading of concessions through linkage–bargain diplomacy was conducted within the GATT whilst function-specific diplomacy was conducted within WIPO. It was the interaction of actors within these two arenas that was crucial to the success of the final negotiations.

Conclusion

It was suggested at the start of this introduction that the growing complexities inherent in the trade agenda demand that we adopt more nuanced approaches to its analysis than are associated with the more traditional conceptions of foreign economic policy. In part, this reflects the fact that trade policy has evolved beyond a concern with border issues and now reaches deep into the recesses of national societies, their cultures and social preferences. As such, it is one dimension of broader processes of boundary erosion that are producing a multilayered policy environment marked by a growing diversity of actors, enhanced complexity in the strategies which they deploy in seeking policy objectives and the arenas in which these goals are pursued.

The resultant image is one in which trade and trade-related issues are emerging at the centre of political debate in an international political economy marked by complex processes of integration and fragmentation. Within this complexity, actor roles and relationships are being redefined in such a way as to cast doubt on conventional distinctions between state-centric and pluralistic approaches to policy making. Thus much of the texture of emerging trade politics described by the contributors to this book rests on images of enhanced interaction and mutual dependency as reflected in the often intricate patterns of linkage between government, business and NGOs. The scenarios provided in this volume may, therefore, be viewed as portraying apparently paradoxical processes wherein trade policy, as traditionally conceived, has become subsumed under broader trends reflecting processes of globalisation and the erosion of the international–domestic divide whilst, at the same time, these very processes are helping to elevate the significance of more densely configured patterns of trade politics. The outcomes are proving as intriguing for analysts to explore as they are testing for practitioners to manage.

Notes

1   See Rosenau (1987).
2   See Dicken (2003: 16–46).

Bibliography

Cable, V. (1996) 'The new trade agenda', *International Affairs* 72: 227–246.

Clark, I. (1999) *Globalization and International Relations Theory*, Oxford: Oxford University Press.

Cox, R.W. (1996) 'Introduction: bringing business back in – the business conflict theory of international relations', in R.W. Cox (ed.), *Business and the State in International Relations*, Boulder, CO: Westview.

Das, D. (2000) 'Debacle at Seattle: the way the cookie crumbled', *Journal of World Trade* 34: 181–201.

Davis, L. (2003) 'Globalizations' security implications',RAND Issue Paper.

De Jonquières, G., Alden, E. and Buck, T. (2003) 'Sowing discord: after Iraq, the US and Europe head for a showdown over genetically modified crops', *Financial Times*14 May.

Dicken, P. (2003) *Global Shift: reshaping the global economic map in the 21st century*, 4th edn, London: Sage.

Dymond, W. and Hart, M. (2000) 'Post-modern trade policy: reflections on the challenges to multilateral trade negotiations after Seattle', *Journal of World Trade* 34: 21–28.

Dunkley, G. (2000) *The Free Trade Adventure: the WTO, the Uruguay Round and globalism: a critique*, London: Zed.

Dunne, N. (1998) 'Commerce's diplomatic decline', *Financial Times*, 7 August.

Evans, P.B., Jacobson, H.K. and Putnam, R.D. (eds) (1993) *Double-Edged Diplomacy: international bargaining and domestic politics*, Berkeley, CA: University of California Press.

Gill, S. (2003) *Power and Resistance in the New World Order*, Houndmills: Palgrave.

Gilpin, R. (2001) *Global Political Economy: understanding the international economic order*, Princeton, NJ: Princeton University Press.

Haass, R.N. (ed.) (1998) *Economic Sanctions and American Diplomacy*, New York: Council on Foreign Relations.

Held, D., McGrew, A., Goldblatt, D. and Perraton, J. (1999) *Global Transformations: politics, economic and culture*, Cambridge: Polity.

Henderson, D. (1999) *The MAI Affair: a story and its lessons*, London: Royal Institute of International Affairs.

Hill, C. (2001) *International Business* (International Edition), London: McGraw-Hill.

Hines, C. (2000) *Localization: a global manifesto*, London: Earthscan.

Hirst, P. and Thompson, G. (1999) *Globalization in Question: the international economy and the possibilities of governance*, 2nd edn, Cambridge: Polity.

Hocking, B. (1998) 'Catalytic diplomacy: beyond "newness" and "decline"', in J. Melissen (ed.), *Innovation in Diplomatic Practice*, London: Macmillan.

Hocking, B. and Smith, M. (1997) *Beyond Foreign Economic Policy: the United States, the single European market and the changing world economy*, London: Pinter.

Hoekman, B. and Kostecki, M. (2001) *The Political Economy of the World Trading System: from GATT to WTO*, 2nd edn, Oxford: Oxford University Press.

Ikenberry, G.I., Lake, D.A. and Mastanduno, M. (1988) 'Introduction: approaches to explaining American foreign economic policy', *International Organization* 42: 1–14.

Johnstone, R. (1996–7) 'Globalization and distinct societies: trade policy in the 1990s', *Behind the Headlines*, Winter, 54: 16.

Jones, R.J. (1995) *Globalization and Interdependence in the International Political Economy*, London: Pinter.

Kapstein, E.B. (1991/2) 'We are US: the myth of the multinational', *The National Interest* Winter: 55–62.

Keohane, R. and Nye, J. (1997) *Power and Interdependence: world politics in transition*, Boston: Little, Brown.

Knight, S. (2003) 'The bomb in the box', *The World Today* 59: 17–18.

Kobrin, S.J. (1997) 'The architecture of globalization: state sovereignty in a networked global economy', in J.H. Dunning (ed.), *Governments, globalization and international business*, Oxford: Oxford University Press, 146–172.

Krugman, P. (ed.) (1986) *Strategic Trade Policy and the New International Economics*, Cambridge, MA: MIT Press.

Lang, T. and Hines, C. (1993) *The New Protectionism: protecting the future against free trade*, London: Earthscan.

Legrain, P. (2002) *Open World: the truth about globalisation*, London: Abacus.

Lenain, P., Bonturi, M. and Koen, V. (2002) 'The economic consequences of terrorism', OECD, Economics Department Working Papers No. 334, Paris.

Mercado, S. (1995) 'Towards a new understanding of international trade policies: ideas, institutions and the political economy of foreign economic policy', in J. Macmillan and A. Linklater (eds), *Boundaries in Question: new directions in international relations*, London: Pinter.

Meyer, M. (1998) 'The trials of big business', *Newsweek* 3 August: 34–35.

Mitchell, J.V. (1998) 'Editor's overview', in J.V. Mitchell (ed.), *Companies in a World of Conflict: NGOs, sanctions and corporate responsibility*, London: Royal Institute of International Affairs/Earthscan.

Monbiot, G. (2003) *The Age of Consent: a manifesto for a new world order*, London: Flamingo.

Moon, B.E. (1987) 'Political economy approaches to the comparative study of foreign policy', in C.F. Hermann, C.W. Kegley and J.N. Rosenau (eds), *New Directions in the Study of Foreign Policy*, Boston: Allen and Unwin.

North, D (1991) 'Institutions', *Journal of Economic Perspectives* 5: 97–112.

Ohmae, K. (1995) *The End of the Nation State: the rise of regional economies*, London: HarperCollins.

Ostry, S. (1997) *The Post-Cold War Trading System: who's on first?*, Chicago: University of Chicago Press.

Pirages, D. (1989) *Global Technopolitics: the international politics of technology and resources*, Pacific Grove, CA: Brooks/Cole.

Preeg, E.H. (1995) *Traders in a Brave New World: the Uruguay Round and the future of the international trading system*, Chicago: University of Chicago Press.

Reich, R.B. (1991) *The Work of Nations: preparing ourselves for 21st century capitalism*, New York: Knopf.

Rosecrance, R. (1986) *The Rise of the Trading State: commerce and conquest in the modern world*, New York: Basic Books.

Rosenau, J.N. (1987) 'Introduction: new directions and recurrent questions in the comparative study of foreign policy', in C.F. Hermann, C.W. Kegley and J.N. Rosenau (eds), *New Directions in the Study of Foreign Policy*, Boston: Allen and Unwin.

Rugman, A. (2000) *The End of Globalization*, London: Random House.

Ryan, M.P. (1998) *Knowledge Diplomacy: global competition and the politics of intellectual property*, Washington, DC: Brookings Institution.

Sampson, G. (ed.) (2001) *The role of the World Trade Organization in Global Governance*, Tokyo: UN Press.

Schattschneider, E.E. (1935) *Politics, Pressures and the Tariff*, New York: Prentice Hall.

Scholte, J.A. (2000) *Globalization: a critical introduction*, Houndmills: Macmillan.

Schott, J.J. (2000) *The WTO after Seattle*, Washington, DC: Institute for International Economics.

Sjöstedt, G. (1991) 'Trade talks', in V.A. Kremenyuk (ed.), *International Negotiation: analysis, approaches, issues*, San Francisco: Jossey-Bass.

Sklair, L. (2001) *The Transnational Capitalist Class*, Oxford: Blackwell.

Strange, S. (1992) 'States, firms and diplomacy', *International Affairs* 68: 3–14.

Strange, S. (1996) *The Retreat of the State: the diffusion of power in the world economy*, Cambridge Studies in International Relations No. 49, Cambridge: Cambridge University Press.

Twiggs, J.E. (1987) *The Tokyo Round of Multilateral Trade Negotiations: a case study in building domestic support for diplomacy*, Lanham, MD: University Press of America, vii.

Tyson, L. (1992) *Who's Bashing Whom?: trade conflict in high-technology industries*, Washington, DC: Institute for International Economics.

Underhill, G. (2000) 'Global money and the decline of state power', in T. Lawton, J. Rosenau and A. Verdun (eds), *Strange Power: shaping the parameters of international relations and international political economy*, Aldershot: Ashgate.

Vogel, D. (1997) *Barriers or Benefits? Regulation in Transatlantic Trade*, Washington, DC: Brookings Institution.

Weiss, L. (1998) *The Myth of the Powerless State: governing the economy in a global era*, Cambridge: Polity.

Winham, G.R. (1977) 'Negotiation as a management process', *World Politics* 30: 87–114.

Winham, G.R. (1992) *The Evolution of International Trade Agreements*, Toronto: University of Toronto Press.

World Trade Organization (1995) *Focus* 1: 4.

PART I

Environments and issues

Key part issues

- What is the role of business in developing regional trade policies?
- To what extent are regional trade agreements a replacement for multi-lateral negotiations at the WTO? Can they complement each other?
- To what extent does greater economic integration require political integration?

A central premise of the volume is that the international trade agenda has become more complex – and more contested – than ever. One level of complexity can be grasped by understanding how more and more countries are active participants in multilateral or regional trade agreements. In contrast to even the late 1990s, there are very few states left out of the global economic system. Partly as a result of this new inclusiveness, policy challenges have changed; development issues, for example, are no longer about 'aid' but rather how to integrate developing states into the trading system most effectively. Moreover, as many chapters make clear, a 'state-centric' model of trade policy will prove very misleading: in many regions, policy now develops out of networks of government, corporate and societal actors. In his chapter, Moon provides a tour d'horizon of the current political economy of trade. He notes that the wrecked meeting of the WTO in Seattle was symptomatic of the inability of the WTO system to accommodate either a broadening trade policy agenda or the claims made by anti-globalisers about the organisation's legitimacy.

The trade arena is made all the more complex due to the simultaneous development of multilateralism and regionalism. Peterson's chapter explores what in many ways remains the most important economic relationship in the world: that between Europe and the USA. It is a policy environment of amazing complexity, as one would expect from a relationship with extensive trade and investment links. Peterson shows how both the USA and the EU rely on a blend of public and private mechanisms to manage the transatlantic economy. In contrast to the complex and well-institutionalised policy environment across the Atlantic, regionalism in Asia is much less developed. Yet, Asia presents us with a situation of rapid evolution. China's emergence as one of the world's largest economies has implications far beyond the Pacific Rim. Asian regionalism is in its infancy, and many factors may limit the ability – or desire – of Asian states to develop along NAFTA-like lines, yet efforts to build more formal regional links continue. Ravenhill shows how business groups have been important drivers in this process – and how both regional and multilateral tracks are pursued by states.

The North American Free Trade Agreement, now a decade old, remains along with the EU the most important regional agreement in existence. Cooper notes how the agreement has helped catalyse even greater levels of economic integration. Cooper's chapter, perhaps more than any other, shows how security issues impinge on trade. In the wake of 11 September 2001, the enhanced security at the Canada–US border, whilst understandable, none the less caused economic chaos as firms on opposite sides of the border found themselves cut off from key supplies. Whether NAFTA will eventually be supplanted by a free trade agreement encompassing both North and South America is the topic of Wrobel's chapter. He notes how various pressures have brought Latin American states to look for ways to 'lock in' the stable economic growth that has proved so elusive over the decades. Finally, Africa's relationship to the global economy is considered in the contribution from Shaw and van der Westhuizen. Whilst some African states remain in a situation of desperate marginalisation, others, notably South Africa, are using bilateral trade agreements, investment, aid and other tools gradually to integrate themselves.

1 From Seattle and Doha to Cancún

The trade agenda in the new millennium

Bruce E. Moon

Summary

This chapter provides an overview of recent global trade negotiations by
chronicling the rocky road they have followed since the creation of the
World Trade Organization (WTO) in 1995. The 1999 WTO conference,
dubbed "the battle of Seattle," interrupted the march toward globalization
by questioning the distribution of its costs and benefits and by raising
doubts concerning the legitimacy of the WTO itself. Whether Seattle will
prove to have been a decisive turning point is not yet clear. The outcome of
2001's WTO ministerial in Doha, Qatar, hinted that it represented more a
temporary hiatus than a permanent change of direction. However, the stunning lack of progress in the run-up to the 2003 ministerial in Cancún,
Mexico, suggests that without a more fundamental alteration of orientation
the WTO risks a descent into illegitimacy and irrelevance. A detailed look at
the negotiating positions of various nations and groups, each designed to
achieve its own interests, reveals little cause for optimism that the deadlock
can be easily broken.

Global trade negotiations have followed a rocky road since the creation of the World Trade
Organization (WTO) in 1995. This chronicle will show that the tumult is at once a micro-
cosm of the broader debate about globalization, a forum for alternative voices concerning
the proper role of international institutions, and a struggle over the economic interests of
various nations. The first stop was Seattle in 1999, where large and violent public protests
contributed to the disastrous collapse of the first effort to construct an agenda for those
negotiations. "The battle of Seattle" reflected nagging questions about the legitimacy of the
WTO, which stem from anti-globalization perspectives in developed countries and charges
of ideological and political bias coming from poor countries. The second stop, the ministerial meeting in 2001 in Doha, was designed to put the negotiations back on track, largely by
ignoring the most fundamental philosophical questions, but this account will show that the
effort served only to highlight the very different priorities among nations. The contested and
confused outcome meant that achieving a focused negotiating agenda was largely deferred

to the 2003 ministerial in Cancún, but this meeting too failed in narrowing the gap in positions produced by the very different economic interests of nations.

The debacle at Seattle

The Third Ministerial Conference of the World Trade Organization (WTO), held in the fall of 1999 and quickly dubbed "the battle of Seattle," is universally and rightly regarded as a landmark event for the still-fledgling organization.[1] It is also an unmistakable sign that protagonists in the greater war over globalization have found in the WTO an institutional venue to serve as the battleground. The Seattle Ministerial was meant to launch the "Millennium Round" of trade negotiations, the first since the formation of the WTO in 1994, but the ninth since the process was initiated by the General Agreement on Tariffs and Trade (GATT) fifty years previously. The ministerial was to produce an agenda for those negotiations.

Even though the creation of the WTO had reinvigorated a process that had been faltering for a decade, trouble was visible on the horizon prior to Seattle. The USA, whose global hegemony is symbolized by its dominant role within the GATT/WTO and other Bretton Woods institutions, sought a narrow agenda centered on its own immediate economic interests: tariff reductions in a few sectors, duty-free e-commerce, transparency in government procurement, extending intellectual property rights, and tinkering with the WTO's dispute resolution mechanism.[2] Notably absent was the breadth of vision normally expected of a hegemon, one that incorporated the interests and perspectives of others while responding to systemic imperatives. Gone too was US tolerance for asymmetric benefits, a stance that had sustained trade negotiations in the past. Both had been fading from their peak in the 1950s, as the USA slowly lost the economic dominance that had allowed it to endure the minor threats to its interests posed by trade competitors.

The EU, characteristically less single-minded in its appraisal of trade consequences, sought a more comprehensive agenda that included investment and competition policy, the trade–environment interface and sustainable development, as well as various WTO rules. However, it was neither able to grasp leadership for itself nor willing to follow the US direction, not least because its constituent countries placed the precarious unity of the EU before the vitality of the WTO. The USA and EU also had irreconcilable interests, even though both recognized the need to deflect criticisms of their agricultural policies (especially from one another, but also from the Cairns group of agricultural exporters and other developing countries).[3] They also shared a desire to co-opt the poor countries whose agenda was far different.

From the standpoint of the developed nations, the negotiations seemed destined to replay a theme familiar from fifty years of the GATT. Each party sought to claim the moral high ground by calling for liberalization in products where they had a competitive advantage while citing special circumstances and normative imperatives that justified the prevention of market access to foreign competition where their producers were vulnerable. In this scenario, compromise between liberalization and protectionism was always possible, but the range of the agenda itself was key: it must be broad enough to permit all the parties to achieve their major objectives, but narrow enough to be tractable. Entering Seattle, expectations were modest for achieving consensus on a relatively routine agenda of trade liberalization, most elements of which represented issues left over from previous negotiations, especially the Uruguay Round of the GATT that had created the WTO itself five years earlier.

A more profound critique of the fairness of WTO processes and the validity of its underlying economic and philosophical assumptions came from poor countries, who also complained that the protectionism of developed countries, especially with respect to textiles and agriculture, made a mockery of their liberalization rhetoric. Significantly, many poor countries, led by India, wanted to revisit the outcome of the Uruguay Round before going forward, seeking to roll back their obligations in areas such as intellectual property, investor protection, subsidies, and anti-dumping. They contended that poor countries were unable to meet the many burdens imposed on them by the previous round, such as to upgrade customs valuation procedures or enforce food-safety or intellectual property standards.

In the event, for the first time in the history of trade negotiations, the squabbles among developed country governments were drowned out by louder and angrier voices. Inside the hall, representatives of developing countries refused to be ignored and forced organizational paralysis. They objected not only to the proposed agenda, but to the process of creating it that had excluded them. For years, the agenda has been forged largely in meetings of small groups of developed countries before being presented for the rubber stamp of the entire membership. From this point forward, such "green room" meetings and mini-ministerials became themselves the target of charges of illegitimacy. Both WTO officials and the Clinton Administration that hosted the meetings seemed caught off guard and were unable to keep the conference on track.

Outside the hall, representatives of progressive NGOs and a very loose coalition of protesters made clear that the anti-globalization forces increasingly visible at other international economic forums could also disrupt the WTO. Nearly 800 NGOs from around the world attended and the series of public events they sponsored drew huge crowds. At its peak, 45,000 protesters filled the streets of Seattle. They were strange bedfellows, most voicing support for the critique put forth by poor countries, but the positions of some directly contradicted others. Organized labor and environmental activists were especially strongly represented. Left-wing opponents of capitalism marched alongside right-wing opponents of any organization poised above the nation-state. Protestors succeeded more in polarizing the general issue of globalization – whatever that might mean – than in presenting any coherent position of their own. But they did disrupt the conference, prevent delegates from reaching meetings, demoralize advocates of liberalization, and energize its opponents.

The "tear-gas ministerial" ended prematurely and in embarrassing chaos. No new negotiations had been scheduled, no agenda agreed upon, and no consensus reached on the future of either the WTO or the international trade system it nominally supervised. Most parties focused apprehensively on the Doha ministerial scheduled for the fall of 2001, with only the largely ineffectual negotiations on agriculture and services scheduled for Geneva in early 2000 left intact.

The Seattle breakdown did not offer a pure test of the relative strength of pro- and anti-globalization forces, not least because the US position was far more ambivalent than normally expected from a hegemonic leader. For example, while rhetorically committed to liberalization, President Clinton, under political pressure from US labor unions, also voiced support for the inclusion of labor standards, which are widely seen in poor nations with low wage rates as an explicitly protectionist "poison pill" for negotiations. With the US economy doing well, the pressure from US business to improve access to foreign markets had also waned. (Of course, the priority attached to global trade fell even further just prior to Doha in response to the 9/11 attacks.) Further, denied fast-track negotiating authority by Congress, the US President was in no position to promise rapid progress on any negotiations to emerge from the ministerial anyway, diminishing the urgency of even pro-liberalization advocates. Finally, the prospect of an expansion of NAFTA to the entire Western hemisphere and bilateral trade deals with other countries offered the USA an attractive fall-back position in the event global negotiations failed. In short, a push for greater liberalization lacked strong leadership whereas a variety of forces emerged to impede the launching of a new round under the old assumptions.

Seattle was unquestionably a turning point in several regards. Progressive social movements and advocacy NGOs "discovered" the WTO as the heart of the global capitalist system and committed to playing a role in affecting its processes. Globalization became associated with its institutional regulator. The poor countries affirmed that while they had no capacity to make global rules in accord with their own interests and perspectives, they could prevent – or at least delay – the establishment of rules by others. More mundanely, the WTO learned, like the Global Economic Forum before it, that controversial meetings should be held outside the range of global rabble, like Doha in remote, secure, and authoritarian Qatar. The irony was not lost on activists that saw organizations like the WTO as a threat to global as well as national democracy.

The road to Doha

At stake in Doha was the legitimacy of the WTO itself, which was openly challenged by the anti-globalization backlash centered in developing countries and the rapidly growing NGO movement. Also in doubt was the WTO's future as the institutional core of the world trade order, which was more guardedly questioned by the developed countries. By this point, neither the USA nor the EU could be considered ardent champions of the WTO, with each bristling at complying with its contentious rulings and facing strong domestic opposition to further concessions. A failure at Doha could have further undermined the USA's already shaky faith in the WTO, and thus driven the leading advocate for multilateral negotiations to bilateral or regional trade deals instead.[4] Unilateralism seemed to be growing in the USA, where Congress was far more responsive to the protectionist farm lobby than the liberal executive branch. The new Bush Administration antagonized everyone with politically inspired steel tariffs that openly violated WTO rules and raised anew the controversial issue of regulating protectionist practices cynically justified by anti-dumping rhetoric. Further, Doha was being counted on to squelch bilateral disputes that threatened to explode into trade wars, especially those involving agriculture, the USA's steel tariffs and tax regime for exports, and the EU's ban on imports of genetically modified food. Finally, all this was occurring in an environment in which the theoretical case for free trade was being weakened daily by assaults from prominent academics, NGOs, and policy makers.

To complicate matters further, by 2001 Doha benefited from no momentum whatsoever in ongoing negotiations. The talks on agriculture and services that had barely survived the Seattle debacle were stalled. Regional trade organizations and bilateral arrangements were continuing to grow, not only to fill the void left by lagging global negotiations, but even to push them aside in areas where regional progress was being made more rapidly. Thus, this Fourth Ministerial Meeting was approached with trepidation by almost everyone. In effect, the WTO placed a premium on avoiding disaster, rather than on finding innovations that could bring real progress. This was accomplished with a conservative and carefully prearranged agenda and with the choice of Doha with its attending security arrangements as a locale, which limited participation to fewer than a dozen NGOs and much smaller official national delegations than in Seattle.

Most developed country governments hoped that the Seattle debacle could be largely forgotten and that the WTO negotiation process could be resumed in Doha on the familiar terms that had dominated previous global trade negotiations. At base, the US and EU positions for the Doha ministerial were virtually identical to their Seattle preparations, seemingly signaling that they saw the Seattle episode as merely a public relations problem to be eased with more artful rhetoric and more precisely targeted political pressure.

In contrast, anti-globalization forces sought a new direction in talks that would be less about expanding and deepening integration than about slowing globalization while shaping it to the broader ends of sustainable development, poverty reduction, environmental protection, human rights, and the sharing of economic benefits among rich and poor alike. NGOs hoped that Doha would initiate a new era in international governance with a deeper commitment to transparent and democratic processes inside the WTO and a new vision for the global economic system as a whole. Poor nations sought to roll back liberalization in those areas that had required increasing intrusion into domestic arrangements and threats to their national sovereignty. Simultaneously they hoped to more fully implement already agreed-to liberalization principles in ways that would now constrain rich countries and benefit poor ones in a better balance of obligations.

Doha: something was launched, but what was it?

None of these visions accurately describes the amorphous and contested outcome of Doha, the implications of which, like all agenda setting, can only be judged when the negotiations themselves are complete. That is likely to be a long time away. Delays, finesses, and obfuscations abounded at Doha, all designed to paper over fundamental disagreements that would be exposed whenever substantial discussions neared fruition. Indeed, in the most telling rhetorical sleight-of-hand – designed to recognize yet overcome the poor country position that a new round of negotiations should not commence before the old one was fully implemented – the Seattle goal of a "Millennium Round" was transformed into the "Doha Development Agenda" and a decentralized "work programme" (Bello and Mittal 2001).[5]

By reinventing agriculture as a development issue, two major concerns that had blocked progress in Seattle were ingeniously recast. Developing countries could claim a victory in that agriculture (and therefore development) was placed at the center of the agenda, and Europe could not block agricultural negotiations without being seen as anti-development. This finesse was a public relations success that allowed the negotiations to go on, but was so substantively vacuous that it provided no energy to achieve progress in them. It ignored the reality that the deepest divisions on agriculture were not between developed and developing countries at all, but rather between the USA (supported by the Cairns group) and Europe (supported by Japan). It also failed to highlight the development issues and concerns of developing countries, the bulk of which had nothing to do with agriculture.

As a result, the time frame first envisioned in Seattle and codified in Doha – three years of negotiations to be completed by January 1, 2005 – would be more at home in a *Hitchhiker's Guide* than in a formal international treaty. Surely humorist Gordon Adams, who famously noted, "I love deadlines! I love the Whoosh sound they make as they go flying by," would find much to admire in the Doha declaration. It stipulated that the negotiations would be completed less than sixteen months after the establishment of modalities at the Fifth Ministerial Conference in Cancún in the fall of 2003. That 2005 deadline was conveniently identical to that of the FTAA, the regional challenger to the WTO's global multilateralism, and just in time for President Bush to sign before his term expired. However, this time frame was never realistic in light of the history of previous talks. The Uruguay Round, negotiated in a far more friendly environment, took eight years, not counting the four years between the first effort to begin talks in 1982 and the actual launch of negotiations in Punta del Este in 1986.[6]

Especially binding was the central commitment to accept several sets of negotiations as "a single undertaking," diplomatic code for "nothing is agreed until everything is agreed" and an arrangement that essentially awards veto power to every individual negotiation. Moreover, given the confusion and ambiguity with which the conference ended (one day late and after some delegates had already departed), it was not at all clear what was included in this "single undertaking." With respect to what are variously called Singapore issues or "new issues" (investment, competition, trade facilitation, and transparency in government procurement) it was not even clear whether agreements had been reached to commence negotiations. Post-Doha, the EU contends that its proposals are part of the single undertaking, but many developing countries, which oppose them, disagree. They cite an oral clarification by the chairman that negotiations would begin only after the 2003 Cancún Ministerial expressed "explicit consensus," which would seem to allow any nation that objects to veto them. In other areas, what was up for negotiation was left similarly vague, in part to allow all countries to maintain that they had won. On agriculture, for example, the USA trumpets the phrase in Article 13 of the declaration that members will negotiate reductions of export subsidies "with a view to phasing them out" (Larson 2002: 7).

The agenda better reflected the influence of the richest countries than the developing countries that make up the majority of the WTO membership. Indeed, many of the poor did not want to launch a new round at all, preferring to adjust and amend previous outcomes. However, the USA used all the tools at its disposal, including many side deals and bilateral agreements involving aid, debt renegotiation, and other arrangements. With Doha occurring a scant two months after the September 11 attack, the USA also suggested that launching a new trade round was an important element in the fight against terrorism.

The agenda priorities of nations were as vastly different as their eventual negotiating positions on the issues themselves. Pascal Lamy, European Trade Commissioner, referred to the liberalization of market access for industrial goods as the "big prize" in the talks, because manufactured goods account for 80 percent of world trade. Meanwhile, almost everyone else saw agriculture as the make-or-break issue – since industrial tariffs average around 4 percent compared to agricultural tariffs above 60 percent – and the EU as one of the principal barriers to progress in it.

Agriculture

Agricultural trade policy is politically sensitive and economically significant in virtually all nations. It is a special priority for many developing countries who felt short-changed by its absence from the agenda in previous rounds because it forms a sizable share of their national product and trade. While agricultural exports represent an opportunity to enhance national income, imports threaten food security and the livelihood of their rural masses. Though it is not as important *economically* in developed countries, the EU has proclaimed that agricultural protectionism can be justified by the "multi-functionality" of agriculture, including, for example, its centrality to rural life and national culture. Thus, agriculture certainly presents the most complex challenges to negotiators. Furthermore, because it was not on the agenda until the Uruguay Round, progress has been limited even in achieving cross-national convergence in the *type* of trade barriers in place. Without that, it is difficult to accurately compare the actual protectionist effects of different nations' policies, a necessary first step toward reducing them.

As a result of different policy structures, the EU and USA continue to clash sharply over which is responsible for greater distortions in global agricultural trade. In a recent editorial, *The Washington Times* wrote, "The ongoing Doha trade round is collapsing under Europe's stubborn adherence to its hefty farm tariffs."[7] Most analysts agree that the EU Common Agricultural Policy (CAP) is, in the words of *The Economist*, "the acknowledged paragon of farm-trade lunacy," because the EU accounts for 90 percent of global export subsidies (*The Economist* 1992: 65). However, that was prior to the US Farm Bill of May 2002 that increased subsidies by 63 percent, mostly through direct payments for eight crops important for developing country producers: cotton, wheat, corn, soybeans, rice, barley, oats, and sorghum.

US farm policy, though different than that of the EU, is hardly a model of liberalism. It is, however, better insulated from challenge by the WTO's complex and controversial set of rules governing domestic support programs. The WTO places various payments to farmers into one of three "boxes," each of which is regulated to a different degree. The USA has been especially successful in influencing this scheme so that its programs are tolerated. For example, the USA accounts for about half of all export credits globally, which support (and thus subsidize) US exports by guaranteeing payments of loans to purchase them. US food aid also undercuts other exporters and erodes incentives for indigenous production with free food. Neither program was covered in the Uruguay Round and the USA has thus far kept them off the post-Doha agenda by deflecting export credits to moribund negotiations at the OECD and insisting that the proper place to discuss food aid is the Food and Agricultural Organization (FAO). Furthermore, a so-called "peace clause" negotiated by the USA and EU exempted these programs from challenge until the end of 2003.

At Doha, poor countries, led by India and the so-called "Like-Minded Group," proposed a "development box" that would designate as tolerable those policies designed to protect food security and aid rural development despite their effect on trade.[8] They also sought protection against the dumping of excess agricultural products by developed countries and reductions in the barriers that block access to the markets of developed countries. Post-Doha, agricultural negotiations were centered on a text drafted for a "mini-ministerial" in Tokyo in February 2003 that does not contain any of the main proposals advanced by developing countries.

Thus, very little progress has been made in agreeing on modalities for agricultural negotiations. The current agenda draft is more acceptable to the USA and the Cairns group than to Japan, which seeks to further close its markets to imported rice, and the EU, which is hemmed in by internal disagreements. The USA has proposed the abolition of export subsidies and a reduction of production subsidies to 5 percent of product value, but the EU has failed to produce any serious proposals to reform its CAP. France and Germany are especially opposed, having reached agreement to keep spending that protects their farmers broadly unchanged until 2013. If agriculture is blocked, developing countries have made clear that no agreement on the "single undertaking" is possible.

The remainder of the post-Doha agenda

Unlike previous rounds, these trade negotiations have not been dominated by the issue of market access for industrial products, nor has the service sector been emphasized. Indeed, no agreement has been reached on the fundamental modalities concerning how the negotiations on trade barriers will proceed, that is, whether they will begin from a specific formula or rely upon bilateral request-and-offer processes.[9] For example, developing countries have attacked the tariff structures of developed countries rather than their overall rates. Very high tariff peaks in products of particular interest to them and the escalation of rates for more highly processed products relegate developing countries to less profitable primary products. Developing countries have also pressed for enhancements of the special and differential treatment for LDCs that has been part of recent agreements.

In place of the traditional GATT emphasis on industrial tariffs, attention has been focused on previously peripheral issues. The EU has championed environmental considerations, successfully seeking, for example, a clearer relationship between the obligations under multilateral environmental agreements and the WTO. The USA obtained a commitment to a zero duty on e-commerce until the next ministerial. Now on the agenda – directed principally at the USA in the wake of its steel tariffs – is the proposed reform of WTO rules to discipline the anti-dumping practices which nations frequently employ as protectionist measures under the guise of compensating for dumping violations by trade partners. The issue of labor rights has been largely removed from the agenda, being directed to the ILO at the behest of developing countries.

In general, most experts think the agenda favors the interests of developed over developing countries. One exception concerns the intersection of trade-related intellectual property (TRIPs) and health issues – especially the honoring of pharmaceutical patents by poor nations – where the Doha language was based upon the draft of the developing countries rather than that of the USA. However, that success seemed to disappear post-Doha when the deadline to find a way for LDCs to access affordable drugs was missed.

Still, it is noteworthy that since Seattle the option of rolling back and cleaning up previous agreements has been discussed alongside proposals for greater liberalization. On the one hand, the EU continues to push new agenda items cited by the Singapore Ministerial as priorities upon the completion of the Uruguay Round. These include national competition policy, the role of investment in trade, enhancing transparency in government procurement, and the facilitation of trade by developing countries (for example, through more effective customs procedures). On the other hand, developing countries, led by India, have not only rejected the inclusion of these new "Singapore issues," but have demanded a return to the incomplete implementation of the Uruguay Round itself, which covers multiple issues within each of eleven different agreements. The formal status of both are indeterminate, awaiting resolution at Cancún, but will surely be dealt with in some fashion.

Process issues

On the road from Seattle to Doha to Cancún, changes have been more evident in process than in outcome. Developing countries are far better informed, organized, and led than in previous negotiations, though there remains a huge imbalance in power. In 2000, twenty-four countries had no permanent representation in Geneva at all, and those that did had an average delegation of only three to four members to cover not only the WTO but all other organizations in Geneva as well. To compensate for the limited capacity of individual nations, a greater role has been played by regional associations, especially the Africa Group, CARICOM (Carribbean Community and Common Market), and ASEAN (Association of South-East Asian Nations) as well as the so-called Like-Minded Group.

Still, significant procedural issues involving fairness have been raised by developing countries. They have sought improvements in technical assistance, capacity building, and WTO processes. Developing nations challenge the power of the WTO staff and developed countries to set the agenda and thus to dominate the early stages of the process that often render final votes insignificant. Among these are the mini-ministerials held in the run-up to Cancún – in Sydney in November 2002, Tokyo in February 2003, and Cairo in June 2003 – and the so-called Green Room meetings during the ministerials themselves. Agendas, which often predetermine outcomes, are controlled by concentric circles of decision making centered on the USA and EU, followed by Japan and Canada. Only then do LDCs friendly to liberal ideas (for example, South Africa, Chile, Singapore) and those too large to be ignored (India, Malaysia, China) enter the process. But these processes are not at all transparent and other members are frequently unaware that "Friends of the Chair" meetings are even taking place. Such institutional and procedural deficiencies are said to marginalize the majority, as does the neoliberal bias of the WTO secretariat, about 80 percent of which are economists from developed countries.

Limping toward Cancún

The fall 2003 Cancún ministerial was planned as a halfway point revision, giving a fresh impetus to a trade negotiation intended to be concluded at the end of 2004. However, the road from Doha to Cancún has not been a smooth one, with a series of issues that should have been concluded early in 2003 remaining unresolved. As the Seattle disaster illustrated, unless substantial disagreements are sorted out in advance, it is unrealistic to expect trade ministers to resolve issues in a five-day meeting. Thus, with impasses unresolved, it is evident that negotiations will not be complete by the January 1, 2005 deadline. Supachai Panitchpakdi, Director-General of the World Trade Organization, conceded in mid-2003 that negotiators have "a lot of catching up" to do before the WTO's ministerial meeting in Cancún, Mexico, but said it was too early to talk about postponing the deadline for agreement.

However, the actions of the other Bretton Woods institutions suggest even greater concern. Supachai was joined by Horst Köhler, Managing Director of the IMF, and James Wolfensohn, President of the World Bank, in appealing to the heads of government at the May 2003 G8 summit to provide the political guidance needed to move the trade negotiations forward. Also, in April 2003, the Board of Chief Executives of the United Nations System, which consists of the executive heads of twenty-seven UN organizations, expressed concern

> that WTO Members were unable to meet the 2002 deadlines relating to special and differential treatment, access to essential medicines for countries lacking capacity to manufacture such drugs themselves, and implementation of existing WTO Agreements and Decisions, as well as the March 2003 deadline for agreeing to modalities for reductions in support and protection in agriculture.

Nicola Bullard (2003: 1) summarizes more plainly:

> With just five months to Cancún, an agenda that's simply not moving and a long summer holiday in between, it's a good idea to start lowering expectations and looking for scapegoats. The state of play in the WTO at the end of March is this: There is no agreement on how to proceed with the agriculture negotiations. There has been no progress in the implementation of special and differential treatment (a key issue for

developing countries) and there is no resolution in sight on the application of the TRIPs and Public Health Declaration, hailed as the biggest gain for developing countries at Doha. The agenda is totally blocked and there is no sign of movement on any front.

That is especially true for the agenda items most closely related to development, such as the Doha Agreement on TRIPs and Public Health that was supposed to allow poor countries to get access to generic drugs to fight AIDS and other diseases. After the US Administration blocked an agreement in December under strong lobbying from the pharmaceutical industry, the WTO Council, having missed its 2002 deadline, gave up and left it to the Ministerial Conference in Cancún. With other negotiations headed in the same direction, there is great fear that Cancún will look like Seattle, though, it must be acknowledged, missed deadlines are hardly unique to this round.

Legitimacy concerns remain

Regardless of whether the process can be put back on track in the short run, it is apparent that no twenty-first-century trade framework can be built upon a mid-twentieth-century intellectual foundation. Neither the backlash against globalization nor the growing power of nations that make up 80 percent of the world's population can be ignored. The difficulty is reflected in the comment of Sophia Murphy of the Institute for Agriculture and Trade Policy:

> The Doha Declaration [that] calls for improving public understanding of the benefits of liberalized trade betrays an outlook that points to another problem: ... The WTO's mandate is to regulate trade, remove barriers that damage other nations' interests, while controlling aspects of trade that undermine the economic benefits that trade can bring. The WTO does not have a mandate – except in the minds of some of its current champions – to liberalize trade without regard to the consequences. The continued use of WTO resources to promote a monolithic vision for trade is part of the reason that the WTO attracts such strong opposition... The simplistic assertion that trade liberalization only has benefits does not reflect real life experience.
>
> (Murphy 2001: 3)

Substantial long-run progress cannot be made until opponents recognize the legitimacy of the WTO – and that cannot happen until the WTO is seen to recognize the legitimacy of other issues and the organizations designed to deal with them. That includes the environment, human rights, social justice, and development. Indeed, critics note a persistent over-reach in WTO efforts. The very first preambular paragraph of the Marrakech Agreement that established the WTO recognizes that "relations in the field of trade and economic endeavour should be conducted with a view to raising standards of living, ensuring full employment and a large and steadily growing volume of real income and effective demand." As Elaine Gross notes in her criticism of the proposed government procurement agreement, however,

> forbidding governments from upholding the values and preferences of their citizens to protect their environment and human health, to be a catalyst for local economic and community development, to promote human and worker rights, to protect food secu-

rity, and to safeguard social, environmental, and economic justice is clearly outside of that purview.

(Gross 2000: 107)

Conclusion

The outcome of 2001's Fourth WTO Ministerial Meeting in Doha, Qatar, hinted that Seattle represented more a temporary hiatus than a permanent change of direction in the drive for a solid architecture for the global trading system. It appeared that the developed countries were committed to business as usual, despite the clear evidence that the international climate had changed. However, the stunning lack of progress in the run-up to the Fifth Ministerial Meeting in Cancún suggests that without a more fundamental alteration of orientation – specifically, the adoption of a more candid assessment of globalization's costs as well as its benefits and a more realistic acknowledgment of the changing balance of power among nations – the WTO risks a descent into illegitimacy and irrelevance.

As it now stands, the "bicycle theory" – that trade negotiations can remain upright only so long as forward progress continues – offers a dark prediction. Forward progress has, unmistakably, stopped, not least because some of the world community, principally the USA, seeks to continue to expand globalization along the same path it has sought for more than half a century, despite the changing landscape through which that path must now be carved. Meanwhile, a rather larger fraction is groping for a strategy that involves some mixture of reducing unconstrained globalization and refining its regulation so as to limit its costs, which are not only increasingly difficult to bear, but increasingly seen to lie in the political, social, cultural, and normative realms as well as the economic.

Notes

1   Since its inception in January 1995, the World Trade Organization has been mandated to hold ministerial conferences at intervals no greater than two years. The first was held in 1996 in Singapore with later meetings in Geneva (1998), Seattle (1999), Doha (2001), and Cancún (2003).

2   The Bretton Woods meeting of 1944 set out the institutional structure of the post-World War II international economic system, centered on the International Bank for Reconstruction and Development (World Bank), the International Monetary Fund (IMF), and the International Trade Organization (ITO). After the ITO failed ratification votes, the GATT, designed initially as a temporary legal framework, assumed the governance role of international trade until it was superseded by a true institution, the WTO, in 1995.

3   The Cairns Group of Fair Trading Nations, so named because it was formally constituted at a ministerial in Cairns, Australia, in August 1986, now consists of Argentina, Australia, Brazil, Canada, Chile, Colombia, Hungary, Indonesia, Malaysia, New Zealand, the Philippines, Thailand, and Uruguay. Fiji was briefly a member and the USA, EU, and Japan were invited observers at the early meetings.

4   The foremost example is the Free Trade Area of the Americas (FTAA) that would encompass the entire Western hemisphere, but these also include the 2000 Africa Growth and Opportunity Act, a proposed Middle East free trade area, and a variety of bilateral arrangements.

5   A group of more than fifty NGOs (WTO Watch 2001) called it "Everything But Development." Walden Bello, from the NGO Focus on the Global South (Bello and Mittal 2001: 1) wrote "Something was launched at Doha, but to call it a 'round' of trade negotiations might be stretching the concept of a round." Gary Horlick (2002: 195) referred to it as "a new Round/Agenda/Work Program/Whatever."

6   The first five rounds of GATT negotiations, which focused almost exclusively on tariff reductions for industrial products and usually involved only about two-dozen countries, were relatively easy

and concluded quite quickly: Geneva, 1947; Annecy, 1949; Torquay, 1950–1951; Geneva, 1955–1956; Dillon Round in Geneva, 1960–1961. When the agenda became more complex, the negotiators more numerous, and the issues more politically difficult, however, the pace slowed markedly, with each round taking more time to initiate and then longer to negotiate than the previous one: the Kennedy Round, 1962–1967; Tokyo Round, 1973–1979; and Uruguay Round, 1986–1994. By 2003 WTO membership had reached 146.

7 "Doha going down," *Washington Times*, April 4, 2003. Available HTTP: <http://nl.newsbank com/nlsearch/we/Archives?p_product=WT&p;_theme=wt&p_action=search&p_maxdocs=200 &p;_text_search0=The%20AND%20ongoing%20AND%20Doha%20AND%20trade%20AND %20round%20AND%20is%20AND%20collapsing%20AND%20under&s_dispstring=The%20 ongoing%20Doha%20trade%20round%20is%20collapsing%20under%20AND%20date(last%2 0180%20days)&p_field_date-0=YMD_date&p_params_date-0=date:B,E&p_text_date-0=- 180qzD&p_perpage=10&p_sort=YMD_date:D&cal_useweights=no> (accessed 30 July).

8 The Like-Minded Group of developing countries from Asia, Latin America, and Africa have met regularly in Geneva on WTO issues: Cuba, Dominican Republic, Egypt, Honduras, India, Indonesia, Jamaica, Kenya, Malaysia, Mauritius, Pakistan, Sri Lanka, Tanzania, Uganda, and Zimbabwe.

9 Possible approaches include a single cross-sector formula for tariff reductions, tariff cuts in specific sectors, the elimination of low tariffs, or a reduction in tariff peaks.

Bibliography

Bello, W. and Mittal, A. (2001) "The meaning of Doha." Available HTTP:<http://www.foodfirst.org /progs/global/trade/wto2001/meaningofdoha.html> (accessed 6 June 2003).

Bullard, N. (2003) "Lowering expectations and looking for scapegoats," *Focus on Trade*, No. 86, April. Available HTTP:<http://www.focusweb.org/publications/Fot2003/fot86.html> (accessed 6 June 2003).

——*The Economist* (1992) "Free trade's fading champion," 11 April.

Gross, E. (2000) "The Seattle WTO Ministerial: complex challenges for the 21st century," *Development* 43: 106–108.

Horlick, G.N. (2002) "Over the bump in Doha?" *Journal of International Economic Law* 5: 195–202.

Larson, A. (2002) "A new negotiating dynamic at Doha," *Economic Perspectives* 7. Available HTTP: <http://usinfo.state.gov/journals/ites/0102/ijee/larson.htm> (accessed 27 July 2003).

Murphy, S. (2001) "The Doha Ministerial: measuring success" 1 December. Available HTTP:<http://www.wtowatch.org/library/admin/uploadedfiles/Doha_Ministerial_Measuring_ Success.htm> (accessed 6 June 2003).

WTO Watch (2001) "International civil society rejects WTO Doha outcome and the WTO's manipulative process." Available HTTP:<http://www.tradeobservatory.org/library/uploadedfiles /International_Civil_Society_Rejects_WTO_Doha_O.htm> (accessed 6 June 2003).

Key readings

Beierle, T.C. (2002) "From Uruguay to Doha: agricultural trade negotiations at the World Trade Organization," Discussion Paper 02–13, Resources for the Future, March. Available HTTP: <http://www.rff.org/disc_papers/PDF_files/0213.pdf> (accessed 6 June 2003).

Bhagwati, J. (2002) "After Seattle: free trade and the WTO," *International Affairs* 77: 15–29.

McMichael, P. (2000) "Sleepless since Seattle: what is the WTO about?", *Review of International Political Economy* 7: 466–474.

Moon, B.E. (2000) *Dilemmas of International Trade*, 2nd edn, Boulder, CO: Westview.

Wolfe, R. (1998) *Farm wars: the political economy of agriculture and the international trade regime*, New York: St. Martin's Press.

Useful websites

http://www.unctad.org (United Nations Conference on Trade and Development).
http://wto.org (World Trade Organization).
http://www.tradeobservatory.org (WTO Watch).

2 The politics of transatlantic trade relations

John Peterson[1]

Summary

Europe and the USA may seem to be drifting apart in economic terms, but they remain collectively powerful enough to determine much of the international trade agenda. Their frequent inability to avoid bilateral conflict or 'export' bilateral cooperation reflects how far economics has run ahead of politics, in both the transatlantic and the international economies. Globalisation is outpacing the capacity of states (including the USA and those of the EU) and international institutions to govern it. Transatlantic trade politics remains atomistic and issue based, with the WTO system clearly identifying winners and losers, thus promoting trade policies and institutions that tend to serve relatively narrow interests. Transatlantic economic relations remain mostly immune to wider diplomatic tensions over, say, the Iraqi war of 2003, but the USA and EU struggle to show collective leadership in international economic diplomacy.

The post-war politics of multilateral trade have overwhelmingly been transatlantic trade politics. Consistently and repeatedly, the USA and Europe have set the agendas, brokered the key compromises, and built multilateral agreements around the bilateral deals they have struck to settle their differences with each other. Transatlantic reconciliation has always been a necessary, sometimes nearly sufficient, condition for advancing the multilateral trade agenda. Yet, in economic terms, Europe and the USA sometimes seem to be drifting apart. Higher volumes of US trade now go to Canada or Asia than to Europe. The expanding EU is, by some estimates, becoming more self-sufficient and focused on its 'near abroad' of Central and Eastern Europe and the Mediterranean. Meanwhile, the combined economic power of the transatlantic partners is subject to new challenges. Asia has become an incubator for fast-growing aspirants to global economic power status, notably China and India, who often defy US and European policy preferences. Today's WTO of nearly 150 member states is far more difficult for the transatlantic powers, or anyone else, to lead compared with the old GATT or even the original WTO.[2] The rise of a rambunctious coterie of non-governmental organisations (NGOs) does not make 'leading' any easier.

Nevertheless, the USA and EU remain by far the world's two most powerful actors in trade politics. Their economies are far more similar to one another and far more interlinked than are those of any other two major traders. The depth of transatlantic economic interdependence means that the trade relationship will always be subject to conflict; indeed it is surprising that there are not more US–EU trade disputes. The wider point is that Europe and the USA remain the twin pillars of a 'convergence club' of advanced industrialised states (Ostry 1997), which itself remains powerful enough to determine most of the terms on which global trade takes place. Europe and the USA's declining shares of total global wealth will, on balance, strengthen – not weaken – their incentives to cooperate in future global trade diplomacy.

Given this backdrop, one of the most puzzling paradoxes of modern trade politics is the frequent inability of the USA and EU to work together. This chapter is mostly concerned with explaining why the USA and Europe have been so often unable to avoid bilateral conflict or 'export' bilateral cooperation to the rest of the world. Three main lines of argument are developed.

First, transatlantic trade relations illustrate clearly how decidedly issue based trade politics remains. In the WTO era, trade disputes are specific legal matters and mostly the domain of lawyers, not diplomats. Moreover, the so-called 'new trade agenda' is far more complex than the old goods-based, tariff-centred agenda: trade politics is increasingly about 'behind the border' regulatory issues, which are both highly technical and touch upon core social values (see Hocking 1999). It is difficult for the USA and EU, together or singly, to subject such a highly atomised agenda of trade issues to any single vision, liberal or otherwise. Second, the clearer identification by the WTO's system of dispute resolution, compared with the old GATT system, of winners and losers in trade politics makes for far more partisan and bitterly contested trade policy processes, particularly in the USA but also in Europe. Trade policy institutions tend to serve relatively narrow interests, who gain from winning specific WTO cases, as much or more than they serve more diffuse interests that benefit from broad agreements to liberalise. Third and finally, the EU has emerged as the clear locus of European trade power as the USA has become a more reluctant leader. Yet, the EU frequently fails to live up to injunctions that it must become a more 'effective and credible actor in international trade diplomacy' (Woolcock 2000: 375). It remains entirely unclear whether the new, enlarged EU of twenty-five or more will be a more or less reliable partner to the USA.

This chapter's central argument is that the US–EU relationship reveals how far economics has run ahead of politics in the international economy. Economic globalisation has dramatically outpaced the capacity of states, including the USA and those of the EU, and international institutions to govern it in ways that are widely accepted as politically legitimate. One upshot is that economic interdependence is a weak 'glue' for holding the USA and Europe together politically.

Economic interdependence, political discord

The historical development of the transatlantic economic relationship is well covered elsewhere (Featherstone and Ginsberg 1996; Ostry 1997; Pollack and Shaffer 2001a). Here it suffices to note three points. First, the reconstruction of the international economy in the early post-war period was very much a US-led exercise, even if its success was reflected eventually in the rise of Europe as a trading power. Second, the relative decline of the US economy led to a variety of US trade measures or acts in the 1970s and 1980s that appeared to be highly protectionist, but never seemed to cause as much damage as was feared by anxious US trading partners. Third, US trepidation that the EU would become an economically discriminatory 'fortress Europe' as a consequence of its political relaunch in the late 1980s proved unfounded (Hanson 1998). The successful conclusion of the Uruguay Round, based very much on a transatlantic bargain, could be cited as proof.

The roots of interdependence

Today, even if their own bilateral economic relationship were considerably smaller or less intimate, the USA and EU would dominate the politics of international trade. Together, they account for roughly half of both global GDP and exports. The USA and Europe are the purveyors of nearly 40 per cent of all trade in goods, and an even higher share of trade in services.

Not only are the USA and EU major traders. They are major traders with each other: no two other large economies in the world are anywhere near as interdependent. Proposals for a 'Transatlantic Free Trade Area' (or TAFTA) tend to run into the sand because there is simply not very much transatlantic trade to free, leaving aside a few politically sensitive sectors (see European University Institute 2002). Each side accounts for about one-fifth of the total trade of the other. Transatlantic trade is remarkably balanced given its massive size (see Figure 2.1).

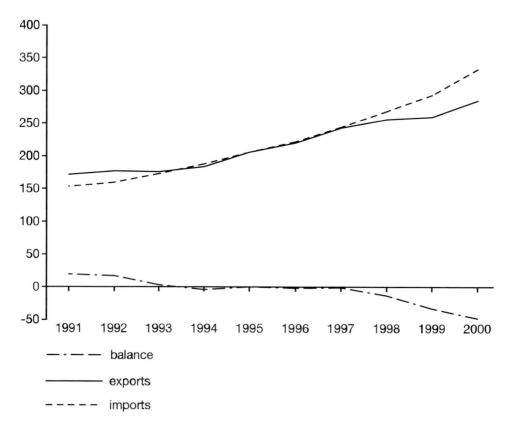

Figure 2.1   US exports, imports and balance of trade (goods and services) with Europe, 1991–2000
          ($US billion)
Source: EABC (2002). Reproduced with the permission of the EABC.

Moreover, trade per se is actually a relatively unimportant element in the US–EU economic relationship. Volumes of cross-investment – the purchase of land, factories, or other assets by investors on one side of the Atlantic in the economy on the other side – dwarf trade volumes. In 2000, US investors accounted for no less than 77 per cent of new foreign direct investment in Europe. Meanwhile the USA was the destination for nearly two-thirds of all foreign investment by Europeans. By way of comparison, Europe invests more annually in Texas than Japanese investors invest in all fifty US states combined (EABC 2002). Many firms produce and sell from where they invest: 'direct sales' by German and French subsidiaries doing business within the US market – that is, sales of goods they make in the USA to US firms or consumers – are now around four times higher than German and French exports to the USA.

It is sometimes claimed that both the USA and EU – and, especially, the Eurozone – are relatively self-contained economies.[3] For example, exports to the USA account for barely more than 2 per cent of the Eurozone's GDP. However, cross-investment by European and US multinational corporations (MNCs) make a mockery of such claims. Around a quarter of all US–EU 'trade' simply consists of transactions within firms with investments on either side of the Atlantic. Investors on each side employ around 3 million workers on the other, mostly in good jobs with high wages and generous benefits. US and European MNCs have become thoroughly intertwined by mergers and cross-fertilisation. Naturally, they can be counted on to lobby for measures that further free transatlantic economic exchange, or at least against ones that disrupt it.

Yet, the disconnection between the economics and politics of transatlantic trade relations is both striking and puzzling. US and EU trade policy processes (treated in greater depth in Chapters 19 and 21) tend to be focused on very narrow economic interests or 'corners' of the North Atlantic economy where competitive advantages may be advanced or weak industries defended.

The policy implications

Public policy making in Washington and Brussels has not been entirely unresponsive to the spinning by (mostly) private actors of dense webs of interdependence. Regulatory cooperation on standards and competition policy became a growth industry in the 1990s, particularly under the Clinton Administration (Vogel 1997; Devuyst 2000; Egan 2001). The 1995 New Transatlantic Agenda (NTA) committed both sides to seek mutual recognition agreements (MRAs) of the kind naturally desired by firms that wished to sell the same products in both markets. The NTA also created a dense array of transatlantic 'people-to-people dialogues', particularly to try to replicate the aggregation of private interests facilitated by the Transatlantic Business Dialogue (TABD), launched in 1994 (Cowles 2001). Consumer, environmental and trade union NGOs, as well as judges and parliamentarians on both sides, were all given new forums in which to liaise, and define and pursue common interests. Most were given assurances – usually vague ones – that their deliberations would be taken into account in future transatlantic policy cooperation.

By the time that the George W. Bush Administration took power in 2001, the NTA as well as transatlantic regulatory cooperation more generally seemed to have run out of steam. No major new MRAs were agreed after a 1999 Veterinary Equivalence Agreement. Nearly all of the transatlantic dialogues either stagnated or withered away, with speculation that even the TABD was on the rocks in early 2003.[4]

On the trade front, the appointment of two extremely able chief negotiators – Robert Zoellick as Bush's US Trade Representative (USTR) and Pascal Lamy as European Commissioner for Trade – led to a dramatic breakthrough in April 2001 in the long-running bananas war, previously a source of bitter recriminations after a judgement against the EU in one of the WTO's first major cases. Still, trade relations hit what many regarded as a new low in 2002. Three very particularistic but highly politicised trade rows came to a boil almost at once: US action to protect its steel industry; a farm bill that massively increased public support for US farmers; and a huge dispute over America's export subsidies, administered via the US tax system.

The last, the Foreign Sales Corporations (FSC) case, saw an EU complaint upheld by a WTO disputes panel, which also approved retaliatory sanctions against the US to a value of $4 billion, an amount many times larger than those approved in the bananas case or a separate case (also lost by the EU) on hormone-treated beef. Claims from Brussels that the FSC case was brought to the WTO in response to pressure from European industry were mostly unconvincing. The case seemed quite purely tactical: a way for the EU to gain leverage in the bananas and beef cases and chalk up a victory in the WTO after several humiliating defeats (see Hocking and McGuire 2002).

European Commission officials openly acknowledged that the WTO-approved sanctions in the FSC case were so huge that there was no way that the EU could avoid 'shooting itself in the foot' by applying them in full: that is, slapping sanctions on goods produced in the USA by European firms or for which the USA was the only or cheapest producer.[5] The case caused enormous political problems for both the Clinton and Bush Administrations, which faced the unenviable task of convincing Congress that US tax law had to be changed as a consequence of international pressure. Many private actors with a stake in transatlantic economic exchange lobbied governments, sometimes on both sides, to settle the case amicably. But the FSC case illustrated two broader points. First, transatlantic economic interdependence often failed to deter one side from inflicting political pain on the other. Second, even longstanding political understandings, such as on the need to live with the distortions caused by differences between taxation systems, were prone to breakdown in the WTO era.

One of the best explanations for the persistence of discord in transatlantic trade relations is an institutional one. Any bias towards cooperation that arises from intense economic interdependence or political agreements such as the NTA seems trumped by the potency of US and EU institutions that often are far more concerned about defending their turf, prerogatives and relationships with favoured societal patrons than with cordial transatlantic relations (see below). Meanwhile, the WTO remains a fragile, legalistic and decidedly intergovernmental institution (see Esserman and Howse 2003). It often appears poorly equipped to provide effective governance of the global economy or the transatlantic economic relationship.

The USA in the WTO era

Throughout the post-war period, US trade policy has been consistently determined by three principal elements: economic theory, federal legislation and political necessity. Yet, the relative power of one factor over the others, or the hierarchy of all three, has been subject to constant flux (see Cohen *et al.* 1996). What seems, thus far, to be different about the twenty-first century is how much any US Administration, George W. Bush's or any other, must struggle to keep a grip on trade policy. In the hierarchy of the three, political necessity frequently looks like the current and future winner.

It is important to acknowledge the counter-evidence. Despite being battered by powerful anti-liberalisation currents, and often appearing not to know its own mind in trade politics, the Clinton Administration still managed an ambitious record of successful trade deals, particularly on the Uruguay Round, NAFTA and trade with China. Essentially, the 'system held' (see Destler 1995), the 'system' being a trade policy process designed to protect Congressional trade policy prerogatives, yet which delegates enough discretion to the executive to make it a credible international negotiator.

Yet, this system was also profoundly challenged by the rise of a new and different brand of US trade politics. On balance, pro-liberalisation forces remained a source of more campaign finance than protectionist ones. However, the skyrocketing cost of Congressional campaigns led to accusations that the US system had become almost 'privatised'. One senior EU official claimed that it 'almost entirely lacks intellect ... it simply processes cheques'.[6] Moreover, the system strained to accommodate 'confounding new issues on the trade agenda', specifically labour and environmental standards, that were both 'here to stay' (Destler and Balint 1999: 48) and an anathema to developing countries.[7] The expansion of the trade agenda partly reflected the rise of a noisy, media-savvy coterie of NGOs, particularly trade unions and environmental groups, which lobbied hard (particularly on Capitol Hill) and generally against trade liberalisation. Its growing power seemed particularly evident after the collapse of the 1999 Seattle ministerial of the WTO, which had intended to launch a new, post-Uruguay trade round. The new US trade politics encouraged a sort of 'scuttle diplomacy', or the constant scurrying of trade officials to cope with the latest bilateral conflict, to become the norm in transatlantic relations (Pollack and Shaffer 2001b: 209). There often seemed to be little capacity in the US system for visionary, long-term thinking about how to move the multilateral trade agenda forward.

The George W. Bush Administration

George W. Bush took office bent on a strongly pro-liberalisation agenda and appeared determined to get a firm grip on trade policy. First, the new Administration signalled that it would downgrade the post of US Trade Representative to sub-cabinet status. Second, it sought to transform – perhaps even abolish – the National Economic Council (NEC), created by the Clinton Administration as a new White House grouping to 'coordinate the economic policy-making process with respect to domestic and international economic issues'. Third, it declared that it would rely more on the President's own Council of Economic Advisors as well as the National Security Council on trade matters, thus suggesting more linkage of trade to foreign policy and security concerns.

Congressional howls of protest about downgrading the USTR led the Bush Administration quietly to confirm Zoellick's cabinet status.[8] The NEC did not wither away, but its appointed head – Lawrence Lindsay – seemed neither very interested in trade nor influential within the Administration.[9] Linkages between trade and foreign policy were often direct and public, particularly as the Bush Administration sought support for its hardline policy towards Iraq in early 2003. But linking trade to wider diplomatic objectives is always complicated by the power of private actors and market forces to determine trade patterns. A far tighter, more obvious linkage was the one the Bush Administration clearly made between trade policy and its domestic political calculations, particularly when it unveiled massive sanctions against imported steel and large increases in support for US farmers ahead of the 2002 mid-term elections. Both measures showered benefits on constituencies that Bush's Republican Party needed in order to take control of Congress in 2002 and ensure his own re-election in 2004, and incidentally hit Europe hard and directly.

The USTR and WTO

The politics of trade policy may have changed, but the central role of the USTR has not. It is a remarkably small agency, with fewer than 100 permanent officials, which has barely grown in size since the 1970s despite massive increases in US trade. It is an exaggeration to claim that 'the US policy process is now almost totally dependent on domestic BIA [Business Interest Associations] for the American perspective on trade disputes' (Jacek 2000: 50). Still, USTR officials admit that they are almost entirely reliant on firms to provide information for use in WTO cases.

The tenor and behaviour of the USTR are very much determined by who heads the agency. Zoellick is, by comparison with his predecessors, something of a renaissance man who has held a variety of public (including in the State and Treasury Departments) and private sector posts. Generally, however, the USTR is a highly legalistic agency that mostly pursues specific cases on the behalf of 'clients'. It is mostly focused on litigation – winning specific WTO cases – not diplomacy, or the fostering of political agreements which open markets. The USTR's focus is logical given that the WTO system is based on retaliation against the losers of cases, instead of (say) compensation of the winners (see Charnovitz 2001; Esserman and Howse 2003).

However, a number of new, burning trade issues are not clearly amenable to purely legal solutions. One is food made with genetically modified organisms (GMOs), a growing industry which is almost entirely US based. Years of food scares in Europe have yielded a powerful aversion to GMOs on the part of many European consumers despite evidence that suggests (if not entirely unambiguously) that most pose no health threat. On one hand, the WTO has an agreed legal text on the so-called 'precautionary principle' – even if it is notoriously vague – to guide policy regulating new types of food. On the other, whether the WTO is the appropriate forum for solving trade disputes that concern new technology, consumer sovereignty and health remains an open question.

The Doha development agenda

The claim that the USA generally misses the big picture in trade diplomacy might seem misguided when considered alongside the US approach to the Doha development agenda of world trade talks, launched in late 2001. On one hand, the Bush Administration's 2002 proposal to abolish tariffs on all manufactured goods globally could be seen as an ambitious attempt to kick-start the negotiations. (An earlier US proposal, designed to smoke out the EU, proposed reducing agricultural tariffs from a global average of 62 per cent to just 15 per cent.) Proposing radical cuts in tariffs exposed the Administration to the ire of protected US sectors, particularly textiles, but Zoellick insisted that: 'Tariffs are just another word for taxes, and when taxes are cut the economy grows.'[10] The proposal for zero tariffs on goods seemed to exonerate the Administration's claims that its earlier actions on steel and agriculture had been purely tactical, and designed to win Trade Promotion Authority from a reluctant Congress for the Doha talks.[11]

On the other hand, the zero-tariffs proposal had zero chance of adoption, particularly as it required considerable sacrifices by developing countries, most of which maintained far higher tariffs than did the USA or EU. A subsequent US proposal to liberalise services allowed Zoellick to claim that he had tabled 'big picture' initiatives in every major trading area – goods, services and agriculture. However, his claim that 'modernizing services can help developing countries jump start the economic growth necessary for reducing poverty' seemed an obvious façade for a proposal that would clearly benefit US firms (not least by opening up Europe's highly fragmented market) far more than those based in the developing world.[12] Meanwhile, the USA remained profoundly reluctant to reform its own trade instruments, such as anti-dumping measures, in response to the insistent urgings of many of its trading partners (particularly in the developing world), despite agreeing to place them on the agenda for negotiation at Doha. At times, the fact that this trade round was meant to be a *development* round seemed to be forgotten in Washington, but in a way that was hardly surprising given past US trade policy behaviour during the WTO era.

Europe: 'quiet superpower', weak leader

In so far as the US record trade deficits of recent years have been viewed as a problem, this has been far more one of major, even structural, imbalances with Japan and China than any deficit with Europe (see Peterson 2001: 50). Nevertheless, deterioration in the US trade balance with Europe in the five years after 1997 was greater than against China or Japan. The simple reason was that the US economy grew much faster during the period than did Europe's (Norris 2003). An economic consequence of Europe's economic stagnation was that it became considerably harder for the USA to generate export-led growth. A political consequence was general disillusion with the EU in Washington.

The Community method and trade policy

A major part of Europe's problem was its patchy record of economic reform since the creation of the euro. The EU's so-called Lisbon agenda, after its launch in 2000, sought to make the EU 'the most dynamic economy in the world' by 2010 through coordinated EU and national actions on labour market reform, electronic commerce, telecommunications, and so on. Arguably, the disappointing record of the Lisbon agenda reflected the failure of European governments to give the EU's institutions stronger powers to make and enforce truly integrated policy at the Brussels level. The so-called 'Open Method' of ostensibly voluntary coordination of national actions with each other and those of the EU was generally far less successful in generating decisive action than the so-called Community method, according to which considerable powers were vested in EU institutions (see Hodson and Maher 2001; Stubb *et al.* 2003).

In fact, a particularly robust form of the Community method is used to determine the EU's external trade policy. The EU has exclusive competence, decisions are taken by majority votes on the EU's Council of Ministers, and the European Parliament has little power to unpick trade deals. Claims that the EU has become a 'quiet superpower' (see Moravcsik 2002) which 'negotiate(s) as equals with the US over trade' (Hain 2003: 21) rest largely on the conviction that its member states wield their economic weight effectively and collectively. The notion that trade policy is the most coherent and effective tool the EU brandishes as a global actor is widely held amongst both European academics (Smith 1998; Smith 2002) and policy makers (Lamy 2002b).

Still, the EU's trade policy is frequently criticised as conservative and protectionist (see Hoeller *et al.* 2000; Winters 2002). By one estimate, the total cost of the EU's discrimination against non-EU producers is equal to as much as 6–7 per cent of its total GDP, or the equivalent of the annual economic output of Spain (Messerlin 2000). Many US officials and observers would blanch at the suggestion that EU trade policy is 'coherent' all or even most of the time. Especially on matters of 'consumer sovereignty', such as cultural products (films and TV programmes) or GM foods, members of the US political class often bitterly condemn the EU. For example, the chair of the US House of Representatives Sub-Committee on Europe does not mince words: 'Americans are becoming increasingly disturbed by EU trade-distorting policies and the Union's restriction of imports on the basis of emotion instead of sound science' (Bereuter 2003: 12).

Creative Brussels?

To be fair, the EU has made significant and substantive contributions to the resolution of several of the most thorny bilateral trade disputes. A good example is aircraft 'hush kits', or equipment designed to lower the noise levels of older aircraft. The EU moved to ban them on environmental grounds, since older aircraft fitted with hush kits pollute more, thus provoking a furious US response, as hush kits were exclusively manufactured in the USA. In the end, the row was defused by an EU agreement in 1999 to replace an outright ban with a more nuanced regulation on aircraft noise and a commitment to work towards a global solution within the International Civil Aviation Organisation.

Another instance of creative European economic diplomacy was the 2000 Safe Harbour Agreement. The need for it arose from a 1998 EU regulation banning the processing of data on individuals by private firms without unambiguous consent from individuals. Firms in the USA, which mostly relied on self-regulation on issues of data protection, seemed set to fall foul of the regulation. A nightmare scenario thus presented itself for firms with investments in both the USA and Europe: an inability to transfer data gathered in Europe to US recipients. The solution was to allow US firms to certify to the US Department of Commerce that they complied with a set of principles governing data transmission – thus giving them 'safe harbour' from the EU regulation. Safe Harbour represented a hybrid set of arrangements that borrowed from both US and European methods of regulation. It was a prime example of positive-sum regulatory cooperation that would have been impossible without inventive thinking in Brussels.

The logical, primary source of such thinking on the EU's side is the European Commission. However, its putatively powerful role in the Community method does not mean that it is an automatic source of leadership or consensus. Commission officials admit that 'negotiations between the Member States can sometimes be far more gruelling than negotiations with third countries', including the USA (Paemen and Bensch 1995: 95).[13]

A large part of the problem is that European private sector lobbies are still over-whelmingly national in structure, thus frequently leaving the Commission with few allies when it presses a recalcitrant member state to accept its own position (Peterson and Bomberg 1999: 110–115). In thorny transatlantic regulatory disputes, the Commission is sometimes actually undermined by private actors: such as when the President of the UK Institute of Chartered Surveyors cast doubt publicly on whether the Commission would succeed in securing an exemption for European auditors from tough new US legislation which threatened to impose huge extra costs on them, prompting fury within the Commission in 2003.[14] US negotiators tend to concur that the Commission is less powerful in EU trade policy than either it appears to be or it would be in a more perfect world.

EU enlargement

The EU's proposed enlargement in 2004 from fifteen to twenty-five member states raised new questions about both the Commission's role and the EU's coherence in trade policy. On one hand, Poland will join with a strong interest in preserving the number one irritant to transatlantic economic relations, the Common Agricultural Policy (see below). Several other new EU states could be expected to insist on protection of their traditional industries. On the other, only four of ten new EU member states had higher overall tariffs than the EU.[15] In any event, the Commission's job in marshalling European economic power into unified, truly common EU positions was about to become considerably more complicated.

An optimistic prognosis would note that the Commission sometimes did win internal European battles in an EU of fifteen and achieve impressive results. A case in point was the agreement to offer the world's least developed countries duty-free access to the EU's market for 'everything but arms' in 2001, which France opposed but was unable to veto. Although modest in impact, 'everything but arms' compared favourably to, say, the Clinton Administration's much hyped Africa Growth and Opportunity Act, which coddled US producers, rammed the US position on labour standards down the throats of African states, and was bitterly attacked by leading commentators (see Bhagwati and Panagariya 2000: 13). By way of contrast with the US system, the EU's system could be viewed as offering a 'systematic bias towards liberalisation over increased protectionism' (Hanson 1998: 56), with the Commission operating at a critical distance from both private lobbies and member governments. Even on the new trade issues such as trade in services and investment, the EU often negotiates with surprising flexibility and effectiveness (Young 2002).

Linking economics and politics?

The extension of European cooperation to areas where the EU lacked legal competence was indicative of a wider point. By the early twenty-first century, the EU had emerged as a far more powerful interlocutor to the USA, with more diverse and important policy tools, than it was even in the early 1990s. However, the Administration of George W. Bush had always been clear that, compared with its predecessor, it would be far less Eurocentric, instinctively supportive of European integration, or wedded to the USA's traditional alliances. Especially after the terrorist attacks of 11 September 2001, new questions arose about whether the economic and security agendas in transatlantic relations would become linked as never before. A benign view was that transatlantic solidarity in the security realm might spill over and smooth agreement in economic relations. For example, the Doha development agenda was successfully launched just over two months after 9/11.

The less benign view was that wider diplomatic tensions could poison economic relations. Soon after the launch of the new WTO round, the USA and EU were back to active bickering on the Doha agenda. There was little sign that cooperation in the war on terrorism was spilling over into the economic realm. By early 2003 there was evidence – including US consumer boycotts of French products and the tabling of a WTO case against the EU on GM foods – that the diplomatic rupture over war in Iraq would have negative economic consequences.

Perhaps above all, there appeared to be no substitute – in the form of non-economic policy cooperation that could renew US–EU relations – for a breakthrough on agriculture. Brussels tried to sell a ten-year EU ceiling on farm spending, agreed in October 2002, as a guarantee that EU subsidies would fall, since nearly static spending levels would be spread amongst twenty-five or more member states in the new, enlarged EU. Yet, the rejection of Commission proposals to switch funding from price support to rural development by a blocking minority of member states, led by France, seemed to justify cynicism about the EU's intentions.

More generally, however, it was difficult to lay the blame for stagnation on Doha on diplomatic tensions over Iraq. Punditry of the 'transatlantic partnership is finished' variety usually did not even mention the economic relationship (see Gordon 2003; Kupchan 2003). The security and economic realms rarely seemed to connect outside of selected sectors, such as the arms and aerospace industries. Even here, where the connection was clear, the Chairman of Boeing, Phil Condit, insisted – along with US officials – that transatlantic economic relations were 'still working' despite frictions over Iraq.[16] Powerful private actors on both sides clearly mobilised to keep the political fall-out from poisoning economic relations.[17] Indicative was the line taken by the *Wall Street Journal*– traditionally the most Eurosceptic of all major US newspapers – on calls to boycott French (and German) products:

> In today's global economy a boycott against a 'French' or 'German' company can easily be a blow against American workers. Exploiting patriotic feeling as a way to block domestic US competition isn't the American way. Come to think of it, it's positively French.[18]

Thus, whatever the state of diplomatic relations between Europe and the USA, the transatlantic economic relationship is sustained by large doses of technology, lobbying and profits. At the first signs that political tensions might harm economic relations, a sizeable coterie of firms with large investments on both sides of the Atlantic can be relied upon to pressure officials and politicians to show restraint.

Still, even in a globalised world, public power remains formidable in trade politics. In most cases, it is directed or constrained by private sector pressure only at the margins. The point applies even in the EU, whose institutions remain young and insecure. But Europe's main problem in trade politics remains the dispersion of Europe's formidable trade power between a range of institutions – including the EU Commission and Council – and its member states. One consequence is that Europe is only rarely an effective leader in global trade politics.

Conclusion

The USA and Europe have powerful incentives to work together on most major questions of economic diplomacy, but struggle to do so. The transatlantic economic relationship may be mostly immune to infection by diplomatic tensions. But the rupture over the 2003 Iraqi war led Peter Sutherland (2003: 17), the WTO's first Director-General, to warn that the USA and EU were 'putting at stake a system of international interdependence and decision-making through painstaking consensus building that has, for the most part, stood the test of time', adding ominously 'this is particularly true of the WTO'.

A particularly burning question – barely touched upon here but a major theme throughout this volume – is whether the regionalism that both the USA and EU have recently embraced in trade policy is compatible with a robust multilateral economic order. Since the early 1990s, both Washington and Brussels have actively sought region-to-region agreements, especially with Asia and Latin America, in ways that often seem politically haphazard but in practice often pressure their transatlantic opposite number to make concessions in bilateral exchanges. This practice is, for many analysts, deeply dangerous (Bhagwati and Panagariya 2000; Gordon 2001), and certainly not a recipe for either transatlantic harmony or 'better', more legitimate global economic governance.

The latter clearly requires reform of the WTO, particularly in view of the deep discontent of much of the developing world with it. Regardless of what the rules say, agenda setting in the WTO remains very much dominated by the USA and EU. In fact, the WTO's consensual, largely intergovernmental rules of decision making are a form of organised hypocrisy. They allow all to respect the instrumental reality of asymmetrical power while maintaining a fiction of sovereign equality: for instance, the WTO has no equivalent of the United Nations Security Council (Steinberg 2002; Moore 2003). Regardless of the latter's recent credibility problems, the WTO could well be a far more effective and efficiently run international organisation if it were given one.

The WTO is not without defenders. Most point out that there are actually very few dispute cases, with most complaints settled amicably and informally. This view claims that the WTO has sufficient capacity for diplomacy and politics. Yet, the WTO has many critics. Most bemoan its phoney egalitarianism, strict state-centrism and elevation of brittle law over more supple politics. According to this view, in the WTO, as in the transatlantic relationship and wider global economy, economics continues to outrun politics, and by margins that remain wide.

Notes

1 For helpful comments on early drafts of this chapter, I am grateful to Matthew Baldwin, Alasdair Young, and the editors.
2 The WTO was 'born' with fewer than 130 member states in 1994.
3 As of 2003, twelve of fifteen current members of the EU were members of the euro and thus in the Eurozone. The 'outs' were Denmark, Sweden and the UK.
4 See 'Europe and America stop talking', *Financial Times* 3 March 2003: 19. A possible exception to the general decline of transatlantic dialogues was the Transatlantic Consumer Dialogue, which was still active with a secretariat in London by mid-2003. See HTTP: <www.tacd.org>.
5 The point was confirmed in interviews in Brussels (October 1999) and Washington, DC, at the European Commission delegation to the USA (September 1999).
6 Interview, Brussels, 19 January 2000.
7 The Clinton Administration's attempts to achieve agreement on 'core labour standards' that all trade agreements would respect (i.e. eschewing child or prison labour) and linking of environmental protection goals to trade deals were largely in response to Congressional pressures. Developing countries instinctively opposed agreeing to measures that, first, had not been imposed on the USA and other advanced economies as they industrialised; and, second, threatened to raise (generally low) costs of production in developing countries.
8 The USTR is an artefact of the US Trade Expansion Act of 1962, which originally created the post and linked it to Congressional powers to regulate international commerce. Thus, Congress can always be expected to defend the sanctity of the post. Bush's attempt to downgrade it was by no means the first time a Presidential Administration sought tighter control over the USTR (see Destler 1995: 105–106).
9 Lindsay was replaced in late 2002 by Stephen Friedman, who focused overwhelmingly on selling Bush's tax-cut plans domestically.
10 Quoted in *Financial Times* 27 November 2002: 9.
11 'Trade Promotion Authority' is the newer, more positive-sounding label for 'fast-track' authority, which a US Administration must win in a Congressional vote but then means that Congress votes on a trade agreement on a straight up or down vote and without amendments.
12 USTR, 'US offers to expand access to the already open American services sector in WTO trade talks', Press Release, 31 March 2003. Available HTTP:

<http://www.ustr.gov/releases/2003/03/03–19.htm> (accessed 15 April 2003).

13 Lamy estimated that his predecessors as External Trade Commissioners spent about two-thirds of their time negotiating with EU member governments, leaving only one-third of their time for negotiating with the EU's trading partners, but also claimed to have reversed these percentages during his own tenure (see Baldwin *et al.* 2003: 35).

14 See Francesco Guerrera, 'EU threatens US with reprisal on auditor rules', *Financial Times* 15 April 2003: 13. See also 'Comments of European Commission on S7–02–03'. Available HTTP: <www.sec.gov/rules/proposed/s70203/aschaub1.htm> (accessed 24 April 2003).

15 The Commission's own assessment of the trade policy implications of the 2004 enlargement are summarised at HTTP: <www.europa.eu.int/comm/enlargement/negotiations/chapters/chap26/index.htm> (accessed 25 April 2003).

16 Quoted in *Financial Times* 8–9 March 2003: 7. For US official views, see 'US official says ties to Europe remain strong'. Available HTTP: <www.useu.be/TransAtlantic/Mar1303JonesUSEU.html>. And 'Treasury official reviews scope of US-EU economic relations'. Available HTTP: <www.useu/be/Categories/Tax%20Finances/Feb1303DamUSEU.html>. And 'US Undersecretary Larson on the transatlantic partnership'. Available HTTP: <www.useu.be/TransAtlantic/Mar2703LarsonTransatlanticRelations.html> (all accessed 13 April 2003).

17 Two indicative examples were a campaign by Medef, the French employers' federation, to convince US firms and consumers to ignore the calls for a US boycott of French products, and lobbying of the US Congress by the Washington-based European–American Business Council on the dangers of letting 'foreign policy differences … spill over into the multi-billion dollar transatlantic trade and investment relationship'. See Robert Graham, 'French business chief in appeal to US over trade', *Financial Times* 16 April 2003: 11, and 'EABC members meet with new chairman of House International Relations Europe subcommittee'. Available HTTP: <www.eabc.org> (accessed 24 April 2003).

18 Quoted in the weekly press review of *European Voice* 17–23 April 2003: 11.

Bibliography

Baldwin, M., Peterson, J. and Stokes, B. (2003) 'Trade and economic relations', in J. Peterson and M.A Pollack (eds), *Europe, America, Bush: transatlantic relations in the 21st century*, London and New York: Routledge.

Bereuter, D. (2003) 'EU must be a partner not a counterweight', *European Voice* 17–23 April.

Bhagwati, J. and Panagariya, A. (2000) 'A trojan horse for Africa', *Financial Times* 13 June 30.

Charnovitz, S. (2001) 'Rethinking WTO trade sanctions', *American Journal of International Law* 95: 792–832.

Cohen, S.D., Paul, J.R. and Blecker, R.A. (1996) *Fundamentals of US Foreign Trade Policy*, Boulder, CO, and Oxford: Westview.

Cowles, M.G. (2001) 'The Transatlantic Business Dialogue: transforming the New Transatlantic Dialogue', in M.A. Pollack and G.C. Shaffer (eds), *Transatlantic Governance in the Global Economy*, Lanham, MD, and Oxford: Rowman and Littlefield.

Destler, I.M. (1995) *American Trade Politics*, 3rd edn, Washington, DC: Institute for International Economics with the Twentieth Century Fund.

Destler, I.M. and Balint, P.J. (1999) *The New Politics of American Trade: trade, labor and the environment*, Washington, DC: Institute for International Economics.

Devuyst, Y. (2000) 'Toward a multilateral competition policy regime?', *Global Governance* 6: 319–338.

EABC (European–American Business Council) (2002) *The United States & Europe: jobs, investment and trade*, 8th edn, Washington, DC: European–American Business Council. Available HTTP: <http://www.eabc.org/publications.htm> (accessed 9 June 2003).

Egan, M. (2001) 'Mutual recognition and standard setting: public and private strategies for governing markets', in M.A Pollack and G.C. Shaffer (eds), *Transatlantic Governance in the Global Economy*, Boulder, CO, and Oxford: Rowman and Littlefield.

Esserman, S. and Howse, R. (2003) 'The WTO on trial', *Foreign Affairs* 82: 130–140.

European University Institute (2002) *The Political Economy of the Transatlantic Partnership*, San Domenico di Fiesole, Italy: Robert Schuman Centre for Advanced Studies, 15 March.

Featherstone, K. and Ginsberg, R. (1996) *The European Community and the United States in the 1990s: partners in transition*, 2nd edn, London and New York: Macmillan and St Martin's Press.

Gordon, B.K. (2001) *America's Trade Follies*, London and New York: Routledge.

Gordon, P.H. (2003) 'Bridging the Atlantic divide', *Foreign Affairs* 82: 70–83.

Hain, P. (2003) 'Diplomacy by resolution is Europe's weakness', *Financial Times* 15 April: 21.

Hanson, B.Y. (1998) 'What happened to fortress Europe? External trade policy liberalization in the European Union', *International Organization* 52: 55–85.

Hocking, B. (1999) 'Introduction – trade politics: environments, agendas and processes', in B. Hocking and S. McGuire (eds), *Trade Politics: international, domestic and regional perspectives*, London and New York: Routledge.

Hocking, B. and McGuire, S. (2002) 'Government–business strategies in EU–US economic relations: the lessons of the foreign sales corporations issue', *Journal of Common Market Studies* 40: 449–470.

Hodson, D. and Maher, I. (2001) 'The open method as a new mode of governance', *Journal of Common Market Studies* 39: 719–746.

Hoeller, P., Girouard, N. and Colecchia, A. (2000) *The European Union's Trade Policies and Their Economic Effects*, Paris: Organisation for Economic Cooperation and Development.

Jacek, H. (2000) 'The role of organized businesses in the formulation and implementation of regional trading agreements in North America', in J. Greenwood and H. Jacek (eds), *Organized Business and the New Global Order*, Basingstoke: Palgrave.

Kupchan, C.A. (2003) 'The Atlantic alliance lies in the rubble', *Financial Times* 10 April. Available HTTP: <www.cfr.org/publication.php?id=5838> (accessed 18 April 2003).

Lamy, P. (2002a) 'Europe's policy-makers live in the real world', *Financial Times* 28 October: 27.

Lamy, P. (2002b) *L'Europe en Première Ligne*, Paris: Editions Seuil.

Messerlin, P. (2000) *Measuring the Costs of Economic Protection in Europe*, Washington, DC: Institute for International Economics.

Moore, M. (2003) *A World Without Walls: freedom, development, free trade and global governance*, Cambridge and New York: Cambridge University Press.

Moravcsik, A. (2002) 'The quiet superpower', *Newsweek* 17 June. Available HTTP: <www.people.fas.harvard.edu/~moravcs/library/quiet.pdf> (accessed 24 April 2003).

Norris, F. (2003) 'That other problem with "Old Europe"', *New York Times* 31 January 2003: D1.

Ostry, S. (1997) *The Post-Cold War Trading System: who's on first?*, Chicago and London: University of Chicago Press.

Paemen, H. and Bensch, A. (1995) *From the GATT to the WTO: the European Community in the Uruguay Round*, Leuven: Leuven University Press.

Peterson, J. (2001) 'Get away from me closer, you're near me too far: Europe and America after the Uruguay Round', in M.A Pollack and G.C Shaffer (eds), *Transatlantic Governance in the Global Economy*, Lanham, MD, and Oxford: Rowman and Littlefield.

Peterson, J. and Bomberg, E. (1999) *Decision-making in the European Union*, Basingstoke and New York: Palgrave.

Pollack, M.A. and Shaffer, G.C. (2001a) 'Transatlantic governance in historical and theoretical perspective', in M.A Pollack and G.C Shaffer (eds), *Transatlantic Governance in the Global Economy*, Lanham, MD, and Oxford: Rowman and Littlefield.

Pollack, M.A. and Shaffer, G.C. (2001b) 'Who governs?', in M.A. Pollack and G.C. Shaffer (eds), *Transatlantic Governance in the Global Economy*, Lanham, MD, and Oxford: Rowman and Littlefield.

Smith, H. (2002) *European Union Foreign Policy: what it is and what it does*, London and Sterling, VA: Pluto.

Smith, M. (1998) 'Does the flag follow trade? "Politicisation" and the emergence of a European foreign policy', in J. Peterson and H. Sjursen (eds), *A Common Foreign Policy for Europe? Competing visions of the CFSP*, London and New York: Routledge.

Steinberg, R.H. (2002) 'In the shadow of law or power? Consensus-based bargaining outcomes in the GATT/WTO', *International Organization* 56: 339–374.

Stubb, A., Wallace, H. and Peterson, J. (2003) 'The policy-making process', in A. Stubb and E. Bomberg (eds), *The European Union: how does it work?*, Oxford and New York: Oxford University Press.

Sutherland, P. (2003) 'Reflections of a frustrated global governor', *Financial Times* 22 April: 17.

Vogel, D. (1997) *Barriers or Benefits? Regulation in transatlantic trade*, Washington, DC: Brookings Institution.

Winters, L.A. (2002) 'European Union trade policy', in H. Wallace (ed.), *Interlocking Dimensions of European Integration*, Basingstoke and New York: Palgrave.

Woolcock, S. (2000) 'European trade policy', in H. Wallace and W. Wallace (eds), *Policy-Making in the European Union*, Oxford and New York: Oxford University Press.

Young, A.R. (2002) *Extending European Cooperation: the European Union and the 'new' international trade agenda*, Manchester and New York: Manchester University Press.

Key readings

Destler, I.M. (1995) *American Trade Politics*, 3rd edn, Washington, DC: Institute for International Economics with the Twentieth Century Fund.

Ostry, S. (1997) *The Post-Cold War Trading System: who's on first?*, Chicago and London: University of Chicago Press.

Peterson, J. and Pollack, M.A. (eds) (2003) *Europe, America, Bush: transatlantic relations in the 21st century*, London and New York: Routledge.

Pollack, M.A. and Shaffer, G.C. (eds) (2001) *Transatlantic Governance in the Global Economy*, Lanham, MD, and Oxford: Rowman and Littlefield.

Vogel, D. (1997) *Barriers or Benefits? Regulation in transatlantic trade*, Washington, DC: Brookings Institution.

Young, A.R. (2002) *Extending European Cooperation: the European Union and the 'new' international trade agenda*, Manchester and New York: Manchester University Press.

Useful websites

www.eabc.org (European–American Business Council).
www.tabd.org (Transatlantic Business Dialogue).

3 Trade politics in East Asia

John Ravenhill

Summary

East Asian countries are playing increasingly significant roles both in international trade and in the determination of the rules of the international trade regime.[1] Double-digit annual rates of economic growth sustained for more than two decades in China have transformed its economy into the 'workshop of the world'. By the turn of the century, China was set to become the world's fifth largest exporter (in fact, if China's exports through Hong Kong are included, it is already the world's third largest exporter after the USA and Germany). Despite the setbacks of the financial crises of 1997–1998, most other East Asian economies continue to grow more rapidly than less developed economies in other parts of the world. Korean exports are now 50 per cent above those of Russia; the value of Malaysian exports exceeds those of Switzerland or Sweden; Thailand exports more than Australia or Brazil (WTO 2003).

The new millennium coincided with dramatic developments in the trade policies of East Asian states. Other members of the World Trade Organization (WTO) finally agreed to the accession of China and Taiwan, fourteen years after these countries had first lodged their applications for membership in the WTO's predecessor, the General Agreement on Tariffs and Trade (GATT). The implementation of the Uruguay Round commitments accelerated the pace of trade liberalisation in these two countries and elsewhere across the region. But East Asian states were not passive bystanders in the global trade regime. The advent of the WTO afforded them new opportunities for trade policy activism. In particular, they made effective use of the new Dispute Settlement Mechanisms to defend their policies against unilateral US action. At the same time, East Asian countries for the first time joined the worldwide trend, which gathered rapid momentum in the 1990s, of negotiating regional preferential trade agreements.

The global level

The advent of the WTO brought new challenges and new opportunities for East Asian countries. The timetable for the implementation of the Uruguay Round agreements brought new pressures on governments to remove protection provided to domestic economic sectors, many of which, especially agriculture in North-East Asian states, were of great political sensitivity. On the other hand, the new dispute settlement mechanisms in the WTO afforded East Asian governments a new avenue for resisting unilateral pressure from the USA in particular for changes not just in trade policies but also in various dimensions of their domestic economic structures that trade partners believed impeded imports. Meanwhile, the admission of China to the WTO will have important consequences not just for the Chinese economy and those of its trading partners but also for the WTO itself.

The WTO and liberalisation

From the end of the Second World War until the start of the 1990s, most East Asian economies (the exceptions were the city-states of Hong Kong and Singapore) maintained relatively high levels of protection in an effort to build up a domestic industrial base. Tariffs and non-tariff barriers had been valued both as economic policy tools and as instruments for maintaining a social compact between governments and those segments of domestic society (most notably the agricultural sector in Japan, Korea and Taiwan) that were vulnerable to international competition. The success of export-oriented industrialisation brought new pressures – both from trading partners and from export industries dependent on access to foreign markets – for the removal of barriers preventing foreign traders and investors from accessing domestic markets. Japan significantly reduced its tariffs in the 1980s; Korea, Taiwan and many of the South-East Asian countries followed suit in the 1990s.

The advent of the WTO brought new pressures for trade liberalisation. The Uruguay Round and subsequent WTO negotiations produced lower tariffs across the board and their complete elimination in some sectors of great significance for East Asian economies, most notably information technology products. For the first time in the post-war period, the agricultural sector became subject to multilateral discipline. Although the Uruguay Round agreements themselves imposed little immediate pressure on the heavily protected agricultural sectors of North-East Asia, they were important symbolically in bringing agriculture under WTO jurisdiction and in signalling that the international community in the future would inevitably move towards imposing further limitations on government intervention in this sector. Similarly, the General Agreement on Trade in Services, GATS, although far from comprehensive, brought new pressures on East Asian governments to open up areas of the economy, such as banking and other financial services, that had traditionally received heavy protection.

For some of the less developed economies in the region, other aspects of the Uruguay Round agreements were equally important. The Trade-Related Aspects of Intellectual Property Rights (TRIPs) agreement provided new weapons for patent owners (mainly from industrialised economies) in their struggle against intellectual piracy in the region (particularly important, for instance, in computer software and in music CDs). The Trade-Related Investment Measures (TRIMs) agreement prohibited a number of trade policy instruments that had been used by governments in their attempts to increase the gains to the local economy from foreign investment. These included demands that foreign investors should source a specific percentage of the value of their inputs from local companies (local content requirements) and that a certain percentage of their output should be exported (trade balancing requirements). Several countries, including Indonesia, Malaysia, the Philippines and Thailand, took advantage of the provision that allowed less developed countries to apply for an extension of the transitional period allowed for implementation of the TRIMs agreement. These countries remain under pressure to phase out their TRIMs; the agreement itself, however, has come under increasing criticism from less developed countries during the Doha Round negotiations (part of their complaint about the inadequacy of the WTO's provisions for 'special and differential treatment' for LDCs) and its future at the time of writing is uncertain (details of the implementation of the TRIMs agreement and of the issues in its renegotiation in the Doha Round are available on the WTO's website, http://www.wto.org).

East Asia and the WTO dispute settlement mechanisms

While the WTO imposed new constraints on the trade policies of countries in the region, it also provided them, through the new Dispute Settlement Understanding (DSU) agreed in the Uruguay Round negotiations, with a significant new instrument for resisting attempts by trading partners to interfere with their domestic economic processes.

As the trade imbalances between the USA and North-East Asian countries grew in the 1980s, the US government had increasingly resorted to unilateral action in an attempt to force its trading partners in the region to change what it perceived to be 'unfair' trading practices. This was particularly the case for its relations with Japan. Having induced an appreciation of the yen and other North-East Asian currencies against the dollar following the Plaza Agreement of the G7 in 1985, and with Japanese tariffs and official non-tariff barriers having been significantly reduced by the late 1980s, the USA turned its attention to the domestic economic structures of East Asian partners and to their policies that it saw as barriers to its exporters. The most dramatic development was the first Bush Administration's Structural Impediments Initiative of 1989–1990, a series of bilateral talks with the Japanese government aimed at removing impediments to market access such as government purchasing regulations, health and safety standards, and regulations governing investment and retail distribution (especially Japan's limitation of large stores under the Large Scale Retail Stores Law). Various policy instruments backed this US initiative, most notably those provided in section Super 301 of the US Omnibus Trade and Competitiveness Act of 1988, which authorised the Administration to determine whether other countries engaged in unfair trading practices and to take retaliatory action against them.[2]

US pressure against Japan under Section 301 of the Trade Act had produced the Semiconductor Trade Agreement in September 1986, in which the Japanese government, *inter alia*, agreed to a target for the share of foreign companies in sales of semiconductors in Japan. For the Japanese government and for most economists this was a dangerous precedent in providing for a new form of state interference in international markets. The Bush Administration and the Clinton Administration in its early years, however, attempted to force a similar agreement on Tokyo for trade in auto parts, which the Japanese government successfully resisted. The new WTO disputes process offered Japan and other East Asian countries an opportunity to test the legitimacy of external pressures brought to bear on them to change their domestic trade structures.

The test case was an action brought by the US government on behalf of the US photographic film company, Kodak, which alleged that its Japanese competitor, Fujifilm, benefited from government policies that restricted access to the Japanese market. Because Japanese tariffs were low and trade was not affected by border non-tariff barriers, the US government (whose case was supported by the EU) had to rely on arguments that Japan's domestic economic policies 'nullified or impaired' previously granted tariff benefits, that government notifications of policies lacked transparency, and that Tokyo effectively accorded foreign products inferior treatment to that granted to domestic ones. In particular, it identified government measures that encouraged vertical and horizontal integration in the film industry to assure greater control by domestic manufacturers; restrictions on the establishment and operation of large stores, the primary outlets for foreign photographic film; and regulatory controls on price competition and advertising. The WTO dispute panel, however, determined in 1997 that Washington had failed to provide sufficient evidence that the Japanese government had discriminated against foreign interests. The verdict had significance far beyond the specific case in that it established a narrow interpretation of some WTO articles and limited the possibilities for Western governments to use the WTO agreements and the DSU against the domestic economic policies and structures of their East Asian trading partners (for further discussion see Lincoln 1999 and Ostrom 2000).

Contrary to its behaviour during the years when world trade was governed by the GATT (whose dispute settlement procedure was largely ineffective), the Japanese government has actively used the WTO's DSU to protect itself from unwanted pressure from the USA and, to a lesser extent, the EU.[3] An initial indication of this new use of multilateral institutions came in 1995 when the Clinton Administration threatened Tokyo with punitive tariffs on imports of Japanese luxury cars, in retaliation for alleged Japanese restrictions on vehicle and car part imports. The Japanese government chose to strike pre-emptively by filing a case with the WTO charging that US import duties on Japanese autos violated GATT Articles I and II. A negotiated settlement resulted in which the Japanese government succeeded in avoiding any imposition of numerical targets on its imports. It followed this up with a challenge, supported by the EU, to the legality of the 1965 US–Canada Auto Pact; the WTO upheld its challenge. Subsequently, it has taken to the WTO its disputes with the USA over US anti-dumping regulations (the Anti-Dumping Act of 1916) and US steel import restrictions.

Other East Asian countries, notably Korea, have followed Japan's new trade policy activism in the WTO. The USA has again been the principal target of these actions, primarily over restrictions it imposes on imports of Korean steel and semiconductors. Even the less developed countries of the region have found the WTO mechanisms a useful way of defending their interests – the Philippines, for instance, has lodged action against Australia, Brazil and the USA.[4] This traffic of course has not been a one-way street and East Asian governments, especially the more developed economies of North-East Asia, have regularly found themselves hauled before the WTO to account for their alleged violations of its rules. But the new activism demonstrates how the improved legal framework of the WTO can protect relatively weak countries against unilateral action by the world's economic superpowers.

China and Taiwan join the WTO

The accession of China and Taiwan to the WTO, agreed at the Doha ministerial meeting in November 2000, closed a long chapter that had frustrated traders and trade negotiators in many parts of the world. The accession negotiations for China had proved tortuous for several reasons. Some WTO members believed that the organisation had been too lenient with the trading practices of a number of economies in transition that were permitted to enter the GATT/WTO in the 1980s and 1990s, which enabled them to avoid their obligations under the rules of these institutions, and were determined not to make the same mistake with China's admission. The sheer size of the Chinese economy, the world's sixth largest according to the World Bank (2003), and its potential both as a market and as a leading source of manufactured imports for industrialised economies, made due diligence even more of an imperative. And consideration of China's application became hostage to political developments: the Tiananmen Square suppression, accusations by the US Congress of other human rights abuses, and tensions between Washington and Beijing over security issues all delayed finalisation of the agreement.

China's admission to the WTO illustrates the significance of the global institution in de-politicising international trade. With its entry into the organisation, other countries could no longer withhold most-favoured-nation treatment from China or, as had been the case in the USA, subject the grant of this status to an annual review of China's human rights policies. Among the most important domestic policy changes arising from Chinese entry to the WTO were a lowering of tariffs (some of the major reductions occurred in preparation for entry – tariffs were reduced from an average of 56 per cent in the early 1980s to 15 per cent in 2001, roughly equivalent to levels in Brazil and Mexico and substantially below those of India, and are scheduled to fall to an average of 9 per cent by 2005),[5] the elimination of non-tariff barriers (to be completed by 2005), the abolition of state trading monopolies, and agreement that treatment for domestic private enterprises would be equal to that accorded the state sector (for further discussion of China and the WTO see Lardy 2002, and Supachai and Clifford 2002).

The prospect of liberalisation of access to the Chinese market and greater respect for the rule of law with WTO entry has made China an even more attractive destination for foreign direct investment, with annual inward flows increasing from about $25 billion at the beginning of the 1990s to $400 billion in 2000. In 2002, China surpassed the USA as the world's largest recipient of direct foreign investment.[6] Manufactured exports, of which approximately half come from 'foreign-invested' firms (joint ventures with TNCs), have soared with China proving a strong competitor across a wide range of goods from low-technology, labour-intensive products to sophisticated manufactures. These exports have posed new challenges for industrialised economies (especially Japan where a vigorous debate on de-industrialisation, similar to that which occurred in North America and Western Europe in the 1980s, has accompanied China's growth) and the USA, where the trade deficit with China has overtaken that with Japan as a focus of Congressional concern. China also poses new challenges for other less developed economies, especially those of the Association of South-East Asian Nations (ASEAN), which fear not only competition from China in export markets but also a long-term loss of competitiveness given foreign investors' increasing preference for China, which now accounts for more than two-thirds of all foreign direct investment into East Asia.

The initial period of China's entry to the WTO has brought mixed results in terms of compliance with its terms of entry. Given the complexity of many of the issues, the fact that adjustment periods will extend for several years, and uncertainty over whether liberalisation will be 'clean' or whether tariffs will be replaced with other barriers, observers from a variety of perspectives have found plenty of evidence to support their prejudices on whether the Chinese government is complying with its obligations.[7] Overall, however, there is no evidence to suggest that the Chinese government has engaged in any wholesale manipulation of its new commitments. Many observers have been surprised at China's defence of the current trade regime. China was a founding member of the group of 22 developing nations, but other less developed economies have expressed disappointment that it has not thrown its considerable political weight behind their demands for a significant restructuring of the trade regime and how the WTO itself operates. Meanwhile, the terms of China's accession have given other members a breathing space before facing the full effect of new competition: China had to accept an

Table 3.1 Participation of East Asian countries in negotiations on preferential trade agreements

Country/grouping	Partners	Status of agreement, May 2003
ASEAN	China	Under negotiation
	EU	Proposed
	Japan	Proposed
China	ASEAN	Under negotiation
	Hong Kong	Proposed
	Macau	Proposed
Hong Kong	China	Proposed
	Macau	Proposed
	New Zealand	Under negotiation
Japan	ASEAN	Proposed
	Canada	Proposed
	Chile	Under study
	Korea	Under study
	Malaysia	Proposed
	Mexico	Under negotiation
	Singapore	Agreement signed
	Thailand	Proposed
Korea	Australia	Under study
	Chile	Agreement signed
	Japan	Under study
	Mexico	Under negotiation
	New Zealand	Under study
	Peru	Proposed
	Singapore	Under study
	Thailand	Under study
	USA	Under study
Malaysia	China	Proposed
	Japan	Proposed
	USA	Proposed
Philippines	Japan	Proposed
	USA	Proposed
Singapore	Australia	Agreement signed
	Canada	Under negotiation
	EFTA	Agreement signed

	EU	Proposed (rejected by EU)
	India	Under negotiation
	Japan	Agreement signed
	Korea	Under study
	Mexico	Under negotiation
	Taiwan	Proposed
	USA	Agreement signed
Taiwan	Costa Rica	Proposed
	Japan	Proposed
	New Zealand	Withdrew from negotiations
	Panama	Under negotiation
	Singapore	Proposed
	USA	Proposed
	Vietnam	Under negotiation
Thailand	Australia	Under negotiation
	Japan	Proposed
	Korea	Under study
	New Zealand	Under study
Vietnam	Taiwan	Under negotiation

Source: Government websites and various newspapers.

Notes: 'Proposed' refers to agreements that have been officially proposed with varying degrees of formality by one government to another (numerous other proposals have been made, primaril y by business groups). Most proposals are then referred for study to either national think -tanks or to consultants and/or to joint working parties from the partners. Negotiations usually do not begin until governments have received these studies.

adjustment period in which countries could maintain limitations on imports of its textiles and more restrictive anti-dumping rules than apply to other WTO members.

The regional level

With the partial exception of ASEAN, established in 1967, East Asian countries have traditionally eschewed discriminatory trade agreements (and even ASEAN had very ineffective arrangements for preferential trade amongst its members until the 1990s). As countries with unusually diverse export markets, and as principal victims of discriminatory trading agreements elsewhere, most notably the EU, they had traditionally been strong supporters of the global trading regime. Their preferred form of trade liberalisation was unilateral action on a non-discriminatory basis, an approach adopted by the region's most comprehensive grouping, APEC, as its original *modus operandi*.[8] US opposition to an East Asian regionalism that would exclude North America and Oceania reinforced these preferences.

At the end of 2001, only China, Hong Kong, Japan, Korea, Mongolia and Taiwan among the WTO's then 144-member economies were not parties to a discriminatory trade agreement. By this date, however, all these countries were included in one or more proposals for bilateral or plurilateral PTAs. In the previous three years more than twenty such schemes involving Western Pacific countries had been put forward; by 2003, the number had mushroomed (Table 3.1). The sudden development of these arrangements caught observers by surprise. A leading theorist of regional integration had commented in 1997 that 'Regionalism in Asia (by itself or with the Pacific nations) would certainly be an important event but has yet to happen. Nor is it likely to happen soon ... discriminatory integration has not caught on there and is unlikely to do so' (Baldwin 1997: 867, 884).

What explains the new enthusiasm of East Asian countries for preferential trading arrangements? The sudden switch in their foreign economic policies suggests that explanations that draw on long-term developments in international relations, such as changes in global or regional power balances, have little relevance to this new approach. Similarly, contrary to the liberal interdependence school, it is not the case that levels of interdependence among East Asian economies have grown rapidly in the years immediately preceding the new bilateralism – indeed, the economic crises of 1997–1998 had a significant negative effect on intra-East-Asian trade. Japan's continuing economic stagnation ensures that the region's largest economy is unable to play the role of engine of economic growth for other East Asian economies. And while China has emerged as a significant trading partner for other North-East Asian economies, it currently is as much a rival as a partner for most South-East Asian economies. For some observers, the economic crises generated a new sense of East Asian identity, which helped lay a foundation for the new preferential agreements. Yet, while containing some elements of truth, such explanations are difficult to reconcile with the decision by East Asian governments to negotiate a significant number of the new preferential arrangements with countries from outside the region (Ravenhill 2002). Another line of explanation that is not very persuasive is the argument that the new enthusiasm for preferential agreements was a response to the failure of the Seattle ministerial meeting of the WTO. Here the timing is simply wrong: the negotiation of the preferential agreements began in earnest in 1998, well before the November 1999 WTO ministerial.

The primary reasons for East Asian enthusiasm for the new preferential arrangements seem to be a belief that regionalism elsewhere has been beneficial for member economies, and a fear of damage to domestic economic interests if access to foreign markets similar to that enjoyed by competitors is not negotiated (Dent 2003; Lloyd 2002). The perceived weaknesses of existing regional schemes in East Asia and, more broadly, the Asia–Pacific, also encouraged a search for alternatives.

Positive experiences in regionalism elsewhere in the global economy

Japan's Ministry of Economy, Trade and Industry (previously MITI, the Ministry of International Trade and Industry) has provided the most comprehensive East Asian official assessment of the benefits of regionalism in other parts of the global economy. Drawing on econometric studies, the Ministry concluded that regionalism had brought a number of positive effects to participating countries, while any welfare loss caused to the rest of the world was minor. Preferential trade agreements had led to increased trade among their members, to a positive competition impact on domestic economies, and to faster economic growth; these effects had often been accompanied by a spurt in direct investment flows. Preferential trade arrangements had also sometimes led to widening participation as excluded states clamoured to join, and to deeper integration, the most obvious example being the EU. But such positive effects, the study noted, also applied to Mercosur and to NAFTA. Moreover, the regional groupings had enhanced the role that their members were able to play in global trade negotiations. Meanwhile, the increase in the share of intra-regional trade and investment in the total flows of East Asian economies that occurred in the 1990s would reduce any negative welfare effects from trade diversion should preferential agreements be negotiated in the region (Ministry of International Trade and Industry 1999).

For governments previously reluctant to jump on the PTA bandwagon, the experience of regionalism in other parts of the world in the 1990s had provided some reassurance. Contrary to the alarmist scenarios popular at the beginning of the decade, the global economy had not fractured into warring trading blocs. Fortress Europe had not materialised. Overall, the trend towards liberalisation of trade throughout the global economy had been maintained (World Bank 2000). The 'defection' of the USA from multilateralism through its bilateral free trade agreements with Israel, Canada and then through NAFTA made it unlikely that Washington could continue to mount any credible opposition to East Asian countries that sought to negotiate similar preferential arrangements. Pro-liberalisation forces saw bilateral agreements as a means of sustaining the momentum towards freer trade and as foundations on which global agreements might subsequently build. They could act as a stepping-stone by gradually exposing protected sectors to international competition. And once the PTA bandwagon gathered pace, as it did in the 1990s,[9] it created a dynamic of its own: governments jumped on board from concerns that they might miss out on something that could be advantaging their competitors. WTO purists had the consolation that they were merely following the lead of others rather than themselves initiating a trend of defection from multilateralism.

The role of domestic economic interests

So far, this discussion on the move to PTAs has followed the practice of much of the literature on international relations in referring to states as if they are unitary actors ('Japan's concern … etc.'). That is, no attention is given to divisions within governments or to the domestic interests that are pushing government agencies in different directions on trade policies. Until recently, such an approach appeared reasonable in studying Asia–Pacific regionalism. As in other parts of the world, the origins of regional cooperation often lay primarily in the security concerns of states rather than in the economic interests of private sector actors. Moreover, states frequently appeared to be little constrained by domestic interests in their pursuit of regional agreements. Indeed, governments have often found it difficult to generate private sector involvement in the regional arrangements they negotiated.[10] The supply of regionalism that governments offered through concluding various negotiations often exceeded the societal demand for it.

Yet, much of the best work on the political economy of South-East Asia in the last two decades highlighted the increased importance of business interests in policy making, and focused on divisions within domestic business communities on key foreign economic policy issues such as levels of protection (Robison 1986; Hewison 1989; Doner 1991; MacIntyre 1991; Doner and Ramsay 1993).[11] Not only were business communities divided on many issues pertinent to regionalism, but so too were bureaucracies. The focus of some of the literature on the financial crises on the resentment of Asian governments at Western responses in general and IMF conditionality in particular frequently obscured the welcome that some government agencies in crisis economies gave to this external intervention, which was seen as providing a significant boost for their pro-liberalisation agendas. In many countries in East Asia, the struggle between pro-liberalisation and anti-liberalisation forces between various agencies of the state continues, and the negotiation of regional trade agreements is an important arena in which this struggle is played out.

The increased interest of business groups in PTAs was stimulated by the growth of such arrangements elsewhere and by the start of the schedules for their implementation. Domestic business interests found themselves disadvantaged in markets where their competitors enjoyed preferential access. The clearest example of new expressions of business interest in the negotiation of PTAs again comes from Japan, where Keidanren,the Federation of Economic Organisations, became increasingly outspoken in support of such agreements in the late 1990s (Keidanren 1999). It particularly voiced concern over access to the Mexican market where US business enjoyed preferential treatment through NAFTA, as did EU business through the EU–Mexico Free Trade Agreement, whereas Japanese exporters faced average tariffs in excess of 16 per cent. Moreover, tariff concessions available to some Japanese companies had been diminished by modifications to the Maquiladora system that were demanded by the USA when NAFTA was negotiated. These concerns were not confined to the Japanese private sector. In a similar vein, Korean auto and tyre exporters complained that they were having difficulties competing in the Chilean market because of its free trade agreements with Mexico and Canada. The Federation of Korean Industries has been an enthusiastic supporter of Korea's negotiating PTAs.

The overall value of trade affected in all cases may have been relatively small but was concentrated in particular sectors – and of sufficient consequence to those affected to prompt political action in support of government negotiation of a PTA.[12] And elements of panic appear to have affected some business communities, leading to expressions of concern disproportionate to any likely negative repercussions of exclusion from preferential arrangements.

The poor performance of existing regional institutions

Disappointment with existing regional institutions also fuelled the enthusiasm for new bilateral approaches. This was particularly the case for APEC, the trans-regional (it spans Europe, Asia, Oceania and the Americas) grouping created in 1989. APEC had made rapid progress in the first half of the 1990s, culminating in the 1994 adoption of an ambitious target of the removal of all trade barriers by its members by 2020.[13] This momentum was lost in the mid-1990s because of ongoing fundamental disagreements among members over both its principal objective (trade liberalisation, favoured by its North American and Oceania members, versus trade facilitation/economic cooperation, favoured by its East Asian members) and its *modus operandi* (unilateral non-discriminatory liberalisation versus negotiated preferential liberalisation).[14] The task of forging agreement within APEC had also been complicated by the rapid expansion of its membership, from twelve in 1989 to twenty-one in 1999.[15]

For some members, especially its Western industrialised economies (and to some extent Singapore and Hong Kong), APEC had achieved too little and was moving too slowly towards realising its goal of free trade. For others, APEC was attempting too much, too quickly. In particular, its effort to expedite the process of liberalisation by negotiating sectorally based agreements, and thereby to move beyond the provisions for trade liberalisation reached as part of the GATT's Uruguay Round, had alienated some of its previously strongest supporters in East Asia, notably Japan and Korea, by posing a threat to sensitive domestic sectors. The East Asian financial crises of 1997–1998 further weakened the grouping. While APEC could hardly be blamed for the crises, its failure to go beyond endorsing IMF programmes for the region was seen by even its most enthusiastic supporters as a lost opportunity (Garnaut 2000). And its preoccupation with sectoral trade liberalisation at a time when East Asian economies were facing their most severe crisis for half a century suggested a lack of sensitivity on the part of its Western members. Trade liberalisation largely disappeared from APEC's agenda after the breakdown of talks on sectoral liberalisation in 1999. None of its key members saw much prospect for significant improvement in APEC's performance in the short to medium term. Consequently, they were unwilling to invest political or bureaucratic resources in attempting to revitalise the institution as a forum for trade liberalisation. APEC's principal role in recent years has been to provide a venue for summit meetings of leaders from around the Pacific Rim, meetings that have been dominated by security issues.

The response to the financial crises of East Asia's most developed regional partnership, ASEAN, also disappointed several of its members. ASEAN, partly in response to the perceived threat of investment diversion to China and concerns that it was falling behind the pace of integration efforts elsewhere, had accelerated its programme for trade liberalisation on several occasions in the 1990s. The deadline for implementation of its free trade area was brought forward to the end of 2002. But progress remained painfully slow and several members opted to continue protection for significant domestic industries beyond the liberalisation deadline. By realising the aspirations of its founders for a truly region-wide grouping by extending the association to cover all of South-East Asia in 1997–1998, member states gave priority to a geographical widening of the grouping. This development inevitably came at the expense of a deepening of cooperation given the lack of capacity of the new members – the low-income economies of Cambodia, Laos and Myanmar – to participate fully in ASEAN's trade programmes.

In contrast to member states' lack of interest in advancing APEC's trade agenda, ASEAN members did respond to the grouping's perceived ineffectiveness by attempting to strengthen the institution. Besides accelerating the implementation of the free trade arrangements, it issued new comprehensive blueprints for the institution's future (the 1997 'ASEAN Vision 2020' and, more significantly, the 1998 Hanoi 'Plan of Action'), and attempted to increase its attractiveness to potential foreign investors by providing them with more liberal conditions. While the possibility of serving an integrated South-East Asian regional market of 500 million people from one plant has been attractive to TNCs in some industries, most notably automobiles, the free trade area has yet to generate much interest from outsiders or from some ASEAN states themselves (one reason being that intra-ASEAN trade has failed to reach even one-quarter of member states' total trade). The most developed of the ASEAN members, Singapore, has cited slow progress in economic cooperation in ASEAN as one of the factors motivating its negotiation of preferential agreements with countries from outside of ASEAN.

Conclusion

Despite the setbacks of the financial crises of 1997–1998, East Asia continues to grow in significance as a global centre for manufacturing, most recently spurred by the rapid growth of China (whose economy depends far more heavily on exports than Japan has ever done). East Asian countries as an aggregate now account for over one-quarter of all world exports, more than double the share of the USA. As they have become more integrated into the global economy so East Asian states have become more active players in negotiating the rules of the global trade regime. In particular, the WTO has provided new means for East Asian governments to defend their interests against unilateral pressure from their Western trading partners. In comparison with the Uruguay Round era, they have also become more outspoken in their defence of measures, such as agricultural protectionism, that sustain the domestic compacts between state and society (and have more actively sought alliances with other countries/groupings perceived to be sympathetic to their cause, e.g. with the EU in the Doha Round negotiations over agricultural protectionism).

The other major development in East Asian trade policies in recent years, the negotiation of PTAs, has also been primarily a defensive response to the proliferation of such arrangements between other countries in the trading system. It also reflects, as discussed in the previous section, the growing role of export-oriented interests in trade policy formulation, a significant recent development in the political economy of trade policy in East Asian states. For governments concerned about maintaining domestic political support, the advantage of the new preferential agreements compared with negotiations in the WTO is that, by excluding some sensitive sectors especially agriculture from liberalisation, they enable the maintenance of social compacts with those employed in non-competitive sectors.

Notes

1   By East Asia, I mean the countries of North-East and South-East Asia (the ten members of ASEAN plus the five North-East Asian economies of China, Hong Kong, Japan, Korea and Taiwan).

2   Super 301, originally known as the Gephart Amendment, built on Section 301 of the 1974 revision of US trade law. This allowed US trade representatives to apply sanctions where trading partners were judged to be discriminating against US exporters. In the intervening years, US trade policy representatives rarely made use of the provision that authorised retaliation against imports from countries regarded as unfair traders. Super 301 reduced the scope of discretion afforded trade administrators, requiring them publicly to identify countries regarded as unfair traders, and the course of action being adopted to redress trade policy grievances. In retaliation, Japan and the EU began publishing lists of what they perceived to be unfair trade practices of the USA.

3   Before 1986, Japan was a defendant in eleven cases at the GATT but chose to settle all but one of them bilaterally. By 1988 Japan had filed only four formal complaints before the GATT. For further discussion of Japan's new use of the multilateral trade dispute mechanisms see Pekkanen (2001).

4   The WTO website has a very useful section on the DSU, which allows for searching by topic or by country:
    <http://www.wto.org/english/tratop_e/dispu_e/dispu_e.htm>.

5   Tariffs on autos, one of the most significant sectors of manufacturing, are scheduled to fall from 62 per cent in 2001 to 25 per cent by mid-2006. Some tariffs, notably but not exclusively on agricultural products, will remain above 35 per cent in 2010. The protected products include motorcycles, photographic film and cameras.

6   For data on FDI flows see UNCTAD's annual *World Investment Report*, various years.

7   China made more than 700 individual pledges on trade policies ranging from agriculture to intellectual property rights in its accession treaties, which total more than 800 pages. For an assessment of early progress on implementation see United States General Accounting Office (2002). This paper and other useful analyses on China and the WTO can be accessed from:

<http://frwebgate.access.gpo.gov/cgibin/useftp.cgi?IPaddress=162.140.64.21filename;&=d03
7r.pdf&;directory=/diskb/wais/data/gao>.

8   In Aggarwal's (1995) terminology, these countries were 'GATT purists'.
9   As of March 2002, the WTO had been notified of the existence of 197 customs unions and free
    trade areas.
10 For discussion of the lack of interest of private sector actors in APEC and of the grouping's
    problems more generally see Ravenhill (2001).
11 Jayasuriya and Rosser (2001) and Stubbs (2000) are rare examples of authors who have examined
    the link between changing domestic economic interests and states' enthusiasm for regionalism.
12 Wall (2001) estimates that the value of Japan's exports to Mexico was 19 per cent lower than it
    would have been in the absence of NAFTA and Mexico's preferential agreement with the EU.
13 APEC members agreed to remove their trade barriers on a unilateral, non-discriminatory basis.
    Because APEC members will remove their barriers to all countries regardless of whether they are
    members of the grouping, it is not a preferential trade institution and therefore complies with the
    WTO requirement for non-discrimination.
14 The USA was the APEC economy most opposed to unilateral, non-discriminatory liberalisation,
    fearing that this would enable the EU to free-ride on the opening up of its markets.
15 APEC's twenty-one members are Australia, Brunei, Canada, Chile, China, Hong Kong,
    Indonesia, Japan, Malaysia, Mexico, New Zealand, Papua New Guinea, Peru, the Philippines,
    Russia, Singapore, South Korea, Taiwan, Thailand, the USA and Vietnam.

Bibliography

Aggarwal, V.K. (1995) 'Comparing regional cooperation efforts in the Asia-Pacific and North
    America', in A. Mack and J. Ravenhill (eds), *Pacific Cooperation: building economic and security regimes in
    the Asia-Pacific region*, Boulder, CO: Westview.
Baldwin, R.E. (1997) 'The causes of regionalism', *World Economy* 20: 865–888.
Dent, C.M. (2003) 'Networking the region? The emergence and impact of Asia-Pacific bilateral free
    trade agreements', *Pacific Review* 16: 1–28.
Doner, R.F. (1991) *Driving a Bargain: automobile industrialization and Japanese firms in Southeast Asia*,
    Berkeley, CA: University of California Press.
Doner, R.F. and Ramsay, A. (1993) 'Postimperialism and development in Thailand', *World Development*
    21: 691–704.
Garnaut, R. (2000) 'Introduction – APEC ideas and reality: history and prospects', in I. Yamazawa
    (ed.), *Asia Pacific Economic Cooperation (APEC)*, London: Routledge.
Hewison, K. (1989) *Bankers and Bureaucrats: capital and the role of the state in Thailand*, New Haven, CT:
    Yale University Southeast Asia Studies.
Jayasuriya, K. and Rosser, A. (2001) 'Economic crisis and the political economy of economic liberali-
    sation in South-East Asia', in G. Rodan, K. Hewison and R. Robison (eds), *The Political Economy of
    South-East Asia: conflicts, crises and change*, Melbourne: Oxford University Press.
Keidanren (1999) 'Challenges for the upcoming WTO negotiations and agendas for future Japanese
    trade policy', Keidanren. Available HTTP:
    <http://www.keidanren.or.jp/english/policy/pol102/proposal.html> (accessed 5 November
    2001).
Lardy, N.R. (2002) *Integrating China into the Global Economy*, Washington, DC: Brookings Institution.
Lincoln, E.J. (1999) *Troubled Times: US–Japan trade relations in the 1990s*, Washington, DC: Brookings
    Institution.
Lloyd, P. (2002) 'New bilateralism in the Asia-Pacific', *World Economy* 25: 1279–1296.
MacIntyre, A. (1991) *Business and Politics in Indonesia*, Sydney: Allen and Unwin.
Ministry of International Trade and Industry, Government of Japan (1999) 'White Paper on Interna-
    tional Trade 1999', Ministry of Economy, Trade and Industry. Available HTTP:
    <http://www.meti.go.jp/english/report/data/gWP1999e.html> (accessed 24 February 2002).
Ostrom, D. (2000) 'The United States, Japan and the WTO: new strategies, uncertain prospects', JEI
    Report 25. Available HTTP:

'Archive/JEIR00/0025f.html> (accessed 7 January 2003).

Aggressive legalism: the rules of the WTO and Japan's emerging trade
v 24: 707–737.

C and the Construction of Asia-Pacific Regionalism, Cambridge: Cambridge

e bloc world? The new East Asian regionalism', *International Relations of the*
... ...

Robison, R. (1986) *Indonesia: The Rise of Capital*, Sydney: Allen and Unwin.

Stubbs, R. (2000) 'Signing on to liberalization: AFTA and the politics of regional economic cooperation', *Pacific Review* 13: 297–318.

Supachai, P. and Clifford, M. (2002) *China and the WTO: changing China, changing World trade*, Singapore:
Wiley (Asia).

United States General Accounting Office (2002) 'World Trade Organization: Analysis of China's
Commitments to Other Members', USGAO, Report to Congressional Committees GAO-03–04
October. Available HTTP:
<http://www.gao.gov/new.items/d034.pdf> (accessed 7 January 2003).

Wall, H.J. (2001) 'Has Japan been left out in the cold by regional integration?', Bank of Japan, Institute for Monetary and Economic Studies, Discussion Paper No. 2001-E-15.

World Bank (2000) *Trade Blocs*, New York: Oxford University Press.

World Bank (2003) 'World Development Indicators 2003', Available HTTP:
<http://www.worldbank.org/data/wdi2003/index.htm> (accessed 19 May 2003).

WTO (2003) 'Statistics: International Trade Statistics 2002: Trade by Subject', World Trade Organization. Available HTTP:
<http://www.wto.org/english/res_e/statis_e/its2002_e/its02_bysubject_e.htm#leading_traders>
(accessed 18 May 2003).

Key reading

Baldwin, R.E. (1997) 'The causes of regionalism', *World Economy* 20: 865–888.

Dent, C.M. (2003) 'Networking the region? The emergence and impact of Asia-Pacific bilateral free
trade agreements', *Pacific Review* 16: 1–28.

Pekkanen, S.M. (2001) 'Aggressive legalism: the rules of the WTO and Japan's emerging trade
strategy', *World Economy* 24: 707–737.

Ravenhill, J. (2001) *APEC and the Construction of Asia-Pacific Regionalism*, Cambridge: Cambridge
University Press.

Ravenhill, J. (2002) 'A three bloc world? The new East Asian regionalism', *International Relations of the
Asia-Pacific* 2: 167–195.

Useful websites

www.apecsec.org.sg (APEC Secretariat).

www.aseansec.org/home.htl (ASEAN Secretariat).

www.meti.go.jp/english/index.html (Ministry of Economy, Trade and Industry, Government of Japan).

www.unctad.org (United Nations Conference on Trade and Development).

www.gao.gov (United States General Accounting Office).

4 NAFTA + chapter 5

A decade on

Andrew F. Cooper

Summary

When the North American Free Trade Agreement (NAFTA) came into existence – ten years ago – it appeared to be highly innovative in terms of its
form and actorness. Far from being revolutionary, however, NAFTA has
taken on a settled – even immobilized – look. This chapter examines the
reasons and the impact of this paradox. Central to the discussion are the
foundational characteristics of the agreement with NAFTA being created not
only as a one-off but a limited arrangement. Furthermore, the argument is
made that what intellectual and instrumental energy exists to extend the
architectural design beyond established institutional and procedural parameters has been drained by the lingering effects of September 11, 2001. For
this traumatic event placed the goal of North American – and more
precisely US – security ahead of economic prosperity. Although there
remains extant the possibility of renewed momentum for the NAFTA project
to be taken to a different and more ambitious stage, these steps will be
uneven and informed by a greater contest between strategic visions.

The North American Free Trade Agreement (NAFTA) has run a paradoxical course over
its ten years of existence. When it came into being this agreement between the USA,
Canada, and Mexico appeared to be in the vanguard of a 'trade policy revolution'
(Winham 1994: 472). Unlike the European Union (EU) and the Asia–Pacific Economic
Cooperation (APEC), the North American regional option was originally driven by its least
developed partner. The speed with which it moved from initial agreement to negotiate in
mid-1990 to formal implementation on January 1, 1994 stood out from the drawn-out
process featured in the other models of integration. Amidst all the controversy over the
implications of the nature of the bargain the significance of NAFTA was marked by its
potential to extend the trade agenda beyond its traditional ambit to encompass non-trade
concerns including investment and social matters.

Looking at the manner by which NAFTA has evolved, however, the dominant image is
no longer one associated with the front lines of regionalism. Debate continues about the
putative winners and losers of the NAFTA architecture (*Foreign Policy* 2002). But the form
and intensity of these arguments have been largely reconfigured. While the negative results
of NAFTA continue to be targeted by its traditional detractors this source of criticism

increasingly has had to share space with the disillusionment felt by many of its original supporters that the NAFTA arrangement has not gone far enough. From this perspective, the deficiency with NAFTA is not its recipe for change, highlighted by sensitivities concerning sovereignty, social fragmentation, and a race to the bottom. Rather the problem is found in its settled – even immobilized – construct. In the words of one such supporter, NAFTA 'did not envisage any unified approach to extract NAFTA's promise, nor did it contemplate any common response to new threats' (Pastor 2001: 2).

The central theme of this chapter is to analyze the limitations of NAFTA by locating this agreement in terms of its foundational characteristics. Instead of acting as a platform for robust and cascading innovation this architectural design established specific institutional and procedural parameters to build in the status quo. This is not to deny the capacity for *de facto* modifications – either toward the future or presently in train – in NAFTA. What stands out though is how much of this pattern has come about not by strategic calculation but by unintended consequences. If there is no prospect for NAFTA to be abrogated there is little appetite either for any type of formal renegotiation to rectify its established faults or to encourage regeneration as a project of integration in North America.

The institutional and procedural parameters on NAFTA

An essential first stage to understanding the limitations on NAFTA is found in the minimalism of its institutional features. In stark contrast to the EU there is no executive built into the design of NAFTA. Nor is there a nascent legislature akin to the European Parliament. The Free Trade Commission established in NAFTA remains not only resolutely intergovernmental but almost invisible in the public context. Instead of presenting a physically grounded or a permanent institution the Commission operates on an ad hoc basis with meetings, aside from an annual meeting, being called only as necessary. Far from an elaborately structured bureaucracy – with masses of NAFTAcrats – the NAFTA administrative apparatus remains small, narrow, and specialized. Each country selects a senior trade official as a NAFTA coordinator to deal with the management and administrative schedule. Much of the technical work is delegated in turn to more specialized work programs managed by working groups and/or committees or as in the case of the dispute settlement understanding in Chapter 19 (subsidy and dumping) cases through binational panels.

The main institutional extensions have come in parallel to the development of the two side accords in NAFTA on the environment and labor standards, the North American Agreement on Environmental Cooperation and the North American Agreement on Labor Cooperation. In the case of the environment, the Commission for Environmental Cooperation (CEC) with headquarters in Montreal, a sixty-person staff from the three countries, and an established work program has been held up as the clearest illustration of working tri-lateralization (Deere and Esty 2002). Individual citizens and/or groups can make use of the CEC's formal machinery for investigation where they believed national environmental laws were not being enforced. In the case of the labor side accord, three National Administrative Offices (NAOs) were established to hear complaints about some areas of working conditions. The Commission for Labor Cooperation, with a coordination role, consists of a small secretariat based in Dallas.

The influence of the 'glare of publicity' ensuing from both of these side accords should not be completely discounted. Complaints on the labor front were permitted on three fundamental sets of issues: the utilization of child labor, health and safety, and on questions to do with minimum wage. As a vehicle for policy advancement, the CEC pushed some degree of transparency onto environmental issues. As the director-general of a Mexican environmental group noted soon after the CEC's inception, civil society was accorded 'a moral power to make things public and to get governments to do things according to the law' (Simon 1996). More recently, the CEC is judged to have been instrumental in nudging Mexico to set out a toxic release inventory based on a mix of the inventories created already in Canada and the USA and the CEC's own Pollutant Release and Transfer Register (Davidson and Mitchell 2002).

Yet with twin disadvantages of a narrowly defined range of authority and the lack of enforcement powers neither should the impact of these add-ons be exaggerated. On the environment, the most contentious issues dealing with cross-border pollution whether in the form of the dumping of industrial wastes or air and water pollution remain untouched. As the CEC's rulings were not binding, even in the area of its domain, there continued to be quite obvious deficiencies in terms of implementation. Because complaints pertaining to it were restricted to the formal sectors of the economy the scope of the labor side deal was extremely narrow. Only cases in its three mandated areas could go to arbitration and potentially to the introduction of sanctions for non-enforcement.

In terms of process, NAFTA lacked the catalytic ingredients for change available in the EU. Without the institutional position of the President of the EU Commission there has been no equivalent within the NAFTA apparatus of a Jacques Delors ready and able to provide a blueprint to take the project to a different stage of development. Nor is there the regular feature of formal NAFTA summitry that concentrates the mind of political leaders (and their policy advisors) on the search for the next big idea and/or deal making in terms of the agenda. The importance of such a site has been reinforced by the results derived by the recent meetings of the NAFTA leaders on the margins of other regional or functional summits. One illustration of this phenomenon emerged in the context of the April 2001 Summit of the Americas in Quebec City, when US President George W. Bush, Prime Minister Jean Chrétien of Canada, and President Vicente Fox of Mexico agreed to set up an Energy Working Group to foster North American cooperation in this area. Another example came to the fore between the same 'three amigos' in the Spring of 2002 at the Monterrey United Nations Conference on Financing for Development when President Fox sought to engage the other two leaders with an ambitious list of NAFTA plus proposals.

Underpinning these institutional limitations were three other contextual ingredients. For one thing, the parameters of NAFTA were shaped by the unique political make-up of the USA. The economic logic of greater commercial efficiencies through reduction of transaction costs and economies of scale was appealing to many within the US elite, including Presidents Bush, both father and son. Still the political contest on NAFTA had been a bruising one, with the anti-NAFTA forces (emanating from conservative isolationists and populists as well the labor movement and influential segments of the environmental movement) mounting a protracted campaign against the project. Although the pro-NAFTA side did win the struggle it was a hard-fought and close result. The US Congress – which in any case maintained its 'deep and enduring skepticism' concerning 'the infringement of sovereignty' – therefore had no incentive to extend the project in any direction that could be interpreted as building a political superstructure on top of an economic arrangement (Talbot 2002: viii).

A second constraint reflected the uneven structural shape of NAFTA. Not only is NAFTA an agreement between highly unequal partners, it is highly asymmetrical in its pattern of relationships. Far from a triangular deal it is a project bringing awkwardly together in a merger two sets of bilateral relationships or double dyads. The special relationship for both Canada and Mexico is with the USA. The connections between Canada and Mexico – while growing (significantly Mexico has become Canada's fourth largest trading partner) – are still totally overshadowed by these main games. In 2001 the Canada–US relationship comprised 60 per cent of North American trade (C$569 billion), with the Mexico–US relationship forming 38 per cent. By way of contrast, the Canada–Mexico relationship formed only 2 per cent of North American trade (Report of the Standing Committee on Foreign Affairs and International Trade 2002: 58–59).

To complicate matters further, Canada and Mexico have attempted to manage their relationships with the USA through quite divergent techniques. Canada has combined the practices of quiet 'routine' diplomacy in the bilateral context with attempts to restrain the USA in a tangle of multilateral institutions and arrangements. All forms of policy linkage are publicly disavowed in favor of the extension of rules-based mechanisms. Mexico has embraced more risky practices. Up to the effort of reinvention undertaken by President Carlos Salinas in the early 1990s Mexico tried to distance itself from the USA in foreign policy terms. Since the advent of the NAFTA era Mexico has pursued aggressive efforts of public diplomacy cum lobbying in the USA on a variety of high-profile issues (Pastor and de Castro 1998; Eisenstad 1997).

A third constraint on NAFTA is the strong element of negative integration contained within the project. Instead of focusing on what can be done the orientation is toward what should be avoided. This feature reflects the commercial bias in NAFTA in which the notion of a North American community is negated. Even on the commercial side, however, the dominant concern is on negation.

The controversy over Article 11 showcases this dimension of the NAFTA paradox. At one level, Article 11 on investor–state provisions or the settlement of investment disputes may be seen as part of the radical spirit of the project in that it points toward a new externally imposed constitutionalism for North America predicated on the dilution of national economic controls generally and the right of corporations to sue governments more specifically (Clarkson 2002). Although sophisticated arguments can be made that this component of NAFTA should be both rethought and reworked (especially with regard to clarification of scope and increased transparency), Article 11 seems consistent with the negative model of integration. Far from opening up NAFTA to some alternative grand design of market-based integration the essence of Article 11 is prevention. In substance this thrust has been consistent with the concern for protection and non-discrimination deemed essential by the architects of NAFTA if investment was to be attracted to Mexico as a developing country. That is to say, the intention was to use Article 11 as a stabilizer reducing the uncertainty of doing business. Notwithstanding the backlash generated by a number of individual cases (most notably, the Methanex case), the impact of these decisions remains isolated and subject to some form of redress. Procedurally, with no standing court NAFTA has no means of expanding case law on the basis of such precedents. Politically, there are some signs that the USA may be bending in its defense of Article 11 in the argument that a 'mere diminution' in the value of an investment does not constitute an expropriation whereas in the Methanex case the company claimed it did do (Ortiz 2002).

Pressures and constraints on innovation

While formidable this array of interconnected constraints did not stymie all forms of innovation. Akin to the catalytic role of President Salinas on the initiation of NAFTA, President

Vicente Fox attempted to kick-start a drive toward a NAFTA plus immediately after his election in July 2000. Confident in his status as a legitimately elected leader of the PAN (National Action Party), not the discredited PRI, Fox circulated a wide number of proposals on how a community of North America could be achieved through freer mobility of people, common currency, a customs union, and even a shared passport. Although much of this initiative composed a symbolic exercise, revealing his willingness to act as a change agent at the apex of a new Mexico, Fox's plan had two important instrumental ingredients attached to it. On one axis, the push for a big idea and solutions (the so-called whole enchilada) on the migration dossier was animated by a desire to propel Mexico–US relations into another era away from the images of illegal/undocumented workers and a militarized border.

Salinas and the Administration of President George Bush Senior had attempted to avoid this issue by adopting the mantra that NAFTA would end the need for migration by delivering prosperity. As Paul Krugman summarized the argument:

> NAFTA is a sort of pledge … a pledge to foreign investors that Mexican reform will continue (and that the US market will remain open to goods produced in Mexico). It is also a pledge to the Mexican population that better times are coming.
>
> (Krugman 1993: 18–19)

Fox not only addressed the migration head-on but merged this issue with a call for greater equity between the developed and developing parts of the NAFTA by emphasizing the salience of regionalism as a development lever. As the former governor of a migrant-oriented state, Fox aimed at a strategy that would benefit not just the relatively prosperous North but the poorer zones of Mexico. Applying a variation of the EU model, via the social cohesion funds, Fox's solution centered on the introduction of a development fund to ameliorate inequities between the regions of Mexico as well as the NAFTA partners.

The logic behind these twin initiatives held some strong impetus in the Mexican political context. By pushing for a migration deal with the USA, the Fox government shifted the debate about human rights away from Mexico's still sensitive record associated with police and judicial corruption and abuse to the question of the rights of Mexicans entering into the USA. Equally, by ratcheting up the NAFTA agenda from a narrow concentration on jobs and investment to a concern with economic/social development the Fox government tackled the question of indigenous rights in a more constructive and long-term manner. The Chiapas revolt in particular had been a source of embarrassment for the image of a new Mexico and Fox and his advisors had a huge incentive to have it disappear.

At least prior to September 11, the possibility was open for Mexico's NAFTA partners to buy into these ideas. In the intellectual/policy domain, a considerable number of proposals were floating around which meshed with the Fox agenda. Arguably the most compelling voice in the USA for a revitalization of NAFTA was Robert Pastor, President Jimmy Carter's former NSC (National Security Council) advisor on the Americas and a co-author of a book with Jorge Castañeda, Fox's first choice as foreign minister (Pastor 2001). Elaborating on Fox's sketch, Pastor laid out a detailed portrait of a NAFTA plus arrangement. If skeptical about some of the details about the EU blueprint (for example, the extension of the social inclusion fund to include the poor regions of rich countries), Pastor drew heavily on the European experience. Indeed, in the vein of the most ambitious proponents of European integration Pastor advocated not only a customs union, but mobile pools of labor, and a development fund akin to a European model. His plan encompassed as well a set of supranational institutions (including a North American Court on Trade and Investment), a common currency, coordination of foreign policy, and a North American plan for transportation and infrastructural development.

Although the scale of Pastor's ambition gives his guidelines pride of place, a host of proposals moving in the same direction were drawn up by a number of other thinkers and institutes. Some, such as the introduction to an edited collection by Hakim and Litan, were somewhat cautious in nature: 'Designing and implementing measures beyond NAFTA will be difficult, if not impossible until policymakers and citizens reach broad agreement on medium- and longer-run objectives' (Hakim and Litan 2002: 11–12). Other formulations, such as that offered by Anthony De Palma in his book, *Here: A Biography of the New American Continent*, were more far-sighted and idealistic about the possibilities of the emergence of a North American community (De Palma 2001).

Canadian ideas on NAFTA plus were less well developed but exhibited a similar sense of urgency about the need to rethink the model of North American integration. Much of this activity – not surprisingly given the concentration of Canadian economic activity vis-à-vis the USA – was directed toward a narrow definition of North America. When the senior foreign ministry official with responsibility for the Americas on leaving government service voiced that the time was ripe for 'a full debate' on policy harmonization the focus was on the Canada–US partnership (Toulin 2001a). A similar theme can be detected in the view expressed just before September 11 by a close advisor to Prime Minister Chrétien, David Zussman, who said 'it's time to ignore taboo and begin "frank talks" with a continental coalition' (Toulin 2001b).

None the less, sneaking out from behind the Canadian obsession with the USA were some indications that a more comprehensive agenda was being considered. Zussman visited Mexico and came back (soaking up the atmosphere of the Fox proposals) full of enthusiasm for thinking about how the EU model could be applied to North America. In a major speech in his capacity as the President of the Public Policy Forum he went so far as to urge that 'Canadians needed to debate … the possibility of a political and economic union with the US and Mexico' (Association of Professional Executives of the Public Service of Canada 2000).

Despite the abundant intellectual attractions, the political optics about seizing the moment to embrace a NAFTA plus agenda were not as one-sided. Showcasing the special relationship between the USA and Mexico held some attractions to President George W. Bush's Republican Administration. Electorally, such a strategy held some potential for weaning Mexican–US voters away from the Democrats. In policy terms, a deal on migration brought with it not only heightened bureaucratic efficiency but commercial advantages. System friction on migration issues contradicted the reality on the ground that without this workforce many parts of the US economy would shrivel away. Concessions on the migration issue also opened the way to a quid pro quo in the form of cooperation between law enforcement officials, an advance most helpful on the narcotics-trafficking front.

At a personal level, their common backgrounds as corporate executives and state governors appeared to facilitate a breakthrough on these terms. The affinity between President Bush and President Fox was apparent when Bush made his first trip abroad to visit Fox at his ranch in Guanajuarto. And there was much fanfare about Mexico being the USA's 'best friend' when Bush played host to Fox in Washington, DC just days before September 11 (Sanger 2001).

These apparent opportunities, however, should still disguise the obstacles to any big deal on migration or NAFTA plus. Neither the Administration nor the Congress wanted to be seen as debating – never mind responding to – a Mexican political agenda. Any deal would be made on the US terms in both terms of timing and administrative detail. As in so many aspects of NAFTA the US political system remained the 800-pound gorilla around which the other actors had to navigate. Whereas a cluster of states could move the EU agenda forward in loose coalition, NAFTA remained dominated by a singe state with a highly localized and highly fragmented decision-making culture.

The constraints on the Canadian side were nuanced but at least equally restrictive. If the logic of moving forward with a NAFTA plus approach was recognized by select individuals in the policy and economic elite, the Canadian political leadership remained skeptical about any great leap forward. In part this caution mirrored the safe political style of Prime Minister Chrétien. Chrétien was willing to test the water as indicated earlier when he allowed the Canadian Ambassador to the USA – his nephew – to put out a trial balloon at the Woodrow Wilson Center on April 29, 1999, in which Raymond Chrétien asked how best: 'Can we deepen and fine-tune our bilateral trade relationship to maximize the prosperity and security of North America?' (quoted in Scoffield 1999).

If willing to talk about a new agenda, Prime Minister Chrétien remained reluctant to do anything in a dramatic fashion to address it. As demonstrated by the public opinion spin put on a June 1999 cabinet retreat to discuss these issues (quoted in Wallace 1999), any notion of a grand vision in terms of rethinking the relationship was played down. Any prospect toward a deepened form of economic integration by way of bold steps, such a customs union or dollarization, was denied.

These stylistic constraints were reinforced by the obvious substantive impediments. Canada and Mexico could tactically use commonalities of positions on world issues with each other to offset the power of the USA, as they did most recently during the 2003 Iraq invasion (with Chrétien and Fox meeting in Mexico to compare positions). Strategically, however, the two countries remained as much rivals as allies. These differences came to the fore when Chrétien treated Fox's proposals for NAFTA plus with public studied coolness and private status anxiety when he visited Ottawa prior to his inauguration as Mexican President (Wilson-Forsberg 2001: 6). Not only were these proposals rejected as being too much too soon, they were rebuffed simply for being a Mexican initiative.

Conundrums on both deepening and widening

The tragedy of September 11 distracted attention away from the NAFTA plus agenda by defining North America in security not trade or economic terms. It would be misleading to suggest that security had been completely absent from the original motivation or earlier crises linked to NAFTA. Much of the original enthusiasm for NAFTA in the USA went well beyond the economic incentives. Foreign policy, and in particular geo-security considerations, played an important role as well. These concerns were rekindled with the 1994–1995 peso crisis, leading to the massive bail-out to ensure the ongoing stability of Mexico (Heath 1999).

September 11 represented a very different type of shock both in scale and in consequence. The earlier crises were made in Mexico, crises that spilled over into the NAFTA relationship. They complicated but did not compromise the economic main game at the heart of the NAFTA arrangement. September 11 threatened to subordinate – or trump – that core dimension to the security nexus.

The immediate rebranding of the North American space post-September 11 was not toward deals that would stimulate a NAFTA plus set of arrangements. Rather it was toward a reconfiguration of its two immediate borders into a security perimeter compatible with homeland defense. In principle, if the model of this exercise was to reproduce the EU model of a hard outer shell combined with a porous inner layer, this concept held some attraction to Canadian and Mexican business. In practice, though, the USA moved to reinforce not reduce the barriers on the points of entry between its NAFTA partners and itself. The image of militarization was exacerbated, moreover, by the changes in the US strategic command structure to give greater prominence to North America and privileged treatment to missile defense.

In their responses to this challenge, the approaches of Canada and Mexico reflected where the two countries fit in with the US 'homeland'. If considerable debate arose in Canada about how far/how much Canadian policies should adjust symbolically and instrumentally to the attack on the USA, the debate in Mexico remained much more in favor of being hands-off influenced by the tradition of non-intervention and sovereignty (*The Economist* 2001). Such a response may be understandable but at least in the short term it plays to the strength of those US political forces that wish to exploit such sentiments to tighten not loosen the border – both because of security concerns and because of a wide number of other issues ranging from migration to trucking practices.

For all of these reasons it is understandable why Canadian politicians and officials have tried to rebrand the frontier not as part of a North American security perimeter but as part of a set of initiatives that reassure the Americans that Canada takes security concerns seriously while not forgetting either its commercial interests or wider foreign policy identity. While a number of alternative slogans appeared from the catchy (ziplock border) to the comprehensive albeit rather laborious zone of mutual confidence, the 'smart border' is the one that has come to the fore, one that is comprehensive in its aims (keeping the bad guys out while allowing the good – and goods – to cross). With an onus on technical fixes contained in the thirty-point agenda are efforts for a more systematic and sophisticated form of pre-clearance system.

On the face of it, Mexico moved in the same direction as Canada. Mexico and the USA also signed a parallel 'smart border' agreement on border security in early 2002. Although not as far reaching as the Canada–US version the US–Mexico Border Partnership Action Plan does represent an important advancement in the ongoing shift in Mexican foreign policy with respect to the USA. The task of convincing the USA that a smart border is not just desirable, but viable, continues to be a very different and more arduous task in Mexico than in Canada.

The alternative route to circumvent this conundrum had long been the widening of NAFTA. The USA had been the traditional champion of this approach from the time of George Bush Senior's call for an 'Enterprise of the Americas' to Bill Clinton's hosting of the December 1994 Miami Summit of the Americas with its goal of an all-encompassing free trade zone by 2005. Not only did this proposal have the advantage of promoting economic liberalization in the region, but it held the promise of consolidating the hemispheric trends toward democratization. Instead of a firm embrace of this strategy through a concerted effort on the Free Trade Area of the Americas (FTAA), however, the USA under George W. Bush had grown more ambivalent and disconnected from the Americas. The only issue for which there continued to be any enthusiasm in Washington, DC was the struggle against Castro's Cuba, an issue on which the USA remained out of step with its neighbors. The USA was viewed as mishandling the crisis in Argentina, a country that under President Carlos Menem had been a close ally. It seemed out of step with the ideological trends – and sense of disillusionment with reform – carrying Lula da Silva to power in Brazil (Naim 2003). Indeed the behavior of Bush's former Treasury Secretary, Paul O'Neill, was taken by regional officials to be indicative of the USA's attitude in making 'offensive' and 'dangerous' remarks about Argentina and Brazil which compounded the damage of the crises (quoted in Dinmore 2003).

There were some diplomatic advantages for Mexico filling this gap of leadership. In a NAFTA enlargement scenario, Mexico had a considerable advantage in terms of voice opportunity, because it would have participated in defining the terms of entry. There was also a price to be paid if the other countries in the region were to think that Mexico had sided with the USA and Canada to deny their access to the US market. Still, these incentives were trumped by the economic disadvantages for the Mexicans because of an enlargement of NAFTA. Following the ratification of the FTAA, Mexican corporations would be on a level playing field with their North American competitors on Latin American markets. Mexico would also see the US market open up to its Latin American competitors. Instead of a privileged position through NAFTA it would be reduced to a role of being one of thirty-four participants in multilateral talks. Furthermore, the regulations of the FTAA would most likely be less strict than those of NAFTA. This means that it will cost less for Mexico's competitors to have access to the US market. For example, unlike Mexico, they would probably not be obliged to sign agreements on labor rights and the environment. These reasons, together, held Mexico back from any assertive posture. While Brazil was allowed to play the role of deal-breaker, Mexican participation in the FTAA negotiations was designed in order to restrict its losses and it is to its advantage that the negotiations drag on. Mexico's energy was placed on diversifying its economic partnerships on a selective basis within Latin America and with the EU (*Latin American Monitor* 2001: 18).

Canada, having lost its unique position derived from the Canada–US Free Trade Agreement, is not as concerned as Mexico about sharing its privileged access to the US market with other countries in the region. It is thus a staunch supporter of a free trade area of the Americas. Indeed, as has often been stressed by its leaders, Canada was the country that insisted that NAFTA include an accession provision. In diplomatic terms, Canada sees the creation of a free trade area as a way to correct the imbalance in terms of voice opportunities that characterizes the close relationship between Canada and the USA. This imbalance was intensified by the ratification of the CUSFTA and NAFTA, which did not provide for any institutional political mechanisms that Canada could use to counterbalance its huge economic dependence. In parallel with its efforts on the FTAA Canada has also pursued separate initiatives, first of all in the form of a bilateral deal with Chile (a move copied by its NAFTA partners) and then negotiations with Costa Rica and other smaller countries.

This interest in using NAFTA to achieve diplomatic gains is all the more understandable given that Canada can only envisage marginal economic gains from trade liberalization with South America and the Caribbean. To illustrate the region's relative economic importance for Canada, it should be noted that trade with all the countries in the region (except Cuba) with which it had not signed a free trade agreement barely amounts to 1.5 per cent of Canadian foreign trade.

Consistent with its long-term diplomatic goals, the Canadian government was also counting on the FTAA to encourage outward-looking and cooperative US economic policies. In other words, this option was consistent with the longer-term Canadian approach of containing through institutions US aggressive unilateral actions with respect to trade remedy laws. The most tangible aspect of this approach was the potential the FTAA negotiations offered for providing a counterweight to anti-dumping and countervailing duties.

The problem for Canada is that its interest in the hemisphere is diluted by competing priorities in Canada's foreign policy. Geographically, the Americas remain but one region competing for attention and resources within the framework of – and tensions between – Canada's perceived role as an activist middle power and the realities of its North American location (Cooper 1997, 2000). On the one side, Canada's membership in a wide number of other organizations (NATO, the Commonwealth, the francophone summit, APEC) detracts from Canada's focus on the Americas. On the other side, the realities of its economic main game (especially in the post-September 11 context) preclude too much ambition.

Conclusion

This analysis of NAFTA a decade on leaves the unmistakable impression of stalling or even reversal of the project. The success of NAFTA was largely predicated on its ability to promote a sense of order through the establishment of a trade regime, rules on investment, and increasing its ambit over some areas of the social agenda. On the basis that the focus of criticisms of the project has tilted from a backward to a forward-looking trajectory, with an eye to reform rather than rejection, the judgment on NAFTA remains positive. Yet, instead of emerging out of its foundational moment in a constructive and progressive fashion, NAFTA has maintained a defensive air about it. Much of the negative impression about NAFTA relates to its closed orientation featuring a lack of public/society access. The image of corporate rights having a status unobtainable by ordinary citizens within the NAFTA countries has been played up by the publicity given to the (still small) number of cases under Article 11. The potential for advances on the side arrangements dealing with the environment and labor standards has, as they have evolved until now, not provided an adequate counterweight to this impression of a democratic deficit.

The constraints on the mode of innovation are numerous and formidable, namely the constraints imposed on an arrangement which remains dominated by its thin intergovernmental structure, the asymmetry between its members, and its lack of innovation beyond its original mandate. These ingredients not only stymie forms of collective action but allow shocks to reverberate through the system as illustrated most vividly by the repercussions from September 11. In direct fashion this traumatic event placed the goal of North American – and more precisely US – security ahead of economic prosperity. More indirectly, by explicitly placing the notion of community at the service of its dominant partners' interests and objectives, it injected a greater sense of acrimony in the project. Questions which might have been viewed as 'low' issues (whether the issue of softwood lumber in the Canadian–US relationship or trucking and agricultural subsidies in the Mexican–US relationship) have taken on a greater profile as litmus tests of the entire state of the NAFTA arrangement.

This is not to suggest that NAFTA or indeed the two bilateral relationships have moved completely off their established moorings. As rehearsed above there is a good deal of emergent intellectual vigor about how NAFTA can be retooled and moved forward. There is if anything a better comfort zone at the technical level not only between state officials but business groups within the three countries than when NAFTA was engineered. Policy makers, regulators, trade bureaucrats, and entrepreneurs mix easily together at events such as the recent 'Partnership for Prosperity' meeting (a forum set up in early 2001 to create jobs in depressed areas of Mexico) (Silver 2003).

What September 11 has done is make the future of NAFTA far more uneven and contradictory. Beset by the imperatives of securitization – or re-bordering – many of the innovations introduced between the NAFTA countries will continue to put the emphasis on keeping threats and enemies out rather than facilitating the efficient flow of goods and services (Andreas 2002). One sign of this approach was the shift toward harmonization between Canada and the USA on common visa policies. Another was the acceleration of the managing of refugee claims through Safe Third Country provisions. Still others came through the establishment of Integrated Border and Marine Enforcement Teams and the sharing of information on customs information and passenger information.

Yet, this concentration on what makes a region (natural or not) safe might have the spillover effect found through other means in the EU. The concept of and connections between North America have been concentrated in an unanticipated fashion. Business leaders in Canada have gone on the offensive in calling for variations of a customs union. Mexican state officials have pushed for innovation even when it has meant risks and departures from accepted practices. Most notably, in October 2002, Fox stated that Mexico

> considers the struggle against terrorism to be part of the commitment of Mexico with Canada and the United States to build within the framework of the North American free trade agreement a shared space of development, well being and integral security.

Although its own response to these initiatives clearly contains a visible downside, it must be acknowledged that the USA has had to take its NAFTA partners seriously and decide how it wants to define its closest and most relevant neighborhood.

Ten years after its signing, then, the future of NAFTA continues to be up for grabs. If NAFTA brought with it a semblance of order, the arrangement has continued to be associated with disorder as well. What was expected to be the projected evolution of events and responses has not taken shape. The commercial logic of NAFTA – while experiencing pressures from representatives of civil society – was thrown off stride by events outside of the realm of imagination in 1994 as we moved through the immediate post-Cold War era. Yet, ten years hence, it is unlikely that what we see now in NAFTA will be what emerges over the next few years. While these new developments will likely be taken in small steps (and in all likelihood at different speeds between the NAFTA partners), they will be informed by a greater contest between strategic visions. After pausing for a deep breath – in the aftermath of September 11 – there remains extant the possibility of renewed momentum for the NAFTA project to be taken to a different and more innovative stage.

Bibliography

Andreas, P. (1998) 'The paradox of integration: liberalizing and criminalizing flows across the US-Mexican border', in C. Wise (ed.), *The post NAFTA political economy: Mexico and the Western hemisphere*, College Park, PA: Pennsylvania State University Press.

Andreas, P. (2002) Remarks made to the conference, 'The re-bordering of North America: integration or exclusion after September 11th?', Watson Institute for International Studies, Brown University, February 5.

Association of Professional Executives of the Public Service of Canada (2000). Notes for an address by Dr. David Zussman, President Public Policy Forum, at the 2000 Apex Symposium 'Canada in the World', May 31.

Clarkson, S. (2002) *Uncle Sam and Us*, Toronto: University of Toronto Press.

Cooper, A.F. (1997) *Canadian Foreign Policy: old habits and new directions*, Scarborough, Ontario: Prentice Hall Canada.

Cooper, A.F. (2000) 'Waiting at the perimeter: making US policy in Canada', in F.O. Hampson and M.A. Molot (eds), *Canada among Nations: vanishing borders*, Don Mills, Ontario: Oxford University Press.

Davidson, D.J. and Mitchell, R.E. (2002) 'Environmental challenges to international trade', in E.J. Chambers and P.H. Smith (eds), *NAFTA in the New Millennium*, La Jolla/Edmonton: Center for US-Mexican Studies, University of California; San Diego: University of Alberta Press.

De Palma, A. (2001) *Here: a biography of the new American Continent*, New York: Public Affairs.

Deere, C.L. and Esty, D.C. (eds) (2002) *Greening the Americas: NAFTA's lessons for hemispheric trade*, Cambridge, MA: The MIT Press.

Dinmore, G. (2003) 'Powell overture fails to impress Latin Americans', *Financial Times* June 11.

The Economist (2001) 'Fair-weather friends?', 20 September. Available HTTP: <http://www.economist.com/displaystory.cfm?story_id=788631> (accessed 23 July 2003).

Eisenstad, T.A. (1997) 'The rise of the Mexico lobby in Washington: even further from God, and even closer to the United States', in R.O de la Garza and J. Velasco (eds), *Bringing the border: transforming Mexico–US relations*, Boulder, CO: Rowman & Littlefield.

Foreign Policy (2002) 'Happily ever NAFTA? A debate', September/October: 58–65.

Hakim, P. and Litan, R.E. (eds) (2002) *The future of North American integration*, Washington, DC: Brookings Institution.

Heath, J. (1999) *Mexico and the Sexenio Curse: presidential successions and economic crises in modern Mexico*, Washington, DC: Center for Strategic and International Studies.

Krugman, P. (1993) 'The uncomfortable truth about NAFTA: it's foreign policy, stupid', *Foreign Affairs* 72 (November/December): 13–19.

Latin American Monitor (2001) 'Mexico moves for more FTAs', November 11.

Naim, M. (2003) 'Lula needs a lift from America', *Financial Times* June 19.

Ortiz, M.A. (2002) 'Dispute settlement under NAFTA', in J.E. Chambers and P.H. Smith (eds), *NAFTA in the New Millennium*, La Jolla/Edmonton: Center for US-Mexican Studies, University of California; San Diego: University of Alberta Press.

Pastor, R.A. (2001) 'Towards North American community: lessons from the old world for the new', DC: Institute for International Economics.

Pastor, R.A. and de Castro, R.F. (eds) (1998) *The Controversial Pivot: the US Congress and North America*, Washington, DC: Brookings Institution.

Report of the Standing Committee on Foreign Affairs and International Trade (2000) 'Partners in North America: advancing Canada's relations with the United States and Mexico', December.

Sanger, D.E. (2001) 'Mexico's President rewrites the rules', *The New York Times* September 8.

Scoffield, H. (1999) 'Canada pushed on several fronts towards integration with US', *Globe and Mail* June 4.

Silver, S. (2003) 'Meeting seeks to repair US–Mexico ties', *Financial Times* June 14/15.

Simon, B. (1996) 'Making the most of moral power', *Financial Times* September 3.

Talbot, S. (2002) 'Foreword', in P. Hakim and R.E. Litan (eds), *The Future of North American Integration*, Washington, DC: Brookings Institution.

Toulin, A. (2001a) 'Union with US on table: PM's advisor Says', *National Post* June 29.

Toulin, A. (2001b) '"Congestion costs business: we should push it as far as we can", chief advisor concludes', *National Post* July 17.

Wallace, W. (1999) 'PM seeks freer trade in Americas', *Toronto Star* June 30.

Wilson-Forsberg, S. (2001) 'Overcoming obstacles on the road to North America: a view from Canada', FOCAL Policy Paper, Ottawa, November.

Winham, G. (1994) 'NAFTA and the trade policy revolution of the 1980s: a Canadian perspective', *International Journal* vol. 49, Summer Issue 472–508.

Key readings

Cooper, A.F. (2000) 'Waiting at the perimeter: making US policy in Canada', in F.O Hampson and M.A. Molot (eds), *Canada Among Nations: vanishing borders*, Don Mills, Ontario: Oxford University Press.

Chambers, J. and Smith, P. (eds) (2002) *NAFTA in the New Millennium*, La Jolla/Edmonton: Center for US-Mexican Studies, University of California; San Diego: University of Alberta Press.

De Palma, A. (2001) *Here: a biography of the new American Continent*, New York: Public Affairs.

Foreign Policy (2002) 'Happily ever NAFTA? A debate', September/October: 58–65.

Hakim, P. and Litan, R.E. (eds) (2002) *The Future of North American Integration*, Washington, DC: Brookings Institution.

Pastor, R.A. and de Castro, R.F. (eds) (1998) *The Controversial Pivot: the US Congress and North America*, Washington, DC: Brookings Institution.

Pastor, R.A. (2001) 'Towards North American community: lessons from the old world for the new', Washington, DC: Institute for International Economics, August.

Report of the Standing Committee on Foreign Affairs and International Trade (2002) 'Partners in North America: advancing Canada's relations with the United States and Mexico', December.

Useful websites

www.naalc.org (Commission for Labor Cooperation).

www.naaec.org (Commission for Environmental Cooperation).

www.iie.org (Institute for International Economics).

www.citizen.org (Public Citizen, Global Trade Watch).

5 The political economy of the Free Trade Area of the Americas

Paulo S. Wrobel

Summary

The chapter describes the initiative to form the Free Trade Area of the Americas (FTAA) in the context of two main economic forces, regionalization and globalization. Extremely ambitious, the FTAA would include all American nations except Cuba, and create the largest regional trade area in the world, from Alaska to Tierra del Fuego. It traces the origin of the idea, describes succinctly the negotiating process, evaluates the progress made so far, and accesses if negotiations are going to be successfully completed by 2005.

Regionalization and globalization seem the two main forces that are shaping the world economy. Despite the fact that they appear to move in opposite directions – the former towards regional concentration of trade and investments while the latter towards a global economy – they are complementary forces. One can see why this is the case by looking at the growth of trade. Indeed, since the end of the Second World War, global trade has been growing three times faster than global output. At the same time, intra-regional trade, that is the proportion that a given country trades goods and services with its regional partners, has also been increasing dramatically in most regions of the world.

Another trend that is fostering the processes of regionalization and globalization is the changes that are taking place in the rules governing world trade. The international community appears to be moving slowly but steadily towards free trade. In recent decades, unilateral, bilateral, and multilateral initiatives have been taken to open markets. At the multilateral level, liberalization of trade took place through several rounds of talks concluded at the General Agreement on Tariffs and Trade (GATT), but barriers remain on the way towards a free trade world.

In the meantime, since the mid-1980s, an explosion of initiatives to promote regional economic integration took place. Economic integration might take five different forms, in progressive order of complexity: preferential trade agreements; free trade areas; customs unions; common markets; and economic unions. Economists have been arguing for decades over the advantages of trade agreements, concerning in particular three major aspects: first, the welfare implications – the debate on trade creation versus trade diversion; second, the role of geographical proximity in creating 'natural' or 'supernatural' regions; and third, whether regional trade agreements might contribute to the ultimate goal of a free trade world (Frankel 1997).

This chapter deals with one form of regional economic integration, that of a free trade area. Along with other regions in the world, the Americas have also embarked on agreements aiming to boost trade among regional partners through granting preferential treatment. A free trade area is an agreement where members commit themselves to abolish all tariffs and quantitative import restrictions, while retaining tariffs and other barriers against non-members.

There are strong non-economic factors that lead countries to form regional trade agreements; they can be formed as a result of geographical proximity, political circumstances, or as a complement to the WTO (World Trade Organization) system.

The FTAA initiative: global, regional, and national factors

On 18–19 April 1998, at the second Summit of the Americas that took place in Santiago de Chile, attended by the heads of state of thirty-four American states, it was announced that the nations of the Americas were ready to start negotiations for the Free Trade Area of the Americas (FTAA).[1] The Santiago summit followed the first Summit of the Americas convened by the USA that occurred in Miami in December 1994. The Santiago agenda included issues such as education, drugs, combating poverty, and organised crime, but it was the FTAA that received most attention.

The proposal to negotiate the FTAA was first put forward by Vice-President Al Gore during a speech in Mexico City in December 1993. More than four years later, in March 1998, after intense debate, high-level diplomacy, and a great number of technical meetings, a consensus document on the format of the FTAA was approved in a meeting of ministers of trade in San Jose de Costa Rica. This document formed the basis on which the heads of state of the Americas were able to announce in Santiago a detailed plan of action to conclude negotiations for the FTAA no later than 2005.

Ideas, proposals, and plans to stimulate trade and investment, and foster economic links, among the countries of the Americas, are certainly not new. There were several attempts in the past to encourage economic integration among the 'American family of nations', but by and large they have failed to transcend the intention of political leaders and catch the imagination of their civil societies (Weintraub 1993).[2] Despite this record of failures, however, it seems that proposals for closer economic links in the Americas did gain a new momentum in the 1990s.

Regional and sub-regional trade and trade-related agreements are a conspicuous trait of the current international economy, and one of the most heatedly debated economic issues of the era. However, given the past record of the Americas, and the sheer number of nations involved in the proposal, Vice-President Gore's initiative was taken with some scepticism. Indeed, initiatives to foster economic links in the Americas – from measures designed to facilitate trade and investment to ambitious schemes for regional economic integration – have been considered many times since the nineteenth century. Immediately after independence, unsuccessful attempts were undertaken by Spanish American leaders to create economic and political unions of the recently created republics; by the end of the century a Pan-American initiative led by the USA had failed to stimulate significant regional commerce; and more recently, several sub-regional groupings were formed, when a number of Latin American and Caribbean countries developed formulae to foster economic integration excluding the USA. Despite all these projects and the moderate success achieved in the recent decades, it was only since the late 1980s that sub-regional economic integration became a significant way of fostering trade and investment among the countries of the Americas (Bulmer-Thomas 1997).

If successfully concluded, the free trade area will include all the nations of the Americas with the exception of Cuba, which was expelled from the Organization of American States (OAS) in 1962 and therefore is excluded from the negotiations. The geographical area will span Alaska to Tierra del Fuego, with a population of around 800 million people, a combined GDP well over US$11 trillion, and total annual exports of more than U$1.5 trillion. The FTAA would become a formidable regional grouping and arguably the largest regional economic grouping in the world.

One should not take for granted the notion that the Americas is anything other than a geographical definition; that is, the thirty-four (or thirty-five with Cuba) nations of the Americas certainly share a continent (or the Western Hemisphere) that embraces a very heterogeneous 'family of nations'. From the largest economy in the world to a number of small states in the Caribbean, they have in common their colonial European past and a forging of nations by a combination of indigenous populations and European, Asian, and African descendants. Inter-American relations in the twentieth century have been characterized by the disparity of hard and soft power between the USA and Canada on the one hand and thirty-three nations of very different sizes, shapes, economic clout, and cultural background on the other. The USA, with around 35 per cent of the Americas' population, has a share of over 77 per cent of their total GDP, and 73 per cent of total industrial output. Mexico and Brazil, the first and second largest economies in Latin America, with about 33 per cent of its total population, are responsible for only 10 per cent of GDP and slightly over 10 per cent of industrial output.

These numbers show that the greatest attraction in the Americas is the sheer size of the US market. In theory then all the countries of the Americas should be equally interested in gaining free access to the US market. In fact, the current access is quite significantly different when one looks at North and Central America and the Caribbean, and South America. Indeed, the ratio of inter-regional trade varies considerably among the sub-regions. In North America – Mexico and Canada – over 80 per cent of their total trade is with the USA, while in Central America and the Caribbean this number is on average around 60 per cent. At the other end of the scale, however, there are the countries of South America. In the southern cone, trade with the USA as a proportion of total trade is just over 20 per cent.

Therefore, the nations of the Americas are quite diverse in terms of geographical distribution of trade and should not be perceived as a single 'natural' region. Moreover, trade negotiations are very complex and time consuming, demanding skilful and technically well-prepared negotiators, a requirement not met by most of the thirty-four nations. Trade negotiations involve hard bargaining and concessions that will affect both well-organized and entrenched interests and vulnerable sectors within all the countries involved and the free trade area, when implemented, will have an unknown impact on the economies and societies of the participating nations. Given these circumstances, it may seem surprising that most of the leaders were so eager to embrace the proposal for a free trade area. This can only indicate the scale of changing global, regional, and national circumstances throughout the Americas.

Global factors

The end of the Cold War was bound to inspire the USA to take some sort of new political initiative towards Latin America and the Caribbean. During the period defined by the East–West confrontation, Latin America and the Caribbean did not figure prominently in

Washington's interests. Its relations were conceived in terms of gains and losses in Washington's overall competition with its main rival, the Soviet Union. Therefore, US attention to the area was principally based on security concerns, for example in its support for authoritarian regimes as well as its several interventions in the domestic affairs of Guatemala, Cuba, Chile, Nicaragua, El Salvador, Panama, and Grenada among others.

This pattern of inter-American relations, namely, putting security above development, pervaded the whole Cold War period. It certainly created resentment amongst Latin American and Caribbean leaders, who could see the contrast between Washington's economic engagement in Europe and Asia, and its apparent neglect of the economic plight of the region. When the USA initiated a project that had economic prosperity as its main goal – the Alliance for Progress during the Kennedy Administration – it was short lived, lacking continuity, and easily subverted by other priorities.

The dramatic change in the international scene after the demise of the Soviet Union, and the reaffirmation of the international leadership of the USA, created the conditions for the launching of a new economic policy towards Latin America and the Caribbean. This took the form of a proposed series of initiatives to stimulate trade and investment, and to deal with the foreign debt crisis, the most urgent economic problem in Latin America and the Caribbean in the late 1980s. President George Bush announced his regional proposals in 1990 under the name of the Enterprise for the Americas Initiative.

Regional factors

A more optimistic climate was created in the region after the Latin American countries were able to deal with the main factor responsible for their dreadful economic performance for most of the 1980s, the so-called 'lost decade'. Starting with the Mexican debt default of September 1982, the area suffered its worse economic downturn since the 1930s, and much needed resources were sent abroad to pay debts incurred during the boom years of the 1970s. Furthermore, the debt crisis forced economic authorities in most countries to close further their already closed economies in an effort to save hard currency and repay the spiralling costs of foreign debt. As a result, in most countries of the area, the 1980s were a decade of sluggish economic growth, deteriorating living standards, high rates of inflation (even hyperinflation in some countries), and a last attempt to protect their economies from foreign competition. Economic policies that had served the area reasonably well for some decades – import substitution, industrialization and extensive state intervention in economic affairs – finally collapsed under zero growth, fiscal crisis, and hyperinflation.

Some countries realized sooner than others that the economic model which had prevailed for so long had collapsed, and started unilaterally implementing policies to open up their economies to foreign trade and investment and to stimulate export-led growth. From the mid-1980s Chile, followed by Mexico, pioneered new trade policies, drastically reducing tariff and non-tariff barriers to trade, and stimulating competition and foreign investment. Every other Latin American and Caribbean country would eventually follow these market-oriented measures (Rajapatirana *et al.* 1997). The opening up of their economies, the end of policies favouring import substitution and the bias against exports, ended up forging a new climate for economic prosperity as the area followed the guidance of a series of market-oriented reforms which became known as the 'Washington Consensus' (Kucynski and Williamson 2003).[3] These reforms, which by and large went further than economic management and included other areas of public policy, contributed to a more market-friendly atmosphere in the area, closing the period of 'defensive nationalism' that for so long characterized Latin American and Caribbean cultural, political, and economic relations with the USA.

Another important feature of the regional environment of the 1990s was the setting up (or relaunch) of schemes for sub-regional economic integration throughout North, Central, and South America and the Caribbean. Latin America and the Caribbean had already gained quite substantial experience in sub-regional economic integration, after the Central American Common Market, the Latin American Free Trade Association, and the Andean Pact were formed in the 1960s. However, in spite of their good intentions, these did not contribute to a significantly expanded trade, investment and economic integration.

A new era of economic integration in the Americas started, however, with the conclusion in 1988 and the entering into force in 1989 of the Canada–US Free Trade Agreement. It marked a downturn in Washington's policy of favouring multinational over regional or bilateral trade agreements as a result of changing perceptions among US trade policy authorities about the role of multilateralism, bilateralism, and unilateralism in US trade policy making. The USA had been, since 1945, the champion of multilateral negotiations to liberalize trade but as the multilateral negotiations conducted at the Uruguay Round of talks of GATT seemed to be going nowhere, a bilateral agreement was perceived as a way to foster business links with Canada. By and large Canada was already the USA's main trade partner, therefore a free trade agreement would serve to stimulate still further trade and investment connections. From the Canadian point of view, it would boost its exports to the USA and the latter's investments in Canada.

After the conclusion of the Canada–US Free Trade Agreement, Mexico followed promptly. In fact, Mexico was undergoing a period of revising its economic and trade policies, opening up a closed economy, which included its membership of GATT. Hence, President Carlos Salinas proposed in 1990 a free trade agreement with the USA. The proposal reflected, among other factors, a historical change in Mexican relations with its powerful northern neighbour. President George Bush accepted President Salinas's proposal, and, with Canada, they formed in 1992 the North American Free Trade Agreement (NAFTA). After a fierce debate, NAFTA was finally approved by Congress in the following year and entered into force on 1 January 1994.

Since then, the USA has embarked on a series of bilateral trade negotiations. Even though it took longer than originally envisaged, Washington concluded a number of bilateral trade agreements, and it seems that it is prepared to continue fostering bilateral partnerships. Those already in force include Israel and Jordan, while Singapore and Chile have already concluded free trade treaties. Meanwhile, Morocco, Australia, New Zealand, and the nations of Central America, southern Africa, and South-East Asia are, or will soon start, negotiating bilateral trade agreements with Washington, while many other countries have voiced their interest.

In the meantime, in Latin America and the Caribbean, old schemes for sub-regional integration were relaunched and new ones were formed. The most significant new initiative was the setting up of the Common Market of the South (Mercado Comun del Sur – Mercosur) in 1991 through the Treaty of Asuncion. Mercosur resulted from initiatives jointly taken since 1985 by Argentina and Brazil, aiming to improve their bilateral relations after decades of suspicion and rivalry. After the conclusion of a series of bilateral agreements, Argentina and Brazil invited Uruguay and Paraguay to join in and a new scheme for economic integration was created. Since 1 January 1995, Mercosur has been a customs union in the making. As a result, trade between its partners has multiplied fivefold between 1990 and 1999. Since 2000, however, the countries of the area have gone through a period of economic and financial turbulence that stalled intra-regional trade. After three years of sharp decline, it is only in 2003 that intra-Mercosur trade is bound to recover the pre-crisis level.

Other examples of economic integration currently in force in Latin America and the Caribbean are: a relaunched Central American Common Market, the Andean Community (previously the Andean Pact), and a strengthened Caribbean Community and Common Market (CARICOM). Moreover, a large number of bilateral free trade agreements were concluded in recent years while many others are under negotiation, resulting in a quite substantial boost in trade and investment flows among the Latin American countries.

Domestic factors

The most important change that took place in almost all the nations of Central and South America and the Caribbean was the rise of leaders more willing to embrace economic cooperation and in favour of expanding trade and investment. In addition, the transition to and the consolidation of civilian rule and democracy was a powerful drive in changing their attitude towards the USA. Furthermore, with few remaining exceptions, old territorial rivalries were resolved, and leaders of different political persuasions seem convinced of the need to move forward in order to deepen political and economic cooperation. Recent radical political changes in the region, including the end of the seventy-five-year rule of the PRI in Mexico and the election of left-of-centre governments in Venezuela, Brazil, and Ecuador, have not, at least so far, contributed to a radical reappraisal of the importance of expanding trade and attracting foreign investment.

Meanwhile, a change of direction was also taking place in North America. Canada, for so long a reluctant player in inter-American affairs, joined the OAS in 1992, and began improving its economic and political links with Latin America and the Caribbean. In the USA, there was a more pragmatic approach to its southern neighbours. The opening up of the economies in Latin America and the Caribbean contributed to create a more benign perception of the opportunities for trade and investment within the Americas.

Canada and Mexico are the first and the second largest US trade partners respectively and the surge in US exports to South America has put the area in the strategic, long-term vision of US trade and investment interests. Contrary to the US trade deficit with Asia and its stagnant trade with Europe, inter-regional trade has boomed and the USA has a substantial trade surplus with Latin America. Furthermore, it exports to the area products of high-valued-added contents such as capital goods and machinery.

In sum, after decades of being perceived as a region of intractable economic, political, and social problems, Latin America and the Caribbean began to be seen as an area of even greater opportunities by US business. This more pragmatic approach, initiated by President George Bush Snr, and continued by Presidents Bill Clinton and George W. Bush, made trade and investment, instead of aid, the name of the game in inter-American relations.

Thus, a number of global, regional, and domestic factors contributed to turn the Americas into a region much more receptive to the idea of a free trade agreement. Nevertheless, a series of unsuccessful attempts, and the difficulties of implementing agreements, made analysts sceptical about the real commitments of the American leaders. So, one must now turn to the negotiating process itself, and look into how free trade moved to the top of the political agenda.

The Miami summit

President Bush Snr announced his Enterprise for the Americas Initiative (EAI) in June 1990, prior to a visit to Latin America. The initiative consisted of a foreign debt relief plan, foreign investment promotion along with the Inter-American Development Bank, and a free trade component. The free trade aspect of the EAI lingered on and, despite the words about a partnership for a new era of prosperity, the only tangible result was the debt relief plan, which succeeded in developing imaginative ways to solve the debt crisis (de Paiva Abreu 1993).[4] Concerning trade and investment, NAFTA absorbed all the energies of the Bush Snr Administration.

The Congressional approval and entering into force of NAFTA, which required a great effort by President Clinton, raised great expectations throughout the area, and it was in this mood that Vice-President Gore announced the Administration's intention to hold a summit of all the republics of the Americas. In doing so, Washington was seeking to broaden the scope of the EAI and NAFTA.

The Summit of the Americas took place in December 1994 in Miami. Prior to the summit, the US government circulated a draft document to its Latin American and Caribbean partners, containing its main proposals. After contentious rounds of talks, a consensus document was approved, known as the Airlie House, which reflected the views of all main players (Feinberg 1997).[5] The centrepiece of the document was the commitment to conclude negotiations on a free trade area of the Americas no later than 2005. It was a declaration of intention that was warmly received by most leaders of the Americas, pleased by what was then perceived as an extension of NAFTA.

Perhaps the most important aspect of the Miami summit was that, for the first time after a declaration of such ambition, a mechanism to follow up and implement the agreement was established. Contrary to what had happened so often in the past, momentum was not lost after the end of a heads of state meeting. In this case, a concrete goal, with a time frame and commonly agreed procedures, was created to move it forward.

From Miami to Santiago

The main document signed by the presidents in Miami contained a Declaration of Principles and a Plan of Action. A few months later, in June 1995, a first meeting of trade ministers took place in Denver, Colorado. There, twelve Working Groups at Vice-Ministerial level were set up, each one chaired by different countries, to discuss each topic of the agreement in great detail and to prepare background technical information. From Denver to San Jose, passing through Cartagena, Colombia, in March 1996 and Belo Horizonte, Brazil, in May 1997, the Working Groups met nine times, and succeeded in generating inventories from every nation involved and a great amount of technical information about several aspects of trade and trade-related issues.

It is interesting to note that the main objective of the negotiating process is to achieve a free trade area, but under US pressure it intends to go beyond the traditional issues of removing tariff and non-tariff barriers. According to the US plan, it should include issues such as, among others, services, investment, competition, intellectual property, and government procurement. Another novelty of the Miami summit was the creation of a tripartite commission, consisting of the OAS, the Inter-American Development Bank (IDB), and the United Nations Economic Commission for Latin America and the Caribbean (ECLAC). Here it appears that the main objectives were to use the resources and technical expertise developed by the IDB and ECLAC as well as revamping the role played by the OAS in inter-American affairs. A trade unit of the OAS was set up in 1995 and, despite the bad image of the OAS as a Washington-led organization, its participation in this initiative was sought as a way of giving it a new lease of life (OAS 1995).

Negotiations after Santiago

As expected, fierce disputes occurred during the negotiations. I will only highlight the most relevant. First, there were different perceptions about how a free trade area should come about. The initial US view was that the FTAA would be a gradual extension of NAFTA to the other Latin American and Caribbean countries (Feinberg 1997). At the Miami summit, Chile was formally invited to become the next country to join NAFTA, while other nations were mentioned as next in line. However, there were opponents to this approach. Led by Brazil, they argued that the FTAA should not be an extension of trade preferences granted unilaterally by the USA to well-behaved countries, but a truly new initiative, negotiated by equal partners. Eventually, this dispute was resolved to accept the approach advocated by Brazil.

A second and related issue was the disagreement about the role of the existing sub-regional groupings in the negotiating process. The USA argued that countries should negotiate individually, while other members, Brazil in particular, argued in favour of a 'building bloc' approach: that is, sub-regional groupings such as the Andean Community, Mercosur, or the Central American Common Market could, if they wished, speak as one voice during the negotiations. In the end, the view that prevailed was that each country would be allowed to choose how it wished to be represented: some opted to do so individually such as the USA and the other NAFTA members, while others, such as Mercosur, opted to negotiate as a group.

A third cause of friction related to the way the free trade area should enter into force. Some countries favoured the idea that agreements should be progressively implemented as soon as they were concluded. On the other hand, other countries favoured the idea, by and large agreed in Miami, of a 'single undertaking': that is, all the agreements would enter into force at the same time, when all the negotiations had been concluded. The latter view prevailed.

The main body created to direct negotiations is the Trade Negotiating Committee, composed of the Vice-Ministers of Trade of the thirty-four nations. The Committee, chaired by different countries, is responsible for the work of nine negotiating groups in the following areas: market access; investment; services; government procurement; dispute settlement; agriculture; intellectual property rights, subsidies, anti-dumping, and countervailing duties; and competition policy. In addition, a Consultative Group on Smaller Economies was attached to the Trade Negotiating Committee (Harker *et al.* 1996). The Tripartite Committee – IDB, OAS, ECLAC – continues giving support to the FTAA process as well as technical assistance to sub-regional groupings and individual countries.

After the approval in Santiago, negotiations were formally launched at the Fifth Ministerial Conference that took place in Toronto in November 1999. Following eighteen months of intensive talks, the negotiating groups prepared a first-draft text of their respective chapters which were presented at the Sixth Ministerial Conference, held in Buenos Aires, and at the Third Summit of the Americas held in Quebec City in April 2001. Following Quebec, a first draft of the FTAA agreement was made public in July

2001, designed to enhance the transparency of the process and involve civil society in the discussions.[6]

According to the principles agreed at Quebec, negotiations will end before January 2005, and the deadline for the agreement's entry into force is December 2005. Negotiations took place in Miami, Panama City, and Mexico City, chaired respectively by Canada, Argentina, and Ecuador. The last stage of the negotiating process is being co-chaired by the USA and Brazil.

Two main aspects of the negotiations stand out: first, in spite of the unequal partnership between the USA and the other members it has been a negotiation, if not between equals, at least between less unequal partners where Washington has been unable to impose its view on most of the competing issues. Second, Brazil stands out as the main interlocutor of the USA. Owing to its sheer size, economic might, as well as diplomatic skills, Brazil was able to galvanize support from its Mercosur partners and other South American countries to confront US views.

According to the original timetable, the thirty-four nations presented, in February 2003, a first list of trade concessions, setting out the hard bargaining about lowering tariffs and abolishing non-tariff barriers, procedures, and the phasing-in timetable required to achieve the final goal of a free trade area. Then, they presented an improved list in June 2003, preparing for the final, and harder, phase of mutual concessions, which started in July 2003. In November 2003, a ministerial summit convened in Miami to grant the political support at the highest level for the last year of negotiations.

We can now turn very briefly to some issues concerning the current global and regional trade agendas and the political and social obstacles that could potentially hamper the successful conclusion of the FTAA before the end of January 2005.

Free trade areas versus multilateral negotiations

There is no consensus whatsoever among trade economists about the role played by regional trade agreements in economic growth (Anderson and Smith 1997; Hufbauer and Schott 1994) and whether these initiatives help or hinder the ultimate goal of a free trade world (Panagariya 1996; Sager 1997). Nevertheless, whatever the political obstacles in the way towards freer trade, the fact is that multilateral negotiations are moving forward; the WTO Doha Round of talks to further liberalize world trade was launched in November 2001.

The Doha Round, named the 'development round', was in part conceived as a process to benefit developing nations. However, the negotiating agenda includes the rules governing extremely contentious issues such as agriculture, investment, services, government procurement, and other themes that polarize developed and developing nations. Among the latter, there are those that argue that they had unilaterally liberalized their trade, committing wholeheartedly to free and fair trade while developed nations continue to use tariff and non-tariff barriers to restrain access to their markets by more competitive developing countries, particularly in agriculture (Bhagwati 1997; Finger and Nogués 2002). The difficulties faced by the initial negotiations to reach a consensus on agriculture and developing nations' demands for special trade concessions led to the failure of the meeting that took place in September 2003 in Cancún, Mexico. As a consequence, a more contentious round of multilateral trade talks might absorb all the energy of participants and, perhaps, make regional negotiations for preferential trade agreements redundant.

A return to protectionism

Another challenge to a successful free trade agreement would be the return to protectionism as a result of economic and financial turmoil or as a result of lobbying by special interests. Almost ten years of economic difficulties in developing nations, from the Mexican peso crisis of December 1994 up to the Argentine economic collapse of 2001 and Brazil's financial scare of 2002, showed once again that emerging markets suffer periodic crises of confidence, partly due to the excessive deregulation of international capital flows. Indeed, the economies of Latin America and the Caribbean deregulated their financial markets and attracted large amounts of volatile capital. Much better macroeconomic management and a series of other measures were implemented in order to boost trust from foreign investors, but the financial turbulence of recent years has, once again, shaken investors' confidence. Another financial crisis could eventually lead to a return of measures to close capital accounts and, perhaps, trade protection.

In addition, it is not implausible to see risks over the return of protectionism in the USA. Indeed, despite its commitment to free trade, George W. Bush's Administration has been acting unilaterally in most foreign policy issues, introducing new measures to protect the domestic market from foreign competition, ranging from steel to agriculture. Both the President and Congress have being under heavy pressure from well-organized sectors to raise trade barriers, and to use trade as a tool to achieve foreign policy and defence goals.

Worsening social conditions

Another potential hindrance for the conclusion of a free trade agreement might well be the reversal of free trade as a political goal in some countries of Latin America as a result of worsening social conditions. The liberal reforms that took place throughout the region in the 1990s contributed to better macroeconomic management and economic efficiency, less state interference, privatization of utilities and other public companies, and an exceptional surge in the inflows of foreign direct investment. In 1997, at the height of foreign investment in Latin America, the region received seven times what it had received in 1990, by all accounts a quite impressive record. However, deregulation, privatization, and the steep increase in FDI did not lead to a decisive improvement in social indicators. On the contrary, despite an increase in real terms of the level of spending on education and health, social conditions did not improve as expected. It was even mentioned that, in social terms, the 1990s were a second 'lost decade', which seems plausible given that Latin America's huge social divide remains untouched. With few exceptions, Latin American societies are extremely unequal: according to data from ECLAC, in 2002 over 200 million Latin Americans still live in poverty, with high levels of unemployment and social exclusion, while corruption is widespread and social insecurity and violence pervade the social fabric. These factors have undoubtedly contributed to the election of left-of-centre politicians in recent years.

Moreover, as society became more organized and vocal, trade liberalization turned out to be a highly politicized issue, and different sectors of civil society have voiced their concerns about the high costs of trade liberalization. So, it is not implausible to conceive that, particularly in nations where left-of-centre parties now govern, the FTAA could become entangled in political arguments that could turn the last phase of negotiations much more acrimonious.

Conclusion

The proposal for the FTAA was born out of a quite unique set of circumstances: the end of an era of confrontation in international affairs and the transition towards another where trade and economic links seemed the right answer to peace and prosperity; a move towards regional economic integration; a regional climate conducive to economic openness, trade, and foreign investment as legitimate tools to development, after the exhaustion of decades of closed economies; and a new climate among democratically elected leaders of the Americas. These factors have persuaded reluctant leaders that a new vision of development, relying much more than in the recent past on robust civil societies and market-oriented economies, is the vital component for prosperity. Indeed, for the first time ever in negotiations for a common inter-American project, both business and labour associations participated intensively in the debates, and it appears that their involvement reflects the mobilization of organized sectors of the civil society. In sum, what could have been empty rhetoric became serious negotiations.

The USA was the originator and main supporter of the initiative for the FTAA, even though not every country in the Americas, in particular Brazil, seems totally convinced that a free trade area would serve its best interest. Nevertheless, despite the caveats mentioned above, it seems that a free trade area is now a *fait accompli*; it remains to be seen, however, if it will be concluded on time.

In the meantime, most of Latin America has not sat still while the negotiations are taking place. There have been several initiatives undertaken by Latin American nations to develop stronger economic links with extra-regional partners. Chile and Mexico, for example, have in the recent past concluded free trade agreements with the EU, while Mercosur is negotiating with the latter a free trade agreement to be concluded in 2005. Caribbean nations, Central America, and the Andean Community are also seeking to reinforce their economic and political links with the EU. At the same time, most Latin American countries are pursuing strategies to diversify their trade partners, and open new markets and business opportunities in Asia, Africa, and Central and Eastern Europe.

If and when successfully concluded, the FTAA will require a long transitional period of ten–fifteen years to become fully operational, that is zero tariffs and no non-tariff barriers imposed on trade among its members. This is due to the fact that every trade agreement needs a period of adjustment to new rules. This seems a reasonable period of time to prepare all the nations involved to reap the benefits of free trade.

Notes

1   The thirty-four countries are: Antigua and Barbuda, Argentina, Bahamas, Barbados, Belize, Bolivia, Brazil, Canada, Chile, Colombia, Costa Rica, Dominica, Dominican Republic, Ecuador, El Salvador, Grenada, Guatemala, Guyana, Haiti, Honduras, Jamaica, Mexico, Nicaragua, Panama, Paraguay, Peru, Uruguay, St Kitts and Nevis, St Lucia, St Vincent and the Grenadines, Suriname, Trinidad and Tobago, the USA, and Venezuela.
2   See the special issue edited by Weintraub (1993).
3   The expression was originally created by the British economist John Williamson. For a recent reappraisal of the agenda for reforms in the region see Kucynski and Williamson (2003).
4   A critical assessment of the EAI from a Latin American perspective has been undertaken by de Paiva Abreu (1993).
5   See Feinberg (1997).
6   The draft text might be accessed at www.ftaa-alca.org.

Bibliography

Anderson, M. and Smith, S.L. (1997) 'NAFTA expansion: US imports upon Chilen, Andean Pact and MERCOSUR accession', *The World Economy* 20: 477–496.

Balassa, B. (1987) 'Economic integration', in *The New Palgrave Dictionary of Economics*, London: Macmillan.

Bhagwati, J. (1997) 'The global age: from a sceptical South to a fearful North', *The World Economy* 20: 259–283.

Bulmer-Thomas, V. (1997) 'Regional integration in Latin America since 1985: open regionalism and globalisation', in Ali M. El-Agraa (ed.), *Economic Integration Worldwide*, Basingstoke and London: Macmillan.

de Araujo Jr, J.T. (1997) 'ALCA: riscos e oportunidades para o Brasil', Paper prepared for the Instituto de Pesquisas de Relações Internacionais do Ministério das Relações Exteriores, Brasília.

de Paiva Abreu, M. (1993) *Brazil–US Economic Relations and the Enterprise for the Americas Initiative*, Texto para Discussão No. 296, Departamento de Economia, PUC-Rio de Janeiro.

Edwards, S. (1995) *Crisis and Reform in Latin America: from despair to hope*, New York: Oxford University Press for the World Bank.

El-Agraa, A. (ed.) (1997) *Economic Integration Worldwide*, Basingstoke and London: Macmillan.

Feinberg, R.E. (1997) *Summitry in the Americas: a progress report*, Washington, DC: Institute for International Economics.

Finger, J.M. and Nogués, J. (2002) 'The unbalanced Uruguay Round outcome: the new areas in future WTO negotiations', *The World Economy* 25: 321–340.

Frankel, J.A. (1997) *Regional Trade Blocs in the World Economic System*, Washington, DC: Institute for International Economics.

Harker, T., El-Hadj, S.O., and Vinhas de Souza, L. (1996) 'The Caribbean countries and the Free Trade Area of the Americas', *Cepal Review* 59: 97–111.

Hufbauer, G.C. and Schott, J.J. (1994) *Western Hemisphere Economic Integration*, Washington, DC: Institute for International Economics.

Irwin, D.A. (1996) *Against the Tide: an intellectual history of free trade*, Princeton, NJ: Princeton University Press.

Kucynski, P.P. and Williamson, J. (eds) (2003) *After the Washington Consensus: restarting growth and reform in Latin America*, Washington, DC: Institute for International Economics.

OAS, Trade Unit (1995) *Towards Free Trade in the Americas*, Washington, DC: OAS.

Panagariya, A. (1996) 'The Free Trade Area of the Americas: good for Latin America?', *The World Economy* 19: 485–515.

Rajapatirana, S., de la Mora, L.M., and Yatawara, R.A. (1997) 'Political economy of trade reforms, 1965–1994: Latin American style', *The World Economy* 20: 307–338.

Sager, M. (1997) 'Regional trade agreements: their role and the economic impact on trade flows' *The World Economy* 20: 239–252.

Schott, J.J. (2001) *Prospects for Free Trade in the Americas*, Washington, DC: Institute for International Economics.

Weintraub, S. (1993) 'Free trade in the Western Hemisphere: probability of pipe-dream?', *The Annals of the American Academy of Political and Social Science* 526: 9–24.

Useful websites

www.eclac.org (Economic Commission for Latin America and the Caribbean).

www.sice.oas.org (Foreign Trade Information System of the Organization of American States).

www.ftaa-alca.org (Free Trade Agreement for the Americas official website).

www.iadb.org (Inter-American Development Bank).

www.ustr.gov/regions/whemisphere/ftaa.shtml (Office of the United States Trade Representative, Western Hemisphere webpage).

6 Trade and Africa

Transforming fringe into franchise

Timothy M. Shaw and Janis van der Westhuizen

Summary

At the start of the new century, trade remains crucial to Africa's political economies even if the continent is increasingly marginal in global trade. Yet, while over the last quarter of the twentieth century, Africa came to constitute a declining share of formal sector global exchange, niches do exist for competitive African companies and sectors in the twenty-first century, concentrated around 'African democratic developmental states' (Mkandawire 2001) like Botswana, Mauritius and Uganda and 'new' industries like mobile telephones and fresh fruit, flowers and vegetables, let alone South African franchises. Moreover, if we recognize informal as well as formal trade along with the roles of diasporas and mafias, then the continent becomes less peripheral and less distant in the global marketplace.

In macroeconomic terms Africa may be the most marginal of the continents. But it contains a range of economies and polities, companies and civil societies: there are many 'Africas'. So it is not unimportant in all sectors or for all companies, notwithstanding Amin's (2002) continued concern about the continent being at the fringe. Moreover, if we recognize that there may be an 'African' variant of capitalism, just as there are Anglo-American, Asian and European varieties, then we can include informal and illegal as well as formal and legal trade. Given the cornucopia of resources on the continent, inclusion of unrecorded trade in 'new' regionalisms would boost Africa's numbers and status. In the first edition of this collection and contribution at the end of the last century, we emphasized a trio of characteristics of the continent in the global political economy – (a) growing marketplace; (b) expanding post-Fordist production; and (c) role in global negotiations over the ACP, WTO, etc. – as well as persistent economic activities – production and accumulation as well as consumption – despite ubiquitous and resilient regional conflicts (Shaw and van der Westhuizen 1999: 247).

In brief, traditional aggregate measures of production and exchange are misleading given the continent's very distinctive and uneven characteristics, although a half-dozen of its economies are larger than US$30 billion per annum (in descending order of size): South Africa, Egypt, Algeria, Nigeria, Morocco and Libya. If we analyse its 'real' economy and trade, then it presents a much more interesting and varied picture. This is especially so if we include a 'political economy of conflict' perspective; at least some of Africa's wars are about economic survival and gain, which in turn impact terms and contents of trade both on and off the continent.

Africa: global and regional trade

The scale and character of trade around Africa has changed as a consequence of the evolving global political economy, from imminent demise of the 'Washington Consensus' and Asian crises in the late 1990s to the myriad reverberations of 9/11 and wars in Central Asia in the first half of the first decade of the twenty-first century. The former couple of 'economic' factors give the continent a little more room for manoeuvre which has been transformed by the latter pair of 'strategic' shocks which spilled over into the continent as indicated by terrorist attacks in Kenya, Morocco and Tanzania. Moreover, in a world increasingly concerned about ecology, the relatively organic character of African agriculture means that its products can anticipate charging a premium in global markets. Its rich, largely untapped, store of biodiversity gives it potential bargaining power in global trade and investment forums. In the WTO Doha Round, along with other G77 states, African states are increasingly insisting on the reduction and elimination of northern, especially EU, subsidies for agriculture to give African farmers wider access to lucrative markets.

Africa has become a much more interesting and challenging continent in terms of the possibilities for development since majority rule in South Africa and because of a trio of current leaders' definition and advocacy of the New Partnership for Africa's Development (NEPAD) launched in mid-2001 around the new African Union (AU) (AU Directory 2002). The former has led in less than a decade to a dramatic push of South African companies and franchises into the rest of the continent. The latter development constitutes the latest attempt by leading states and presidents to articulate an indigenous direction for the continent at the start of a new century as the overconfidence of neoliberalism at the global level is yielding to a somewhat less triumphalist version of 'development'. Whilst this vision of an 'African Renaissance' may be less creative or critical than Amin (2002: 50) would wish, at least he recognizes that it possesses some authenticity and possibility.

Africa already had a distinctive – albeit marginal – place in a world characterized by globalization. As already suggested, this has been reinforced by the intense impacts of 9/11 and subsequent wars in Afghanistan and Iraq. To be sure, multicultural relations become more problematic in as well as around the continent, especially in those states and regions with significant Moslem communities. But at the same time its oil and gas reserves as well as UN votes become ever more valuable. In a world of some 200 states, the more than 50 in Africa together have some credibility, even if they constitute a smaller proportion of the total in 2000 (25 per cent) than in 1990 (33 per cent).

Moreover, some of these 50 are not insignificant global economic players although Sub-Saharan Africa (SSA) produces but 0.4 per cent of the world's manufactured exports or just under 2 per cent of those from developing countries (0.5 per cent if South Africa's significant contribution is excluded). If the continent includes some Fourth World 'countries' which control very little, such as Liberia and Somalia, it also contains some Second World economies, such as Botswana, Mauritius and South Africa. In addition, there is a large majority of relatively impoverished but not hopeless political economies (Kenya, Morocco and Senegal), a few of which may yet become 'democratic developmental states' like Ghana and Uganda. It also can boast a few regimes – Angola is the best example – that have excelled in replicating Mobutu-style avarice. As some of its established economies decline at the start of the century (Côte d'Ivoire and Zimbabwe) so others rise, phoenix-like

(Ghana and Tanzania). Some of its newer, smaller economies (Botswana, Lesotho and Uganda) have grown much faster over the last decade than some of its established larger ones (Côte d'Ivoire, Nigeria and Zimbabwe). Such diversity on the continent means that inter- as well as extra-continental trade has significant possibilities in the twenty-first century if 'competition states' (Cerny 2003), entrepreneurial companies and flexible labour are sufficiently agile and ready to take risks.

The combination of the anti-globalization movement in Seattle at the end of the 1990s and US unilateralism in the twenty-first century has complicated the context for global trade negotiations, so that the compromise of Doha may not be sustainable. In terms of the continent's position, the transformation of the OAU into the AU should advance its cohesion and determination in the WTO. However, the tendency of South Africa to nego- tiate its own bilateral deals with the EU – bilateral free trade agreement rather than multilateral ACP Cotonou terms – in turn undermines any tenuous Pan-African unity. Furthermore, parallel multilateral negotiations over conflict diamonds (the Kimberley Process), the tobacco framework agreement and HIV/AIDS drugs reveal the complexity of any global regime. The Monterrey talks about Official Development Assistance (ODA) may reinforce the G8 African Action Plan in response to NEPAD. Moreover, notwithstanding its tendency towards unilateralism, the USA has actively pursued the global health agenda as well as provided the export prospects of the Africa Growth and Opportunity Act (AGOA).

Whilst the continent faces daunting development challenges in the new century – from street children to HIV/AIDS – the rise of civil society, especially in the 1990s, gives cause for some hope. The proliferation of NGOs along with other civic groups/social move- ments, from ecological and feminist to governance and peace-keeping, serves to balance oppressive regimes and rapacious corporations. Bi- and multilateral donors increasingly recognize the imperative of such 'social capital' in sustainable development. In particular, the proliferation of focused campaigns against particular companies, such as Shell, along with the popularization of anti-corporate and anti-government demands from the HIV/AIDS lobby in South Africa, should inform future policies of states and companies alike.

Such antagonism may moderate enthusiasm in World Bank and OECD circles for 'part- nerships' yet the latter constitute something of a foretaste of the future as indicated by their proliferation in the North, symbolized by the UN's Global Compact. Indeed, MNCs' part- nerships constitute something of a growth industry as major global companies seek to polish their image and protect their reputations, reflecting the proliferation of corporate codes of conduct, social responsibility and best practice. So in South Africa, as with other major economic players, there are now annual reports on the best companies to work for.[1]

Beyond structural adjustment: what prospects for African trade and investment?

At the start of a new century, following two decades of Structural Adjustment Programmes (SAPs), given the undeniable mix of anti-globalization forces and economic difficulties in countries from Argentina and Mexico to Russia, let alone the lingering Asian crisis from the late 1990s, there are the beginnings of a global shift backwards to greater concern for sustainable social development rather than just short-term efficiency and profitability. Given the very mixed record of twenty years of neoliberalism, development policies may now be beginning to move towards a post-SAP era in the first decade of the twenty-first century, encouraged by the challenge of Millennium Development Goals (MDGs) and fears about inequalities exacerbating inclinations towards global tensions and terrorism – hence the North–South 'consensus' around Monterrey and NEPAD which rendered the notion of an emerging 'African Renaissance' at least plausible.

In the first edition of this collection we focused on the African political economy at the end of the twentieth century (Shaw and van der Westhuizen 1999: 252–254) with an emphasis on (a) globalization, including the growing role of diasporas and sports (e.g. World Cricket Cup in South Africa in early 2003); (b) niche markets (e.g. organic African 'boutique' coffees featured in major global coffee franchises like Starbucks and new supply chains around fresh flowers, fruit and vegetables); (c) digital connections, both Internet and cell phone; and (d) tourism (expanding in South Africa and Uganda while declining in Zimbabwe and resilient in Kenya despite two bomb attacks), in part encouraged by threats elsewhere such as war in the Middle East and the Severe Acute Respiratory Syndrome (SARS) virus in East Asia. Such possibilities remain crucial, particularly given global supply and production chains. But here we also analyse emerging trends in terms of FDI in- and outflows and new micro-regional initiatives, with profound implications for trade prospects.

Despite striving to meet myriad conditionalities, from SAP to Heavily Indebted Poor Countries Initiative (HIPC), still only 1 per cent of global FDI flows into Africa. Such inflows towards the continent averaged some US$10 billion per annum around the turn of the century, rising to $11.8 billion in 2001 (Economist Intelligence Unit 2002). But this was concentrated in a minority of economies: South Africa, Angola and Nigeria (oil), Botswana (diamonds), Côte d'Ivoire, etc. In general, UNCTAD's survey of the continent's economies which are attractive to FDI coincides with the World Economic Forum's African Competitive Index. In 1996–1998, those industries which attracted most FDI were telecommunications, food and beverages, tourism, mining, textiles and agriculture; those which were expected to be most attractive to FDI at the dawn of the millennium (2000–2003) included tourism, food and beverages, textiles, telecommunications, etc. (UNCTAD 1999: 50). In the early 1990s, like other 'emerging markets', the continent received more FDI than usual, yet still less than other developing regions (UNCTAD 1999: 45). In 2000, it was just under $10 billion at $9.1 billion, falling from $10.5 billion in 1999, yet in 1998 it was $8.3 billion down from $9.4 billion in 1997, in part a spillover from Asian crises.

According to an UNCTAD (1999: 49) opinion survey, the most attractive African states in terms of progress towards creating a business-friendly environment for trade and investment by 2000–2003 were: Botswana, South Africa, Namibia, Uganda and Côte d'Ivoire. In general, of course, these are the more liberal economies, which are more likely to be willing to be evaluated in terms of economic governance under any NEPAD peer review mechanism. FDI *outflows* from the continent were similarly concentrated. South African firms have been listed on the London Stock Exchange in search of cash to fund operations in the rest of the world, not just Africa.

Three current developments indicate that some parts of the continent may be able to turn globalization (Held *et al.*1999) to advantage, with implications for its pattern of trade and investment in the future. First, some companies and sectors have been expanding, such as the minerals sector in Tanzania, where mining for emeralds – and more recently gold – has expanded. New mines and technologies have led to a gold-rush in the boomtown of Mwanza on Lake Victoria, where the Anglo-American Corporation, in association with Ashanti Goldfields of Ghana, is a key player. This joint venture has led to merger talks. Large-scale mining commenced in mid-2000 at Geita, where 720,000 ounces (22 tonnes) were produced by early 2003 (www.ashantigold.com). Ashanti already operates in Ghana,

Guinea and Zimbabwe as well as Tanzania and is exploring in seven African states. However, given the use of cyanide around Mwanza, there is concern about the health of Lake Victoria if such gold extraction and refining continues (MacDougall 2001).

Second, Africa has begun to develop some innovative development partnerships of its own – existential as well as conceptual 'triangles' – involving a range of heterogeneous actors: local and city governments and communities and large and small companies. The most advanced of these is the Maputo corridor with its toll road, electricity, oil and water pipelines, etc., between Maputo and Gauteng with the Mozal aluminium refinery as its centrepiece (capacity being doubled by 2005) (Soderbaum and Taylor 2003). Similarly, in the Eastern Cape, the area outside Port Elizabeth has seen major infrastructure development to facilitate Pechiney's new aluminium smelter and proposed platinum mining and refining further along the 'Wild Coast'. And in a less formal way, 'clusters' of informal and formal industries may stimulate sustainable growth, such as motor vehicle repair/rebuilding in Eastern Nigeria and around Nairobi and clothing production in South Africa's Western Cape and Eastlands in Kenya.

Third, by exploiting new technologies as well as market supply chains linking Africa to Europe (and sometimes Asia) fresh fruit, flowers and vegetables are proliferating (Ponte and Gibbons 2004). The producers use refrigerated trucks, warehouses and airfreight, typically linked by computers, to supply major supermarket chains and others with fresh, often organic produce on a just-in-time basis. The primary producers with the necessary infrastructure and connections have been Kenya and South Africa with Zimbabwe in decline and Uganda an emerging source. But some produce also reaches Europe from the Gambia and Senegal. This includes the highly profitable wine industry, in terms of backward and forward linkages to the tourism and food and beverages as well as agricultural industries. The Western Cape in South Africa is the world's seventh largest wine producer. It is also one of the world's most productive, with grape yields at some 6 tonnes per acre. This is superior to France and Italy (around 3–4 tonnes) and Spain at (1 tonne only) but less than the USA where yields of 8 tonnes per acre are typical (Shaw 2001: 93). In recent years, partly due to greater political stability, globalization and better distribution networks, the continent's only other Mediterranean micro-climates for viticulture, in Tunisia, Algeria, Morocco and Egypt, have been able to expand production despite limited domestic demand due to both religious and cultural practices.

Finally, there are three leading airlines on the continent which facilitate global and regional trade and communication and all with major Airbus or Boeing fleet replacement programmes underway: South African Airways which connects southern Africa to the continent, Europe, Asia and the USA through Africa's hub, Johannesburg; Kenya Airways with its Nairobi hub, which is part of the KLM/Northwest alliance; and Ethiopian Airlines, which is smaller than SAA but also connects the continent to the rest of the world. British Airways now has two major regional carriers operating under its franchise in southern and eastern Africa, reflecting increased demand for short- and medium-haul flights.

Increased linkages, including direct connections to New York and Atlanta on SAA and a nine-hour overnight flight from Johannesburg to Europe, enable novel niche markets to emerge in the export of services: from a growing demand for upmarket residential property for German and British tourists in suburbs of opulence along Cape Town's Atlantic seaboard – not unlike similar French 'retreats' in Morocco and Tunisia – to the popularization of cosmetic surgery vacations. Offering first-class private medical care, elective surgery becomes much more affordable in dollar or pound terms – and more pleasant if recuperation includes staying in a luxury safari resort or hotel.[2]

The emerging picture is complex and – in spite of considerable progress – a noticeable feature of recent economic performance has been the variability in growth rates around the continent. As the African Development Bank observes,

> Despite the modest performance of the African economy as a whole, it is encouraging to note that 17 African countries achieved rates of growth in excess of 5 per cent, with 16 others registering growth rates of between 3 and 5 per cent. The number of countries recording negative growth also declined from nine to five.
>
> (African Development Bank 2002: i)

However, with a gross continental product equivalent to that of Spain there is much to be done (Griffith 2003).

NEPAD as Africa's response to globalization: renaissance of trade?

At the start of the 1980s, African leaders responded to growing disappointment with the limited fruits of independence with a contrary development blueprint: the Lagos Plan of Action. It sought to overcome growing debt, drought and underdevelopment with a return to state-centric autonomy when the embryonic neoliberal order was heading towards the liberation of the market. Two decades later, a new generation of more democratic leaders is concerned not to make the same mistake. After some reflection and hesitation a trio of 'modern' presidents have formulated NEPAD as the continent's attempt to accept and take advantage of the neoliberal nature of globalization rather than deny or resist it. This section looks at seven dimensions of the 'new' Africa's quest for more rapid growth and expanding trade through rather than against globalization.

First, in the 1990s, privatization initiatives proliferated as internationally sponsored, but nationally agreed, Poverty Reduction Strategy Programmes (PRSPs) aimed to wrest economic activity out of state hands. The PRSPs were generated through distinctive national discussions and negotiations, typically involving major elements from civil society and the private sector. Such 'triangular' talks led to enhanced debt reduction and ODA provision, the former encouraged by global campaigns such as Jubilee 2000, the latter by growing ODA budgets, at least among many OECD donors, if not the USA.

Second, in recognition of the continent's continuing conflicts and development deficit, the G8 became increasingly concerned and invited leading African presidents to its Genoa summit in mid-2001. This novel dialogue was continued at the G8 summits in Kananaskis in Canada and in Evian, France, in 2003. Given the particular commitment of G8 leaders like Tony Blair and Jean Chrétien, new programming for the continent has been provided by at least some G8 countries, notably the UK, Canada and France. Japan has also continued its Tokyo International Conference on African Development (TICAD) initiative and USAID has pledged US$500 million to healthcare. Furthermore, the EU has replaced its Lomé Agreement with the ACP countries with the Cotonou Convention, including formulating an 'Everything but Arms' trade policy, and finalized a bilateral free trade agreement with South Africa. Further, the Global Coalition for Africa (GCA), 'An Intergovernmental Forum for African Development', now headed by Hage Geingob, continues to network among states and NGOs on and off the continent on corruption, governance, private sector development, security, etc. (www.gca-cma.org). Meanwhile, the WEF draws attention to the continent in both annual Davos discourses and regular conferences on and about the continent.

Third, the US African Growth and Opportunity Act (AGOA) announced by the Clinton Administration in the late 1990s has provided significant opportunities for new manufacturing exports from Africa by countries which meet its criteria: from some US$1 billion in investment so far, some US$3 billion exports to the USA from the continent in 2001. To date, the primary sources of such exports, mainly clothing, have been Lesotho, Nigeria, Kenya, South Africa and Uganda.

Fourth, reaching out post-apartheid, some larger South African companies are increasing their extra- as well as intra-African investments. For example, SABMiller is now the second largest global brewer, with activities concentrated in emerging markets in Eastern Europe and China, and de Beers is active in new diamond mines and exploration in Canada.

Fifth, conversely, major global MNCs are increasingly active on the continent, especially in its higher-growth countries and regions, with implications for growing intra-company international trade. For example, Bata (Canada) operates its shoe business in eight African states mainly in SADC (Botswana, Congo, Malawi, South Africa, Zambia and Zimbabwe) along with Commonwealth members like Kenya and Uganda (www.bata.com); Parmalat (Italy) has a major presence in South Africa with milk/yoghurt outlets also in Botswana, Mozambique, Swaziland and Zambia and many in RSA (www.parmalat.co.za); and Danone (France) manufactures and sells food products in South and North Africa. After fifty years, Volkswagen now produces one in five of the cars sold in South Africa and by 2001 had exported 100,000 units, mainly Golfs (www.vw.co.za). Similarly, having advanced from the assembly of Completely Knocked-Down (CKD) imported parts to full manufacture, BMW invested a billion rand in the mid-1990s and now exports 60,000 units a year, and plans another 2 billion rand investment in its plant at Rosslyn (*Business Day* 29 November 2002). Moreover, the German company has taken advantage of tariff-free access to the US market under AGOA to double exports from 11,000 to 22,000 units from 2000 to 2002. Indeed, BMW shipped some R3.8 billion worth of cars to the USA in 2002, with the president of the South African operations calling AGOA a 'significant anchor' for foreign investment in South Africa (Fraser 2002).

Sixth, regional organizations have been one familiar means by which African states have sought to achieve growth. But, at least at a formal level, such arrangements have rarely realized their targets in terms of expanding formal regional trade, even if more informal regionalisms – ecological, ethnic, social, etc. – have proven more creative and resilient. Whilst the East African community has risen phoenix-like from the ashes, ECOWAS is still largely moribund and SADC has overstretched by admitting further members, notably the Congo. In turn, COMESA and CBI compete with SADC's credentials while micro-level SACU and the Rand Common Monetary Area look ever more promising. As SADC has expanded to include the 'state' of Congo, so more micro-level arrangements from a renegotiated SACU (finally agreed in mid-2003) to corridors and triangles from a Highland water scheme to a Maputo corridor look more attractive and manageable.

Finally, NEPAD has begun to spawn ambitious sectoral plans for agriculture, communications, industry, telecommunications, etc., with implications for future global as well as regional trade. And the ADB has committed finance of some US$200 million in 2003 for seventeen projects. These infrastructural developments are also not unconnected with the expansion of South African capital into the rest of the continent – triggered by pressures for market expansion by erstwhile state-owned monopolies to privatize – of which electricity supplier Eskom and Vodacom, the telecoms supplier, are the most salient. Given the current inability of supply to match demand, Eskom's ambitions extend way beyond the southern African region and include investment plans for 2000–2005 comprising US$240 million in southern African projects: $445 million dedicated to West Africa, $86 million to North and Central Africa as well as $245 million to East Africa. Eskom is also expected to generate 20 per cent of Nigerian capacity by 2004 through a joint venture with Shell. Likewise, Sasol, the former state-owned oil company, will supply oil to Gauteng, from the Pande en Temane fields in Mozambique, along an 865 km pipeline and estimated to boost Mozambique's GDP by 20 per cent! In fact, South African capital has invested a total of R25 billion in Mozambique over the past five years (*African Business* July/August 2002).

Rainbow continent? from semi-developmental states to economies without states

While Africa contains many very small, poor and weak economies, it also includes a half-dozen economies that are larger than US$30 billion: South Africa, Egypt, Algeria, Nigeria, Morocco and Libya (in order of total size), i.e. mainly oil-producing and North African economies. Its biggest oil producers are Libya and Nigeria followed by Algeria, Egypt and Angola. The World Economic Forum (WEF) has produced a competitiveness report on the continent's 'tigers'. And for the first time in early 2003, the annual 'Globalization Index' from *Foreign Policy*/A T Kearney included some African states. This index ranks countries according to a mix of economic, personal, political and technological dimensions, such as trade/FDI, travel/phone calls, numbers of memberships of international organizations/embassies and IT, respectively. The top eight African countries according to 'Measuring Globalization: who's up, who's down?' (Kearney 2003: 65) are: Botswana (#33), Uganda (#36), Nigeria (#37), South Africa (#38), Tunisia (#39), Senegal (#41), Kenya (#43) and Egypt (#46). Interestingly, these include the trio of initiators of NEPAD, which suggests ways in which Africa can take advantage of globalization, especially increased trade, via the G8.

Nevertheless, there is a growing minority of states on the continent which control little even in the capital city: these contain 'economies without states' (emerging banking and cellular telephones as well as traditional drug trafficking networks in the Horn). Piracy along the coast of Somalia and Puntland, on the south-east coast of the Horn in particular, has prompted shipping companies to dramatically increase their insurance costs or refuse to provide any cover whatsoever, contending that piracy constitutes an act of war when bombs or rockets are employed, prompting cargo to be excluded from PandI insurance cover. Armed attacks have also been reported in Abidjan, Bonny River, Lagos, Conakry, Dakar, Dar es Salaam, Douala, Luanda, Owendo and Tema (*African Business* July/August 2002).

Political economy of conflicts: economies without security

Africa is not marginal in terms of role in illegal networks of trade and investment. Neither is it marginal in numbers of conflicts that have their roots in the political economy of human insecurity. 'The illegal trade in drugs, arms, intellectual property, people and money is booming. Like the war on terrorism, the fight to control these illicit markets pits governments against agile, stateless and resourceful networks empowered by globalization' (Naim 2003: 29). Whilst it is recognized that some of the continent's contemporary wars are functions of 'national security' imperatives, most have causes in the deficiency of human development/security. Moreover, the continent has to deal with related threats such as endangered species, toxic waste and trade in human organs, all informal/illegal niche markets. The human, economic and ecological costs of such regional conflicts are incalculable, posing a fundamental challenge to the claims and ideals of NEPAD (MacLean *et al.* 2002).

At the turn of the century, a new genre of analysis began to emerge from scholars and development agencies on the economic causes of conflict on the continent, characterized by Duffield (2001) as the 'merging of development and security'. He argues that this is a function of new insecurities associated with growing inequalities in the global political economy along with changes in the character of war itself: intra- rather than inter-state involving a range of actors: 'The focus of the new security concerns is not the threat of traditional interstate wars but the fear of underdevelopment as a source of conflict, criminalized activity and international instability' (Duffield 2001: 7).

Interestingly, such a perspective has been articulated by both conservative and radical political economists. The former includes classical macroeconomists from the World Bank etc. while the latter includes scholars like William Reno as well as Duffield and a range of NGOs, especially Partnership Africa Canada.

The political economy of war and conflict is also not unrelated to the significance of the African diaspora as both a conduit for trade and transnational expressions of national identity, despite the extent to which the phenomenon remains marginal to debates about development and Africa's role in the global political economy (Mohan and Zack-Williams 2002a). For, despite the difficulties of determining empirically the extent to which remittances, social networks and migration interact, it has for example been estimated that for the Cape Verde, remittances account for around 17 per cent of GDP; whilst Ghanaians in the USA remitted between US$250 and 350 million per annum throughout the 1990s, 'with remittances outstripping FDI for every year between 1983 and 1990' (Mohan and Zack-Williams 2002b: 225). Although the difficulty of calculating remittances is due partly to the fact that only about 50 per cent are sent through official channels, the size and prevalence of money transfer agencies such as Western Union and Money Gram provide some indication of the significance of such networks to those with poorer and often impoverished extended families in Africa.

Challenges to human security also partly explain the prevalence of African professionals, academics, medical doctors and engineers in North America and Europe – the export of skilled people – due not only to better pay and career prospects but to the inability of African economies to retain their highly skilled people. Nowhere is the international division of labour as vividly portrayed as in the case of medical care or IT professionals in southern Africa. The migration of Canadian medical staff – often reflecting an unwillingness to work in rural locations – to the USA, has meant that Canada has had to recruit staff from other countries, leading to the accusation of 'poaching' South African personnel. It is estimated by the South African government that 3,500 of its 26,000 practising doctors work overseas, whilst up to 20 per cent of doctors in the Canadian province of Saskatchewan are South African trained. To make up for the serious shortfall, Pretoria has similarly actively recruited from Cuba, eschewing similar poaching practices from the rest of the region, such as Zimbabwe. The effect, however, as Crush (2002: 160) notes, is that 'Zimbabwean doctors and nurses have simply left for other places, particularly the United Kingdom. … South Africa's principled stand has benefited neither South Africa, nor Zimbabwe nor the region.'

In some cases, notably the Ottawa and Kimberley Processes, more reliable African governments have been instrumental in coordinating with NGOs novel, mixed actor coalitions to deal with the problems of landmines and blood diamonds. Whereas the political-economic significance of the former only becomes apparent in relation to questions of ecological sustainability and human security, the latter is decidedly economic. Yet what makes the Kimberley Process significant is not only the degree to which it involves de Beers as a South African MNC and erstwhile operator of one of the world's most successful cartels, now turned private company, but that this process was partly triggered by NGO activism and a threatened consumer boycott, underlying the potential of consumerism to effect North–South alliances. Indeed, in collaboration with George Soros, over a hundred NGOs are now clamouring for MNCs to publish clearly how resource-related funds – taxes, royalties and fees – paid to African governments are managed and distributed, revealing the potential of consumer activism to emulate the Kimberley Process in relation to oil, gas and mining (www.publishwhatyoupay.org).

The 'new' South Africa in Africa

There is now more FDI in the rest of the continent from South Africa than elsewhere, with implications for the volume and direction of trade: states and companies north of the Limpopo now have a choice not only between old capital like that from the EU/UK and USA and new capital from Japan and the rest of Asia, but now also of capital from South Africa with its relative proximity as well as relative relevance/familiarity.

Such FDI and franchises balance South Africa's sometimes aggressive foreign policy, such as 'humanitarian interventions' in Lesotho and Burundi and the political economy of its arms industry and recent weapons acquisitions with concomitant regional insecurities thereby created.

Symptomatic of the possibilities of 'leap-frogging' is the explosion of cell phones throughout the continent at the century's turn. By the early twenty-first century, there were twice as many cell phones on the continent as fixed lines, concentrated in North and southern Africa. And in 2001 alone, cell phone usage on the continent was up by 50 per cent, especially in MTN's (South Africa's largest mobile phone company) latest (and very challenging) market, Nigeria.

South African franchises and related logistics have managed to 'invade' the continent in ways more sustainable than the early trekboers and subsequent 'anti-communist' soldiers were able to. We turn here from retail chains to the service sector. First, in terms of food, clothing and related sectors, for example, by the early twenty-first century, while Pick-'n-Pay had supermarkets in Botswana, Swaziland, Tanzania and Zimbabwe (as well as Australia!), Shoprite had become the continent's largest retailer with ninety-two super-markets in thirteen countries from the Cape to Cairo (Botswana, Egypt, Lesotho, Madagascar, Malawi, Mozambique, Namibia, Namibia, Swaziland, Tanzania, Uganda, Zambia and Zimbabwe) in addition to South Africa, leading to exports from the latter of over R400 million per annum. Similarly, for the less affluent and street traders, Metro Cash and Carry warehouse outlets are now located in Angola (six!), Botswana, Kenya, Malawi, Uganda and Zimbabwe, and the lower middle classes can shop at Edgars in Botswana, Lesotho, Namibia, Swaziland and Zimbabwe. For the emerging upper middle classes, Woolworth franchises are now found in Botswana (nearly a dozen), Kenya, Lesotho, Mauritius, Namibia, Swaziland, Tanzania, Uganda, Zambia and Zimbabwe. Interestingly, with the exception of Tanzania and Zambia, these franchise locations all fall well within the 2002 Human Development Report medium human development category, suggesting that not unlike the 'Big Mac index', Woolworth stores may be suggestive of the size and presence of a middle class!

Second, meanwhile, in the service sectors, from finance to communications, Stanbic Bank operates in Botswana, Congo, Ghana, Tanzania, Uganda, Zambia and Zimbabwe (not to mention Moscow!) and is contemplating opening in Angola and Kenya. Two South-African-originated financial companies are becoming both continental and global: Investec operates in the SADC, especially Botswana, Mozambique and Namibia along with the UK and USA plus Australia, Ireland and Israel, while Old Mutual is already in Kenya, Namibia and Zimbabwe as well as the UK. Two major South-African-based hotel companies are increasingly active in the SADC and COMESA: Protea prides itself on being the largest hotel company in the continent: in a dozen African states from Egypt to South Africa, including a half-dozen in Tanzania; and Sun International occupies a more exclusive segment around casinos and golf in the SADC. MTN has mobile phone licences in Cameroon, Rwanda, Swaziland and Uganda as well as Nigeria. MNet/DStv operates satellite TV facilities throughout the continent via a series of concentric circles from its RSA hub, franchises and joint ventures in the SADC and Commonwealth, and agents in the francophone/Sahelian states plus Congo: almost all of SSA including the islands – some 850,000 subscribers!

Conclusion

Our analysis of Africa's current pattern of trade and investment poses challenges to a set of interrelated development approaches, disciplines and debates, with relevance beyond the continent. In particular, we suggest that lingering state-centrism is misplaced in both explanation and prescription: 'success stories' in Africa as elsewhere require innovative coalitions or partnerships involving non-state actors (Lewis 2002). Policy responses from state and non-state actors at all levels need to be creative in a world of 200 states and competing companies, regions, sectors, etc. The very diversity found in Africa today should be cause for some optimism, which NEPAD tries to capture. But whether the AU, ECA and/or NEPAD are compatible or sustainable remains an open question. Nevertheless, the dynamism of civil society in and around Africa should provide some reassurance despite Amin's scepticism that human development/security indicators may improve rather than worsen for some of the continent's countries/communities/companies in the new millennium.

Notes

1   The survey can be found at: www.researchfoundation.com.
2   See, for example, www.surgeon-and-safari.co.za.

Bibliography

Abrahamsen, R. (2000) *Disciplining Democracy: development discourse and good governance in Africa*, London: Zed.
African Business (2002) July/August. Available HTTP:
   <http://www.mbendi.co.za/> (accessed 25 July 2003).
African Development Bank (2001) *African Development Report 2001: fostering good governance in Africa*, Oxford: Oxford University Press.
African Development Bank (2002) *African Development Report 2002: rural development for poverty reduction in Africa*, Oxford: Oxford University Press.
African Union Directory (2002) *First Heads of State Summit*, Port Louis, Mauritius: Millennium.

Amin, S. (2002) 'Africa: living on the fringe', *Monthly Review* 53: 41–50.

Barnett, T. and Whiteside, A. (2002) *AIDS in the Twenty-first Century*, London: Palgrave.

Beavon, K. (1997) 'Johannesburg: a city and metropolitan area in transformation', in C. Rakodi (ed.), *The Urban Challenge in Africa: growth and management of its largest cities*, Tokyo: United Nations University Press.

Business Day (2002) 'From car assembler to major exporter', 29 November. Available HTTP: <http://www.bdfm.co.za/cgi-bin/pp-print.pl> (accessed 25 July 2003).

Cerny, P. (2003) 'Globalization and other stories', in A. Hulsemeyer (ed.), *Globalization in the Twenty-first Century*, London: Palgrave.

Chabal, P. and Daloz, J.P. (1999) *Africa Works: disorder as political instrument*, London: James Currey.

Cornellissen, S. (2000) 'Nodal points of economic growth: a perspective on urban governance and sustainability in Southern Africa', Paper presented at the International Studies Association Annual Convention, 14–18 March, Los Angeles, California.

Corporate Research Foundation (2002) *South Africa's Most Promising Companies*, Cape Town: CRF.

Crush, J. (2002) 'The global raiders: nationalism, globalization and the South African brain drain', *Journal of International Affairs* 56: 147–174.

Desai, V. and Potter, R. (eds) (2002) *The Companion to Development Studies*, London: Arnold.

Duffield, M. (2001) *Global Governance and the New Wars: the merging of development and security*, London: Zed.

Economist Intelligence Unit (2002) *South Africa Country Report*, December, London.

Fraser, J. (2002) 'Multinational BMW to benefit from AGOA scheme', *Business Day* 8 November. Available HTTP: <http://www.bday.co.za/bday/content/direct/1,3523,1219527-6078-0,00.html> (accessed 25 July 2003).

Griffith, P. (ed.) (2003) *Unbinding Africa*, London: Foreign Policy Centre.

Hart, M. (2001) *Diamond: the history of a cold-blooded love affair*, Toronto: Penguin.

Held, D., McGrew, A., Goldblatt, D. and Perraton, J. (eds) (1999) *Global Transformations: politics, economics and culture*, Cambridge: Polity.

Kearney, A.T. (2003) 'Measuring globalization: who's up, who's down?', *Foreign Policy* 134: 60–72.

Klare, M.T. (2002) *Resource Wars: the new landscape of global conflict*, New York: Owl.

Lewis, D. (2002) 'Civil society in African contexts: reflections on the usefulness of a concept', *Development and Change* 33: 569–586.

MacDougall, A.K. (2001) 'Lake Victoria: casualty of capitalism', *Monthly Review* 53: 38–42.

MacLean, S.J., Quadir, F. and Shaw, T.M. (eds) (2001) *Crises of Governance in Asia and Africa*, Aldershot: Ashgate.

MacLean, S.J., Harker, H.J. and Shaw, T.M. (eds) (2002) *Advancing Human Security and Development in Africa: reflections on NEPAD*, Halifax: Centre for Foreign Policy Studies.

Makhan, V.S. (2002) *Economic Recovery in Africa: the paradox of financial flows*, London: Palgrave.

Mkandawire, T. (2001) 'Thinking about Developmental States in Africa', *Cambridge Journal of Economics* 25: 289–313.

Mkandawire, T. and Soludo, C.C. (eds) (2001) *Our Continent, Our Future: African perspectives on structural adjustment*, Dakar: CODESRIA.

Mohan, G. and Zack-Williams, A.B. (2002a) 'Editorial: Africa, the African diaspora and development', *Review of African Political Economy* 92: 205–210.

Mohan, G. and Zack-Williams, A.B. (2002b) 'Globalisation from below: conceptualising the role of the African diasporas in Africa's development', *Review of African Political Economy* 92: 211–236.

Mshomba, R.E. (2000) *Africa in the Global Economy*, Boulder, CO: Lynne Rienner.

Naim, M. (2003) 'Five wars of globalization', *Foreign Policy* 134: 29–37.

Parpart, J.L and Shaw, T.M. (2002) 'African development debates and prospects at the turn of the century', in P.J. McGowan and P. Nel (eds), *Power, Wealth and Global Equity: an international relations textbook for Africa*, 2nd edn, Cape Town: University of Cape Town Press.

Ponte, S. and Gibbons, P. (2004) *Globalization and Economic Change in Africa*, London: Palgrave.

Sassen, S. (1991) *The Global City: New York*, London, Tokyo, Princeton, NJ: Princeton University Press.

Shaw, T. (2001) 'South Africa and the political economy of wine: from sanctions to globalizations/liberalizations', in S. MacLean, F. Quadir and T. Shaw (eds), *Crises of Governance in Asia and Africa*, Aldershot: Ashgate.

Shaw, T.M. (2003) 'Africa', in M. Hawkesworth and M. Kogan (eds), *Routledge Encyclopedia of Government and Politics*, 2nd edn, London: Routledge.

Shaw, T.M. and van der Westhuizen, J. (1999) 'Towards a political economy of trade in Africa: states, companies and civil societies', in B. Hocking and S. McGuire (eds), *Trade Politics*, London: Routledge, 246–260.

Soderbaum, F. and Taylor, I.C. (eds) (2003) *Regionalism and Uneven Development: the case of the Maputo Corridor*, Aldershot: Ashgate.

UNCTAD (1999) *World Investment Report 1999: foreign direct investment and the challenge of development*, New York and Geneva.

UNCTAD (2001) *World Investment Report 2001: promoting linkages*, New York and Geneva.

Van der Westhuizen, J. (2001) 'Marketing the Rainbow Nation: the power of South African music, film and sport industry', in K.C. Dunn and T.M. Shaw (eds), *Africa and International Relations Theory*, London: Palgrave.

Van der Westhuizen, J. (2003) 'How (not) to sell big ideas: argument, identity and NEPAD', *International Journal* (in press).

Key readings

Crush, J. (2002) 'The global raiders: nationalism, globalization and the South African brain drain', *Journal of International Affairs* 56: 147–174.

Parpart, J.L and Shaw, T.M. (2002) 'African development debates and prospects at the turn of the century', in P.J. McGowan and P. Nel (eds), *Power, Wealth and Global Equity: an international relations textbook for Africa*, 2nd edn, Cape Town: University of Cape Town Press.

Soderbaum, F. and Taylor, I.C. (eds) (2003) *Regionalism and Uneven Development: the case of the Maputo Corridor*, Aldershot: Ashgate.

UNCTAD (2001) *World Investment Report 2001: promoting linkages*, New York and Geneva.

Van der Westhuizen, J. (2001) 'Marketing the Rainbow Nation: the power of South African music, film and sport industry', in K.C. Dunn and T.M. Shaw (eds), *Africa and International Relations Theory*, London: Palgrave.

Useful websites

www.researchfoundation.com (Corporate Research Foundation).
www.nepad.org (New Partnership for Africa's Development).
www.oneworldtrust.org (One World Trust).
www.sadc.int (Southern African Development Community).
www.agoa.gov (United States African Growth and Opportunity Act).

Part II

The politics of the World Trade Organization

Key part issues

- What kind of organisation can or should the WTO be?
- How can the disputes process be improved? Do you think that non-governmental organisations or firms should become eligible participants?
- What handicaps do developing states face in their efforts to participate fully in the WTO?
- Does engagement with civil society enhance the WTO's credibility of legitimacy, or merely overwhelm the organisation with yet more demands?

The WTO exploded into public consciousness in late 1999 when violent protests in Seattle disrupted the organisation's key ministerial meeting. Until that date, most people probably knew little of this key international organisation: afterwards, it seemed that most people had a view – informed or otherwise! The WTO is central to our understanding of international trade politics. It is the key international institution dedicated to trade and, as such, occupies the centre of a dense web of state and societal interests. Moreover, its operations have for many critics epitomised the democratic deficit that characterises modern political economy. Critics charge that important decisions about national economies are made, not by elected politicians, but by technical experts and bureaucrats.

Sally opens this part with a survey of the current issues confronting the WTO. He shows how the organisation has evolved from its previous incarnation as the General Agreement on Tariffs and Trade (GATT). He notes how a widely perceived strength of the WTO, its enhanced status and rules-based operations, has undermined the ability of members to come to a politically arranged compromise over trade conflicts. Lee's chapter on the dispute settlement process is a key complement to Sally's argument. The Dispute Settlement Understanding (DSU) was seen as a key achievement of the Uruguay Round negotiations; by instituting a rules-based disputes process, the power of strong states to bully the weak would be attenuated. Lee shows that things have not turned out as planned. Large and powerful actors like the USA and EU still dominate the process, though as developing states become more confident, this dominance may diminish.

One of the central criticisms of the WTO is that it is essentially a club designed by and operated for rich Western states and their firms. Narlikar's chapter shows the obstacles that stand in the way of developing countries as they seek full participation in the organisation. The GATT was indeed the child of the post-war Bretton Woods settlement; the concerns of developing countries were not considered. Yet, as Narlikar shows, emerging economies in Asia, Africa and Latin America now constitute the bulk of the WTO's membership. These states are no longer passive players but seek to shape the current Doha negotiations which are, after all, called the 'Development Round'. Developing states are not the only actors making their presence felt in Geneva: civil society is too. Scholte's chapter illuminates the growing linkages between the WTO and a myriad of civil society groups representing causes as diverse as labour rights activists, anti-pollution groups and animal conservationists. The WTO remains a state-centred body, yet its efforts to engage with interest groups reflect the importance attached to the legitimacy of the organisation's operations and decisions.

7 The WTO in perspective

Razeen Sally

Summary

Four underlying trends characterise the shift from the GATT to a wider and deeper WTO: standards harmonisation; legalisation; politicisation; and regionalisation. There are three scenarios for the WTO's middle-distance future, crystallised by the Doha Round agenda: (1) a GATT-style market access focus; (2) an EU-style regulatory agency with a standards harmonisation agenda; (3) a UN-style development agency, with more aid and carve-outs for developing countries. Intergovernmental politics – a bundle of old and new forces – will largely determine the outcome.

Much has changed in the transition from the GATT to the WTO. The Uruguay Round agreements take the WTO wider, with broader sectoral coverage, and deeper into domestic regulations, all underpinned by much stronger dispute settlement. WTO membership has expanded, with the accession of almost twenty developing and transitional countries since the end of the Uruguay Round – including China. The WTO appears more politicised than the GATT, internally fractured by intergovernmental divisions and externally buffeted by hostile NGOs. Finally, after a false start at Seattle, a new round of multilateral trade negotiations was launched in Doha at the end of 2001.

Symptoms of change have nevertheless to be set alongside elements of continuity from the GATT era, with the combination placed in a broader trade policy context. Only then can one grasp underlying trends in the WTO since its inception.

Accordingly, this chapter begins by way of brief scene-setting, taking a *tour d'horizon* of recent trade policy developments on national, bilateral and regional tracks, all of which influence WTO business. Then it moves to structural shifts – economic, political and legal – from the GATT to the WTO, and attempts to identify the key underlying trends in the WTO today. Based on the latter, the following section asks fundamental questions: What is the WTO's *raison d'être*? Where is it heading? What are the scenarios for its middle-distance future? To a large extent, the answers lie in the changing intergovernmental politics of the WTO, which plays into the present Doha Round and which will determine its course and result. This is the focus of the final section of the chapter.

Extended background: trade policy reforms and 'multi-track' trade policy

Overall, trade policy has become progressively more liberal in the last couple of decades as part of wider packages of economic policy reform, although this trend is patchy and uneven. The OECD countries have gradually opened their markets further, consolidating the liberalisation of trade and capital controls since the late 1940s. The real trade policy revolution, however, has occurred in developing and transitional countries, and in Australia and New Zealand (Henderson 1998).

About 20–25 relatively recent 'globalisers' – nearly all middle-income countries from East Asia, Latin America and Eastern Europe – have liberalised significantly and integrated fast and deep into the world economy. In stark contrast, the overwhelming majority of developing countries, bunched in the low-income and least developed brackets, retain higher protection and have low or stagnant growth. Many, particularly the least developed (LDCs), are mired in political and economic instability (Michalopolous 2001: 45–88).

The bulk of recent trade-and-investment liberalisation in developing and transitional countries has taken place unilaterally, that is governments have liberalised independently and not via international trade negotiations. This has been driven by domestic political momentum (especially in the recent globalisers) and external pressure (especially in the LDCs through IMF and World Bank structural adjustment programmes).

The realities of modern politics – interest group lobbying for protection, ingrained mercantilist thinking, the perception that trade liberalisation hurts the poor and vulnerable – make sustained unilateral liberalisation very hard to achieve, except in situations of political and economic crisis (Haggard and Williamson 1995). Given the practical difficulty of undertaking unilateral liberalisation, there is some merit to the 'multilateralised reciprocity' that the GATT/WTO embodies. The following advantages come to mind (Krugman 1997; Hoekman and Kostecki 2001: 25–36):

- Intergovernmental negotiations and binding international obligations help protect governments against powerful protectionist interests at home, and mobilise the support of domestic exporters.
- WTO rules provide rights to market access for exports; and rights against the arbitrary protection and predation of more powerful players. This is particularly important for developing countries.
- Multilateral rules can bolster domestic reform efforts and reinforce the clarity, coherence and credibility of national trade policy reform in the eyes of exporters, importers, local and foreign investors, and, not least, consumers. This is another way of saying that the WTO, at its best, is a helpful auxiliary to good national governance.

Regional trade agreements (RTAs), sandwiched between unilateral measures and the WTO, have proliferated in practically all regions of the world economy since the 1980s. Activity on the regional track has accelerated since the failure of the WTO's Seattle Ministerial Conference in 1999, especially in Asia–Pacific. The WTO secretariat estimates that about 250 RTAs are either in force or under negotiation. Intra-RTA trade could soon account for over half of international trade (WTO 2002: 40).

Structural shifts from GATT to WTO

The GATT provided rules for progressively more open trade, at the border, in (some) industrial goods. The edifice was – and remains – underpinned by the principles of non-discrimination, reciprocity and transparency (Box 7.1). As a result of the Uruguay Round agreements, the WTO goes much wider and comes closer to universal coverage, providing market access rules for the bulk (if not all) of international trade. As important, the agreements go well beyond the coverage of border barriers (tariffs and quotas) to encompass a much broader range of 'behind-the-border' non-tariff barriers, i.e. domestic regulations that hinder international trade.

Box 7.1 WTO principles

Non-discrimination: The principle of non-discrimination has two components: Most Favoured Nation (MFN) status and National Treatment. They are enshrined in GATT Articles I and III respectively, and are to be found in other WTO agreements on goods, services and intellectual property.

The MFN rule requires that a product made in one member country be treated 'no less favourably' than a 'like' (very similar) product that originates in any other member country. Thus, if the best treatment granted a trading partner supplying a specific product is a 5 per cent tariff, then this rate must be applied immediately and unconditionally to the imports of this product originating in all WTO members.

The National Treatment rule requires that foreign products, once they have satisfied whatever border measures are applied, be treated 'no less favourably' than like or directly competitive products produced domestically in terms of internal taxation. That is, products of foreign origin circulating in the country should be subject to the same taxes and charges that apply to identical products of domestic origin.

MFN applies unconditionally, i.e. it is a general obligation, though with exceptions for free trade areas and customs unions, and for preferential treatment of developing countries. National Treatment is a general obligation in the GATT but not in the GATS.

Reciprocity: The reciprocity principle is fundamental to trade negotiations, with liberalisation occurring on a quid pro quo basis. Import barriers are reduced through an exchange of 'concessions'. This can take place bilaterally or in regional club-like arrangements. Multilateral reciprocity in the GATT/WTO entails extending concessions granted in bilateral negotiations to all other member countries via the MFN rule.

Transparency: This is a legal obligation embodied in GATT Article X and GATS Article III. It is intended to aid the enforcement of member countries' legal commitments and reduce the scope for circumvention of obligations. WTO members are required to publish their trade regulations, to establish and maintain institutions allowing for the review of administrative decisions affecting trade, to respond to requests for information by other members, and to notify changes in trade policy to the WTO. These internal transparency requirements are supplemented by multilateral surveillance of trade policies by WTO members. This process is facilitated by periodic country-specific reports (Trade Policy Reviews).

(Hoekman and Kostecki 2001: 29–31, 34–35)

The General Agreement on Tariffs and Trade 1994 (GATT 1947 as amended by Understandings and Agreements negotiated during the Uruguay Round) continues the

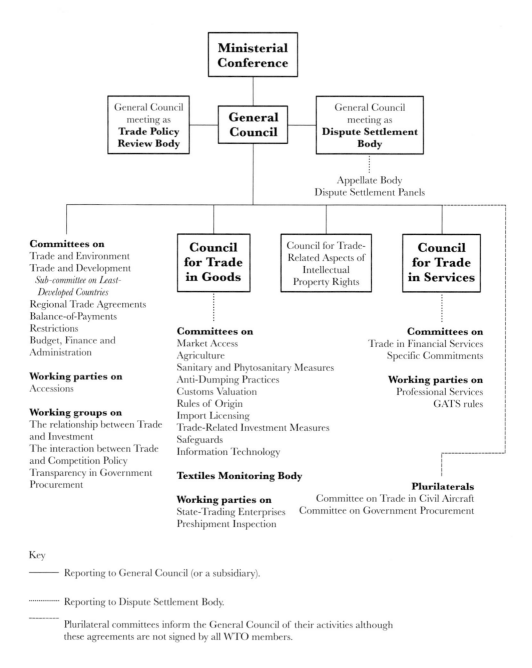

Ministerial Conference

General Council meeting as **Trade Policy Review Body**

General Council

General Council meeting as **Dispute Settlement Body**

Appellate Body
Dispute Settlement Panels

Committees on
Trade and Environment
Trade and Development
Sub-committee on Least-Developed Countries
Regional Trade Agreements
Balance-of-Payments Restrictions
Budget, Finance and Administration

Working parties on
Accessions

Working groups on
The relationship between Trade and Investment
The interaction between Trade and Competition Policy
Transparency in Government Procurement

Council for Trade in Goods

Committees on
Market Access
Agriculture
Sanitary and Phytosanitary Measures
Anti-Dumping Practices
Customs Valuation
Rules of Origin
Import Licensing
Trade-Related Investment Measures
Safeguards
Information Technology

Textiles Monitoring Body

Working parties on
State-Trading Enterprises
Preshipment Inspection

Council for Trade-Related Aspects of Intellectual Property Rights

Council for Trade in Services

Committees on
Trade in Financial Services
Specific Commitments

Working parties on
Professional Services
GATS rules

Plurilaterals
Committee on Trade in Civil Aircraft
Committee on Government Procurement

Key

———— Reporting to General Council (or a subsidiary).

·········· Reporting to Dispute Settlement Body.

- - - - - - Plurilateral committees inform the General Council of their activities although these agreements are not signed by all WTO members.

The General Council also meets as the Trade Policy Review Body and Dispute Settlement Body

Figure 7.1 The World Trade Organization

fifty-year-old process of reducing tariff and non-tariff barriers to trade in manufactures. The Agreement on Agriculture and the Agreement on Textiles and Clothing, although relatively weak and shot through with loopholes, have GATT-style rules and procedures for gradually liberalising important but hitherto highly protected chunks of goods trade. The General Agreement on Trade in Services (GATS), although architecturally complicated and with modest commitments to date, nevertheless establishes the framework for the liberalisation of trade *and* factor movements in cross-border services transactions. The GATS also has provisions for making the domestic regulation of services sectors more transparent and non-discriminatory – a vital consideration given that opaque and discriminatory domestic regulations hinder services trade far more than classic border restrictions. A strong Agreement on Trade-Related Intellectual Property Rights (TRIPs) provides international minimum standards for the protection of patents, copyrights and trademarks. A considerably weaker Agreement on Trade-Related Investment Measures provides disciplines on government investment measures (e.g. local content, export and technology transfer requirements) that discriminate against imports.

New or revamped trade procedures, notably on subsidies, technical barriers to trade, sanitary and phytosanitary measures, customs valuation and import licensing, furnish some of the regulatory infrastructure for tackling behind-the-border trade restrictions and taking better advantage of trade opportunities. This is especially important for developing countries that lack such regulatory infrastructure. Previously, such trade regulation was largely confined to plurilateral codes, mostly negotiated during the Tokyo Round, which were only binding on signatories. Nearly all developing countries were not party to these codes. Post-Uruguay Round, these agreements are binding on all WTO members.

Uruguay Round negotiations on GATT rules led to a strengthened Agreement on Safeguards, which abolished Voluntary Export Restraints and modified provisions on the use of safeguard measures covered by Article XIX GATT. The WTO Antidumping Agreement (covering the use of anti-dumping measures under Article VI GATT) is much weaker, as is the Understanding on the Interpretation of Article XXIV GATT (covering preferential trade agreements in goods among subsets of WTO members).

Finally, the Uruguay Round Dispute Settlement Understanding gives WTO dispute settlement procedures much more teeth and bite compared with the GATT record. Dispute settlement is now quasi-automatic, reliant more on law and due process than on the vagaries of diplomacy.

All the agreements mentioned above form part of the Single Undertaking, another Uruguay Round innovation. All WTO members have to comply with the obligations of all Uruguay Round agreements, with the relatively minor exceptions of agreements on public procurement and civil aircraft subsidies. The latter are updated Tokyo Round codes with rules and obligations binding only (overwhelmingly developed country) signatories.

The Single Undertaking breaks new ground in at least one very important respect: it changes the nature of Special and Differential Treatment (SDT) for developing countries. Previously, SDT, as codified in the Tokyo Round's Enabling Clause, legitimised the GATT practice of 'non-reciprocity' for developing countries: they received tariff concessions negotiated among developed countries through the Most Favoured Nation clause (in Article I GATT), but they were not obliged to reciprocate with own tariff reductions. They were also granted additional tariff preferences by developed countries, albeit on a non-binding basis. In general, developing countries were given sweeping carve-outs and exemptions from GATT rules and obligations. The Single Undertaking has effectively whittled down

SDT: common rules and obligations are binding on developing countries, though with provision for longer transition periods for implementing agreements, and promises of increased technical assistance.[1]

Figure 7.1 maps the architecture of the WTO, which was established as an international organisation with legal standing on 1 January 1995. (The GATT, in contrast, was an intergovernmental treaty serviced by a secretariat which did not have such legal standing.) The WTO is headed by a Ministerial Conference, which meets at least once every two years. Four Annexes contain the agreements mentioned above, as well as the Trade Policy Review Mechanism, an instrument for the regular surveillance of members' trade policies established early in the Uruguay Round. Between Ministerial Conferences, the WTO is supervised by a General Council comprised of senior officials from member governments (usually heads of national delegations to the organisation). The General Council also meets as the Trade Policy Review Body and the Dispute Settlement Body. Three subsidiary councils, covering the core agreements, operate under the guidance of the General Council. Separate committees, working parties and working groups deal with specific issues. The WTO secretariat, still largely resembling the GATT secretariat of old, is relatively small and has limited powers. As was the case with the GATT, the WTO is a 'member-driven' organisation reliant primarily on national capitals and Geneva delegations for negotiations and the operation of the covered agreements (Hoekman and Kostecki 2001: 50–55).

In sum, it could be said that with a wider and deeper rule base, enforced through stronger dispute settlement, the WTO has moved more in the direction of a law-governed system and away from the power (or diplomacy)-governed system that characterised the GATT (Jackson 1998: 6–10). And prima facie, observers might get the impression that the WTO is an edifice for free trade – a house built by and for free-traders. This kind of WTO would supply, and help to enforce, a transparent and non-discriminatory rule base for market access in cross-border transactions. Thus, 'from above' as it were, it would be a helpful, more effective auxiliary to liberal trade policies in member states, dovetailing with unilateral liberalisation and domestic regulatory reforms 'down below'.

The WTO, however, is more complicated than that: following GATT precedent, it is the offspring of delicate, finely balanced political compromise, certainly not a blueprint for free trade. Underlying trends point to a more complex, many-sided evolution and future for the WTO. Viewed benignly, these trends correct free trade's defects and complement it with other legitimate objectives for the multilateral trading system. More anxious observers from the free trade camp would ring alarm bells.[2]

The evolving WTO

Four underlying trends, or structural shifts in the transition from the GATT to the WTO, need to be addressed: standards harmonisation; legalisation; politicisation; regionalisation. Let us take each in turn.

First, the WTO has an in-built and gradually expanding standards harmonisation agenda. The TRIPs agreement sets the precedent. TRIPs contains harmonised legal standards on the protection of patents, trademarks and copyrights to be applied across the WTO membership, regardless of differences in levels of development. It differs fundamentally from classic GATT-type market access rules, which are reasonably simple and 'negative', in the sense that they enjoin governments *not* to discriminate in international trade but otherwise leave them free to do anything not specifically forbidden. In other words, GATT rules are *proscriptive*. TRIPs, in contrast, houses 'positive' regulatory measures, with detailed *prescriptions* on how they should be enforced within domestic juris-dictions.[3]

The main point to bear in mind is that TRIPs takes WTO rules in a new direction – not necessarily farther in the direction of opening markets, but elsewhere, towards a complex, regulation-heavy standards harmonisation agenda intended to bring developing country standards up to developed country norms. It sets the precedent for raising developing country standards in a range of other areas, such as labour, environmental health, food safety, product labelling and other technical standards, armed with stronger WTO dispute settlement and the Damoclesian Sword of trade sanctions in case of non-compliance. To Jagdish Bhagwati, such an agenda constitutes backdoor *intrusionism*, an attempt to iron out the asymmetries in developing countries' domestic institutions and raise their costs out of line with comparative advantages. The effect is the same as classic frontal protectionism against cheap, labour-intensive developing country exports (Bhagwati 2002: 51–52, 67).

Admittedly, the issue is complicated and to some extent these pressures are inevitable. As border barriers come down and technology advances, globalisation inexorably runs up against all sorts of new barriers behind borders. If the WTO disregarded these regulatory barriers, lower protection at the border would be nullified by higher protection behind it. This means the WTO has to tackle standards relating to production and processing methods that lie deep in the structure of the domestic economy, in addition to tackling remaining (and substantial) border barriers. Negative (proscriptive) rules continue to be crucially important; but the WTO needs to have some positive (prescriptive) procedural disciplines to make domestic trade-related policies more transparent. Otherwise market access would not be a reality. This is the original intention behind the WTO's agreements on subsidies, services, sanitary standards, technical barriers to trade, customs valuation and import licensing.

Hence a minimum standards approach to domestic regulation in the WTO could cut both ways: in some cases hindering market access, in other cases promoting it. In general, WTO members need to be very sensitive to constraints in developing countries – especially the LDCs – with scarce administrative, technical and financial resources to implement high-quality international standards. Arguably, an intrusive, one-size-fits-all regulatory approach, driven by developed country benchmarks and political agendas, is neither politi-cally nor economically appropriate.

Second, the creeping legalisation of the WTO is not all good news. On the one hand, it is widely recognised that the new dispute settlement mechanism has, on balance, func-tioned well: increasing numbers of developed and developing countries have had recourse to it; and compliance has generally been good. On the other hand, trade negotiators have a perhaps unavoidable tendency to conclude vaguely worded final texts that give legal expression to political compromise and fudge. In WTO-speak this is known as 'constructive ambiguity'. Many Uruguay Round agreements contain numerous gaps and ambiguities, especially in the dense thickets of domestic regulation. Inevitably, there are limits to legal certainty on the nitty-gritty of this-or-that regulatory measure, with ample room for diverging legal interpretations – more so than with simpler, clearer border measures. Given quasi-automatic dispute settlement, there is more incentive for governments to fill in these regulatory gaps through litigation in panels and Appellate Body rulings rather than through negotiation and quiet, behind-the-scenes diplomacy (Dunkel *et al.* 2001; Barfield 2001).

This could be a dangerous and slippery slope. The WTO, like the GATT before it, is a 'contract organisation' bringing together a large, diverse group of sovereign nation-states

(Winham 1998). The Dispute Settlement Body probably does not enjoy the political consensus to sustain 'creative' judicial interpretations of legal texts and policy driven by litigation, as happens from time to time in the US Supreme Court and the European Court of Justice. The risk inherent in such judicial activism is that policy may be driven in crucial areas by those large and powerful WTO members able to commit significant legal resources to dispute settlement cases. This could conceivably lead to rulings inimical to developing country interests, such as an expansive, open-ended interpretation of the precautionary principle on food-safety issues, and discrimination against imports based on their production and processing methods. Thus, to those who fear excessive legalisation, the bottom line is that governments and not international judges should determine the boundary between WTO rules and domestic policy space (Ostry 2001: 9).

Third, the WTO is manifestly more politicised than the old GATT. Externally, it faces the brunt of the anti-globalisation backlash, and is constantly buffeted by a combination of old-style protectionist interests and new-style NGOs, the latter subsuming well-funded, high-profile groups in the West purporting to represent causes (such as protection of the environment, food safety and other consumer issues, working conditions, human rights and animal welfare). The arcana of trade policy, previously handled through low-key diplomacy and negotiation, now seem to be the crucible for global controversies, with their fair share of adversarial sloganeering and point-scoring.

As important – perhaps even more so – are the deeper internal, intergovernmental divisions within the WTO. These are many and cross-cutting, by no means restricted to traditional and new developed–developing country cleavages – though the latter are perhaps the most attention grabbing. The hyperinflation of the GATT/WTO, i.e. the accession of so many developing and transitional countries during and after the Uruguay Round, has added new sets of interests and preferences to the WTO's ongoing business. Decision making has become even more unwieldy and snail-like, more often than not distracted by rhetoric and political grandstanding in the WTO General Council, on the one hand, and the Geneva trade officials' obsession with procedural minutiae, on the other. There is also greater pressure to boost developing country representation when making new appointments to the WTO secretariat – with the attendant risk that appointments will be made on the grounds of political expediency and not on merit.

All the above – grandiloquent speechifying, political point-scoring, running around in procedural circles, the temptation to make appointments on political rather than meritocratic grounds – are signs of the 'UN-isation' of the WTO. The GATT escaped the pitfalls of other international organisations, particularly within the UN system, because it had a reasonably clear purpose, a well-framed negotiating agenda, a small number of key players, and, not least, a high-quality secretariat. If present UN-style trends continue, the WTO will quite possibly be unable to function as an effective multilateral forum for trade negotiations. It could well become a marginalised talking shop; and attention would shift elsewhere, particularly to bilateral and regional negotiating settings.

Fourth, the accelerating regionalisation of the world economy, i.e. the proliferation of discriminatory RTAs, seems to be pre-programmed, not least in reaction to stalled multilateral liberalisation. So far, there is little evidence that RTAs have retarded the overall liberalisation of trade and foreign direct investment (WTO 1995). Advocates of RTAs argue that small clubs of like-minded countries could take trade-and-investment liberalisation faster, wider and deeper than would be possible in the WTO. RTAs could in turn act as 'building blocks' for multilateral liberalisation (Bergsten 1997).

Sceptics counter that RTAs are 'stumbling blocks' in the multilateral trading system. The danger is that they could lead to a 'spaghetti bowl' of opaque, overlapping and discriminatory procedures, particularly in the form of incredibly complex rules of origin requirements that tie governments and firms in knots of red tape. In addition, RTAs could divert political attention and negotiating resources away from the WTO – by no means a trivial point given minimal trade policy capacity in many developing country administrations, especially in the LDCs. Finally, major powers, acting as RTA 'hubs', could force weaker 'spoke' countries, especially in the developing world, to accept inappropriate conditions in bilateral and regional agreements, such as minimum labour, environmental and other regulatory standards. This would in turn make it easier to sneak these issues into the WTO (Bhagwati 2002: 106–118).

The evidence on RTA effects is perhaps ambiguous. Nevertheless, the discriminatory, rule-evading potential of RTAs cannot be overlooked, particularly as multilateral disciplines on them (in Article XXIV GATT and Article V GATS) are rather weak. The risk is that RTAs will coalesce into discriminatory big blocks, revolving around the USA, the EU and perhaps China, competing and cooperating with each other according to power relationships rather than (non-discriminatory) multilateral rules. This would really put the squeeze on poorer and politically weaker developing countries effectively excluded from preferential access to the markets of major developed *and* developing countries.

Regionalisation is a fact of life. The effective way of mitigating its potentially negative effects, particularly for weaker developing countries, is to ratchet up non-discriminatory multilateral liberalisation in the context of a well-functioning WTO. That is not how things stand at the moment.

Given this cocktail of underlying trends, the missing ingredient in the WTO today happens to be the traditional virtue of the GATT: its ability to deliver results in the form of stronger rules for progressively more open international trade, through effective diplomacy and negotiation. This is not to say that the WTO should return to a golden yesterday. Far from it: the pressure for a wider agenda with domestic regulatory content has to be accommodated, especially if it enhances transparency and facilitates market access; legalisation is to some extent welcome as it makes the system more rules based for smaller and weaker players; and politicisation is simply a fact of modern trade policy. Put another way, it would be pie-in-the-sky to rely unduly on GATT-style diplomacy. However, the latter has been squeezed too tightly. It needs to be revived, for without it the WTO will not get out of its rut and advance.

The WTO, in short, needs to find a new balance: for dealing with domestic regulation so that it becomes more transparent and does not lead to regulatory overload and standards harmonisation; for dispute settlement so that legal procedures do not result in judicial policy making; for accommodating an increasing and overwhelming developing country majority without a headlong descent into UN-isation. These considerations go to the heart of the WTO's *raison d'être*, and set the scene for scenarios of its future.

The WTO's *raison d'être* and future scenarios

In trade policy, whether one is a negotiator or an academic expert, it is all too tempting to master details and techniques but perhaps overlook the big picture and macro-strategy. Identifying trees is of little use without a view of the forest. Thus it is important to rise above policy detail and pose fundamental questions: What is (or should be) the WTO's core purpose? Given recent trends, where is it heading? What might it look like in five, ten or fifteen years' time?

The heart of the matter is that there is no consensus among WTO members on the Organization's *raison d'être*. It is being pulled in different directions; and the predictable result is drift and deadlock. This contrasts with the GATT record. Then there was reasonable consensus (more or less), at least among the developed countries which ran the system, about what to do and how to go about doing it.

Based on the trends outlined in the previous section, it is possible to throw up basic scenarios of the WTO's future. Three come to mind:

- *Scenario One* would rediscover the *raison d'être* of the GATT: the progressive reduction and removal of barriers to trade, underpinned by simple, transparent, non-discriminatory rules, as embodied in the National Treatment and Most Favoured Nation principles. Admittedly, the GATT had lots of loopholes and a restricted remit of tackling border barriers on (most) industrial goods. Now a much expanded market access agenda subsumes agriculture, textiles and clothing, and services, as well as dealing with non-border trade barriers.

    This scenario is traditionalist in the sense that it restores a GATT-like compass to the WTO. But it is also reformist in that it ranges wider (broader sectoral coverage than the GATT) and ventures deeper (procedural disciplines to make trade-related domestic regulations more transparent, as covered by Article X GATT and Articles III and VI GATS).[4] It is a scenario that would accommodate a lowest common denominator of rules and obligations applicable to all WTO members; but still one that would allow plenty of leeway for different countries, at different levels of development (and with different histories and preferences), to have different sets of economic policies with different institutional mixes of state and market. This scenario would be sufficiently open-ended to encourage bottom-up unilateral experimentation by national governments in response to local circumstances and challenges. This would in turn promote a decentralised, market-like competitive emulation among governments in search of better policy and institutional practice.[5]

- *Scenario Two* is an EU-style future for the WTO. The EU is now the leading *demandeur* for a range of 'new issues' to be brought into the WTO. These comprise labour and environmental standards, and the 'Singapore issues' (investment rules, competition rules, trade facilitation and transparency in government procurement). With the exception of labour standards, they form part of the Doha Development Agenda (DDA).[6]

    The EU argues that as globalisation casts its net wider and becomes more complex, so these new issues need to be brought into the WTO fold. This is partly for market access reasons, i.e. to liberalise trade and investment further, as is the case with the Singapore issues and the liberalisation of environmental goods and services. But other motivations figure at least as prominently, such as addressing NGO and other interest group concerns on labour, food-safety, product labelling, environmental and animal welfare standards in developing countries. However, cynics among the WTO membership retort that the EU's main motivation is to use the new issues to deflect attention from the agricultural negotiations in the Doha Round, in which the EU is the main obstacle to liberalisation.

    Sceptics of the EU Commission's agenda hold that it is less interested in market access (along the lines of Scenario One), and more interested in turning the WTO into a regulatory agency in its own image. The EU proposes to add complex regulation to the WTO agenda, some of which could conceivably impose burdensome environmental and other standards on developing countries. This would extend the scope of standards harmonisation in the WTO, aimed at raising developing country standards in the direction of developed country levels. The door was opened with TRIPs; the environmental aspects of the Doha Round threaten to open the door wider. Developing countries fear this could result in an extra layer of developed country regulatory barriers that would restrict their labour-intensive exports and negatively affect inflows of foreign investment.

•   *Scenario Three* is a UN-style future for the WTO, the prospects for which have increased with the accession of so many developing countries to the organisation. Given one-member–one-vote, consensus-based decision making in the WTO, developing country issues and concerns clearly have to be accommodated to a much greater extent than was the case with the GATT. Accordingly, the DDA places these issues (notably implementation of Uruguay Round agreements, SDT, TRIPs and public health, technical assistance and capacity building) at the heart of its Work Programme.[7]

In the Doha Round there has been much pressure to reopen Uruguay Round agreements and grant blanket exemptions to developing countries on the grounds of Special and Differential Treatment. There is also a clamour for technical assistance (i.e. aid) (Sally 2003: 18–22). At the same time, the WTO is becoming more a forum for adversarial political grandstanding and procedural nit-picking than one for effective decision making. The risk is that a more politicised WTO would look more like a profligate and not terribly effective UN development agency than the pre-1995 GATT. It would disburse more aid and steer back in the direction of old-style non-reciprocal SDT, with greater developing country exemptions from common rules and obligations. The danger is that if the WTO goes too far down this road, it will be too crippled to do much else.

In a sense all three scenarios are built into the DDA, which, following the events of 11 September 2001, reflected the spirit of all-round compromise that allowed the new round to be launched. Its large, complex and messy agenda contains a market access core (Scenario One). The constituency in favour of further liberalisation is led by the present US Administration, notwithstanding protectionist interests in US domestic politics. The Cairns group (of developed and developing country agricultural exporters), as well as a clutch of others from Latin America and East Asia, have an even stronger stake in this kind of WTO. Since its accession in 2001, China has shown every sign of becoming a leading member of this constituency. However, EU and developing country issues are also prominent in the DDA (more in line with Scenarios Two and Three) (Sally 2003: 9–10, 13–14).

In reality, no one constituency commands sufficient support to swing the Doha Round, and with it the future of the WTO, decisively in any one direction. Drift and gridlock might continue to prevent movement altogether. Also possible is a compromise that would attempt a synthesis of all three scenarios. The risk inherent in such a 'third way' is a resulting dog's breakfast: market access gains could be gutted by a combination of regulatory protectionism and politically correct giveaways and exemptions for developing countries.

Intergovernmental politics, in this round and beyond, will largely shape the WTO's future. To this I now turn.

The intergovernmental politics of the WTO

Politics among the WTO membership is a mix of the old (GATT) and new. Three old and four new features deserve to be highlighted.

First, since the Kennedy Round, the necessary condition for progress is for the major players, the USA and the EU, to contain domestic political difficulties, defuse bilateral conflicts and cooperate intensively. However, given a large and diverse WTO, this is far from sufficient.

Second, following Uruguay Round precedent, success in this round and beyond will require the effective participation of a core of about twenty-five developed and developing countries which are already active in the WTO. Canada, Japan, Norway, Switzerland, Australia and New Zealand from the OECD come to mind. In the developing country camp, Brazil, India and now China stand out, but this group also includes other Latin American and East Asian countries.

Third, multi-country coalitions will be important.[8] Broad-based, informal '*café au lait*'-coalitions will be useful to share information and act as sounding-boards for ideas (the 'chat group' phenomenon). The drawback of these groups is that they are too big and heterogeneous to forge common positions. Perhaps more important will be small, discrete, issue-based developed–developing country coalitions. The Cairns group and the International Bureau on Textiles and Clothing (ITCB) are the pathfinders in this respect. More probable in other negotiating areas are looser, informal coalitions (so-called Friends Groups), with membership fluid and varying across issues.

The first novel element is that the active, 'first-division' developing countries will be negotiating with each other and other developing countries, especially on the tariff and non-tariff barriers that throttle South–South trade. During the Uruguay Round, the active developing countries tended to go head to head with developed countries but not with each other. The present situation is but a reflection of the increasing differentiation within the developing world and the porousness of the North–South divide.

The second novel element will be the more active participation of many more developing countries, including some traditionally weaker developing countries and even some LDCs, than was the case in previous rounds. The countries concerned are too small and weak to sustain effective participation on their own, so they will have to create like-minded (or 'common characteristic') coalitions for this purpose (Page 2002).

However, there are distinct limits to the active participation of the second- and third-division developing countries with limited-to-very-limited trade policy capacity, even in coalition formation.[9] During the long haul of complex and multiple negotiations, they are likely to remain followers, not initiators and proactive players, most of the time. This applies particularly to the LDCs, but, albeit to a less extreme extent, also to large low-income countries such as Pakistan, Bangladesh, Egypt and Nigeria. All may have more 'negative' bargaining power than before, i.e. the ability and willingness to block agreement, but they will not have significant 'positive' bargaining power for the foreseeable future.

The third factor is the entry of China and Taiwan ('Chinese Taipei') into the WTO. Russia too may join while the round is ongoing, although Russian unwillingness to initiate WTO-compatible reforms may drag out the accession process. Taiwan, with a track record of relative openness to the world economy, and having liberalised further in order to join the WTO, is in a good position to play an active role.

China is now the most important developing country in the WTO and is bound to play a major role. WTO accession was the crowning point of the most comprehensive set external liberalisation and domestic regulatory reform measures seen anywhere in the world in the 1990s. China's WTO commitments are the strongest of any developing country in the organisation, and it is roughly on track with their staged implementation. After a fifteen-year WTO accession negotiation, China has capable, savvy trade negotiators who will want to extract maximum benefit from the WTO and use it to further bolster domestic reform – not to destroy the WTO system. Indeed, it appears that China is adopting more a 'Brazilian' than an 'Indian' strategy in the WTO. It is not being negative and blocking on several fronts; rather it is shaping differentiated interests and pursuing a mixture of offensive and defensive positions, forming overlapping coalitions with other WTO members along the way. Overall, it is increasingly apparent that its objectives are market access focused (Scenario One rather than Scenarios Two or Three).

Fourth, but by no means least, is the tantalising possibility of more clear-cut and robust US leadership in the WTO under the Bush Administration – in contrast to the vacillation and drift of the Clinton years. Early signs of a more vigorous US approach emerged during the course of 2002, when it advanced ambitious market access proposals in the Doha Round.

This cannot be divorced from the broader strategic picture of an increasingly confident and assertive US superpower on the international stage, compared with an internally sclerotic and externally pusillanimous EU. Since the Tokyo Round, the USA and the EU have shared co-equal leadership in the GATT/WTO. To be sure, it will still take two to tango, but is the USA about to lead the dance for the first time since the 1960s? It is too early to tell, and this scenario is hedged about with ifs and buts. If the USA is to lead from the front, it will need 'coalitions of the willing' also favouring a market access future for the WTO.[10] Many potential allies are to be found in Latin America and East Asia. China stands prominent among them.

Conclusion

Trade policy is increasingly 'multi-track', with simultaneous movements taking place unilaterally, bilaterally, regionally and multilaterally. The WTO, like the GATT before it, provides rules for progressively more open trade on the basis of non-discrimination, reciprocity and transparency. However, much has changed from the GATT to the WTO. The latter's rules and procedures have wider and deeper coverage; its membership is ever larger; and it has much stronger dispute settlement. Underlying trends – standards harmonisation, legalisation, politicisation and regionalisation – throw up daunting challenges. What worked well in the GATT – diplomacy-based negotiations – does not seem to be working well in the WTO. Moreover, the WTO lacks a basic consensus on its *raison d'être*, with different members pulling it in sometimes contradictory directions. The intergovernmental politics of the WTO contains elements from the GATT, with an admixture of increasing but highly differentiated developing country participation. Finally, the wider 'high politics' context of US leadership and the rise of China are bound to influence the WTO's future course, though its direction is as yet unclear.

Notes

1   On the Uruguay Round agreements, the Single Undertaking and SDT, see Hoekman and Kostecki (2001), Croome (1999) and Jackson (1998).
2   For a flavour of such contrasting views, see Esty (2002a), Henderson (2002) and Esty (2002b).
3   On the distinction between negative, classical-liberal-type rules and positive regulation in international transactions, see Sally (2002: 15–18).
4   I owe this form of words to my former student Joakim Reiter, now dealing with trade policy at the Swedish Ministry of Foreign Affairs.
5   It is the classical liberal tradition, from Hume and Smith to Hayek, which highlights the merits of national (unilateral) freedom of action and an intergovernmental institutional competition, all in search of better practice in a complex world of uncertainty and flux. See Sally (1998: 198–203).

6 See WTO (2001a: paras 6, 13, 20–27, 31, 32). Also see Sally (2003: 22–26) for discussion of these issues.
7 See WTO (2001a: paras 2, 3, 12, 18–19, 35–44, 50), WTO (2001b) and WTO (2001c).
8 On formal and informal coalitions in the Uruguay Round, see Croome (1999).
9 On trade policy capacity in developing countries, see Page (2002) and Sally (2003: 28–30).
10 The US Trade Representative, Robert Zoellick, seems to be thinking along these lines (Zoellick 2002).

Bibliography

Barfield, C. (2001) *Free Trade, Sovereignty, Democracy: the future of the World Trade Organisation*, Washington, DC: American Enterprise Institute.
Bergsten, C.F. (1997) 'Open regionalism', *The World Economy* 20: 545–565.
Bhagwati, J. (2002) *Free Trade Today*, Princeton, NJ: Princeton University Press.
Croome, J. (1999) *Reshaping the World Trading System: a history of the Uruguay Round*, Geneva: WTO/Kluwer.
Dunkel, A., Ruggiero, R. and Sutherland, P. (2001) 'Joint statement on the multilateral trading system', *WTO News*, 1 February. Available HTTP:
  <www.wto.org/english/news_e/news01_e/jointstatdavos_jan01_e.htm> (accessed 19 June 2003).
Esty, D. (2002a) 'The World Trade Organisation's legitimacy crisis', *World Trade Review* 1: 7–22.
Esty, D. (2002b) 'Rejoinder', *World Trade Review* 1: 297–299.
Haggard, S. and Williamson, J. (1995) 'The political preconditions for economic reform', in J. Williamson (ed.), *The Political Economy of Policy Reform*, Washington, DC: Institute for International Economics.
Henderson, D. (1998) *The Changing Fortunes of Economic Liberalism: yesterday, today and tomorrow*, London: Institute of Economic Affairs.
Henderson, D. (2002) 'WTO 2002: imaginary crisis, real problems', *World Trade Review* 1: 277–296.
Hoekman, B. and Kostecki, M. (2001) *The Political Economy of the World Trading System: the WTO and beyond*, 2nd edn, Oxford: Oxford University Press.
Jackson, J. (1998) *The World Trade Organisation: constitution and jurisprudence*, London: Pinter/Royal Institute of International Affairs.
Krugman, P. (1997) 'What should trade negotiators negotiate about?', *Journal of Economic Literature* 38: 13–20.
Michalopolous, C. (2001) *Developing Countries and the WTO*, London: Palgrave.
Ostry, S. (2001) 'WTO: institutional design for better governance', in R.B. Porter et al. (eds), *Efficiency, Equity and Legitimacy: the multilateral trading system at the Millennium*, Washington, DC: Brookings Institution.
Page, S. (2002) 'Developing countries in GATT/WTO negotiations', *Working Paper No. 20*, February. London: Overseas Development Institute. Available HTTP:
  <www.odi.org.uk/iedg/participation_in_negotiations/wto_gatt.pdf> (accessed 23 July 2003).
Sally, R. (1998) *Classical Liberalism and International Economic Order: studies in theory and intellectual history*, London: Routledge.
Sally, R. (2002) 'Whither the World trading system? Trade policy reform, the WTO and prospects for the new round', *Stockholm: Timbro*. Available HTTP:
  <www.timbro.se/pdf/whither.pdf> (accessed 23 July 2003).
Sally, R. (2003) 'Whither the WTO? A progress report on the Doha Round, trade policy analysis no. 23', 3 March, Washington, DC: *Cato Centre for Trade Policy Studies*. Available HTTP:
  <http://www.freetrade.org/pubs/pas/tpa-023es.html> (accessed 23 July 2003).
Winham, G. (1998) 'The World Trade Organisation: institution-building in the multilateral trading system', *The World Economy* 21: 349–368.
WTO (1995) *Regionalism and the World Trade System*, Geneva: WTO.
WTO (2001a) 'Ministerial declaration', WT/MIN(01)/DEC/W/1, Geneva: WTO, 14 November.

WTO (2001b) 'Declaration on the TRIPs Agreement and Public Health', WT/MIN(01)/DEC/W/2, Geneva: WTO, 14 November.

WTO (2001c) 'Implementation-Related Issues and Concerns', WT/MIN(01)/W/10, Geneva: WTO, 14 November.

WTO (2002) *Annual Report*, Geneva: WTO. Available HTTP: <www.wto.org/english/res_e/booksp_e/anrep_e/anrep02_e.pdf> (accessed 23 July 2003).

Zoellick, R. (2002) 'Unleashing the trade winds', *The Economist* 5 December. Available HTTP: <http://www.economist.com/displaystory.cfm?story_id=1477509> (accessed 23 July 2003).

Key readings

Bhagwati, J. and Hudec, R. (eds) (1996) *Fair Trade and Harmonisation*, Cambridge MA: MIT Press, 2 vols.

Drabek, Z. and Laird, S. (1998) 'The new liberalism: trade policy developments in emerging markets', *Journal of World Trade* 32: 244–269.

Finger, J.M. and Nogues, J. (2002) 'The unbalanced Uruguay Round outcome: the new areas in future WTO negotiations', *The World Economy* 25: 321–340.

Hudec, R. (1999) *Essays on the Nature of International Trade Law*, London: Cameron May.

Irwin, D. (2002) *Free Trade Under Fire*, Princeton, NJ: Princeton University Press.

Krueger, A. (ed.) (1998) *The WTO as an International Organisation*, Chicago: University of Chicago Press.

Moore, M. (2003) *A World Without Walls: freedom, democracy, free trade and global governance*, Cambridge: Cambridge University Press.

Sampson, G. (ed.) (2001) *The Role of the World Trade Organisation in Global Governance*, Tokyo: UN University Press.

Viner, J. (1951) 'Conflicts of principle in drafting a trade charter', in J. Viner (ed.), *International Economics*, Glencoe, IL: Free Press.

WTO (1999) *The Legal Texts: the results of the Uruguay Round of multilateral trade negotiations*, Cambridge: WTO/Cambridge University Press.

WTO (2000) *From GATT to the WTO: the multilateral trading system in the new Millennium*, Geneva: WTO/Kluwer.

8 Understanding the WTO dispute settlement process

Donna Lee

Summary

Much has been made of the shift from a politically based system of dispute settlement in the GATT era to the legally based system in the WTO. The introduction of stronger rules and tighter procedures suggests a more reso-lute and fairer system for settling trade disputes than existed until 1995. This chapter highlights and assesses this new system. It finds significant modifications and improvements, but also immutability and continued fail-ings in WTO dispute settlement.

The WTO can only be effective if the procedures for enforcement and implementation of its rules are efficient and credible. The WTO's dispute settlement system must be able to administer properly the sweeping rules agreed at Marrakech in 1995. The system is seen to work well by most commentators (Jackson 2000; Krueger 2000; Hoekman and Kostecki 2001). First, it is very busy – with much higher levels of dispute activity in the WTO compared with the GATT. Second, the key flaws in the GATT system – blocking, delay and failure to implement rulings – have been pretty much eradicated. Third, it is more compre-hensive in that it covers all the WTO agreements while the GATT only covered goods. And finally, resorts to unilateral retaliation by members, such as those practised by the USA under Section 301 of the Trade Act of 1974 (amended in 1988), have become less frequent. At first glance, therefore, it would appear that the new procedures for dispute settlement are a huge improvement on the GATT system. The system has certainly been resuscitated and by supplying the WTO with greater authority over its members, dispute settlement is seen to be not only more reliable, but also more impartial. This chapter, however, argues that while much has changed procedurally in dispute settlement, the impact of institutional reform has done little to alter the politics of dispute settlement in terms of either the international or domestic dimensions of trade politics. There is little difference in fact in the political struc-ture of trade conflict resolution between the GATT and WTO systems. The political issues that tested the credibility of the GATT dispute settlement – the lack of transparency in procedures, the dominance of powerful states, the weakness of developing countries, the marginalisation of the least developed members, the relative lack of domestic legislative input, and the absence of civil society contribution – remain. Dispute settlement is still an opaque intergovernmental process, dominated by developed states. While there are much lauded claims of a shift from a power-oriented diplomacy towards a rule-oriented diplomacy – what is more often described as the judicialisation of dispute settlement – in the WTO

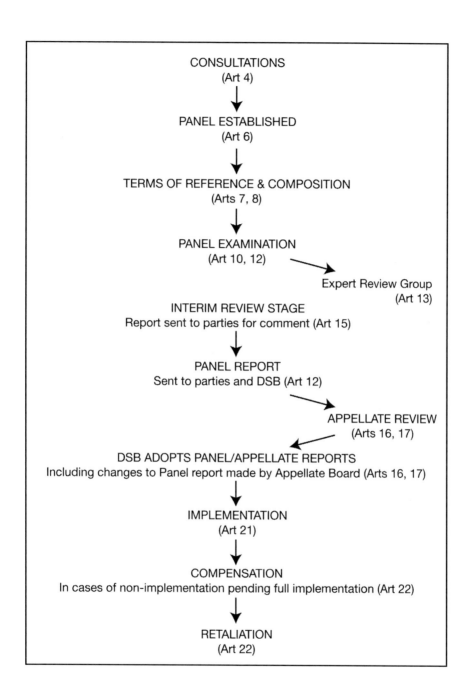

Figure 8.1: The dispute settlement process

Source: WTO homepage.

Notes: During all stages the WTO Director-General provides good offices, conciliation or mediation to encourage and support the parties to diplomatically resolve the dispute 'out of court'.

(Jackson 1997; Wilkinson 2000; Young 1995) the rules, norms and practice of dispute settlement are still largely determined by power politics.

This first section of the chapter discusses the process of WTO dispute settlement and highlights the procedural changes from the GATT system. The second section discusses the practice of dispute settlement using current WTO data to focus on the internal political processes. The concluding section considers the international and domestic dimensions of dispute settlement.

The judicialisation of dispute settlement

The rules and norms of WTO dispute settlement are set out in detail in the Dispute Settlement Understanding (DSU), a text that runs to twenty-seven Articles (WTO 2001) and applies to all disputes arising under the GATT agreements, the WTO agreements, as well as disputes regarding the operation of the DSU itself. The main body responsible for the DSU is the Dispute Settlement Body (DSB) – essentially the WTO General Council by another name. The DSB has sole authority in the dispute settlement process and is responsible for establishing panels, adopting final Panel Reports, overseeing the implementation of the Panel Reports and, where necessary, authorising retaliation and/or compensation measures (Hoekman and Kostecki 2001; Wilkinson 2000; WTO 2001). As a process, the WTO dispute settlement progresses through a number of quite distinct and time-bound stages as illustrated in Figure 8.1. Overall, the process is designed to settle disputes quickly and impartially using a rigorous set of procedures.

A dispute is triggered when a WTO member complains that a benefit guaranteed under the GATT or WTO agreements has been 'nullified or impaired' by another member. Third parties to the dispute can also at this time declare they have an interest. Once a complaint is lodged then the DSB administers the settlement of the dispute through what Hoekman and Kostecki (2001) have identified as five stages. Note that thereafter the DSB rather than the members controls the process, but with the proviso that during each stage the WTO actively encourages diplomatic settlement of disputes before a ruling has to be made, and clearly members have an interest in early settlement in the dispute if only to avoid expensive litigation. As a result, almost half of disputes are settled without a ruling. The USA, for example, settles almost half of its disputes, whether as a defendant or complainant, in the initial stages; these have included disputes over salmon imports with Australia, copyright protection with Greece, intellectual property rights with Sweden, and patent protection rights with Pakistan. Less than 20 per cent of conflicts go through all stages of the process.[1] Implicit in the whole process is that each stage is automatic, and that decisions reached at the final stage are indeed final, with no possibility for further appeal. The process, which takes between eighteen and twenty-four months to complete plus an additional fifteen months for implementation, develops as follows (WTO 2001):

- The process begins when a member believes it is a victim of a violation of WTO trade rules and requests consultations. This stage is best described as a diplomatic one involving bilateral consultations to try to solve the dispute. Indeed, many disputes are settled in the first sixty days. The WTO works in the background in this stage, providing 'good offices, consultation and mediation' and factual information on the legal context of the dispute in order to encourage settlement. The onus is, however, clearly on the conflicting parties to settle outside of the WTO machinery where at all possible. Consultations are given sixty days to resolve the dispute; should they fail then the complaining member can request a panel.

- In the second stage rule orientation really kicks in and the DSB creates a panel to settle the dispute. It defines the terms of reference and also the composition of the panel. There are usually three panellists but this can be increased to five on request of the members. Panellists are nominated from a list drawn up by members and are experts who act independently of any government or organisation. If a dispute involves a developing country, there is a proviso that the panel include an expert from a developing country.

- The third stage involves information gathering, mediation and reporting over a period of between six and nine months. The panel meets with the parties, including third parties to the dispute, to hear arguments and, where necessary, collect information from external bodies. It uses this information to write a draft ruling – an Interim Review. Throughout this stage the primary aim of the panel is to find a 'mutually satisfactory solution' (Article XI) and the Interim Review should be an 'objective assessment' (Article XI) of the dispute. Where a dispute involves a developing country, the panel is required to explain in its report how it met the WTO's commitment to provide 'differential and more-favourable' treatment for developing countries (Article XI:11). It is important to note that the proceedings of this stage and the next are confidential.

- In the fourth stage the panel submits its report which must then be adopted by the DSB within sixty days unless one of the parties makes an appeal in writing or unless the DSB 'decides by consensus not to adopt' (Article XVI:4). Only parties to the dispute – not third parties – can appeal the Panel Report. Moreover, the appeal must be 'limited to issues of law covered in the panel report and legal interpretations developed by the Panel' (Article XVII:6). The latter is most improbable and has, to date, never occurred. The former is, however, frequent practice and when an appeal is lodged the DSB must launch an Appellate Review of the dispute. The Appellate Review consists of three independent experts appointed on a rotation basis from the Appellate Body (composed of seven such experts) to analyse the original Panel Report and issue a ruling – Appellate Review – within 60–90 days (Article XVII:1). Appellate Reviews are adopted by the DSB and must be 'unconditionally accepted' by the parties unless there is a consensus in the DSB not to adopt (Article XVII:14). Unlike Panel Reports, Appellate Review Reports are binding and final and cannot be appealed. Members are given a 'reasonable period of time' to comply with the ruling; this should not extend beyond fifteen months. Most cases are resolved in this stage and compliance takes place in less than a year.

- In the fifth and final stage of the DSU process, the DSB acts to ensure compliance with the report or authorises some means of compensation. The DSB scrutinises compliance with the recommendations of the report and should parties fail to comply with the ruling – a very rare occurrence – then Article XXII of the DSU gives the plaintiff the right to demand compensation or, should the parties fail to agree adequate levels of compensation, retaliation against the offending member. This involves the suspension of most favoured nation rights – that is, the plaintiff introduces bilateral tariffs to the equivalent value of the tariff imposed in the first instance. In the dispute over beef hormones involving the USA and the EU, the DSB ruled in favour of the USA in May 1998, and following non-compliance by the EU, authorised US retaliatory tariffs worth $116.8 million (a figure it calculated to be equal to the level of damage to US exporting companies) against the EU in July 1999. Similarly, in May 2003 in the Foreign Services Corporations case, the DSB authorised the EU to apply $4 billion trade sanctions against the USA following non-compliance.[2]

How this differs from the GATT dispute settlement system

An agreed system for settling disputes had existed in the GATT since its inception, although this system evolved gradually into a more formal system than was originally conceived, especially in the last fifteen years of the GATT (Hudec 1993). For example, the practice of using working groups was replaced by the use of panels of experts not unlike the panels in the WTO and the right to a panel is carried over from the GATT's *1989 Dispute Settlement Procedures Improvements* (Wilkinson 2000). But because of the absence of fixed time schedules and also because panel rulings were very easy to block, some disputes would drag on for years, as in the case of the notorious bananas dispute that was never resolved in the GATT system; the EU simply refused to adopt the 1994 panel ruling. But examples of such blatant blocking were quite rare and the system did work reasonably well. Busch and Reinhardt (2003) find that in 64 per cent of GATT disputes, full or partial concessions were offered indicating that 'Overall the system was very efficacious, despite its legendary shortcomings' (2003: 154). Effective for developed countries that is, whose combined cases as defendants and complainants constituted 80.7 per cent of the total. The GATT system was much less effective for developing countries whose combined cases constituted 19.3 per cent and less developed countries (LDCs) who were not involved in any cases as either defendant or complainant,[3] clearly illustrating that the GATT 'system is ... more responsive to the interests of the strong than to the interests of the weak' (quoted in Busch and Reinhardt 2002: 465).

The DSU represents an attempt to overcome both these failings in the GATT dispute settlement system. It aims to bring errant members to 'trial' and to encourage greater participation by developing countries. Built into the DSU are a number of reforms of the GATT system of dispute settlement that have created a more robust judicial form of dispute settlement. These changes include: a mechanism to prevent members from blocking decisions; a strict timetable for decision making in the various stages of dispute settlement; the creation of a high court of international trade – the Appellate Body – to make final and binding rulings on dispute cases; and an implementation system which allows for retaliatory and compensatory measures in the event of non-compliance. They were introduced to correct the perceived procedural weaknesses in the GATT system, the chief frailty being the practice of 'positive consensus' in which members could block the establishment of panels and also block the adoption of Panel Reports. 'Positive consensus' enabled members unilaterally to prevent the GATT from implementing its trade rules. That this occurred – however rarely – undermined members' faith in the whole GATT system, particularly the USA and the developing countries who led the charge for reforms of the dispute settlement system in the Uruguay Round of negotiations. Moreover, without an effective means of enforcing trade rules, countries may well revert to unilateral action to remedy unfair trade practices.

The DSU, by contrast, works on the basis of 'negative consensus'. All WTO members must agree *not* to establish a panel and agree *not* to adopt a panel or Appellate Report. Thus opportunities for delaying and blocking of dispute settlement unilaterally have been all but eradicated in the WTO. Furthermore, implementation procedures have been strengthened by the introduction of non-compliance measures such as negotiated compensation and cross-retaliation. Though rarely used, retaliation was authorised and used in the late 1990s in two high-profile cases, the bananas dispute and the beef hormones dispute. The key changes to dispute settlement in the WTO can be summarised as follows:

- Decision making by 'negative consensus'.
- Time limits introduced at every stage of the process.
- Automatic establishment of panels.
- Automatic adoption of Appellate Reports.
- Standard terms of reference for panels and Appellate Reviews.
- Creation of an appeals process.
- Strengthening of the implementation of reports.
- Provision of compensation and retaliation measures in the event of non-compliance.

In essence, the process of dispute settlement is now automatic from the point of initial registration of a complaint to the implementation of a ruling. It is the automatic factor that, according to most, ensures that once a complaint is triggered, rule-based diplomacy drives the process. The process has, it is argued, become a judicial one in which politics plays little if any role so as to ensure a more even-handed system of dispute resolution (Jackson 1997). No longer, it is thought, can powerful states force weaker states into agreement against their interests. Neither can powerful states ignore the legitimate complaints of weaker states and thwart the implementation of multilateral trade rules. Disputes in the WTO, so the argument goes, are resolved by *rules not force*; by negotiation and decision with reference to the norms and rules agreed by WTO members rather than by reference to relative diplomatic and economic capabilities (Jackson 1997: 109–110). In the change from the GATT to the WTO, dispute settlement has passed through 'a critical juncture' into a multilateral rather than bilateral system governed by agreed rules and norms (Wilkinson 2000). And a rule-orientated system should mean, among other things, that dispute settlement is more responsive to smaller, and especially developing, countries (Jackson 1997). The provision of special and differential treatment in the WTO dispute settlement process, including rulings on panel composition to ensure that developing countries are represented on panels where disputes involve a developing country, as well as the general ruling found at various points in the DSU that developing countries be afforded 'differential and more-favourable' treatment in dispute settlement, would, in theory, also add weight to Jackson's conclusions.

Yet in order to make such conclusions we would need to pay as much attention to the political changes in dispute settlement as we have to the procedural changes.[4] As Wolfe argued in the first edition of *Trade Politics*, 'The WTO has an *economic* logic and a *legal* basis, but it is fundamentally a *political* entity' (1999: 218). To what extent has the political character of dispute settlement changed since the inception of the DSU? Having highlighted how the DSU is supposed to operate, this chapter now discusses how it actually works and, significantly, who works it.

The political economy of dispute settlement

The international dimension

Participation in the DSU matters not because high levels of dispute settlement serve to legitimise the WTO as Jackson and others would have us believe, but because participation determines the rules and norms of the international trade system. Those who are most active in the DSU are more able to shape the interpretation and application of trade rules and norms to their advantage (Shaffer *et al.* 2003). When we look at the data on comparative participation of WTO members in dispute settlement, what is most obvious is that nothing much has changed from the GATT period. Dispute settlement continues to be dominated by the developed countries in general, and the USA and the EU in particular, especially in terms of initiating complaints. Of the total 277 cases brought before the WTO between 1995 and mid-2003, the USA was the plaintiff in 73 and the EU was the plaintiff in 62; together they account for 48.8 per cent of the total number of complaints.[5] More broadly, developed countries brought 71 per cent of the total number of complaints between 1995 and 2000, and significantly, 56 per cent of all complaints were lodged by developed countries *against* developing countries. By contrast, developing countries initiated just 26 per cent of cases (Park and Umbricht 2001). Furthermore, the USA and the EU have been third parties in most of the cases that have reached the Appellate Stage, where the impact on shaping WTO rules is greatest (Shaffer *et al.* 2003). Although there has been an increase in developing country participation, this increase is as defendants in disputes. Developing countries are increasingly the targets of developed country complaints. Furthermore, developing countries, unlike the USA and the EU, are also seldom repeat players in the system, especially the LDCs of Sub-Sahara Africa (Shaffer *et al.* 2003).[6]

What these figures illustrate is that the international dimension of dispute settlement is little changed. The WTO process is just as much dominated by power politics as the GATT process. Developing countries continue to play at best a supporting role in the dispute settlement system.[7] The endurance of power asymmetries in world trade relations rather than any lack of developing country trade complaints best explains the low levels of developing country participation in WTO dispute settlement. Asymmetries of power work in a number of ways to create barriers to developing country activism in the DSU. One obvious factor is the prohibitive cost of pursuing a trade dispute. Developing countries lack the human and financial resources to pursue disputes. They have few trained lawyers expert and experienced enough in WTO jurisdiction, and they lack the financial resources to hire expensive private lawyers to do their bidding. In addition, structural economic inequalities between states can create political and economic pressures to discourage developing countries from pursuing trade complaints. Developing countries, for example, are often dependent on developed countries, receiving bilateral aid and development assistance. Clearly, the risks of pursuing a trade complaint are great. International trade structures also reduce the efficacy of the implementation measures of the DSU for developing countries. As small economies they have little, if any, trade leverage in their relations with larger economies. Furthermore, the DSU compensatory measures involve trade concessions rather than monetary awards. Thus, even if a developing country runs the risk of lodging a complaint, incurs the expense of hiring private lawyers to make its case, and goes on to win, in the event of non-compliance, there is little in fact to gain. The remedies available are often meaningless to small economies.[8] The experience of Ecuador in the bananas dispute illustrates the point. To compensate Ecuador for EU non-compliance the DSB authorised retaliation. It then recognised that Ecuador had too few imports from the EU to have an important effect and so allowed Ecuador to suspend concessions relating to TRIPs (Anderson 2002).

In a broader sense, the operation of dispute settlement in the WTO tends to treat disputes as discrete, isolated events rather than as evidence of the imbalances and inequalities of international trade relations in general. The international dimensions of trade conflict have expanded in recent years; as membership has grown so have the economic and political divisions and tensions between North and South and the USA and Europe. In the transition from the GATT to the WTO, dispute settlement has not overcome the structural imbalances of the international political economy.

The domestic dimension

Despite procedural changes, the WTO, like the GATT, is entirely an intergovernmental body with little public or domestic political input in dispute settlement. This lack of access and transparency – features carried over from the GATT system – generates public and government criticism of the process. Current debates on DSU reform show that some governments support the idea of increased public access to the DSU as well as improved transparency of the workings of the panels and Appellate Body. Interestingly enough, developing countries opposed the one occasion when the Appellate Body received briefs from NGOs. This was in the shrimp–turtle dispute in which the Appellate Body used information provided by an NGO in its report. Developing countries felt that in doing so the Appellate Body was far exceeding its authority. Furthermore, the NGO provided information in support of the defending member – which in this case was the USA – which was advantaged at the expense of the others in the dispute (India, Thailand, Malaysia and the Philippines). Based on their experience of this example of what others might view as minimal public participation in dispute settlement, developing countries argue against consideration of private briefs in the process.

It is the domestic dimension of the process that now raises the most penetrating questions about the DSU's political legitimacy in the context of debates about state sovereignty and public accountability. The lack of legislative involvement in the settling of disputes raises sovereignty issues that are aggravated by the lack of transparency in the Panel and Appellate Stages of the DSU. The US Congress, perhaps the most vocal legislative critic of WTO dispute settlement, has claimed the Appellate Body rulings frequently exceed its authority, threatening US trade policy sovereignty. Were it not for the fact that the USA is the successful plaintiff in more cases than it is the defeated defendant, we might expect frequent US recourse to unilateral retaliation. Previous behaviour in the GATT system – especially during the years leading up to and including the Uruguay Round – suggests the Americans might once again invoke Section 301 to retaliate against unfair trade practices and in doing so undermine the WTO.

The new dispute settlement system does nothing to change the essential fact that trade disputes belong to and pertain to governments (Weiler 2001). Trade is politically and socially significant and public interest in WTO dispute settlement is growing as trade disputes increasingly entail moral issues such as genetically modified foods and animal rights. We have seen that recent disputes that have environmental implications, such as the Tuna–Dolphin dispute over a US measure to try to protect dolphins in tuna fishing, have attracted high levels of public attention. Yet public access to the dispute settlement system – either indirectly through civil society groups or directly through legislatures – is non-existent. The confidential nature of dispute settlement means that WTO dispute settlement continues to work like a private club and, as a consequence of the judicialisation of the process, the political power of those on the inside – lawyers, experts, diplomats – is enhanced and 'the Rule of Law' becomes the 'Rule of Lawyers'. Whether states decide to pursue a trade dispute through the DSU will in many cases be decided not by public assessment but rather by the decisions of private lawyers on whether the case is winnable or not. (Weiler 2001:

Table 8.1 Key proposals for DSU change, 2001–2003*

Clarifications and amendments	Developing country and LDC proposals	Developed country proposals
Procedural issues:		
Appellate Body	Clarify workings to restrict influence of private parties and remove right to private briefs; improve rights of third parties in dispute; procedures should promote development	Make permanent or semi-permanent; increase size to 9 or 11, or authorise DSB to do so on ad hoc basis; develop guidelines on private briefs; improve public access to documents and allow public observer status; improve quality of reports
Function of panels	Extend time periods; procedures should promote development	
Consultations:	Consultations to take place in capitals of LDCs if involved in dispute	Shorten time periods; improve access by third parties in dispute; improve public access; improve quality of reports
Rule change:		
Special and differential treatment	Mandatory throughout the process; enhance role of WTO Trade and Development Committee	
Dispute initiation	DSB decision whether there is a case against an LDC	Strengthen surveillance by creating compliance panel and appeal process; weaken retaliation process and improve incentives to comply with ruling
Compliance	Collective retaliation; improve rights of third parties; recovery of costs for developed countries; developed countries to select trade concessions; trade compensation rather than retaliation	
Resources	Creation of trust fund to support legal costs for developing countries	

Source: The WTO: TN/DS/W series of documents available at http://www.docsonline.wto.

*The list is not comprehensive. It covers only key proposals for procedural and rules -based changes. In addition, it should not be read as indicating consensus. Divisions with in the developed countries are as deep as the divisions between the developing countries and the developed countries. The USA, for example, opposes proposals by Canada, New Zealand and Japan to modify retaliation measures, while the EU opposes some of the transparency measures that other developed countries prioritise. The developed countries have each submitted proposals whereas the developing countries and LDCs enjoy much more cohesion and have submitted joint proposals as the African Group, an LDC group and a large group led by India, as well as a number of individual proposals.

197). In addition, outcomes are decided by the preferences of the experts who sit on panels and the Appellate Body and recent research suggests that the more powerful the defendant the more likely the Appellate Body will be to deliver a conciliatory ruling (Garrett and Smith 1999). This brings us right back to the structural imbalances in international trade dispute settlement. The move to judicialisation and the creation of an Appellate Body may in fact have resulted in an increased accommodation of the interests of the WTO's most powerful members.

Members are currently reviewing dispute settlement in special sessions of the DSB.[9] The Doha Ministerial Declaration of November 2001 called for new negotiations on ways to 'improve and clarify' the DSU. Earlier attempts to negotiate amendments to the DSU in the period 1998–1999 failed and all the indications point to repeated failure this time around. At the time of writing the DSB had failed to reach agreement by the deadline of May 2003, a deadline that itself had been extended from July 2002. After some five years of negotiations on improvements during which over fifty proposals from members have been discussed, the latest report by the chairman of the special session of the DSB on dispute settlement states that on all aspects of the DSU 'convergence remains very limited' because of the 'complexity of the issues' and, perhaps more to the point, because of a 'diversity of participants' priorities and interests'.[10] The developed countries have prioritised increased transparency and procedural changes to the appeal process to make it more effective in the face of ever-increasing workloads. Developing countries, however, are opposed to increased transparency and are wary of strengthening the Appellate Stage of dispute settlement. Instead they prioritise three issues: improvements to the compensation and retaliation process; provision of legal costs to developing countries; and proper implementation of the special and differential treatment provisions of the DSU. Table 8.1 provides some details of the specific proposals of members.

There are also differences of opinion between members on the scope of the Doha Ministerial Declaration mandate. While some interpret the Declaration as a green light for negotiations to agree fundamental changes to the DSU, others read it more literally as a licence to agree only 'improvements and clarifications'.[11] Perhaps this divergence is more a matter of different perspectives on what can practically be achieved in the review process given the short time frame originally set for the negotiations. It may well be that the most members can hope for is clarification on issues such as the authority of the Appellate Body to use briefs from private actors, or the rights of third parties in dispute settlement. So far the work of the special sessions of the DSB has served to clarify positions on issues rather than to reach even a modicum of agreement on specific procedural and rule changes.

Dispute settlement in the WTO continues to work according to the exercise of power politics and it is the powerful members – WTO experts and private lawyers – who work the system. Commentators on the international and domestic dimensions of the practice of dispute settlement have tended to overplay the effects of procedural change and underplay structural political stasis.[12] The system has, without question, become more judicial, and there are notable advantages as a result. Yet the politics of dispute settlement has changed very little. The process remains intergovernmental, dominated by the powerful developed countries, and lacking in transparency. The judicialisation of dispute settlement has meant that the WTO can achieve its stated goal of making international trade relations more predictable and stable, but these conditions mainly benefit the major trading countries such as the USA and the EU. The endurance of power politics in dispute settlement prevents the WTO from achieving the broader goals of promoting the economic growth and sustainable development of the poorer countries set out in some detail in the Marrakech Declaration.

Of course, the DSU cannot be held solely responsible for the lack of development of the developing and LDCs. But its failure to make a positive difference in their trade relations with the developed world is a result of the power-based system of dispute settlement that persists in the contemporary international political economy.

Notes

1 Data from: 'WTO Dispute Settlement – Status in Brief'. Available HTTP: <http://www.wto.org/english/tratop_e/dispu_e/dispu_e.htm#disputes> (accessed 4 May 2003).
2 Ibid. (accessed 8 June 2003).
3 Data taken from Busch and Reinhardt (2002: 466) which is an excellent source for detailed examination of data on participation rates in dispute settlement in the GATT and the WTO up to the year 2000.
4 This inattention probably results from the fact that the growing literature on dispute settlement is found predominantly in law journals and books rather than political science publications.
5 Figures calculated from WTO data. Available HTTP: <http://www.wto.org/english/tratop_e/dispu_e/dispu_e.htm#disputes> (accessed 4 May 2003).
6 In their comparative analysis of developing country participation in the GATT and the WTO, Busch and Reinhardt (2002) go much further and argue that developing countries participate less in the WTO dispute settlement than they did in the GATT.
7 See Footer (2001) for an examination of the experience of developing countries in the DSU.
8 For a detailed discussion of these structural weaknesses see Shaffer *et al.* (2003). For analysis of the problems of retaliation measures in the DSU see Anderson (2002) and South Centre (1999).
9 The special sessions of the DSB were supposed to report on the DSU Review by 31 May 2003. This deadline has passed and no report is tabled at the time of writing (June 2003).
10 Reports of the Chairman, Péter Balás to the WTO Trade Negotiating Committee: 2 April 2003, TN/DS/7; 7 May 2003, TN/DS/8.
11 See minutes of the meetings of the special session of the DSB 12 June 2002, TN/DS/M/1 2002; 3 July 2002, TN/DS/M/2; 9 September 2002, TN/DS/M/3; 2 November 2002, TN/DS/M/4; 27 February 2003, TN/DS/M/5; 21 March 2003, TN/DS/M/6.
12 Hudec (1999) makes a similar observation when comparing dispute initiation in the GATT and the WTO.

Bibliography

Anderson, K (2002) 'Peculiarities of retaliation in WTO dispute settlement', *World Trade Review* 1: 123–134.

Busch, M.L. and Reinhardt, E. (2002) 'Testing international trade law: empirical studies of GATT/WTO dispute settlement', in D.L.M. Kennedy and J.D. Southwick (eds), *The Political Economy of International Trade Law: essays in honor of Robert. E. Hudec*, New York: Cambridge University Press.

Busch, M.L. and Reinhardt, E. (2003) 'The evolution of GATT/WTO dispute settlement', in J.M. Curtis and D. Ciuriak (eds), *Trade Policy Research 2003*, Ottawa: Department of Foreign Affairs and International Trade.

Croome, J. (1995) *Reshaping the World Trading System: a history of the Uruguay Round*, Geneva: World Trade Organization.

Footer, M.E. (2001) 'Developing country practice in the matter of WTO dispute settlement', *Journal of World Trade* 35: 55–98.

Garrett, G. and Smith, J.M. (1999) 'The politics of WTO dispute settlement', Paper presented to the Annual Meeting of the American Political Science Association, Atlanta, GA.

Hoekman, B.M. and Kostecki, M.M. (2001) *The Political Economy of the World Trading System*, 2nd edn, Oxford: Oxford University Press.

Hudec, R.E. (1975) *The GATT Legal System and World Trade Diplomacy*, New York: Praeger.

Hudec, R.E. (1993) *Enforcing International Trade Law: the evolution of the modern GATT legal system*, Salem, NH: Butterworth Legal Publishers.

Hudec, R.E. (1999) 'The new WTO dispute settlement procedure: an overview of the first three years', *Minnesota Journal of Global Trade* 8: 1–53.

Jackson, J.H. (1997) *The World Trading System: law and policy of international economic relations*, 2nd edn, Cambridge, MA: The MIT Press.

Jackson, J.H. (2000) 'Designing and implementing effective dispute settlement procedures: WTO dispute settlement, appraisal and prospects', in A.O. Krueger (ed.), *The WTO as an International Organisation*, Chicago: University of Chicago Press.

Krueger, A.O. (ed.) (2000) *The WTO as an International Organization*, Chicago: Chicago University Press.

Park, Y.D. and Umbricht, G.C. (2001) 'WTO dispute settlement 1995–2000: a statistical analysis', *Journal of International Economic Law* 4: 213–230.

Shaffer, G., Mosoti, V. and Qureshi, A. (2003) 'Towards a development-supportive dispute settlement system in the WTO', Sustainable Development and Trade Issues ICTSD Resource Paper No. 5, Geneva: International Centre for Trade and Sustainable Development. Available HTTP: <http://www.ictsd.org> (accessed 14 May 2003).

South Centre (1999) 'Issues regarding the review of the WTO dispute settlement mechanism', Trade-Related Agenda, Development and Equity Working Paper 1, Geneva: South Centre.

United States General Accounting Office (2002) 'World Trade Organization. The US experience in the dispute settlement system: the first five years', Testimony before the Subcommittee on International Trade, Committee on Finance, US Senate. Statement of Susan S. Westin, Associate Director, International Relations and Trade Issues, National Security and International Affairs Division, GAO/T-NSAID/OGC-00–202.

Weiler, J.H.H. (2001) 'The rule of lawyers and the ethos of diplomats: reflections on the internal and external legitimacy of WTO dispute settlement', *Journal of World Trade* 35: 191–207.

Wilkinson, R. (2000) *Multilateralism and the World Trade Organisation: the architecture and extension of international trade regulation*, London: Routledge.

Wolfe, R. (1999) 'The World Trade Organisation', in B. Hocking and S. McGuire (eds), *Trade Politics: international, domestic and regional perspectives*, London: Routledge.

WTO (2001) *The WTO Dispute Settlement Procedures*, 2nd edn, Cambridge: Cambridge University Press.

Young, M.K. (1995) 'Dispute resolution in the Uruguay Round: lawyers triumph over diplomats', *International Lawyer* 29: 389–409.

Key readings

Busch, M.L. and Reinhardt, E. (2002) 'Testing international trade law: empirical studies of GATT/WTO dispute settlement', in D.L.M. Kennedy and J.D. Southwick (eds), *The Political Economy of International Trade Law: essays in honor of Robert. E. Hudec*, New York: Cambridge University Press.

Busch, M.L. and Reinhardt, E. (2003) 'The evolution of GATT/WTO dispute settlement', in J.M. Curtis and D. Ciuriak (eds), *Trade Policy Research 2003*, Ottawa: Department of Foreign Affairs and International Trade.

Croome, J. (1995) *Reshaping the World Trading System: a history of the Uruguay Round*, Geneva: World Trade Organization.

Footer, M.E. (2001) 'Developing country practice in the matter of WTO dispute settlement', *Journal of World Trade* 35: 55–98.

Hoekman, M.J. and Kostecki, M.M. (2001) *The Political Economy of the World Trading System*, 2nd edn, Oxford: Oxford University Press.

Hudec, R.E. (1975) *The GATT Legal System and World Trade Diplomacy*, New York: Praeger.

Hudec, R.E. (1993) *Enforcing International Trade Law: the evolution of the modern GATT legal system*, Salem, NH: Butterworth Legal Publishers.

Jackson, J.H. (1997) *The World Trading System: law and policy of international economic relations*, 2nd edn, Cambridge, MA: The MIT Press.

Krueger, A.O. (ed.) (2000) *The WTO as an International Organization*, Chicago: Chicago University Press.

Shaffer, G., Mosoti, V. and Qureshi, A. (2003) 'Towards a development-supportive dispute settlement system in the WTO', Sustainable Development and Trade Issues ICTSD Resource Paper No. 5, Geneva: International Centre for Trade and Sustainable Development. Available HTTP: <http://www.ictsd.org> (accessed 14 May 2003).

South Centre (1999) 'Issues regarding the review of the WTO dispute settlement mechanism', Trade-Related Agenda, Development and Equity Working Paper 1, Geneva: South Centre.

Wilkinson, R. (2000) *Multilateralism and the World Trade Organisation: the architecture and extension of international trade regulation*, London: Routledge.

WTO (2001) *The WTO Dispute Settlement Procedures*, 2nd edn, Cambridge: Cambridge University Press.

Useful websites

http://www.wto.org/english/tratop_e/dispu_e/dispu_e.htm (Dispute Settlement Home Page, World Trade Organization).

9 Developing countries and the WTO

Amrita Narlikar

Summary

This chapter traces the evolving degrees of influence that developing countries exercise in the WTO in terms of their visibility in the organization and the bargaining outcomes that they have generated. It begins with a brief overview of the negotiating history of developing countries in the GATT and then analyses more recent bargaining outcomes involving developing countries in the WTO. Some of the outcomes that are adverse to developing countries can be explained as an inevitable result of the international power discrepancies and domestic weakness of developing countries. But this chapter argues that many of the problems of participation and influence facing developing countries in the WTO are a direct product of the institutional design and negotiating processes that underlie this organization. It further argues that unless an effort is made to change the current trajectories of institutional evolution and negotiating processes, the position of developing countries within the WTO is likely to only worsen with time.

Introduction

The overwhelming majority that developing countries enjoy in the WTO goes back to the days of the General Agreement on Tariffs and Trade (GATT). Eleven of the twenty-three original signatories of the GATT were developing countries, and this large proportion soon developed into a decisive majority that has only grown over time (see Figure 9.1). Large numbers, however, do not necessarily translate into influence, and there is little reason to assume that the well over 100 developing countries in the WTO today are effective participants in the organization. This chapter addresses the puzzle: what kind of influence do developing countries exercise in the WTO? There are several ways to assess influence; in this chapter we examine the visibility of developing countries in the WTO as well as the extent to which bargaining outcomes conform to the stated interests of developing countries to gauge influence. Given that the legacy of the GATT still survives in the WTO, as do the results of the Uruguay Round, this chapter begins with an overview of the position of developing countries in GATT negotiations. But the greater part of the chapter focuses on the WTO and bargaining outcomes that the participation of developing countries has recently generated.

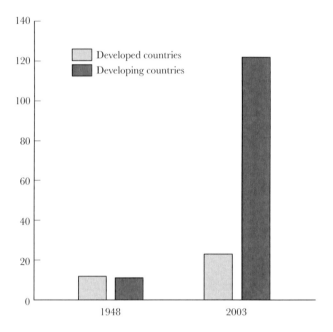

Figure 9.1   The growth in membership of developed and developing countries in the GATT and WTO

The second section examines the history of developing countries in the GATT, and focuses on negotiating processes as well as substantive provisions that related directly to the developing countries until the end of the Uruguay Round. The third section investigates the changes in the participation of developing countries in the WTO and the opportunities and costs that this participation generates. It focuses particularly on the degrees of success that developing countries have achieved recently at the Doha ministerial that launched the Doha Development Agenda. The fourth section traces the explanations for these outcomes. Four sets of explanations are suggested: international structural constraints, domestic limitations, institutional design, and the negotiating process. While the first two are well documented across disciplines, the latter two have only begun to receive attention fairly recently and rarely in the context of developing countries. Hence the fourth section focuses specifically on the effect that the institution of the WTO and negotiating process have on outcomes involving developing countries. The fifth section concludes.

Developing countries in the GATT

It is interesting to note that even though the GATT (like the WTO) was a one-member–one-vote organization, developing countries made few attempts to utilize the power of large numbers to set the GATT agenda. Instead, they remained aloof members of the organization that was often referred to as the 'Rich Man's Club'. Both the substance of GATT rules and the decision-making processes that underlay it contributed to this seemingly recalcitrant behaviour on the part of developing countries, as highlighted below.

The distrust of GATT rules by developing countries derived partly from the free trade ethos that underlay them, which often contradicted the policies of greater protectionism and interventionism in the developing world, especially in the late 1950s and 1960s. Additionally, the GATT was seen as a poor substitute for the stillborn ITO. Unlike the ITO, the original Articles of Agreement made no mention of economic development. GATT membership was based on a formal parity of obligations and did not initially make a difference between strong and weak parties. Until as late as the mid-1960s, there were primarily only two development-specific provisions in the GATT. The first was an infant-industry protection clause in Article XVIII, while the second (introduced in 1954–1955 as Article XVIII:*b*) allowed the use of Quantitative Restrictions (QRs) for Balance of Payment (BOP) purposes whenever foreign exchange reserves were considered below the level necessary for economic development.

Developing countries not only questioned the substance of the GATT in terms of its failure to take differing levels of development into account, but found equal measures of dissatisfaction with the processes that underlay its functioning. Although the GATT was formally a one-member–one-vote organization, in practice decisions were taken by consensus. The consensus principle, now institutionalized in the WTO under Article IX:1, states that consensus is reached 'if no member, present at the meeting in which the decision is taken, formally objects to the proposed decision'. One key problem here was the assumption of presence, whereas some developing countries lacked permanent presence in Geneva and were hence unable to object to the so-called consensus. Further, Green Room meetings and other types of small-group meetings were used to arrive at consensus, from which most developing countries were excluded.[1] Resulting partly from its provisional nature, the GATT secretariat was very small and was not empowered to assist developing countries with the logistics of participation (Narlikar 2003).

In addition to procedural constraints, the GATT operated on the Principal Supplier Principle and hence negotiations directly reflected the strengths of the parties. As per this principle, negotiations took place between principal suppliers and consumers and were then extended to other members on the basis of Article I (granting Most Favoured Nation, MFN, status to all members). Further, developed countries often packed the negotiating agenda with issues of interest to themselves, disregarding or excluding issues where the comparative advantage of developing countries lay (e.g. classically, agriculture and textiles through exceptions). As a result of these constraints, the costs of participation in the GATT were high for developing countries, while benefits were few.

The attempt by the USA and other developed states to bring 'new issues' within the purview of the GATT in the early 1980s, along with a changing international context that prompted trade policy reform, shook developing countries out of their former disengagement. The new issues covered trade in services, trade-related intellectual property rights (TRIPs), and trade-related investment measures (TRIMs). They took the GATT well beyond its initial mandate that had been restricted to border measures and were seen to hold the key to the health of national economies.[2] Developing countries could no longer afford to stand on the sidelines.

The initial reaction of developing countries was to oppose the new measures. In fact, over sixty-one developing countries expressed opposition to the launch of a new round. Subsequently, and partly in response to several trade-offs and issue-linkages that were offered, a 'Grand Bargain' was arrived at. As part of this Grand Bargain, developing countries conceded on the inclusion of the new issues within the GATT in return for concessions by the developed countries on traditional issues such as textiles and agriculture that had eluded GATT remit for years (Ostry 2000). Given the Single Undertaking, it was no longer possible for developing countries to pick and choose the agreements that they would sign up to. Ostry writes, 'So they took it but, it's safe to say, without a full comprehension of the profoundly transformative implication of this new trading system' (2000: 5).

The new imperatives of the WTO

One of the outcomes of the Uruguay Round was the establishment of the WTO in 1995. Many of the problems that developing countries encountered when participating in the GATT – such as the consensual decision-making, member-driven character of the organization, and the importance of informal processes – still persist in the WTO (Narlikar 2001). But the WTO differs from its predecessor in four important ways. First, GATT coverage of behind-the-border measures was limited to plurilateral codes that could be selectively adopted by members, whereas the WTO covers a wider range of measures which cannot be selectively applied because of the Single Undertaking. Second, as a result of the Uruguay Round negotiations, the reach of the WTO goes well beyond border measures into areas where states have traditionally exercised their sovereign rights of legislation. Such areas include Sanitary and Phytosanitary (SPS) Barriers to Trade, Technical Barriers to Trade (TBT), TRIPs, services and so forth. Third, the WTO's Dispute Settlement Understanding (DSU) is far stronger than that of the GATT, mainly because of the rule of 'negative consensus'. As a result, the WTO can authorize cross-sectoral retaliation in cases where its rules are violated, thereby punishing countries on issues where it hurts them most. Finally, the secretariat of the WTO, though still small in comparison with those of the IMF and the World Bank, acquired greater transparency and surveillance functions through the Trade Policy Review Mechanism. In this new institutional context, developing countries found both opportunity but also problems.

The WTO offers considerable opportunity to developing countries by providing them with a more effective system of rules, the possibility of reciprocal gains (with political economy implications at the domestic level), and the possibility of enforcing violations of rules through the strengthened DSU. However, many of these potential benefits have not materialized. While reasons for this are discussed in the fourth section, this section elaborates on some of the costs that participation in the WTO has generated for developing countries by focusing on the aftermath of the Uruguay Round and the outcomes of the Doha ministerial.

The concerns of developing countries that the WTO agreements resulting from the Uruguay Round had not yielded the promised gains go back to the Singapore ministerial. Two broad sets of problems with the Uruguay Round outcomes may be noted. First, academics, governments and NGOs indicated their disappointment with market access payoffs (Hoekman and Kostecki 2001). For instance, in the case of textiles and clothing, back-loading of liberalization meant that import barriers in developed countries remained in place. Any liberalization that did take place was offset by the use of special safeguards, ADDs, more restrictive rules of origins and tariff increases within bound levels (Laird 2002). Industrial tariff peaks remained high, especially in products where developing countries tend to have an export advantage, for instance footwear, leather goods and steel. Similarly, tariff barriers and subsidies on agricultural products continued to persist in many developed countries to the detriment of developing country exporters. Second, implementation of several of the agreements involved some significant costs for developing countries.

These costs have been high in the case of implementing disciplines on domestic regulatory policies and have diverted attention away from urgent development-related priorities (Hoekman and Kostecki 2001). Areas where implementation is especially costly include customs valuation, SPS, TRIPs, and so forth. In fact, a recent study suggests that in some cases involving the Less Developed Countries (LDCs), implementation may involve an entire year's development budget (Finger and Schuler 2002). Not only were the costs of implementation high in themselves, but transitional time periods that allowed developing countries to modify the relevant regimes were found to be too short.

The issues of the unfulfilled promise of the Uruguay Round and continued difficulties in implementing many of the agreements came to the fore at the Seattle ministerial in 1999. The demands raised by developing countries in this context and the resulting impasse contributed to the failure to launch a new Millennium Round at Seattle. The question then arises, how far have these concerns been addressed in the Doha Development Agenda (DDA)? Admittedly, while the DDA is little more than a negotiating agenda, as opposed to the result of a new round, it provides some important insights into the evolving agenda-setting power of developing countries in the WTO.

Perhaps the most significant indicator of a newfound awareness of development concerns in the WTO is the fact that the new set of negotiations has been named the 'Doha *Development* Agenda'. Attention to development concerns appear through the greater part of the DDA, in striking contrast to the GATT's approach to development when such issues were added only later under Part IV. The main ministerial declaration states: 'The majority of WTO members are developing countries. We seek to place their needs and interests at the heart of the Work Programme adopted in this Declaration' (WTO 2001: para. 2). Overall, the text uses the expressions 'least developed' countries twenty-nine times, 'developing' countries twenty-four times, and 'LDC' nineteen times (Panagariya 2002). Many documents of the Doha Declaration relate directly to the concerns of developing countries, e.g. the Declaration on the TRIPs Agreement and Public Health, Implementation-Related Issues and Concerns, the Decision on Procedures for Extension under Article XXVII:4 (referring to subsidies and countervailing measures), the Decision on Waiver for EC–ACP Partnership Agreement, and the Decision on the EC Transitional Regime for Banana Imports.

Besides frequent references to issues of development, developing countries point to several instances where they achieved success in shaping the DDA.[3] First, and among the most widely cited victories, is the Declaration on TRIPs and Public Health, which clarifies the right of members to grant compulsory licensing for the manufacture of patented drugs in a national emergency. The declaration also states that the discretion of determining what constitutes a 'national emergency or other circumstances of extreme urgency' lies with the members themselves (WTO 2001: Article V). For LDCs, the declaration extends the transition period by another ten years, i.e. up to 2016, on pharmaceutical products. Admittedly, this declaration is mainly political, but its importance goes well beyond the symbolic. Schott (2002) argues that the Declaration will make it politically very difficult to bring a dispute against a country that uses compulsory licensing or parallel imports of patented medicines in response to public health emergencies.

Another important success in so far as it displays the influence of developing countries on the DDA (despite its contested benefits), is the reaffirmation in Paragraph 44 of the main declaration that the provisions of SDT 'form an integral part of the WTO Agreements'. The Decision on Implementation contains a work programme on SDT that finds endorsement in the main declaration. References to SDT recur in all the declarations, both as a principle and in terms of its application to specific groups/ subgroups of countries like the LDCs or the small economies.

The symbolic 'triumph' of a commitment of good faith to development came at a heavy price. Perhaps one of the most serious costs is the fact that 2005 was set as the deadline for the completion of the new round. As noted above, the developing countries were not fully aware of what they had signed up to in the Uruguay Round that took eight years to negotiate. The DDA now requires them to negotiate even more complex issues in even less time. Classic examples of the new, complex issues that have been brought within the WTO mandate are the Singapore issues (government procurement, trade facilitation, investment and competition policy) that developing countries have resisted with a fair degree of consistency. The introduction of the complex Singapore issues into the WTO agenda has an air of *déjà vu* about it. It is strongly reminiscent of the way services were brought into the work programme of the GATT in 1982: though the programme initially committed countries to national studies and exchange of relevant information in international organizations, what eventually developed were binding commitments in the Uruguay Round agreements (Narlikar 2003).

In other words, in spite of qualifications on procedures, it is entirely possible that the Singapore issues have already made their backdoor entry into the WTO. On the 'implementation' issues, developing countries had raised the demand that these be addressed before the launch of a new round. But by mention in the DDA, they have been linked to the negotiating process of the new round and in exchange for new commitments. In some ways, this means that developing countries will end up paying twice over for the same commitments (i.e. they had agreed to the Uruguay Round in return for concessions on agriculture, textiles and so forth; they have now agreed to the Doha Round in return for a fulfilment of the same promises of the Uruguay Round). Linkages between the old and the new as well as implementation issues are almost inevitable, especially as the negotiations are being conducted within a Single Undertaking. Paragraph 47 of the declaration states: 'With the exception of the improvements and clarifications of the Dispute Settlement Understanding, the conduct, conclusion and entry into force of the outcome of the negotiations shall be treated as parts of a single undertaking.'[4]

On balance then, though the DDA pays unprecedented lip-service to issues of development, it would be foolhardy to claim a concrete victory for developing countries even in terms of agenda setting. The outcome of the Doha ministerial so far presents developing countries with some procedural promises, few substantive gains and several losses. This outcome merits some surprise, especially as developing countries showed very high levels of preparation for the Doha ministerial and participated actively in the run-up to it (in contrast to their days in the GATT). It becomes crucial to address the question: why is the influence of developing countries on WTO outcomes so weak, in spite of their preparedness and activism?

Explaining outcomes

This section investigates the impact of the WTO as an institution and the negotiation process on the exercise of influence by developing countries in the WTO. As the interplay of these two factors with the structural constraints can sometimes produce a multiplier effect, some reference is also made to the international power differentials and domestic limitations of the developmental state.[5]

Institutional design of the WTO

There has been an increasing recognition in recent writings that the design of institutions is often a product of state interests and has some serious implications on what the institution actually does (Koremenos *et al.* 2001). The reasons as to why the institution of the WTO evolved into its current form lie beyond the scope of this chapter. However, we may note four features of institutional design that critically impact upon the influence that developing countries actually exercise in the WTO, in spite of the level of their preparation or involvement. These broad features of institutional design encompass many of the micro-level decision-making processes that were discussed above (Narlikar 2001, 2003; Rege 2000).

The first feature of GATT/WTO institutional design is the importance of informality that underlies most processes of decision making. Given the nature of the negotiation that typifies the GATT and WTO, the nature and depth of commitments involved, and the trade-offs required to ensure that countries actually take those commitments on, informality is a necessary condition to beat the consensus among 145 members into shape. This informality manifests itself in many ways. For instance, Article IX:1 of the Agreement Establishing the WTO states that 'Except as otherwise provided, where a decision cannot be arrived at by consensus, the matter at issue shall be decided by voting.' But in the entire history of the GATT and WTO, and even when countries have reached impasses, the norm of consensus has prevailed and a disputed decision never been put to an official vote. Similarly, almost all decisions are preceded by informal consultations. These informal consultations can include the entire membership of the WTO (e.g. the Heads of Delegations, HODs meetings), or they can take place in smaller groups. Informal consultations are also used at the levels of the councils, committees and working parties, again which work partly by invitation and partly by self-selection. The Green Room diplomacy of pre-Seattle WTO days and small-group meetings of today epitomize the importance of these informal processes.

Admittedly, while it is difficult to dispose of the role of informal processes in WTO negotiations, informality generates several costs. Even though countries could potentially self-select to attend announced informal meetings, many developing countries are scarcely at the point of being able to identify their interests and claim the right to attendance. Informal meetings, often by their very nature, are ad hoc and leave inadequate time for preparation. Some effort has recently been made to have open-ended small-group meetings, but it is very difficult for developing countries to intervene effectively in the final stage if they have not participated in the initial discussions.

The biggest cost of informality is ambiguity of working procedures. Clarity of rules is especially important when resources are limited and parties weak (Krasner 1985). In the absence of such clarity, developing countries find themselves dealing with the obscure rituals and protocols of what is often still seen as the 'Rich Man's Club'. But the call for more formalization only creates a Catch-22 situation that potentially worsens the position of developing countries. Suggestions for formalization and transparency have included the creation of an Executive Board that would permanently institutionalize the exclusion of developing countries (Narlikar 2001). Alternative proposals that informal consultations are replaced by formal, recorded meetings (Sharma 2002) if implemented would jeopardize the multilateral trading system itself by reducing the negotiating space for deals, trade-offs and log-rolling that are so critical to the formulation of trade agreements. Recourse to increasing bilateralism and regionalism would inevitably follow. Informality is a feature embedded in the WTO as the multilateral institution for trade negotiations, and only minor changes within it seem plausible.

The second characteristic feature of the WTO today is its rapidly evolving role into a risk regulating body.[6] The rise in the regulatory content of international trade legislation can be seen as a direct response by the GATT/WTO to the risks created by globalization (King and Narlikar 2003). Increasing trade, a vehicle and consequence of globalization, created this new regulatory mandate by introducing a new type of 'risk'. As trade increased and products (goods or services) crossed borders, there was a possibility that countries might use national standards as an excuse to discriminate against imported products. To prevent this from happening, and also to guard against the risk that hazardous products might enter importing nations in the name of free trade, the WTO entered the domestic regulatory domain. It began to deal with standards with respect to goods that might pose risks of health or safety and undermine consumer protection, but often also touch upon products that violate national cultural preferences. Examples of the former include products infected with foot-and-mouth disease. To the latter set belong examples of products manufactured using child labour, or goods whose production causes deforestation or endangers certain animal species. Many products, however, cover both categories, i.e. products whose consumption is seen as hazardous by certain cultures but is not easily verifiable objectively or agreed upon universally. In an attempt to deal with such risks, the WTO has become increasingly involved in setting standards of regulation that take it well beyond the cross-border tariff reductions that had formed the centre of trade rules under the GATT.

The expansion of the WTO into risk regulation is more than simply a question of deeper integration. Risk regulation, whether domestic or international, is characterized by highly technical knowledge that is often inaccessible to popular understanding. Often delegates from poorer countries find that they are unable to keep up with the multi-sector, technical discussions on rules and standards in the WTO. Were risk regulation even mainly a technocratic process based on an epistemic consensus, limited participation by some members of international organizations might not prove to be a huge problem to the members themselves or the international organization concerned. But what actually gets selected as a risk to be regulated is a matter of agenda setting that is even more difficult to influence than before owing to the technicalities involved. Implementation of these new standards is an especially expensive process for developing countries as the new standards involve a replication of standards of the developed countries. The WTO agreements on TRIPs, customs valuation, SPS and TBT present examples of 'advanced countries saying to the others, "Do it my way!"' (Finger and Schuler 2002).

If informality and technicality make it difficult for developing countries to exercise influence effectively in the WTO, the third institutional feature of the WTO – increasing legalism – compounds these difficulties. Though developing countries have traditionally sought greater stability in international relations through systems of authoritative rules and regimes, elaborate legal rules do not necessarily work in the same direction. The onus of putting the DSU to effective use falls on the members; it is the members themselves who can bring cases of violation of obligations, and the aggrieved party alone can be given the authority to respond through cross-sectoral retaliations. Even though developing countries have increased their use of the DSU, considerable resources and skill have to be invested by them if they decide to bring a suit against another member country. The process is long and there is considerable scope for delaying the implementation of panel findings (Laird 2002). Developing countries seldom have the time, effort or resources to get locked into this process. Further, if the complainant country is given the right to retaliate, developing countries often find it very difficult to make a major dent in the economy of the other party due to the small size of their markets and trade shares. Some attempts have been made to facilitate the use of the DSU by developing countries through measures such as the establishment of the WTO Advisory Centre on WTO law to provide advice to developing countries. But political pressures, within and outside the WTO, remain a reality, thereby adding to the reluctance of some developing countries to resort to the DSU (Hoekman and Kostecki 2001). All in all, the DSU seems to have been a stick that developed countries find much easier to brandish than at least the smaller developing countries. As a result, many developing countries find themselves more exposed to the threat and use of the DSU and poorly equipped to employ the same machinery in their defence or offence.

In recognition of some of these problems, and partly as a result of the evolution of the GATT into a full-fledged organization, the WTO acquired a new institutional feature of technical assistance and capacity-building provisions. The Integrated Framework on trade-related technical assistance for the LDCs was endorsed in October 1997 and involved six agencies (International Trade Center, IMF, UNCTAD, UNDP, World Bank and WTO). But the impact of the Integrated Framework was limited, and not only because of inadequate financing. Several studies pointed out that it did not address the missing developmental dimension of the agreements with respect to the LDCs (Finger and Schuler 2002; Hoekman 2002). Additionally, many developing countries complained that technical assistance was seldom forward looking or catered to their individual needs. Many alleged that it was actively biased towards a free trade agenda and ignored the interests and even questions of developing countries themselves (Narlikar 2001). Recent years have seen attempts to address some of these limitations. Programmes include training sessions in Geneva, but also some capacity building in capitals. Funding comes from the WTO's regular budget, voluntary contributions from WTO members, and cost sharing either by the host country of an event or by other countries (www.wto.org).

While all the innovations of the DDA are important steps, they evade the critical issue that underlies the expansion of the functions of the secretariat in new directions. The old GATT and the early WTO were mainly member-driven organizations. Today, the WTO seems to be caught between an uneasy balance of the old-style informal, minimalist organization and a maximalist organization with a vastly expanded mandate, encroachments into domestic domains and inaccessible technocratic areas, expanded legalism, and unprecedented responsibilities of technical assistance and capacity building.[7] The countries that are squeezed the most amidst these tensions are of course developing countries, especially as it becomes increasingly difficult for them to control this mammoth and ever-growing institution and its agenda.

Negotiating process

The change in the WTO as an institution is related to the negotiating processes that underlie it. As such, processes of negotiation have an indirect but also direct impact on the influence that developing countries exercise in the WTO. A brief analysis of these processes follows below.

First, and in some ways responsible for the expanding mandate of the WTO, is the old 'bicycle theory' of the GATT, i.e. if the GATT bicycle did not keep moving, it would topple over. For the political economy of the WTO to work, countries must be able and willing to make trade-offs across issue-areas that are valued differently. As patterns of production evolve (e.g. from manufacturing to services in the case of the developed countries in the 1980s), the WTO must expand its rules to include the new areas to retain the relevance of the organization. As developing countries, by the very nature of their development, are on a lower rung in the production ladder, the agenda for expansion into new areas (e.g. the Singapore issues) is driven by developed countries. Developing countries, on the other hand, find it very difficult to keep pace with the moving bicycle of the WTO. The Main Declaration of the DDA, for instance, covers nineteen issues within its work programme, some of which are especially difficult to understand, let alone negotiate. Figure 7.1 in Chapter 7 shows the structure of the organization and illustrates the number of committees, working groups and parties that members need to cover to keep tabs on the WTO's negotiating and evolving agenda. Developing countries often find that they are not even able to attend all the meetings, let alone participate in them in an informed and effective way.

The second feature of WTO negotiations is a product of the institutional feature of informality. The importance of informal processes places substantial reliance on the role and discretion of the chairperson as the broker, mediator and facilitator of the negotiations. In other words, the chair can wield considerable power in deciding who gets invited to meetings, when meetings are held, what is included on the agenda and even formulating a mediating text. This procedure has already come under considerable controversy as developing countries worry that this power will be used to exclude their concerns from the agenda (Raghavan 2001). Additionally, there is a lack of clarity on the procedures for making these appointments and also the limits of their authority. The proliferation of committees and working parties in the wake of the DDA exacerbates these problems, as developing countries now have more meetings to participate in and somehow hold accountable.

The third element of the negotiating process that also works adversely in the case of developing countries is the tendency of developing countries to adopt extreme strategies of either complete bandwagoning or complete balancing. In fact, the larger developing countries often tend towards 'value-claiming strategies' in the WTO rather than value-creating ones.[8] Of course this tendency has sources at the level of the individual member countries and the coalition, but at least one possible additional explanation is simply the fact that value-creating strategies require considerable knowledge and skill. The pace of the negotiations makes it especially difficult for developing countries to adopt a proactive, positive stance that is based on substantial research even while formulating initial negotiating strategies, let alone fallback positions. In most situations, on the application of intense pressure in the end game (sometimes at the capitals' level), they end up abandoning the hard line and gain few concessions in return. Observing this, former Indian Ambassador to the WTO, B.L. Das, writes: 'The transition from the long period of determined opposition to sudden collapse into acquiescence at the end has denied these countries the opportunity of getting anything in return for the concessions they finally make in the negotiations' (Das, n.d.). Some efforts have been made in recent years to correct this by attempting to evolve a more 'positive agenda' but the essential problems remain.

Fourth, while developed countries successfully harness domestic lobbies, interest groups and NGOs to promote their interests, this is rare in the case of developing countries. One of the few instances in which developing countries successfully harnessed domestic lobbies, the media, as well as Northern and Southern NGOs was in the successful public health coalition in the run-up to the Doha Ministerial. Operating through such networks can increase the legitimacy of the demand as well as contribute to research and capacity building for the coalition. Unfortunately, it is all too rare and there is often a remarkable discrepancy between positions taken at Geneva and positions eventually taken by the capitals in the ministerial meetings. Unless corrective measures are taken, these discrepancies are likely only to increase with the increasingly technocratic and legal content of WTO legislation and thereby further undermine the influence of developing countries operating in small delegations.

Finally, no discussion on the negotiating process can be complete without a mention of the state of coalitions involving developing countries today. The late 1980s saw a disaggregation of the bloc of developing countries and the emergence of issue-based coalitions. It is not entirely surprising that the results of the Uruguay Round were adverse, given that developing countries had lost whatever limited collective clout that they had enjoyed in the beginning of the Round (Narlikar 2003). The run-up to Doha, however, saw quite a new phenomenon in operation. While the division of the developing countries into Third, Fourth and Fifth Worlds still persisted, there emerged an unprecedented degree of coordination and log-rolling between coalitions involving developing countries. This may have led to compromises (e.g. the African Group did bow down from its hard line, once the ACP waiver was granted). But coordination also contributed to the strength of coalitions in areas such as public health and SDT. Had coalitions of developing countries been pitted against each other (as they were in the Uruguay Round), it is doubtful if they could have achieved even the little that they did at Doha (Narlikar 2003).

Conclusion

This chapter has argued that while the influence of developing countries in the DDA is unprecedented, it is still far from optimal or remotely equal to the influence of the developed countries. Outcomes even in the Doha *Development* Agenda are development-friendly in only a very limited way. In other words, well over two-thirds of the members of the WTO find it difficult to set the agenda in the organization. While some reasons for this limited influence are intrinsic to the international power divisions and the domestic problems of development, the institution of the WTO and the negotiating process contribute substantially to the limited influence of developing countries. The expanding role of the WTO into a regulatory organization with a vastly expanded, technocratic and legalistic mandate is likely to only worsen the position of developing countries. Hence any attempts at institutional reform must be directed towards limiting the scope of the organization. In terms of negotiating processes, it is true that the nature of the institution predisposes developing countries towards certain negotiating strategies. Limiting the pace of the negotiation may contribute to the ability of developing countries to adopt a more proactive stance. But considerable room for manoeuvre still lies in the hands of developing countries themselves. Coalition formation, greater coordination with other coalitions, and closer links with domestic lobbies and transnational NGOs to their advantage present feasible steps to greater empowerment.

Notes

1   Green Room meetings were exclusive meetings that were called at the initiative of the Director-General of the GATT (in the green room adjacent to his offices). A small number of 'important' delegations would be invited to these meetings to thrash out consensus over contentious issues. Traditionally they worked by invitation only (see Narlikar (2001) for the evolution of the Green

Room format of meetings from the GATT to the WTO) and involved an average of about twenty countries. Only a few developing countries were represented around the table.

2   While GATT legislation had moved beyond border measures in the Kennedy and Tokyo Rounds, these encroachments into domestic economic policy had still been through 'plurilateral' agreements, that is agreements that members could choose whether or not to sign-up to.

3   Interviews with trade diplomats, Geneva, May 2003.

4   In fact, one could argue that the Single Undertaking of the DDA is even more pernicious than the Uruguay Round's owing to its potential murkiness and ambiguities. The first interpretation of the Single Undertaking under the DDA is the notion of the 'early harvest', i.e. 'agreements reached at an early stage may be implemented on a provisional or a definitive basis. Early agreements shall be taken into account in assessing the overall balance of the negotiations' (Paragraph 47). Second, reform of the DSU (an area in which developing countries have demonstrated considerable interest) is excluded from the Single Undertaking. Third and paradoxically, Paragraph 47 also reinforces the notion of the Single Undertaking as per the Uruguay Round as per the quotation above.

5   For example, if the institution and the negotiation have a negative impact on the country's influence, the international power differential is heightened as are the domestic limitations of the 'quasi-state' (Jackson 1990).

6   Similar patterns may be traced in other international organizations as well and need to be seen as moving in tandem with rise of the 'regulatory state' (Hood *et al.* 2001; Majone 1997).

7   The tension between the minimalist and maximalist forms has significant implications for broader questions on the accountability of global governance, especially as there is already a major discrepancy between the expanding role of the WTO and the existing procedures of accountability that survive from GATT days.

8   Odell (2000) conceptualizes value-claiming strategies and value-creating strategies in terms of the opposite ends of a spectrum. He writes: 'At one pole is the pure value-claiming or distributive strategy, a set of actions that promote the attainment of one party's goals when they are in conflict with those of the other party. ... At the opposite pole is the pure integrative or value-creating strategy. It involves actions that promote the attainment of goals that are not in fundamental conflict – actions designed to expand rather than split the pie' (31–33).

Bibliography

Das, B.L. (no date) 'Strengthening developing countries in the WTO', Trade and Development Series, No. 8, Third World Network. Available HTTP:
<http://www.twnside.org.sg/title.tad8.html> (accessed 25 July 2003).

Finger, J.M. and Schuler, P. (2002) 'Implementation of WTO commitments: the development challenge', in B.M. Hoekman, P. English and A. Mattoo (eds), *Development, Trade and the WTO: a handbook*, Washington, DC: World Bank.

Hoekman, B. (2002) 'Strengthening the global trade architecture for development: the post-Doha agenda', World Bank Working Paper, No. 2757, 18 January. Available HTTP:
<http://econ.worldbank.org/view.php?type=5&id=3606> (accessed 23 July 2003).

Hoekman, B. and Kostecki, M.M. (2001) *The Political Economy of the World Trading System: the WTO and beyond*, 2nd edn, Oxford: Oxford University Press.

Hood, C., Rothstein, H. and Baldwin, R. (2001) *The Government of Risk*, Oxford: Oxford University Press.

Jackson, R. (1990) *Quasi-States: sovereignty, international relations and the Third World*, Cambridge: Cambridge University Press.

King, D. and Narlikar, A. (2003) 'The new risk regulators: international organizations and globalization', *Political Quarterly* 74: 337–348. Koremenos, B., Lipson, C. and Snidal, D. (2001) 'The rational design of international institutions', *International Organization*, 55(4): 761–799.

Krasner, S.D. (1985) *Structural Conflict: the Third World against global liberalism*, Berkeley, CA: University of California Press.

Krueger, A.O. and Michalopoulos, C. (1985) 'Developing-country trade polices and the international system', in E. Preeg (ed.), *Hard Bargaining Ahead*, New Brunswick, NJ: Transaction Books.

Laird, S. (2002) 'A Round by any other name: the WTO agenda after Doha', *Development Policy Review* 20: 41–62.

Majone, G. (1997) 'From the positive to the regulatory state: causes and consequences of changes in the mode of governance', *Journal of Public Policy* 17: 139–167.

Narlikar, A. (2001) 'WTO decision-making and developing countries', TRADE Working Paper, No. 11, Geneva: South Centre. Available HTTP: <http://www.southcentre.org/publications/wtodecis/workingpapers11.pdf> (accessed 25 July 2003).

Narlikar, A. (2003) *International Trade and Developing Countries: bargaining coalitions in the GATT and WTO*, London: Routledge.

Neuman, S.G. (1998) 'International relations theory and the Third World: an oxymoron?', in S.G Neuman (ed.), *International Relations Theory and the Third World*, London: Macmillan.

Odell, J. (2000) *Negotiating the World Economy*, Ithaca, NY: Cornell University Press.

Ostry, S. (2000) 'The Uruguay Round North-South grand bargain: implications for future negotiations', *Political Economy of International Trade Law*, University of Minnesota, September 2000. Available HTTP: <http://www.utoronto.ca/cis/Minnesota.pdf> (accessed 25 July 2003).

Panagariya, A. (2002) 'Developing countries at Doha: a political economy analysis', *World Economy* 25: 1205–1233.

Raghavan, C. (2001) 'Harbinson ignores lack of consensus, sends draft to Doha', 1 November. Available HTTP: <http://www.twnside.org.sg/title/lack.htm> (accessed 25 July 2003).

Rege, V. (2000) 'WTO procedures for decision making: experience of their operation and suggestions for improvement', Background Paper, Commonwealth Secretariat, 21 January.

Schott, J. (2002) 'Comment on the Doha material', *Journal of International Economic Law* 5(1): 191–195.

Sharma, S. (2002) 'WTO internal process: democratic principles in question', Geneva Update, No. 2, 26 January. Available HTTP: <http://www.wtowatch.org/library/admin/uploadedfiles/WTO_Internal_Processes_Democratic_Principles_i.htm.> (accessed 7 May 2003).

Wolf, M. (1984) 'Two edged sword: demands of developing countries and the trading system', in J. Bhagwati and J. Ruggie (eds), *Power, Passions and Purpose*, Cambridge, MA: The MIT Press.

WTO (2001) 'Doha Ministerial Declaration', WT.MIN (01)/DEC/1, 20 November.

Key readings

Hoekman, B. and Kostecki, M.M. (2001) *The Political Economy of the World Trading System: the WTO and beyond*, 2nd edn, Oxford: Oxford University Press.

Hoekman, B.M., English, P. and Mattoo, A. (eds) (2002) *Development, Trade and the WTO: a handbook*, Washington, DC: World Bank.

Jackson, J.H. (1997) *The World Trading System: law and policy of international economic relations*, 2nd edn, Cambridge, MA: The MIT Press.

Kwa, A. (2003) *Power Politics and the WTO*, 2nd edn, Bangkok: Focus on the Global South. Available HTTP: <www.focusweb.org> (accessed 26 June 2003).

Krueger, A. (ed.) (1998) *The WTO as an International Organization*, Chicago: Chicago University Press.

Collection of papers on the Doha Round (2002) 'Part II: quick impressions of the Doha results', *Journal of International Economic Law* 5: 191–219.

Useful websites

www.focusweb.org (Focus on the Global South).
www.southcentre.org (South Centre – An Organization of Developing Countries).

10 The WTO and civil society

Jan Aart Scholte[1]

Summary

Civil society activity is one of the striking features of contemporary global trade politics. A host of citizen groups have undertaken studies, disseminated information, provided policy inputs and otherwise tried to shape the WTO regime. The WTO in turn has pursued various initiatives to engage with civil society associations. Relations between civil society actors and the WTO have contributed a number of benefits to global governance of trade, but they have suffered from pitfalls, too. All parties can do more to improve the quality of these exchanges.

Global governance and civil society

The creation of the WTO has reflected and reinforced an important structural shift, in the face of large-scale globalization, from statist to post-sovereign governance. At the start of the twenty-first century, regulatory activities are no longer wholly centred on or subordinated to the national territorial state. Instead, much governance has become spread across a host of substate (municipal and provincial), state and suprastate (regional and transworld) institutions, as well as a number of private organizations such as credit-rating agencies and foundations. None of these sites of authority holds complete and consistent primacy over the others (Scholte 2000).

The contemporary accelerated growth of global flows has made sovereignty (in its traditional sense of absolute, supreme, comprehensive, unilateral state control over a given territorial jurisdiction) unworkable. To be sure, the end of sovereignty has in no way meant the end of the state. On the contrary, many states (especially those of the OECD countries) have in recent history increased in size, expanded their competences, and acquired new policy instruments. However, the unprecedented growth since the middle of the twentieth century of global communications, global ecological problems, global finance, global production, global markets, global travel, global organizations and global consciousness has made the statist mode of governance impracticable.

In these circumstances, regulators have devised numerous substate, suprastate and private sector mechanisms to supplement or even in some respects to supersede rule by states (Hart 1997; Tita 1998). A key challenge in the contemporary globalizing world is to construct efficient, stable, equitable and democratic governance out of what has become multilayered and often fragmented authority. How can policy formulation, implementation and review be properly coordinated in decentred governance? How can post-sovereign conditions be fashioned to yield regulatory arrangements that are adequately participatory, open, transparent and accountable?

As other chapters in this book demonstrate, the WTO is a prominent instance of growing suprastate governance in the contemporary globalizing world. Not surprisingly, given the substantial growth in amount, scope and impact of global trade rules, many civil society groups have developed considerable interest in the WTO. As an important influence on the production, distribution and consumption of resources worldwide, the institution has come to occupy a prominent place on the agenda of numerous business forums, consumer unions, development cooperation groups, environmental groups, farmers' organizations, human rights advocates, labour unions, think tanks, women's associations, and other elements of civil society. Many of these actors have sought direct contact with the WTO, bypassing national government authorities in order to interrogate and lobby the multilateral institution itself.

This increase in approaches from civil society organizations to the WTO is part of a larger trend of growing civil society activity on global issues across most of the world. In the present context, 'civil society' refers to a political space where voluntary associations seek – from outside official circles, political parties and firms (though sometimes closely linked with them) – to shape the rules, norms and/or deeper structures that govern social relations (Scholte 2002).

One leading researcher of civil society has described (albeit perhaps with some hyperbole) 'a global "associational revolution" that may prove to be as significant to the latter twentieth century as the rise of the nation-state was to the latter nineteenth' (Salamon 1994). For example, in the 1990s Kenya counted some 23,000 registered women's groups, and more than 25,000 registered grassroots organizations have operated in the state of Tamil Nadu in India (United Nations Development Programme 1997). Significant parts of this expanding civil society have involved transborder affiliations. The number of active transborder civil society groups (e.g. of religious believers, professionals, human rights campaigners, etc.) has increased more than tenfold since 1960, to some 17,000 in 1999 (Union of International Associations 1999). Many local and national civil society organizations, too, have incorporated global networking into their activities (Smith *et al*. 1997; Keck and Sikkink 1998; Cohen and Rai 2000; Florini 2000; Edwards and Gaventa 2001).

Since the 1970s, most of the major suprastate agencies have experienced a notable growth of direct exchanges with local, national and transborder civil society associations (Willetts 1996; Weiss and Gordenker 1996; O'Brien *et al*. 2000). For example, almost all organs of the UN system have acquired expanded external relations departments, and many UN agencies have instituted liaison committees with participants from civil society groups. Proposals have furthermore circulated for the creation of a UN People's Assembly composed of civil society representatives next to the General Assembly of state delegates. Civil society groups have since the 1990s convened global meetings with fair regularity, for example, alongside the Group of Seven summits, the Annual Meetings of the International Monetary Fund (IMF) and the World Bank, and ad hoc UN conferences on various global issues. A broad consensus has by now emerged that civil society bodies and global governance institutions should have relations with each other. On the other hand, there is far less clarity, let alone agreement, on how these relations should be conducted, and to what ends.

Given this wider context of contemporary world politics, WTO staff and national trade ministry officials ought not to have been surprised to encounter substantial civil society interest in the new multilateral organization. Indeed, a prominent business association, the

World Economic Forum (WEF), was instrumental in launching the Uruguay Round of trade negotiations that produced the WTO. Notable gatherings of civil society actors have accompanied each of the WTO Ministerial Conferences held to date, most visibly in Seattle at the end of 1999. Over 950 associations (with up to three representatives apiece) were eligible to attend the Fifth Ministerial Conference at Cancún in September 2003. This compared with around 150 groups at the First Ministerial Conference in Singapore seven years earlier.[2] Some governments have also included civil society practitioners on their official conference delegations. In addition, civil society organizations have undertaken studies of the WTO, disseminated information about the new organization, pursued dialogues with WTO staff, written official trade policy proposals for governments, and so on (Charnovitz 1996; Dunoff 1998; Esty 1998).

In fact, the Marrakech Agreement of 1994 explicitly acknowledges interest and involvement by civil society associations in the institution. Article V(2) stipulates that the agency should make 'appropriate arrangements for consultation and cooperation with non-governmental organizations'. The GATT never acted on similar provisions in the (unratified) Havana Charter of 1948 for 'consultation and cooperation with non-governmental organizations' (Charnovitz and Wickham 1995). In contrast, the General Council of the WTO within eighteen months after the founding of the successor body elaborated formal guidelines for increased relations with non-governmental organizations (NGOs).[3] In 1998 the Director-General of the day, Renato Ruggiero, announced further measures to improve WTO contacts with civil society groups.[4]

Benefits and pitfalls

Before examining specific relationships between the WTO and civil society associations, it is relevant to reflect in general terms on the possible effects of those exchanges. Civil society actors are not inherently good or bad. They can both improve and undermine efficiency and stability in the world economy. They can both enhance and detract from social justice and democracy. In short, civil society's consequences for post-sovereign governance depend very much on the particular features of individual civil society associations and official institutions and the wider socio-historical conditions in which these actors operate.

Unlike the multilateral development banks and many UN agencies, the WTO does not engage so-called 'operational' civil society groups in the delivery of services. However, civil society activities offer the global trade regime at least six other potential benefits:

1   Civil society associations can provide the WTO with information and insights that are useful in policy formulation, implementation and review.
2   Civil society groups can stimulate debate about WTO policies, particularly by offering alternative perspectives, methodologies and proposals. Such challenges can push the WTO better to clarify, explain, justify and perhaps rethink its positions.
3   Civil society organizations can provide channels through which stakeholders may voice their views on trade issues and have those opinions relayed to WTO staff. With this input officials can better gauge the political viability of proposed measures or programmes.
4   Civil society associations can play an important role in democratically legitimating (or indeed de-legitimating) WTO activities. For example, civil society organizations can influence the respect accorded (or denied) to WTO views and the ratification (or rejection) of WTO-related trade agreements.

5   Civil society bodies can serve as important agents of civic education, increasing public
     understanding of the WTO and its policies. Many civil society associations have in this
     vein prepared handbooks and information kits, organized workshops, circulated
     newsletters, written press articles, maintained Internet sites, developed curricular mate-
     rial for schools, and so on.
6   Relations between the WTO and civil society associations can reverberate to have
     more general democratizing effects. For example, citizen groups that are denied access
     to their national governments may be able to gain a voice through suprastate channels
     such as the WTO.

However, the benefits just reviewed do not flow automatically. If poorly organized and
executed, relations between civil society associations and the WTO can also have detrimental effects on the global trade regime and politics more generally. In a negative vein:

1   The collection of civil society associations that develops relations with the WTO might
     not adequately or fairly represent the various constituencies that have stakes in the
     global trade regime. Civil society inputs could thereby reproduce and even enlarge
     inequalities and arbitrary privileges connected with nationality, class, race, gender, reli-
     gion, age, and so on.
2   The WTO could treat overtures to civil society bodies as merely a public relations
     exercise. The institution would thereby not only miss out on the valuable inputs indi-
     cated above, but also alienate citizen groups.
3   Interventions from civil society associations into global governance of trade could be
     misdirected and/or ill-informed. Such low-quality involvement can unhelpfully disrupt
     institutional operations and policy development.
4   The WTO could, through its exchanges with civil society groups, become embroiled in
     local and national politics of which it has little understanding, perhaps undermining
     democracy in the process.
5   The WTO could focus its exchanges with civil society organizations on supportive
     groups to the neglect of challengers. As a result, the institution might get a false sense
     of public endorsement of its policies. Indeed, such marginalization of critics (delib-
     erate or unconscious) could generate a severe backlash against the global trade regime,
     as was witnessed on the streets of Seattle and at Cancún.

In sum, relations between civil society organizations and the WTO can have significant
consequences – positive or negative – for the design and operation of the global trade
regime. Given the previously described dynamics of politics in the contemporary globalizing world, it seems most unlikely that contacts between the WTO and civil society
associations will decline, let alone disappear. On the contrary, most indications suggest that
these interchanges will further grow in the years to come. The challenge before the WTO
and civil society actors is therefore to develop their mutual relationships in ways that minimize the pitfalls and maximize the benefits outlined above.

Civil society interest in the WTO

Civil society activities encompass huge diversity. The multitude of associations exhibit
widely differing constituencies, institutional forms, sizes, resource levels, geographical
scopes, historical experiences, cultural contexts, agendas, goals and tactics. In short, due
caution is necessary when generalizing about civil society groups.

That said, we may loosely distinguish three types of civil society organizations in terms of their general approach to the WTO. One group, who might be called 'conformers', follow mainstream discourses of trade theory and broadly endorse the existing aims and activities of the WTO. A second group, who might be called 'reformers', accept the need for a global trade regime, but seek to change reigning rules and operating procedures. A third category of civil society associations, who might be called 'rejectionists', seek to reduce the WTO's competences and powers or even to abolish the institution altogether.

Corporate business associations, commercial farmers' unions and economic research institutes have usually taken a conformist approach to the WTO. Prominent business groups that have supported the WTO-based global trade regime include the aforementioned WEF, the International Chamber of Commerce (ICC) and the European Round Table of industrialists. With a narrower agenda, the US Dairy Foods Association, the Pork Producers Council, the National Farmers' Alliance and the American Sugar Alliance have urged a rapid liberalization of cross-border trade in agricultural products. Think tanks that have promoted a broadly conformist line on the WTO include the Brookings Institution and the Institute for International Economics in the USA. In the juridical field, bodies such as the International Law Association Committee on International Trade Law have also broadly shared the prevailing discourse on world trade.

This is not to say that conformist civil society organizations have approved of every WTO rule, procedure and decision. On the contrary, business lobbies have frequently sought to revise or overturn a WTO measure to their commercial advantage, and mainstream researchers have often queried certain WTO actions and analyses. However, these disagreements have remained within the conventional framework of trade debates, namely on a spectrum running from liberalism to mercantilism. Conformists therefore 'speak the same language' as WTO staff and most national trade officials. For these circles, arguments about trade regulation do not go beyond issues concerning the balance between free trade and protectionism and the degree and speed of liberalization.

In contrast, reformers in civil society aim to change the thinking, rules and procedures of the WTO. Most reformist activities have sought to redress alleged undesirable effects of the existing trading order: for example, in respect of labour conditions, underdevelopment of the South, environmental degradation, consumer protection and gender inequalities. Many of these lobbyists have concurrently campaigned for a democratization of WTO operations: for example, in terms of wider public participation, greater public release of information and increased public accountability.

For example, trade unions and human rights advocates have spurred efforts to incorporate protective labour standards into the global trade regime (O'Brien 2000). These reformers maintain that trade liberalization has greatly weakened the power of workers vis-à-vis managers and investors. In order to safeguard basic labour rights and restore a fair balance of class interests – so these civil society groups have argued – the WTO needs a social clause that commits states to respect seven key conventions of the International Labour Organization (ILO) (Evans 1996). Leading voices from organized labour in this campaign have included the International Confederation of Free Trade Unions (ICFTU), the World Confederation of Labour (WCL) and several International Trade Secretariats (ITS). Certain human rights groups have also engaged the WTO on issues of labour protection: for example, the Washington-based International Labor Rights Fund; the Montreal-based NGO, Rights & Democracy; and the Brussels-based SOLIDAR alliance. Significantly, some trade unions and NGOs have viewed this lobbying with scepticism as an effort to perpetuate the privileges of workers in the North at the expense of development in the South.

Indeed, general economic development has been a recurrent major civil society concern regarding the WTO. Given that WTO rules severely restrict the autonomy in trade policy of already weak states in the South, many development NGOs have worried that the Uruguay Round and subsequent global trade accords might well compromise possibilities for equitable human development. Prominent NGOs in trade-and-development debates have included Oxfam, Third World Network and the Harare-based International South Group Network. Several of these organizations, together with other donors, have jointly sponsored the International Centre for Trade and Sustainable Development (ICTSD), established in Geneva in 1996. Trade-and-development issues have also occupied a number of development think tanks, including the Brazilian Institute for Social and Economic Analysis (IBASE, Rio de Janeiro), the North–South Institute (NSI, Ottawa), and so on.

Some of the most persistent civil society efforts to reform the WTO have come from environmental NGOs (Esty 1997; Williams and Ford 1999; Williams 2000). These critics maintain that a liberal global trade regime tends to exacerbate ecological degradation: (a) by encouraging a relaxation of national environmental protection measures in order to maintain international competitiveness; (b) by promoting production for export (more environmentally damaging) rather than for home consumption; (c) by stimulating, with increased exports, unsustainable levels of natural resource exploitation; and (d) by (implicitly) sanctioning trade in toxic wastes. Environmentalists have sought, first, to get sustainable development concerns on the WTO agenda and, second, to institute restrictions on trade where it causes ecological damage. Leading reformist environmental NGOs in dialogue with the WTO have included the World Conservation Union (IUCN), the World Wide Fund for Nature (WWF), the International Institute for Sustainable Development (IISD) and the Centre for International Environmental Law (CIEL).

A fourth issue of notable concern in campaigns to reform the WTO has been consumer protection. Activists on this subject argue that the existing liberal global trade regime has greatly enhanced the power of large (usually transborder) firms. Consumer advocates affirm that global competition policy and a binding code of conduct for global companies are needed to constrain this corporate power in the public interest. Prominent civil society associations in this area have included UK-based Consumers International, India-based Consumer Unity and Trust Society (CUTS) and the International Organization of Consumer Unions (IOCU).

Meanwhile certain other NGOs have sought to bring greater gender awareness to the WTO. Employing feminist political economy, they are concerned that the global trade regime, like the modern economy generally, contains structural biases against women (Joekes and Weston 1995; Mehta and Otto 1996). Some voices in the global women's movement have therefore called *inter alia* for gender assessments of WTO rules and for attention to gender issues in the WTO's trade policy reviews.[5] These associations created an Informal Working Group on Gender and Trade at the Singapore Ministerial Conference in 1996. Prominent actors in these (to date fairly limited) efforts have included the New-York-based Women's Environment and Development Organization (WEDO) and the Brussels-based campaign, Women in Development Europe (WIDE). WEDO has produced several booklets on the global trade regime, and WIDE organized a Women and Trade Conference in Bonn in 1996.[6]

The issues discussed so far relate to policy content, but many reformers in civil society have also sought to change the operating procedures of the WTO. In particular they have advocated a democratization of the organization by giving citizens increased access to, and influence in, its proceedings and decisions (Bellman and Gerster 1996). Some reformers have argued in this vein that relevant representatives from civil society groups should participate directly in WTO policy deliberations, trade policy reviews and dispute settlement procedures (Bullen and Van Dyke 1996). Pursuing a complementary line, some groups have also urged the establishment of a WTO parliament with legislative competence or, in the interim, the formation of an inter-parliamentary group with an advisory role vis-à-vis the WTO.[7] Other proposals have called for a more transparent WTO: that is, one which has open hearings, increased (and more timely) publication of official documents, and greater dissemination of information, particularly in the South. Reformers have also repeatedly called for better representation of Southern governments at the WTO offices in Geneva and increased capacity-building initiatives for trade officials from the South.

Whereas reformers aim in one way or another to alter the WTO, rejectionists in civil society regard the existing global trade regime as incorrigible. They therefore advocate its contraction (back to the original parameters of the GATT, for example) or complete abolition: hence the slogan 'Shrink or Sink' (Keet 2000). In the mid-1990s, rejectionist groups campaigned against the Uruguay Round accords and the North American Free Trade Agreement (NAFTA). In the late 1990s many of the same opponents developed a loose worldwide network called Peoples' Global Action against 'Free' Trade and the World Trade Organization (PGA). The PGA called openly for 'the disappearance of the WTO'. Its rejectionist stance can be broadly likened to the position of the 50 Years Is Enough coalition against the IMF and the World Bank. Rejectionist circles also include some environmentalists who – in contrast to the reformist associations named earlier – refuse to engage with the WTO.

The preceding survey amply confirms the observation made at the start of this section that civil society relations with the WTO encompass a large diversity of organizations, activities and approaches. The distinction of conformist, reformist and rejectionist groups is not always neat in practice, of course. For example, some economic research institutes have straddled conformist and reformist positions. Meanwhile a number of development NGOs have fluctuated between reformist and rejectionist positions. Nevertheless, the three-way categorization of conformers, reformers and rejectionists remains analytically useful in mapping the politics of civil society in regard to the WTO.

WTO overtures to civil society

How has the WTO reacted to the various initiatives from civil society associations described above? The institution has during its first decade taken several steps to implement Article V(2) of the Marrakech Agreement. In brief, the WTO has: (a) adjusted its language to recognize civil society; (b) undertaken various outreach initiatives towards civil society associations; (c) increased its public dissemination of information; and (d) made some alterations to substantive policy that (partly) meet civil society demands. These four developments are detailed in turn below. On the other hand, as the next section elaborates, the WTO has to date done relatively little to institutionalize relationships with civil society bodies or to involve these associations directly in policy deliberations. Nor has the WTO so far made much use of contacts with civil society organizations to gauge the political viability of its policies.

On the first point – namely, recognition of civil society – the WTO has joined other suprastate agencies in acknowledging the importance of civil society inputs to global governance. For example, in his address to the Singapore Ministerial Conference in 1996,

Ruggiero highlighted the presence of many 'representatives of non-governmental organizations, the business sector, and the media' (in Hart 1997: 77). Again at the Geneva Ministerial Conference eighteen months later, Ruggiero and several of the government leaders present publicly endorsed the idea of increased relations between the WTO and civil society associations. The Seattle debacle made Ruggiero's successor, Michael Moore, disinclined to nurture contacts with civil society bodies outside academic and business groups. The third Director-General, Supachai Panitchpakdi, has thus far likewise adopted caution. Nevertheless, the WTO's annual reports have addressed relations with civil society groups since the 2000 edition. At a time when UN bodies and the Bretton Woods institutions are continually speaking of 'stakeholders', 'ownership' and 'participatory development', the WTO can hardly speak another language. In further recognition that civil society bodies have a role to play, the WTO website has since 1996 included a designated 'NGO Room'.

The shift in discourse has been more than rhetorical in so far as the WTO has taken various initiatives to establish dialogue with civil society groups. Its staff have provided many briefings to, and received multiple representations from, business associations, labour unions and NGOs. The secretariat has hosted various seminars at the WTO offices where civil society bodies can present their work. More elaborately, the institution has since 1994 organized regular symposia in Geneva with representatives of civil society on major trade issues. In this vein two-dozen NGOs from four continents participated in 1997 in a Joint WTO/UNCTAD Symposium on Trade-Related Issues Affecting Least-Developed Countries. Around 750 people signed up to attend a WTO public symposium in June 2003 ahead of the Cancún Ministerial Conference. Also in 2003, the WTO secretariat began, in response to requests from governments, to hold symposia with civil society groups and parliamentarians in-country, e.g. in Cape Town, South Africa and São Paulo, Brazil. At Ministerial Conferences the WTO has provided accredited civil society representatives with office space and media facilities.

The WTO has also responded to demands from many civil society groups for greater release of information concerning its activities. The production of official publications has expanded, and the secretariat has since 1995 maintained an elaborate website. In 1996 the General Council adopted Procedures for the Circulation and De-Restriction of WTO Documents. Under these guidelines, reports of dispute panels are now made public as soon as they are adopted. The WTO also publishes completed trade policy review reports and summaries of the proceedings of the Committee on Trade and Environment. In 2002 the Council agreed considerably to accelerate the de-restriction process, from an average of 8–9 months to 6–12 weeks.[8] Some important WTO documentation continues to be restricted, and a proposal by the Canadian government to televise the proceedings of its Trade Policy Review was blocked. Nevertheless, the WTO releases far more information than the GATT ever made available, giving the One World Trust cause to rate the institution quite favourably on transparency in its *Global Accountability Report* (Kovach *et al.* 2003).

Following measures announced in 1998, the WTO secretariat has alerted member governments to all documents, position papers and newsletters submitted to it by civil society organizations. A monthly list of these submissions is posted on the WTO website, although it appears that relatively few people inside or outside the organization consult them.

Several other turns in WTO policy have also responded to demands from civil society associations. For example, the expansion of trade liberalization measures to cover intellectual property matters, telecommunications, financial services and so on has (at least partly) met the wishes of various business lobbies. In response to development questions, the WTO has maintained a Committee on Trade and Development. In 1997 it convened a High-Level Meeting for Least-Developed Countries, and four years later the newest phase of multilateral trade negotiations was dubbed a 'Development Agenda'. In recognition of ecological concerns, ministers assembled at Marrakech decided to launch a wide-ranging work programme on trade and environment in the WTO (Shaffer 2001). (In contrast, the GATT Group on Environmental Measures and International Trade, formed in 1971, met only once, in 1993, to discuss the results of the UN Conference on Environment and Development.) On questions of unfair business practices in global markets, the WTO has established a Working Group on the Interaction between Trade and Competition Policy and a Working Group on Transparency in Government Procurement.

To be sure, these and other policy developments at the WTO have often fallen short of what civil society groups (reformists in particular) have sought. For example, beyond the headline rhetoric it is not clear how far the WTO has substantively moved to become a development-friendly organization. In addition, the WTO has not put labour standards on its agenda or effectively deepened its collaboration with the ILO. Environmental groups have complained about purported inadequacies of the WTO Committee on Trade and Environment.[9] Although the Working Group on Trade and Competition Policy has produced many studies and proposals since its creation in 1996, no intergovernmental negotiations on the subject have started. In spite of these limitations, though, it can still be said that pressure from civil society organizations has contributed to modest policy shifts of the kind noted above.

Shortfalls in relations

Contributions from civil society organizations to the global trade regime have clearly increased in both quantity and quality since the 1990s. Nevertheless, major additional advances would be required before civil society inputs could realize their full positive potentials (on the lines described earlier) vis-à-vis the WTO. The following paragraphs outline three major shortcomings in current relations between civil society associations and the WTO, namely unequal access, shallowness and limited reciprocity. These flaws have caused WTO–civil society exchanges to suffer significantly from the possible pitfalls noted earlier.

A first major way that WTO–civil society contacts have thus far failed to maximize their potential contributions to policy enhancement relates to biased participation. The various elements of civil society have not enjoyed equal opportunities to engage with the WTO. In a rough ranking, conformers like business associations have usually had easiest access. Thus, for example, well over half of the non-governmental actors accredited to attend the Ministerial Conferences have represented business interests. Certain reformist groups such as trade unions, environmental NGOs and development NGOs have generally come (a rather distant) second. Many other civil society bodies, including most grassroots associations, have had no direct entry to the WTO at all. Other inequalities in access have favoured organizations based in the North over groups located in the South (although the WTO has since 1999 paid for around forty persons from poor countries to attend each of its symposia in Geneva).[10] In class terms, civil society contacts with the WTO have principally involved urban-based, university-educated, computer-literate, (relatively) high-earning English speakers. Some development NGOs have attempted to incorporate 'voices from the base' into their advocacy work on the WTO, but the rest of the under-class has been locked out of exchanges with the institution. The dialogue has also shown a gender bias, with disproportionately large participation from men in both the WTO staff and civil society groups (especially academic, business and labour associations).

A second major shortcoming in WTO–civil society relations to date has been their overall shallowness. Although, as seen above, the WTO leadership has in general terms acknowledged the importance of civil society involvement in contemporary global governance, the organization has for the most part lacked clearly formulated objectives and carefully constructed channels of communication for its interchanges with civil society groups. On the whole the WTO's engagement of civil society associations has occurred through improvisation. The 1996 guidelines on relations with civil society actors are very short and general. Its External Relations Division, set up under the GATT in 1989, has remained small, with one director and only three professional staff as of 2003. Moreover, these officials have lacked specific expertise in respect of civil society liaison apart from accumulated on-the-job experience. In contrast to the World Bank, the WTO has not established a permanent liaison committee with civil society groups, although Director-General Supachai in June 2003 announced the formation of a small personal advisory committee of NGOs that he would consult for the remaining two years of his term. (An earlier attempt by Ruggiero to form a similar consultative group collapsed.) In contrast to the United Nations, the WTO has made no arrangements for permanent accreditation of civil society organizations, as opposed to ad hoc admission to specific events. No civil society associations have participated as ex officio observers on WTO committees. Nor have civil society groups been systematically involved in trade policy reviews or dispute settlement procedures. To this extent the WTO has done little to bring civil society organizations into its policy-making processes, and this situation seems unlikely to change in the near future (Lopez 2001).

Approaches from civil society groups towards the WTO have often suffered from similar shallowness. True, since the late 1990s increased numbers of civil society associations have pursued sustained, focused, carefully researched efforts to understand and shape WTO policies, for instance, on agriculture and market access. In Thailand, increased competence regarding WTO matters allowed farmers' organizations and NGOs to play a significant role in drafting national legislation to implement the TRIPs agreement in that country.[11] However, many other civil society groups with concerns about global economic governance have shown only haphazard and superficial interest in the WTO, becoming active only around a particular conference, set of negotiations or trade dispute.

A third general limitation in WTO–civil society relations – namely, a lack of veritable 'dialogue' – has especially affected the institution's contacts with rejectionists. These interchanges have often lacked sufficient openness and reciprocity, where the WTO on the one hand and activists on the other are fully ready to listen to, learn from and be changed by each other. Such 'dialogues of the deaf' were particularly acute, for example, in early contacts between free-traders at the WTO and environmentalists who automatically linked trade liberalization with increased ecological degradation. Many parties to WTO–civil society exchanges are still not as prepared as they could be to consider positions other than their own.

In sum, relations between the WTO and civil society associations have to date often succumbed to the sorts of potential dangers highlighted earlier. First, the exchanges have not been democratically representative. On the contrary, they have sooner tended to reinforce structural inequalities in world politics. Second, on balance the WTO has not yet taken its contacts with civil society actors that far beyond public relations exercises. Third, on the whole civil society groups have not provided the WTO with sufficient precisely formulated and carefully researched inputs. Fourth, the WTO has not given careful thought to the possible repercussions of its contacts with civil society associations on national and local politics in its member countries. Fifth, even after the Seattle protests, the WTO has for the most part skewed its contacts towards conformist groups, to the relative neglect of its reformist and rejectionist critics, thereby obtaining an artificially optimistic assessment of the political viability of its policies.

To note shortfalls in relations between civil society bodies and the WTO is not to advocate an abolition of these links, of course. As stressed before, the dynamics of contemporary governance are such that those exchanges are in effect irrepressible. World politics cannot return to a statist mould where multilateral institutions dealt only with governments. The unavoidable challenge is therefore to forge relationships that maximize the potential contributions of civil society associations to global governance and minimize their possible harms.

Constraints

In order to prescribe measures for improved relations between civil society organizations and the WTO, one needs first to assess the causes of the problems. In a word, the shortfalls just described have arisen primarily from resource limitations and deeper structural forces. That is, the shortcomings in WTO–civil society relations have not resulted in the first place from the personalities and attitudes of individual officials and lobbyists, but from the political, economic and cultural context in which they work.

In terms of resources, the WTO has thus far lacked sufficient personnel, funds, stores of information and coordination capacities to realize the full potential of relations with civil society groups. At present the secretariat has only a modest staff of 560 people to handle a vast global trade agenda (WTO 2002: 154). (In comparison, the IMF currently employs around 3,200 persons, whereas the World Bank payroll is double that size.) In terms of disposition, the professional staff of the WTO are overwhelmingly economists without formal training in socio-political issues such as the organization and operations of civil society. Meanwhile the WTO secretariat runs (as of 2002) on a total annual administrative budget of SF140 million (US$107 million) (WTO 2002: 163). In comparison, the IMF operating budget in 2002 was $737 million (IMF 2002: 82). Of the WTO budget, the External Relations Division obtains less than SF0.5 million per year,[12] hardly a sum that allows for major overtures to civil society. In view of these personnel and funding limitations, it is not surprising that the WTO has accumulated little information on civil society. Its staff are therefore usually poorly briefed on many of the civil society groups that they meet. Nor has the organization developed any mechanisms to coordinate its work on civil society associations with national governments and other global governance bodies that have more experience in these contacts.

In most cases, civil society groups suffer from even more precarious resource situations than the WTO. In terms of personnel, civil society organizations rarely have more than one or two staff with detailed knowledge of the global trade regime. Larger business associations and certain think tanks have operated with fairly substantial and reliable funding, but most trade unions and NGOs have worked on shoestring budgets and/or short-term grants. Most civil society groups have (partly owing to the inaccessibility of some official documents) lacked sufficient data and analysis to mount fully informed campaigns for policy change at the WTO. In addition, civil society groups have developed few arrangements (aside from loose networking as seen in the PGA) to exchange information on and coordinate lobbying of the WTO. As a result, the limited resources of civil society actors have rarely been optimally employed.

That said, improved staffing, funding, information flows and coordination would not by themselves maximize the benefits of exchanges between civil society organizations and the WTO. Indeed, certain deeper conditions of social structure have, if anything, stood as greater barriers to a fuller development of the dialogue.

For example, difficulties of access to the WTO for civil society organizations have resulted in part from the culture of secrecy that has traditionally enveloped both global economic governance in general and global trade regulation in particular. Recent WTO moves towards increased disclosure mark an important shift towards greater openness, but the embedded culture of secrecy has slowed the process and is unlikely to dissolve quickly.

The previously described inequalities of civil society access to the WTO have also reflected deeper structural conditions: in this case pervasive entrenched social hierarchies in contemporary world politics between countries, cultures, classes and genders. Such structures of subordination have figured centrally in producing a lower allocation of resources and opportunities: to South-based civil society organizations relative to North-based groups; to rural bodies relative to urban organizations; to labour unions relative to business associations; to women relative to men; and indeed to civil society bodies relative to official circles.

The power of neoclassical economic orthodoxy has been another important structural force against a more inclusive, deeper and more open dialogue between the WTO and civil society organizations. So-called 'neoliberal' ideology has dominated knowledge of political economy during contemporary globalization, particularly following the dissolution of communist regimes and the collapse of post-colonial socialism. In this situation of near monopoly, ideas of market rationality and comparative advantage have frequently reigned as unquestioned truths, and staff of the WTO have faced little pressure to give alternative perspectives a serious hearing. This knowledge/power structure has put reformers and rejectionists at a marked disadvantage in civil society relative to conformers.

A fourth structural inhibition to greater development of relations between the WTO and civil society associations has been the persistent hold of the sovereignty norm. Although, as indicated at the start of this chapter, states have lost their effective capacity to exercise sovereign governance, most governments have continued to cling jealously to the claim that they always have the complete and final say in regulation. In this vein most members of the WTO have been reluctant to see the secretariat develop extensive contacts with civil society groups and have insisted that these relations are the prerogative of governments. Most WTO officials and civil society activists, too, have continued to work under the spell of the sovereignty myth. Both civil society groups and the WTO have therefore usually limited their direct exchanges to an intensity that governments would tolerate.

Finally, and partly as an extension of the sovereignty issue, structural conditions have limited dialogue between the WTO and civil society in so far as citizen groups have generally experienced difficulty establishing their legitimacy. In the statist mode of governance to which contemporary globalization has brought an end, national governments were normally regarded as the only legitimate actors in world politics. Today's post-sovereign situation allows for a multiplicity of agents, but non-state entities must still work hard to establish their credentials. Civil society associations could secure their legitimacy in terms of their own democratic practices; however, most of these groups have to date attended insufficiently to questions concerning their autonomy, accessibility, transparency and accountability (Scholte 2003).[13] Indeed, some of the organizations that have pressed hardest for a democratization of the WTO have done little to secure democracy in their own operations. This has allowed the WTO and states to take civil society associations less seriously than they might otherwise have done.

Towards the future

If – as seems probable – globalization continues at substantial rates into the foreseeable future, then governance is likely to become increasingly multilayered and diffuse. As indicated above, civil society inputs can contribute greatly to policy in this situation; yet such benefits do not accrue automatically. It is understandable that early phases of relations between the WTO and civil society associations were largely haphazard and improvised. However, future development requires more concerted and carefully constructed efforts. What sorts of practicable measures are available to take relations between civil society organizations and the WTO forward in the short to medium term?

Five general suggestions follow from the analysis presented above. In the first place, the parties to WTO–civil society relations could aim to clarify their objectives. What, more precisely, are they trying to achieve by engaging with each other? The WTO in particular needs more specific policy aims in regard to civil society.

Second, further steps could be taken to institutionalize relations between the WTO and civil society associations. Drawing on the experience of other global governance agencies, the WTO could devise mechanisms for observer status in relevant committees and panels, a regular cycle of consultations (extending current practices of symposia and briefings).[14]

Third, both the WTO and civil society groups could improve relevant staff capacities. For example, the WTO could expand its External Relations Division, including the appointment of at least one civil society specialist. Other relevant staff of the WTO could take a short training course on relations with civil society groups. Likewise, more capacity regarding the global trade regime is needed in civil society, particularly among marginalized groups.

Fourth, the parties could make more efforts to coordinate their activities in WTO–civil society exchanges. For example, the WTO could join the sixteen other global governance agencies that subscribe to the UN Non-Governmental Liaison Service (NGLS). The trade body could also more actively exchange information and advice concerning civil society associations with other multilateral institutions that have more experience in these relationships. Meanwhile civil society groups with interests in the global trade regime could do more in the way of exchanging information, sharing tasks, coordinating initiatives, and so on.

Fifth, both civil society practitioners and WTO officials could consciously nurture attitudinal changes that promote more constructive dialogue. For instance, all participants in the relationships could make more deliberate efforts to include otherwise marginalized circles. The WTO and civil society groups could also cultivate greater mutual recognition, respect and reciprocity. In addition, both civil society organizations and the WTO could become more sensitive to issues of their democratic accountability. To this end, all parties could *inter alia* do more to publicize their activities to each other and to the wider public.

None of the steps just described need be particularly costly or difficult. Given the substantial benefits of well-developed WTO–civil society relations – in terms of increasing information, stimulating debate, educating citizens, legitimating regimes and democratizing politics generally – such initiatives are surely worthwhile.

Notes

1 This chapter originated in team research during 1996–1998 on global economic institutions and global social movements, funded through the Global Economic Institutions Programme of the Economic and Social Research Council in the UK (grant no. L120251027). The first edition version – which also appeared in the *Journal of World Trade* 33:1, February 1999 – drew on research by Robert O'Brien and Marc Williams as well as myself. For the second edition I am also grateful to Ricardo Meléndez-Ortiz of the International Centre for Trade and Sustainable Development and Hans-Peter Werner of the WTO for comments and corrections on an earlier draft.

2 Information on NGO participation can be found at: <www.wto.org/english/thewto_e/minist_e/min01_e/min01_ngo_e.htm> (accessed 10 June 2003).

3 'Guidelines for arrangements on relations with Non-Governmental Organisations', WT/L/162, 23 July 1996. Available HTTP: <www.wto.org/english/forums_e/ngo_e/guide_e.htm> (accessed 10 June 2003).

4 'Ruggiero announces enhanced WTO plan for cooperation with NGOs', WTO Press Release 107, 17 July 1998.

5 See 'World trade and the rights of women', *Women Working World Wide Bulletin* 2, January 1997.

6 *Who Makes the Rules? Decision-Making and Structure of the World Trade Organization*, New York: WEDO, 1995; *How Secure Is Our Food? Food Security and Agriculture under the New GATT and WTO* New York: WEDO, 1995; *Who Owns Knowledge? Who Owns the Earth? Intellectual Property Rights and Biodiversity under the New GATT and WTO*, New York: WEDO, 1995.

7 Cf. J. Bosley, 'Toward a Parliamentary Assembly for the World Trade Organization' Ottawa: World Federalists of Canada Discussion Paper, 2001; interview with Fergus Walsh, Executive Director, World Federalists of Canada, 6 May 2002.

8 On transparency in the WTO see: <www.wto.org/english/forums_e/ngo_e/bernie_derestrictiontext_e.htm> (accessed 10 June 2003).

9 World Wide Fund for Nature, *The WTO Committee on Trade and the Environment – Is It Serious?*, Geneva: WWF, 1996; Friends of the Earth, *A Call to Close the Committee on Trade and the Environment*, Amsterdam: FOE International, 1996.

10 Interview with Hans-Peter Werner, External Relations Division, WTO, 11 June 2003.

11 Interviews with Witoon Lianchamroon, Director of Biothai, in Bangkok, 18 June 2002 and 23 May 2003.

12 Interview with Hans-Peter Werner, 11 June 2003.

13 Cf. J.A. Scholte, *Democratizing the Global Economy: The Role of Civil Society*, Coventry: Centre for the Study of Globalisation and Regionalisation, 2003, Part 5.

14 Cf. *Accreditation Schemes and Other Arrangements for Public Participation in International Fora: a contribution to the debate on WTO and transparency*, Geneva: International Centre for Trade and Sustainable Development, 1999.

Bibliography

Bellmann, C. and Gerster, R. (1996) 'Accountability in the World Trade Organization', *Journal of World Trade* 30: 31–74.

Bullen, S. and Van Dyke, B. (1996) *In Search of Sound Environment and Trade Policy: a critique of public participation in the WTO*, Geneva: Centre for International Environmental Law.

Charnovitz, S. (1996) 'Participation of non-governmental organizations in the World Trade Organization', *Pennsylvania Journal of International Economic Law* 17: 331–357.

Charnovitz, S. and Wickham, J. (1995) 'Non-governmental organizations and the original international trade regime', *Journal of World Trade* 29: 111–122.

Cohen, R. and Rai, S.M. (eds) (2000) *Global Social Movements*, London: Athlone.

Dunoff, J.L. (1998) 'The misguided debate over NGO participation at the WTO', *Journal of International Economic Law* 1: 433–456.

Edwards, M. and Gaventa, J. (eds) (2001) *Global Citizen Action*, Boulder, CO: Lynne Rienner.

Esty, D. (1997) *Why the World Trade Organization Needs Environmental NGOs*, Geneva: International Centre for Trade and Sustainable Development.

Esty, D.C. (1998) 'Non-governmental organizations at the World Trade Organization: cooperation, competition, or exclusion', *Journal of International Economic Law* 1: 123–147.

Evans, J. (1996) 'The trade union's view on international labour standards: a comment', in P. van Dijck and G. Faber (eds), *Challenges to the New World Trade Organization*, The Hague: Kluwer Law International.

Florini, A.M. (ed.) (2000) *The Third Force: the rise of transnational civil society*, Washington, DC: Carnegie Endowment for International Peace.

Hart, M. (1997) 'The WTO and the political economy of globalization', *Journal of World Trade* 31: 75–93.

IMF (2002) *Annual Report* 2002, Washington: International Monetary Fund.

Joekes, S. and Weston, A. (1995) *Women and the New Trade Regime*, New York: UNIFEM.

Keck, M. and Sikkink, K. (1998) *Activists Beyond Borders: advocacy networks in international politics*, Ithaca, NY: Cornell University Press.

Keet, D. (2000) 'Alternatives to the WTO regime: a discussion paper on tactics and strategies', Cape Town: Alternative Information and Development Centre.

Kovach, H., Neligan, C. and Burall, S. (2003) *Global Accountability Report 1: power without accountability?*, London: One World Trust.

Lopez, H.E. (2001) 'Recent trends and perspectives for non-state actor participation in World Trade Organization disputes', *Journal of World Trade* 35: 469–498.

Mehta, A.K. and Otto, C. (1996) *Global Trading Practices and Poverty Alleviation in South Asia: a gender perspective*, New York: UNIFEM.

O'Brien, R. (2000) 'The WTO and labour', in R. O'Brien, A.M. Goetz, J.A. Scholte and M. Williams (eds), *Contesting Global Governance: multilateral economic institutions and global social movements*, Cambridge: Cambridge University Press.

Salamon, L.M. (1994) 'The rise of the nonprofit sector', *Foreign Affairs* 73: 109–122.

Scholte, J.A. (2000) *Globalization: a critical introduction*, Basingstoke: Palgrave.

Scholte, J.A. (2002) 'Civil society and governance in the global polity', in M. Ougaard and R.A. Higgott (eds), *Towards a Global Polity*, London: Routledge.

Scholte, J. (2003) *Democratizing the Global Economy: the role of civil society*, Coventry: Centre for the Study of Globalisation and Regionalisation.

Shaffer, G.C. (2001) 'The World Trade Organization under challenge: democracy and the law and politics of the WTO's treatment of trade and environment matters', *Harvard Environmental Law Review* 25(1): 1–93.

Smith, J., Chatfield, C. and Pagnucco, R. (eds) (1997) *Transnational Social Movements and Global Politics*, Syracuse, NY: Syracuse University Press.

Tita, A. (1998) 'Globalization: a new political and economic space requiring supranational governance', *Journal of World Trade* 32: 47–55.

Union of International Associations (1999) *Yearbook of International Organizations*, Munich: Saur.

United Nations Development Programme (1997) *Human Development Report*, New York: Oxford University Press.

Weiss, T.G. and Gordenker, L. (eds) (1996) *NGOs, the UN, and Global Governance*, Boulder, CO: Lynne Rienner.

Willetts, P. (ed.) (1996) *Conscience of the World: the influence of non-governmental organisations in the UN System*, London: Hirst.

Williams, M. (2000) 'The World Bank, the World Trade Organization and the environmental social movement', in R. O'Brien, A.M. Goetz, J.A. Scholte and M. Williams (eds), *Contesting Global Governance: multilateral economic institutions and global social movements*, Cambridge: Cambridge University Press, 109–158.

Williams, M. and Ford, L. (1999) 'The World Trade Organisation, social movements and global environmental management', *Environmental Politics* 8: 268–289.

WTO (2002) *Annual Report 2002*, Geneva: World Trade Organization.

Key readings

Charnovitz, S. (1996) 'Participation of non-governmental organizations in the World Trade Organization', *Pennsylvania Journal of International Economic Law* 17: 331–357.

Charnovitz, S. and Wickham, J. (1995) 'Non-governmental organizations and the original international trade regime', *Journal of World Trade* 29: 111–122.

Dunoff, J. (1998) 'The misguided debate over NGO participation at the WTO', *Journal of International Economic Law* 1: 433–456.

Edwards, M. and Gaventa, J. (eds) (2001) *Global Citizen Action*, Boulder, CO: Lynne Rienner.

Esty, D. (1998) 'Non-governmental organizations at the World Trade Organization: cooperation, competition, or exclusion', *Journal of International Economic Law* 1: 123–147.

Lopez, H. (2001) 'Recent trends and perspectives for non-state actor participation in World Trade Organization disputes', *Journal of World Trade* 35: 469–498.

O'Brien, R. *et al.* (2000) *Contesting Global Governance: multilateral economic institutions and global social movements*, Cambridge: Cambridge University Press.

Scholte, J. (2002) 'Civil society and governance in the global polity', in M. Ougaard and R. Higgott (eds), *Towards a Global Polity*, London: Routledge.

Scholte, J. (2003) *Democratizing the Global Economy: the role of civil society*, Coventry: Centre for the Study of Globalisation and Regionalisation.

Williams, M. and Ford, L. (1999) 'The World Trade Organisation, social movements and global environmental management', *Environmental Politics* 8: 268–289.

Useful websites

www.ictsd.org (International Centre for Trade and Sustainable Development).

www.iisd.org (International Institute for Sustainable Development).

www.iccwbo.org (International Chamber of Commerce).

www.icftn.org (International Confederation of Free Trade Unions).

www.agp.org (People's Global Action).

Part III

The trade agenda

Key part issues

- Why does agriculture continue to occupy a central role in trade politics? What are the major differences of interest on this issue in current trade negotiations?
- What factors explain the emergence of intellectual property on the trade agenda? Has the TRIPs agreement made the poorer countries worse or better off?
- What factors have strengthened the linkage between competition policy and trade? Why is there pressure towards international convergence in competition policies?
- Why has the issue of a multilateral agreement of investment proved to be so politically sensitive? What progress is being made on this issue in current trade negotiations?
- Explain the factors linking issues on the trade and environmental agendas. To what extent has the WTO adapted to this linkage?
- What are the arguments for and against linking labour standards issues to trade negotiations? What is the significance of 'conditionality' in this debate?
- Evaluate the interests involved in the dispute over trade in genetically modfied food. What does this reveal about the character of contemporary trade politics?

Moving from the context of trade relationships and debates on the nature and role of the WTO, the third part of the book focuses on the range of issues on the trade agenda and how these reflect patterns of domestic and international interests. Obviously, not every issue is covered here, but we can see how contemporary trade politics now embraces what appear to be traditional issues alongside new concerns that reflect both the changing nature of the global economy and technological change.

Balaam's chapter reminds us that one of the oldest issues in international trade, namely agriculture, is still firmly on the agenda. Indeed, the round of trade negotiations which began at Doha in 2001 found itself confronting major disagreements (not least between the USA and the EU) on agriculture. But one of the other major stumbling blocks lay in a very different area, that of intellectual property (more specifically, access to patented drugs) which is outlined in Capling's chapter. This is an area which emerged as part of the agreements resulting from the Uruguay Round negotiations

(1986–1994) and underscores the ways in which the changing character of the global and national economies are reflected in the patterns of international trade.

Similar points can be made about competition policy and investment issues, dealt with by Damro and Bora. As Damro demonstrates, the ways in which the rules governing the operation of business in a globalised economy are shaped and adjudicated are now central concerns in trade negotiations which have moved from a concern with what happens at *national borders to what happens* behind *national borders. Similarly, Bora's evaluation of the pressures for an agreement on international investment reflects the growing importance of direct access to markets for producers of goods and services and, consequently, of a stable environment for international investment.*

In their chapters, Brack and van Liemt highlight two new and important trade issues: the environment and labour rights. That these two appear is testimony to the increasing reluctance of civil society to regard trade issues as the sole preserve of economists, trade lawyers and politicians. Labour standards is an area where human rights meets international trade and the same holds true with the environment.

In both cases, controversy arises out of the perception that some issues ought to be above money. But does agitation for more rigorous international standards signal a genuine concern for human and planetary welfare, or an attempt to raise protectionist barriers? Moreover, as Brack argues, it is by no means clear that market-based approaches to pollution problems are inimical to environmentalism.

A concern with values also underpins Falkner's chapter on agricultural biotechnology. Here, we are confronted by an issue that seems to symbolise the changing character of trade politics: one that not only involves governments and business, but also mobilises civil society organisations and excites public opinion.

11 Agricultural trade policy

David N. Balaam[1]

Summary

Agriculture remains one of the most controversial areas of international trade. Levels of protection remain high, particularly in the European Union, Japan, Norway, and Korea and agricultural industries have powerful political bases in many states. This chapter examines why agriculture figures so prominently in contemporary trade politics and provides an analysis of the most recent efforts to liberalize the sector. It begins by considering three perspectives on agricultural production and trade, then moves to consider both the Uruguay and Doha Rounds of WTO negotiations.

Unlike other trade issues in multilateral trade negotiations, agricultural protection appears to be an intractable problem. Virtually all nation-states protect or otherwise support their agricultural sectors by manipulating trade policies. Many of the world's largest commodity exporters, such as the USA, the European Union (EU), Canada, and Argentina, employ export enhancing measures to assist their agriculture sectors, while nearly all the major importers such as the US, EU, Japan, South Korea, and Norway, utilize a variety of restrictive measures to insulate domestic producers from lower priced imported commodities. Over the last fifty years tariffs on manufactured goods have dropped from 40 to 4 per cent, while agricultural tariffs remained at about 40 per cent. Rich nations spend about $350 billion a year supporting their farmers, as much as the entire gross national product of Sub-Saharan Africa (Gunnell 2002). Why has it been so difficult for nations to liberalize and so decrease the level of protection for agriculture in multilateral negotiating trade rounds?

Agricultural protection is often rooted in the political clout of farm groups and other agricultural interests including big business (multinational food companies, for example), and agribusinesses (such as large corporate farmers). In many countries protection also results from government efforts to generate jobs and income, achieve food security, preserve social customs, and to accomplish a variety of other national goals. Agricultural trade, then, is a politically and economically sensitive issue for states. The purposes and mix of often incompatible public and private interests behind support measures make international agricultural trade negotiations difficult and contentious.

In earlier rounds of the General Agreement on Tariffs and Trade (GATT) states were reluctant or unwilling to collaborate on reductions of agricultural support protection. In the Uruguay Round of GATT negotiations (1986–1994), and in the current round of

World Trade Organization (WTO) talks that got underway in Doha, Qatar, in November of 2001, agriculture has played an important, central role in trade negotiations.

This chapter is an overview of the reasons agricultural trade and farm support measures have been difficult to negotiate and why agricultural trade has played such an important role in recent multilateral trade talks. It begins with a discussion of the connection between national farm policies and international agricultural trade agreements and then outlines three popular political–economic perspectives – mercantilism, economic liberalism, and structuralism (Balaam and Veseth 2001) – ideological rationales, and explanatory frameworks that serve as a basis of academic explanations and different state national objectives and trade strategies. Analytically this work focuses on the state (or coalitions of nation-states), their choices, interests, and strategies, to account for the different negotiating positions and "deals" reflected in trade agreements. While the pluralist (interest) group politics perspective assigns the state the role of merely registering group interests, attention to the state and its representatives captures more of the proactive negotiating, bargaining, and reconciling processes national and international organization officials actually carry out.

The chapter then explores some of the central features of the Uruguay Round Agreement on Agriculture (AoA) and the new Doha Development Round pertaining to agriculture, especially the growing role of less developed countries (LDCs). It concludes that WTO efforts to liberalize agricultural trade have not as yet resulted in *significant* cuts in agricultural protection. In both rounds agricultural trade played a central role in the talks to the extent that agreement on other issues was conditioned on an agricultural accord. In the Uruguay Round states agreed on new rules and enough modest reductions in agricultural protection to pave the way for agreements on other trade issues. At this point in the Doha Round, however, an assortment of political and economic factors severely weakens support for an agreement to further reduce agricultural protection, which because of agriculture's central role in the talks jeopardizes the chances of new agreements in other products and services. The conclusion of the chapter discusses some of the implications of these developments for the future of agricultural trade policy and multilateral trade negotiations.

Domestic farm programs and agricultural trade policy

As societies develop they are transformed (Polanyi 2001) so that as the agricultural base of the economy shrinks its industrial base expands. As more land, labor, capital, and new technologies are applied to the production process in developed regions of the world, the result is often commodity overproduction. This drives down the price of food for consumers as well as the prices farmers receive. When farm receipts cannot keep up with production costs many farmers try to become more efficient by acquiring more land or applying new technologies and capital, thereby increasing their output and productivity. In a competitive environment many farmers cannot earn enough to stay in business and usually end up in debt and leaving their profession. In many LDCs where agriculture remains the largest sector of the economy, the result is often mass migration to and pressure on urban areas. Farmers everywhere usually turn to government for income support and other measures to help them overcome their financial problems and sustain their way of life. It is much easier for poorer and displaced farmers to tolerate their plight in developed nations than it is in LDCs that lack social welfare or other programs that help poor people adjust to some of the difficult consequences of the transformation process.

Table 11.1 Contrasting perspectives on agricultural trade

Theoretical perspectives	Mercantilism	Economic liberalism	Structuralism
Main actors	Nation-state	Individual and business firms	Socioeconomic-based classes
Objectives	Security, increasing wealth, and production	Free trade, increased production, and wealth	Class equity, fairness, equal distribution of wealth and production
Advocates	Frederich List, Alexander Hamilton, Franz Fischler	Adam Smith, David Ricardo, Margaret Thatcher, Ronald Reagan	Karl Marx, Antonio Gramsci
Policies	Tariffs, export subsidies, quotas	Reduce tariffs and export subsidies, decrease domestic support measures	Programs equalizing the distribution of wealth, some subsidies or assistance to farmers

How nations deal with the transformation problem and the role of trade policy in that process generates a good deal of tension in multilateral negotiations involving agriculture. Table 11.1 compares and contrasts three different analytical perspectives that account for the many motives behind countries' trade objectives, strategies, and policies: mercantilism, economic liberalism, and structuralism.

Mercantilism

Mercantilist policies – designed to generate a trade surplus in commodities – are popular in capitalist countries like Japan, Germany, South Korea, and Taiwan. Even though the USA formally adopted a free trade policy in 1934, agriculture has always been a heavily protected industry. The USA has employed acreage control, storage, and price support programs for its grains, oilseeds, and cotton. Import quotas and tariffs along with voluntary export restraints have also protected US cheese, butter, sugar, and some beef items. Along with food aid to assist anti-communist allies during the Cold War, US export subsidies also helped set farm prices closer to world market levels. In the 1970s the USA aggressively marketed grain to the USSR, Western Europe, Japan, and many LDCs in response to the growing demand for imported food products and commodities. When demand slackened by the early 1980s due to self-sufficiency programs in other countries, protectionist support was even more sought after by US agricultural interests.

EU protectionist agriculture policies (Grant 1997) reflect an even tighter connection between farm policies and agricultural trade than in the USA. Since 1968 EU officials have tried to harmonize the national farm and agricultural trade policies of a community that has grown from six to fifteen members. Historically, the goals of the EU Common

Agriculture Policy (CAP) have been: to achieve food self-sufficiency, maintain and increase farm income, and preserve the small-farm character of rural Europe. The CAP has employed various infrastructural support measures along with price support and disposal programs to assist dairy, beef and veal, sugar, cereal grain, pork, and table wine producers. Trade protectionist measures have included a variable levy instead of tariffs, to limit food imports into the community, accompanied by subsidies to encourage exports. As a result of its self-sufficiency programs, in the 1970s the EU became a major agricultural exporter, competing with US disposal programs and drying up US agricultural export markets in Europe, generating a good deal of tension between the USA and EU.

Like the EU, Japan is also famous for its farm support programs, particularly rice, citrus, and beef, aimed at protecting its farmers from international competition. Such programs minimize dependency on overseas food suppliers and manage the structural transformation process in such a way as to help sustain Japan's economic recovery and promote investment in its industrial development. Its domestic commodity programs and especially import protection measures have included tariffs, import quotas, and variable levies, along with import restrictions tied to strict health and safety standards (Honma 1993). The USA and EU have also pressured the Japanese government to correct its growing surplus balance of trade by opening its markets to their agricultural goods and products.

Economic liberalism

Adam Smith and David Ricardo made popular economic liberal ideas in the late eighteenth and early nineteenth centuries, ideas revived by Ronald Reagan and Margaret Thatcher in the 1980s. Support for free trade and minimum state interference in the market are the ideological foundations and recommendations of many WTO and national trade policy officials. Liberals criticize farm and agricultural trade protection as it exacerbates the oversupply problem by setting domestic prices at levels higher than world prices. This in turn stimulates domestic production and leads to demands for more state support, which "distorts" international trade by not allowing markets to clear surpluses.

Economic liberals are usually very critical of the political power and influence of farm groups, who, although decreasing in number, usually have a disproportionate share of influence in national legislatures. In countries like Japan, the USA, and the EU, not only do farm interests dominate the agendas of many local or regional governments, but they support urban interests in exchange for agricultural support and are often the base of political support behind a major party like the Liberal Democratic Party in Japan.

Until the late 1970s many LDCs preferred different versions of mercantilist trade policies and strategies to economic liberal policies to support their agricultural sectors. Officials in some Latin American countries employed import substitution policies and tariffs to assist local peasants and farmers.[2] Yet many encountered problems when the government taxed agriculture to help fund development projects and resisted supporting the rural economy because it would undermine the government's urban base of political support. Based on Japan as a model, some of the more successful East and South-East Asian countries pursued a "developmental capitalist" version of mercantilism that combined exports of value added manufactured products with tariffs on commodity imports.

In the 1980s and 1990s as part of structural adjustment loan (SAL) conditions instituted by the IMF to deal with debt, many LDCs were compelled to reduce or eliminate agricultural support measures and to adopt more economically liberal-oriented policies. Many LDCs opened their markets and imported more of the developed nations' commodities and processed food to meet the demands of growing and higher income-earning urban populations, only to find themselves in more debt and dependent on the developed nations (Bello 1994). After the Asian financial crisis of 1997, the economic liberal policies of the World Bank and WTO came under attack by the anti-globalization campaign, many of whose members have been informed by a structuralist perspective of trade policy (Steger 2002).

Structuralism

The structuralist approach to trade policy is grounded in Marxist thinking about the exploitation of the working class through policies set in place by elites and state officials to protect the interests of the economy's corporate structure and agribusinesses (Krebs and Lehman 1996). Ironically, structuralists feel two ways about protection. Sounding much like economic liberals, some argue that protection is bad, that it benefits agribusinesses and not small farmers. Other structuralists believe that protectionist measures intended to benefit small, poor farmers are justified and should be employed in "flexible" ways to achieve a variety of valuable social goals such as sustaining income for poorer farmers, overcoming malnutrition and hunger, achieving food security, and preserving the environment. Furthermore, the economic liberal policies behind the WTO and other financial institutions do not help LDCs as much as they harm them, generating poverty and hunger. Some structuralists prefer to see LDCs adopt self-sufficiency or "food first"(Lappe *et al.* 1998) measures that cut LDC dependency on the developed nations through trade and food aid.

The Uruguay Round and the central role of agriculture

Up until the early 1980s states were generally reluctant to negotiate reductions in the level of protection for agriculture. But by the opening of the Uruguay Round of the GATT negotiations in 1986 the developed countries were primarily interested in establishing rules for some fourteen goods and services not previously covered by the GATT (Schott 1994). Developed countries recognized that putting agriculture on the negotiating table would help open LDC markets to their commodities as well as value-added goods and services, making it easier to reduce levels of domestic support for their own agricultural interests. LDCs routinely complained about the discriminating trade practices of the developed nations against their primary agricultural products and viewed the talks as an opportunity to export more of their commodities to the developed countries if the developed nations reduced tariffs and use of export subsidies.

The opening session of the Uruguay Round was held in Punta del Este, Uruguay, in September of 1986 and was concluded in April of 1994 at Marrakech, Morocco. Even though members claimed they wanted to reduce agricultural protection, for seven years officials walked a fine line between pressures to protect agriculture at home and to open up their markets for international trade. Briefly, the Uruguay Round's rather technical Final Act included an Agreement on Agriculture (AoA) whose three "pillars" committed members to make provisions to deal with market access, domestic support, and export subsidies (Diakosavvas 2002). Market access measures included a ban on such non-tariff barriers (NTBs) as quantitative import restrictions, variable import levies, and discretionary import licensing. The developed countries also agreed to a new policy of "tariffication" (Brooks and Cahill 2001) that converted various NTBs into tariffs so they could be quantified, added to existing tariffs, and then reduced over the next six years by 36 per cent (with a minimum cut of 15 per cent for each tariff) from their base period. Countries agreed to import a minimum amount of commodities under a tariff-rate quota (TRQ) system. Under a TRQ system, an import is subject to two tiers of protection: a quota of commodities enters under a lower tariff rate, whilst additional imports are subjected to a higher tariff.

An ingenious result of the round was the plan whereby trade protection instruments were sorted into categories – boxes – according to how trade distorting the measure was. Thus, "green box" domestic measures that were deemed not to impact trade that much were exempt from reductions, while "amber" and "blue box" measures, such as administered pricing schemes, input subsidies, and producer payments, were regarded as more trade distorting and would be reduced. States were encouraged to "decouple" their support measures from production and direct support of income. Each country was also to reduce its total aggregate measurement of support (AMS), except when protection fell below a *de minimus* point.

A major provision of the AoA was that export subsidies were to be cut from a 1986–1990 base period by 36 per cent and in volume by 21 per cent over a period of six years for the developed countries, while LDC cuts were 24 and 14 per cent respectively on a product-specific basis over a ten-year period. Other measures of the agreement included sanitary and phytosanitary (SPS) trade controls to protect human, animal, or plant life, a "peace clause" that made members immune from WTO complaints for nine years if they cut subsidies and trade barriers, and several provisions to strengthen the dispute settlement process.

During negotiations, different states employed various strategies that reflected wide discrepancies in their approaches to trade policy. The first Reagan Administration proposed to phase out all trade-distorting subsidies over a ten-year period – a bid similar to the Administration's "zero option" arms control proposal at the time. While at first appearing to be disingenuous, in hindsight it appears that the Administration's objective was a calculated maneuver to force the EU and Japan to either defend their trade barriers or tear them down. This tactic did not mean the end to agricultural protection in the USA. Instead the US strategy was to shift the means used to support agriculture interests by *opening up* markets for US commodities the world over while simultaneously deflating Congressional protectionist pressures, reducing farm program budget costs, and improving the growing balance of trade and payments deficits. The USA also defended itself by seeking out new bilateral trade agreements and promoting regional trade agreements such as the North American Free Trade Agreement (NAFTA) and later the Asia–Pacific Economic Cooperation (APEC). The Administration also stated that if the GATT talks failed or competitors failed to reduce agriculture protection, Congress might increase export subsidies, which it did to protect soybeans.

European Community (EC) officials also acted defensively throughout the talks (Swinbank and Tanner 1996), especially in the face of US efforts to push the anticipated adjustment costs that would come with an agreement on them. Commissioner Ray MacSharry used the negotiations to argue that domestic programs had to be cut back in order to come into line with GATT proposals. An impasse within the EC in 1990 occurred when some member governments faced new elections and were pressed not to significantly reform their agriculture sectors. The French minister accused MacSharry of exceeding his mandate when it came to reform of the CAP.

Japan went into the negotiations supportive of liberalizing trade in other areas but resistant to change in its agriculture structure and reluctant to negotiate its farm and agricultural trade policies. Throughout the talks Japan generally "kept its head low" while US and EC officials engaged one another quite vociferously. Quite often Japan's negotiating style reflected its effort to appear as a cooperative team player in an effort to play a more positive role in the international system.

At the time the Cairns group was composed of some fifteen developed and developing nations that were smaller agricultural exporters and made up roughly one-third the world's agricultural trade.[3] Often praised by the USA and others for its efforts to extensively reduce levels of agricultural protection, the Cairns group gradually found it difficult to negotiate deep cuts in protection and later shifted their role in the talks to become an honest broker between the major parties. Together with the USA, the Cairns group eventually proposed to cut domestic trade-distorting subsidies by 75 per cent and export subsidies by 90 per cent as well over a ten-year period.

After talks stalled for lack of an agricultural agreement, a breakthrough came when MacSharry led a successful two-year effort to reform the CAP by ensuring that deficiency payments to EC farmers would continue despite being decoupled from production. The EC also *increased* set-asides for French farmers by 27 per cent. The new proposal became more acceptable to EC members when domestic support reductions were reduced to 30 per cent based on 1986–1989 levels, which meant that for some commodities support would actually *increase* under the new agreement. Likewise, proposed export subsidy and tariff levels would actually end up *higher* than they might have been without an agreement given the flexibility in determining which products would be covered under the agreement.

A new accord on agriculture was finally reached in 1993, though, when it became clear that an agreement on other major trade issues in the round was linked to success on agriculture. The new Clinton Administration supported the proposed accord and worked hard with the British to isolate the French, who did not veto the new agreement. The USA did, however, make several concessions to the French, exempting 25 million tons of cereal stockpiles from the agreement and shifting the base periods used to average export subsidies.

To gain domestic support for the measures and the final accord state officials constantly enticed farm groups with promises of as much as $1 trillion in economic gains in the next decade and $35 million a year in earnings from trade. EC and other national officials also helped organize community groups to support the new agreement. Meanwhile the voice of farm groups gradually weakened in the developed countries due to increasingly divided views about trade *within* farm communities, the growing number of *non-farm* interests agriculture had to compete with, and when smaller numbers of family farmers had to contend with the pro free trade interests of the food investment, processing, packaging, marketing, and transportation "agro-food" business sector. Many US farmers were upset with President Reagan's proposal to gradually eliminate protection for agriculture. Tariffication would render non-tariff and other barriers more transparent and easier to cut, undermining their support and allowing state officials to more easily compromise farm interests with other domestic and international interests and state objectives.

Even if new rules would help to resolve trade disputes and de-escalate US and EU export subsidy wars, especially over grains and oilseeds, strong supporters of free trade were disappointed that the AoA did not substantially cut or eliminate export subsidies for agricultural commodities and products altogether (Paarlberg 1997). For many economic liberals the AoA did not bite hard enough into protectionist measures and, in effect, sanctioned remaining subsidies and tariffs. Today, support levels remain high and so do commodity surpluses. Agricultural tariffs average 60 per cent of the price of imports while industrial tariffs rarely average above 10 per cent. Ambiguous rules make possible "dirty tariffs" where officials inflate TRQs used as base levels, negating the effort to reduce tariffs. Export subsidy cuts are not commodity specific; countries can group them in any combination to arrive at the required average needed to show a decrease in support. Nations can also shift support for farm programs as long as they stayed underneath the required ceiling of reduction, while some support programs such as milk were exempted from new rules.

Careful analysis of developments in the Uruguay Round surrounding agriculture reveals that much like an arms control agreement, the Uruguay Round's members compromised enough so as to make the claim that they had made a dent in agricultural protection, while as yet *preserving* much of their domestic support and trade protection. Many of the technical problems of the agreement were papered over. More importantly, in the final analysis the major players were not willing to risk losing potential "sweet deals" in areas such as financial services and intellectual property rights for lack of a serious effort to reduce the levels of agricultural protection.

The Doha Development Round

Article 20 of the AoA mandated a new round of multilateral negotiations, which was to start in Seattle, Washington, in November of 1999. Several weeks before in Geneva, delegations could not agree on an agenda for the new round. In Seattle, approximately 50,000 demonstrators made headlines when they protested against, among other things, WTO support for globalization and free trade policies they claim lead to greater income inequality between the world's "haves" and "have-nots," damage to the environment, and exploited labor (Steger 2002). Doha, Qatar, was chosen as the site to kick off the next round of multilateral trade negotiations in November of 2001. The EU recommended that the new round should be called the "Doha Development Round" in recognition of the importance of LDCs in these talks. Some note, though, that the Doha Round might not have started if the 9/11 terrorist attacks had not united WTO members in a show of international solidarity in the face of the attacks (*The Economist* 2003a).

As was the case in the Uruguay Round, once again in the Doha Round failure to reach an agreement on agricultural issues potentially jeopardizes agreements in other trade areas (*The Economist* 2003b). The developed countries are most interested in reaching agreements on industrial tariffs, investments, competition policy, trade-related intellectual property rights (TRIPs), trade facilitation, and environmental issues. Again, they would like to pry open LDC markets as outlets for their agricultural commodities in conjunction with efforts to decrease spending for domestic agricultural programs. For example, Nicolas Stern of the World Bank adopts the often used pro free trade tactic of promising LDCs $100 billion, or two times what they get in development aid, if they sign on to a new AoA. Without an agreement, he argues, a further slowdown of the international economy over the next 12–18 months can be expected, and LDC efforts to reduce poverty will go for naught (Stern 2002).

Because LDCs want access to generic drugs to fight AIDs and other diseases they might be willing to compromise with the developed nations. However, the bottom line for many of them appears to be that implementation of the current AoA should occur first and that progress in other trade issues is contingent on progress on an agreement that benefits them more directly than did the Uruguay Round's AoA.

Once again the USA's opening position is a provocative one; to cut agricultural tariffs around the world by 75 per cent, eliminate export subsidies over five years, and to reduce farm subsidies to 5 per cent of the value of farm production (Schalch 2002). Many consider the proposal to be disingenuous given that the new US 2002 Farm Bill *increases* the level of protection for US farmers and agribusinesses by $170 million over the next ten years, signaling a decided shift away from US efforts to support multilateral international economic institutions to support for more unilaterally oriented national objectives. Curiously, the USA has once again framed trade issues in almost war-like terms: that the US agriculture community is ready to decrease support for agriculture but does not want the USA to unilaterally disarm before doing so (Zoellick 2002). The USA and others blame the EU for spending $2 billion plus a year in export subsidies and three times what the USA does for trade-distorting domestic agricultural programs. It wants the EU to bring down its barriers while simultaneously protecting itself in case no agreement can be reached (*The Economist* 2003b).

Conversely the EU and many other states see the USA as hypocritical and its agricultural trade policy as being all over the map. The USA publicly calls for free trade in agriculture, yet its subsidies and farm protectionist measures would be very difficult to significantly reform. The George W. Bush Administration has not pressured domestic interests to decrease protection nor has it squared its new Farm Bill with efforts to promote free trade and trade system openness. Additionally, support for steel also raises questions about US sincerity.

The EU, Japan, Switzerland, Norway, and South Korea all heavily support their farmers and are not keen to drastically cut the level of farm support. Once again a major issue for the EU is CAP reform, which makes it especially hard to mesh EU internal deliberations on agricultural trade reform with the Doha negotiations. Growing surpluses bring the CAP into conflict with WTO commitments on export subsidies, especially cereal and beef. The EU proposes only a 45 per cent cut in export subsidies, a 36 per cent cut in tariffs, and a 55 per cent reduction in farm subsidies. Moreover, it supports the idea that all countries should reduce the level of tariffs by the *same* amount. EU officials argue that proposals to cut domestic support by 50 per cent would hurt Europe and Japan more than the USA, driving hundreds of thousands of small farmers out of business. The French oppose efforts to significantly reduce agricultural protection and France's Jacques Chirac recently agreed with Germany's Gerhard Schröder to keep CAP spending at its current level until 2013 (*The Economist* 2003a).

To maintain domestic support for reform, Franz Fischler, the EU's agricultural policy commissioner, proposes that the EU follow through on decoupling production from protection and make direct payments to farmers (*The Economist* 2003b), a blue box provision that does not have to be factored into commitments to reduce subsidies. The EU also wants talks to cover a variety of non-trade issues such as food safety and labeling, name protection of certain products from different regions, and the environment. EU consumers are concerned about epidemics like Mad Cow disease and the effects of genetically modified organisms (GMOs) and biotechnology, and EU politicians hesitate to appear soft on these and other issues and expect strong opposition to a new agreement if it means having to reform the CAP, which technically does not expire until 2006. Finally, the EU will also have to deal with the issue of the impact of increasing membership in the next few years.

Economic liberal and structuralist critics of the CAP, however, argue that it mainly benefits large producers and agribusinesses who employ the most powerful lobbyists, and that high levels of CAP support encourage environmental damage and depletion of national treasuries. A wide range of environmentalists, consumers, LDCs, and not unexpectedly the USA, argue that what the EU proposes is not enough, only repackaged subsidies.

Several other issues between the USA and EU have recently added to transatlantic tension: bananas, steel, and EU refusals to import genetically modified crops. The WTO recently ruled the US foreign-sales corporate tax illegal, allowing the EU to impose $4 billion worth of tariffs on the USA. Meanwhile the USA claims the EU is using environmental legislation as a back door to protectionism. Both the USA and EU have raised suspicions about each other and other WTO members because they have pushed for regional and bilateral agreements outside of the WTO – the USA working on a Free Trade Area of the Americas deal and the EU pushing for regional free trade agreements with South Africa and Mercosur in South America (Zoellick 2002). Recently, the most noteworthy source of stress has been EU criticism of the US war on Iraq.

Likewise Japan would like to see agreements on investment regulations and competition laws. With persistent recession at home, at this point in the talks Japan is not very interested in agricultural trade liberalization.

So far the Cairns group has explicitly called for reducing and then phasing out all forms of export subsidies over a three-year period for the developed countries and six years for developing nations. Their proposal would phase out "any export credit transaction" along with credit guarantees or insurance programs. They also want to extend coverage to food aid programs that are often used to dispose of food. However, the newest Cairns group proposal reflects an effort to recognize the (protectionist) needs of LDCs to sustain special and differential treatment for legitimate and varied non-trade needs including rural development, food security and subsistence, and small-scale farming. The fact that fourteen of its members are LDCs is quite likely to diffuse the solidarity of the Cairns group and its proposal for deep cuts in agricultural protection (WTO 2003).

A distinctive feature of the Doha Development Round so far is the increasingly important role of LDCs who make up roughly 100 of the 145 WTO members and who have more political clout in the WTO than they do in the IMF or World Bank. In the WTO, LDCs do not have a cohesive bargaining position; some are pro-liberalization, e.g., fourteen of the Cairns group, while others who belong to the Association of South-East Asian Nations or to the African group are more mercantilistic in outlook or are sitting on the fence (WTO 2003). While their objectives and proposals depend on many factors – what they produce, the demand for their commodities and products, their connection to political allies, and how food secure they are – what most LDCs have in common is great disappointment with the results of the Uruguay Round's AoA. They blame the USA, EU, and Japan for dragging their feet on implementing the Uruguay Round's trade liberalization measures (*The Economist* 2001a). Developed country tariffs, quotas, and NTBs have lowered LDC export net earnings by more than $100 billion a year (Todaro and Smith 2003). The wealthy countries give six times as much to their own farmers as they do to the world's poor. Yet, half the people in LDCs – three-fourths in the least developed countries – are dependent on agriculture.

Brazil for example claims to have one of most efficient agricultural sectors in the world. Yet, import quotas limit Brazil's access to US markets. In the EU, sugar beet subsidies keep Brazilian commodities out of African countries. The developed countries also use "sanitary barriers" to keep Brazilian tropical fruits out of their markets. For Brazil, the Uruguay Round was a lot of lofty rhetoric that added up to "do as we say, not as we do," leaving major trade barriers still standing. Brazil claims that it accepts globalization, but that it cannot be victimized by special rules or massive subsidies that maintain inefficient production in the developed countries or perpetuate ever more asymmetrical gains for the developed countries.

Developed country export subsidies also make it tough for LDCs to market their commodities and textile products (Oxfam 2002). The World Bank estimates that eliminating tariff peaks, defined as tariff rates above 15 per cent that apply to about 5 per cent of developed country imports from all LDCs and 10 per cent from the least developed nations, could yield $500 billion in additional income to LDCs over a ten-year period.

The "Like Minded Group" of India, Pakistan, Egypt, Malaysia, and others is also opposed to a new AoA until Uruguay Round commitments are dealt with and argue that the developed nations are not doing enough to follow through on the deals they made with LDCs in previous negotiations (*The Economist* 2001a). Many LDCs, along with Japan, South Korea, and others, also want to tighten WTO rules to prevent protectionist misuse of anti-dumping laws, a tool the US Congress likes to use to counter competitive LDCs' imports. In fact, sixty US Congressmen told US Trade Representative Zoellick not to touch this legislation (*The Economist* 2001b). But US trade negotiators fear that LDCs, including China, India, South Africa, and Argentina, will likely use the law against US interests.

Many LDCs themselves employ protectionist measures that in some cases depress domestic prices and reduce production incentives for farmers. Many African and Caribbean countries also want to keep preferential access to developed markets. India is worried that cutting tariffs on agricultural goods could harm its rural economy, which is why many LDCs want more time to adjust to new measures when their farmers are unable to compete with imported commodities from other countries or when there are fewer markets for their exports in developed nations.

Conclusion: the future of agricultural trade

This study has explored some of the ways in which agricultural trade shares many of the characteristics of newly traded items, and under the right terms or conditions many states are indeed willing to make deep cuts in protection of their products and to resolve trade issues multilaterally. In many ways, however, the sensitive political, social, and economic interests behind agricultural commodities and products still render them very different from manufactured products, the protection of which is much easier to reduce. As the case of the Uruguay Round demonstrated, WTO members supported an agreement that produced some new trade rules but only *began* the process of reducing agricultural protection.

Today, many LDCs feel that the Uruguay Round did not benefit them enough and that once again the focus of new trade talks is too much on potential gains and not enough on the results of past agreements. The Doha Round could conclude as the Uruguay Round did with an eleventh-hour agreement on agriculture that frees up officials to reach a series of agreements on other trade issues. On the other hand many pundits caution that because of the voting structure in the WTO the developed countries will have to do more to sell trade liberalization to developing nations. Failure to arrive at a new accord for agriculture undermines not only the Doha Round but also the WTO and free trade policy itself.

Despite support for economic liberal trade policies on other issues, efforts to decrease agricultural trade protection in multilateral trade negotiations are likely to encounter strong resistance based on a number of conditions unrelated to any particular state proposal. Many high-income countries such as the USA, EU, and Japan, and LDCs including India, Brazil, and South Korea, feel they have reached the "bottom of the barrel" when it comes to reducing protection. Slowed economic growth and recession pressure state officials to support not only agriculture but any number of industrial products. In an increasingly protectionist climate WTO members are also under constant pressure to balance or reconcile trade liberalizations with a variety of other (non-trade) objectives. In a recent study by the Carnegie Endowment favoring drastic cuts in agricultural protection some pro free trade experts recommended that states have the flexibility to adopt temporary or limited compensatory policies in the case of hardships and threats to important societal values and institutions (Orden *et al.* 2002). Of course what constitutes the *legitimate* needs of LDCs or others negatively affected by trade liberalization is very much a political matter to be decided by member states.

Other difficulties include the split in big business and labor unions over the effects of globalization and who can no longer be counted on to push for trade liberalization. Still another issue is the growing suspicion of trade liberalization as a collective objective WTO members are willing to pursue on its merits alone. Since the Seattle ministerial meeting many protestors but also state officials and academics have become increasingly critical of the results – or lack thereof – of WTO, IMF, and World Bank economic liberal policies.

Finally, multilateral trade negotiations do not exist in a political vacuum; quite often trade is a means states use to deal with much broader issues or priorities. In the case of agriculture trade policy mercantilists win the day analytically to the extent they remind us that economic liberal policies are not the norm of international political economy. Rather, the degree to which economic liberal goals or objectives are achieved reflects the willingness of state officials to pursue common ends, make deals related to cost and benefit trade-offs, and adjust to those agreements. As long as nation-states are the major actors in the international system, interdependence will generate incentives for states to cooperate but also not to cooperate with one another. No wonder many states pursue bilateral and regional agreements with other states while simultaneously participating in multilateral negotiations.

Notes

1 I would like to thank my students Elizabeth Perry and Chris Gulugian-Taylor for research assistance on this version of the chapter.
2 Import substitution policies are efforts to stimulate domestic industries by limiting imports and helping domestic industries produce those or similar products.
3 In the Uruguay Round the Cairns group was made up of Australia, Argentina, Brazil, Canada, Chile, Colombia, Hungary, Indonesia, Malaysia, New Zealand, Paraguay, the Philippines, Thailand, and Uruguay. By the Doha Round, Bolivia, Costa Rica, Guatemala, and South Africa had joined the coalition while Hungary left in preparation for joining the EU, for a new total of seventeen members.

Bibliography

Balaam, D.N. and Veseth, M. (2001) *Introduction to International Political Economy*, 2nd edn, Upper Saddle River, NJ: Prentice Hall.

Bello, W. (1994) "Global economic counterrevolution: how economic warfare devastates the South," in K. Danaher (ed.), *50 Years is Enough: the cases against the World Bank and IMF*, Boston: South End Press.

Brooks, J. and Cahill, C. (2001) "Why agricultural trade liberalization matters," *The OECD Observer*, Paris, November.

Diakosavvas, D. (2002) "The Uruguay Round agreement on agriculture in practice: how open are OECD markets?" in M. Ingco (ed.), *Agriculture, Trade, and the WTO: creating a trading environment for development*, Washington, DC.

Grant, W. (1997) *The Common Agricultural Policy*, New York: St. Martin's Press.

Gunnell, B. (2002) "US hits the poor," *New Statesman* 131, April 20: 14.

Honma, M. (1993) "Japan's agricultural policy and protection growth," in T. Ito and A. Krueger (eds), *Trade and Protection*, Chicago: University of Chicago Press.

Krebs, K. and Lehman, A. (1996) "Control of the world's food supply," in J. Mander and E. Goldsmith (eds), *The Case Against the Global Economy: and a turn toward the local*, San Francisco: Sierra Club Books.

Lappe, F.M., Collins, J., and Rosset, P. (1998) *World Hunger: twelve myths*, 2nd edn, New York: Grove Press.

Orden, D., Kaukaab, R., and Diaz-Bonilla, E. (2002) "Liberalizing agricultural trade and developing countries," Issue brief, Washington, DC: Carnegie Endowment for International Peace.

Oxfam (2002) "Boxing match in agricultural trade," Oxfam Policy Paper, November.

Paarlberg, R. (1997) "Agricultural policy reform and the Uruguay Round: synergistic linkage in a two-level game?" *International Organization* 51: 413–444.

Polanyi, K. (2001) *The Great Transformation: the political and economic origins of our time*, 2nd edn, Boston: Beacon Press.

Schalch, K. (2002) "Worldwide agricultural subsidies and how they affect Third World countries," National Public Radio, November 22.

Schott, J. (1994) *The Uruguay Round: an assessment*, Washington, DC: Institute for International Economics.

Steger, M. (2002) *Globalism: the new market ideology*, Boulder, CO: Rowman & Littlefield.

Stern, N. (2002) "Remove these trade barriers," *The International Herald Tribune* December 19, available HTTP:
   <http://www.iht.com/ihtsearch.php?id=80720&owner=(IHT)&date=20030120033401> (accessed 21 July 2003).

Stiglitz, J. (2002) *Globalization and its Discontents*, New York: W.W. Norton.

Swinbank, A. and Tanner, C. (1996) *Farm Policy and Trade Conflict*, Ann Arbor, MI: University of Michigan Press.

The Economist (2001a) "Playing games with prosperity," 26 July. Available HTTP:
   <http://www.economist.com/displaystory.cfm?story_id=709533> (accessed 21 July 2003).

The Economist (2001b) "Seeds sown for future growth," 15 November. Available HTTP:
   <http://www.economist.com/displaystory.cfm?story_id=863838> (accessed 21 July 2003).

The Economist (2003a) "Deadlocked in Doha," 27 March. Available HTTP:
   <http://www.economist.com/displaystory.cfm?story_id=1667266> (accessed 21 July 2003).

The Economist (2003b) "The Doha squabble," 27 March. Available HTTP:
   <http://www.economist.com/displaystory.cfm?story_id=1666610> (accessed 21 July 2003).

Tangermann, S. (1994) "An assessment of the agreement on agriculture," in *The New World Trading System*, Paris: OECD.

Todaro, M. and Smith, S. (2003) *Economic Development*, Boston: Addison-Wesley.

WTO (2003) *Phase 1: Developing Countries*. Available HTTP:
   <http://www.wto.org/english/tratop_e/agric_e/negs_bkgrnd09_develop_e.htm> (accessed 30 June 2003).

Zoellick, R. (2002) "Unleashing the trade winds," *The Economist* 5 December: 27–29.

Key readings

Bello, W. (1994) "Global economic counterrevolution: how economic warfare devastates the South," in K. Danaher (ed.), *50 Years is Enough: the cases against the World Bank and IMF*, Boston: South End Press.

Grant, W. (1997) *The Common Agricultural Policy*, New York: St. Martin's Press.

Gunnell, B. (2002) "US hits the poor," *New Statesman* 131, April 20: 14.

Josling, T. (1993) "Multilateralism: a constraint on unilateralism and regionalism in agricultural trade," *American Journal of Agricultural Economics* 75: 803–809.

Lappe, F.M., Collins, J., and Rosset, P. (1998) *World Hunger: twelve myths*, 2nd edn, New York: Grove Press.

Oxfam (2002) "Boxing match in agricultural trade," Oxfam Policy Paper, November.

Steger, M. (2002) *Globalism: the new market ideology*, Boulder, CO: Rowman & Littlefield.

Todaro, M. and Smith, S. (2003) *Economic Development*, Boston: Addison-Wesley.

Useful websites

www.ceip.org (Carnegie Endowment for International Peace).
www.oxfam.org.uk (Oxfam).
www.worldbank.org (World Bank).
www.wto.org (World Trade Organization).

12 Trading ideas

The politics of intellectual property

Ann Capling

Summary

One of the most contentious areas of international trade politics concerns the regulation of intellectual property rights. This chapter explores the origins of the WTO agreement on Trade-Related Aspects of Intellectual Property Rights (TRIPs). It explains how a strong global regime to protect and enforce intellectual property came about, despite the lack of an international consensus on the social or economic benefits of the intellectual property protection. A case study on access to life-saving drugs shows how the TRIPs agreement has made developing countries worse off and exacerbated global inequity.

One of the most astonishing outcomes of the Uruguay Round was the inclusion of a new multilateral code governing trade-related aspects of intellectual property, the so-called TRIPs agreement. Certainly the US negotiators who spearheaded the drive to include intellectual property within the auspices of the General Agreement on Tariffs and Trade (GATT) had not anticipated the scope and nature of the final TRIPs agreement. Unlike the GATT itself, which prescribes a set of rules and norms for trade in goods which each Contracting Party is free to implement in its domestic laws as it sees fit, the new TRIPs agreement actually requires members of the WTO to harmonize their legal and regulatory systems in matters concerning intellectual property rights.

This represents a far greater incursion on national sovereignty than has ever been the case in past multilateral trade negotiations, and it represents the globalization of intellectual property rights at a level that benefits only the USA and the European Union, at least for the immediate future. In that sense, it poses a real challenge to the WTO's capacity to maintain the 'embedded liberal compromise', which has been a strength of the multilateral trade system since 1947 (Ruggie 1983). This compromise allowed countries to maintain welfare states whilst allowing for the progressive liberalization of international trade. Moreover, the theoretical rationale for the new TRIPs regime is highly contentious, and its inclusion represents the triumph of powerful economic interests rather than the measured consideration of costs and benefits within the global trade system. Indeed, as this chapter will demonstrate, the debate over intellectual property rights is characterized by competing normative positions, few of which are grounded in either economic theory or empirically demonstrable outcomes. As a result, it is possible that the new TRIPs regime will simply enhance the economic benefits accruing to the holders of intellectual property rights while imposing new and greater economic and social costs for many others.

What are intellectual property rights?

Intellectual property is a somewhat abstract concept which encompasses ideas and images, sounds and symbols, words and music, text and designs, formulae and blueprints. The rationale for intellectual property rights is that most forms of intellectual property have the characteristics of a public good – that is, their use cannot be limited to those who incur the initial cost of its creation. Without a way to prevent 'free-riding' (the unauthorized or uncompensated use of intellectual property), there would be no economic incentive for individuals to create intellectual property. This is the 'market failure' argument for intellectual property rights which sees the creation of intellectual property as purely the outcome of material, instrumental and rational self-interest. Without reward, there would be no incentive to create intellectual property. Moreover, society would suffer from the loss of benefits derived from the creation of intellectual property, whether that be films or computer software or drugs.

This reward/incentive argument is typically used by pharmaceutical companies which claim that they would not develop new drugs if other companies could simply copy the formula and sell an identical product at a lower price, without having incurred the initial research and development costs. Hence the use of patent protection which gives drug companies exclusive control over their new drugs for a set period of time, during which they can recoup the millions of dollars invested in the initial costs of research, development, conducting trials and marketing.

There are many forms of intellectual property rights which can be divided into two main categories: industrial property rights and copyright. Industrial property including novel ideas, inventions, ornamental designs on functional objects, packaging, emblems and logos is protected by *patents*, *trademarks* and *registered designs*. Literary, artistic and musical works are protected by *copyright*. Unlike industrial property rights which protect ideas, copyright protects only the concrete expression of an idea, as might be embodied in a film, a CD, a book or a photograph. Other forms of intellectual property rights include *integrated circuits* which protect semiconductor chips, *plant breeders' rights* which protect some biotechnological processes and products, *moral rights* which assert a creator's right to have some control over the use of his/her artistic, musical or literary work, and *trade secrets*. All intellectual property rights give the holder of the right control over the use of the product. In effect this is a monopoly right which enables the person or firm which holds the IPRs to determine the distribution and price of the product. All of these rights can be sold, traded or licensed in return for royalties being paid to the holder of the right.

National approaches to IPRs

IPRs have traditionally been the domain of national legislation. Because of the monopoly nature of IPRs, considerations of social welfare and the public interest must be balanced against the private monopoly which is bestowed by the IPRs on the property holder. For instance, pharmaceutical companies might be tempted to profiteer from their exclusive rights to manufacture and distribute a new life-saving drug. For that reason, governments limit the monopoly power of drug patents by setting expiration dates on a patent, or by creating a competitive market through compulsory licensing requirements, or by not recognizing patent rights at all. The wide variations in national regimes for IPRs depend on many factors including, most obviously, a nation's economic and industrial structure, its national development objectives and its comparative advantage in trade.

Generally speaking this has meant that IPRs have been weaker in poorer nations which have been unwilling or unable to underwrite the high cost of patent-protected drugs, chemicals and technology, and in nations which are imitators rather than innovators of technology. As Trebilcock and Howse (1995: 251) note:

> A country where innovation is not a major source of economic activity and growth is likely to choose, on balance, a less stringent intellectual property regime than would a country whose economy is highly dependent on innovation. From this perspective, there is nothing suspect or unreasonable with the preference of many developing countries for a relatively lax system of intellectual property rights.

Indeed Deardorff (1990) and Grossman and Helpman (1991) have argued that forcing the developing countries to increase intellectual property protection may reduce global welfare overall.

Cultural and legal traditions also influence a nation's IPR regime. For instance, nations which are not heir to a Western European or British legal tradition, which asserted the primacy of private individual rights over public collective rights, are less likely to have a strong system to protect intellectual property. Moreover, the registration and enforcement of IPRs is a resource-intensive activity that requires high levels of technical and legal expertise. In that sense, the willingness of national governments to recognize and enforce IPRs depends to a great degree on the administrative capacity and sophistication of the state and the judicial system.

Finally, differences in national systems to protect intellectual property can also be attributed to the relative strength of domestic interest groups. Thus in many countries, copyright support for literary, artistic and musical works, film and software tends to be stronger than patent protection for industrial property and technology. This is likely due to domestic pressure from associations representing writers, artists, musicians and film makers. In India for instance, home to the world's biggest film industry and a highly competitive computer software industry, copyright protection is quite strong. On the other hand, as a net importer of technology, India's patent protection has traditionally been quite weak.

A similar situation has developed in the USA. Now the international champion of strong IPRs, the USA had until recently a weak regime for the protection of copyright. US publishers freely reproduced and sold books by foreign authors without paying royalties to either the author or their foreign publisher. In addition, US law prevented the import of English language literary material, written by a US citizen or resident, which was not manufactured in the USA or Canada. This weak copyright protection was motivated by the desire to protect the US publishing industry against competition from cheaper imported books (Benko 1987: 6–7).

Although IPRs remained within the realm of national legal systems, since the late nineteenth century, there have been concerted moves by national governments to create legal and institutional frameworks to foster international recognition of IPRs. Since then, several international agreements have been established which create international disciplines for the protection of intellectual property. These include the Paris Convention for the Protection of Industrial Property (1883) which protects patents and trademarks, the Berne Convention for the Protection of Literary and Artistic Works (1886), the Universal

Copyright Convention (UCC) of 1952 and the Rome Convention for the Protection of Performers, Producers of Phonograms and Broadcasting Organizations (1961). With the exception of the UCC which is administered by the United Nations Educational, Scientific and Cultural Organization (UNESCO), these agreements are administered by the World Intellectual Property Organization (WIPO).

Established in 1967, WIPO has been a specialized agency of the United Nations since 1974. Signatories to any of these conventions are required to accord *national treatment*, that is the same legal protections and remedies to foreigners as to their own nationals in matters concerning IPRs. However, membership in these conventions is voluntary and as a result coverage has been quite uneven.[1] Moreover, the conventions do not require signatories to harmonize their IPRs at a particular benchmark level, and each member country is allowed to determine its own level of protection and its own enforcement mechanisms. Of course it was this 'relatively loose international' system which made it possible for the rich industrialized nations like the USA and Japan to achieve parity with those on the cutting edge of a particular technology (Ringo 1994: 122–123). Indeed at least part of Japan's economic 'miracle' was due to its ability to imitate and then improve upon US innovations.

IPRs on the international trade agenda

The establishment of WIPO was an important step in the development of a framework for international cooperation on IPRs. However, in addition to the problem of uneven coverage, there was no scope within WIPO or its individual conventions to consider trade-related aspects of intellectual property, an issue of increasing importance to the world's leading exporters of intellectual property, especially in the USA and Western Europe. During the 1970s, the manufacturers of luxury items such as expensive watches and designer apparel were concerned about the manufacture of cheap counterfeits, largely in South-East Asian countries which had few domestic laws to prevent such activities. Pirated cassette tapes and videos were also a problem.

This led to US attempts during the Tokyo Round of multilateral trade negotiations (1973–1979) to have IPRs strengthened within the GATT, especially in the area of counterfeit goods. But these efforts failed largely because of the opposition of many of the developing countries which argued that intellectual property issues did not properly belong within the purview of the GATT. From its perspective, WIPO was a UN agency and was perceived to be more open and sympathetic to the perspective of developing nations than the GATT, an institution that tended to privilege the trade interests of the rich industrialized countries. In addition, WIPO already had a considerable track record in providing financial and technical assistance to nations that wished to develop their own intellectual property regimes. But from the US perspective, WIPO was neither an adequate nor an appropriate vehicle to secure the IPRs of US companies.

By the early 1980s, intellectual property had become a trade issue of considerable importance to many rich industrialized countries. As these nations began to lose older, labour-intensive manufacturing to the newly industrializing countries, they sought to locate their future trade competitiveness in technological innovation and research-intensive activities. Areas targeted for growth included pharmaceuticals, chemicals, microelectronics, telecommunications and information technology, biotechnology, medical and scientific instruments, entertainment products such as videos and CDs, and high-value-added luxury items such as wine, fashion apparel and perfume.

Just as the impetus to include trade in services in the Uruguay Round agenda came almost entirely from the US government acting on behalf of US corporations so too did the push for matters relating to trade in intellectual property. Indeed, this was an area where powerful domestic industry interests had been very active in the lead-up to the round (Drahos 1995).

At the forefront of lobbying efforts were the pharmaceutical, information technology, entertainment and clothing industries which commissioned dozens of reports to demonstrate how US firms lost billions of dollars a year due to infringements and inadequate protection of intellectual property. One study by the US International Trade Commission claimed that in 1982 alone, 131,000 US jobs were lost due to foreign counterfeiting of US consumer and industrial goods. Other studies claimed that violations of IPRs cost US industry from $30 to $60 billion each year (Benko 1987: 21; Gadbaw and Richards 1988), although many experts were sceptical of the accuracy of these figures (Maskus 1990: 120). Figures of this magnitude spurred the Reagan Administration to adopt aggressive action to secure improved protection for the IPRs of US industry. As in other areas of its trade policy, the US government adopted a three-pronged approach of unilateral, bilateral and multilateral initiatives to pursue its agenda on IPRs.

Unilateral and bilateral initiatives

In the area of unilateral action, the US government had recourse to Section 337 of the *US Tariff Act of 1930* which allows the seizure of any imports which are alleged to contravene US intellectual property laws. Scope for unilateral measures was considerably enhanced with the passage of Section 301 of the *Trade Act of 1974* which allowed the US Administration to take action against other countries which were deemed to have inadequate intellectual property protection. This was further strengthened with the passage of the *Trade and Tariff Act of 1984* which gave the US President the right to withdraw preferential tariffs or impose punitive tariffs on any goods imported from countries which, in the view of the USA, had inadequate IPR regimes. Under this law, punitive action was taken against Brazil, Mexico, the Republic of Korea and Taiwan.

In 1988 the unilateral thrust of US trade legislation was extended with the *Omnibus Trade and Competitiveness Act*. In particular, the 'Special 301' section required the United States Trade Representative (USTR) to identify all nations which have intellectual property regimes that are deemed to be objectionable to US trade interests. The threat of unilateral trade sanctions was used to extract policy concessions from 'target' countries, and the USTR's 'priority watch list' included developing countries such as Brazil and India, as well as industrialized countries such as Australia, Canada and Norway.

In addition to these acts of 'aggressive unilateralism', the USA also undertook a variety of bilateral initiatives to secure intellectual property protection for US exporters and foreign investors. In the late 1980s, it completed bilateral agreements with Japan and the EU which provided copyright-style protection for semiconductor chips. It is worth noting that these unilateral and bilateral actions were not aimed at promoting a new international multilateral regime for the protection of intellectual property. Indeed, the general effect of these initiatives was to distort international trade further in a way that favoured the USA over its competitors. For instance, Korea responded to US pressure not by improving its system of IPRs, but by granting protection to US technology, while denying that same protection to others (Mody 1990: 205).

Multilateral initiatives: the Uruguay Round

The inclusion of IPRs in the Uruguay Round agenda came very late, practically on the eve of the meeting at Punta del Este which launched the round in 1986. In fact, the US government was divided over the wisdom of trying to include IPRs in the new round, which was already overloaded with serious and longstanding issues such as agriculture and textiles, as well as the contentious new issue of trade in services. Moreover, intellectual property experts were reluctant to support a change in policy forum from the WIPO to the GATT. There was also debate over whether it would be better to pursue IPRs through the negotiations to liberalize trade-related investment measures (TRIMs). In these negotiations, countries could have agreed to strengthen particular aspects of their intellectual property protection, thus enabling US companies to undertake foreign investment knowing that their patent rights in these markets would be secure. Despite the differences of approach, the growing importance of intellectual property in international trade and investment could not be ignored.

Prior to the Uruguay Round, there were few GATT rules concerning trade in intellectual property. Articles IX and XX recognized the right of contracting parties to prevent imports of counterfeit goods, but GATT rules did not establish a clear set of binding IPRs. In effect, the TRIPs negotiations were beginning from a blank slate and, as such, the negotiating mandate established at the beginning of the Uruguay Round was both broad and general. Specifically, the TRIPs negotiators were required to consider 'the need to promote effective and adequate protection of IPRs' in order to reduce distortions and obstacles to international trade (quoted in Croome 1995: 130).

From the outset, there were deep divisions within the TRIPs negotiating group. In one corner was the USA, which was pushing for a new and comprehensive agreement on intellectual property. Such an agreement would establish minimum standards for the protection and enforcement of a wide variety of IPRs including patents, trademarks, trade secrets, semiconductor layouts and copyright. In effect, the USA wanted all other GATT members to raise their levels of intellectual property protection up to US levels. In addition the US proposal included provisions for a dispute settlement mechanism and strong penalties including 'cross retaliation' (the withdrawal of other trade benefits) for GATT members which violated or failed to live up to any aspect of a new agreement. The US position was supported, with varying degrees of enthusiasm, by other members of the Organization for Economic Cooperation and Development (OECD). The strongest support came from the EU and Japan, where powerful domestic lobbies, working in collaboration with the intellectual property lobby in the USA, pressured their governments to take a strong stand on TRIPs (Sell 1999).

In the other corner were the G10 countries, a group of influential non-OECD nations led by Argentina, Brazil, Egypt and India. This group was willing to negotiate a stronger GATT discipline to prohibit trade in counterfeit goods, which the USA had pushed for during the 1970s. But these nations objected to any broader discussion of intellectual property, arguing that IPRs were properly the domain of the WIPO not the GATT. Indeed, Brazil and India argued that IPRs were by their very nature trade restricting and anti-competitive, the implication being that they violated the fundamental rules and norms of the GATT. If that claim sounds capricious, it is worth considering their objections in some detail.

The case against strengthening IPRs

The main objections to strengthening intellectual property protection are based on pragmatism and principle. There are social and economic dimensions to these arguments as well. For instance, many nations have traditionally given little or no patent protection to pharmaceuticals on the grounds that patent protection for drugs will inflate prices to a level beyond the reach of many of their citizens. Argentina, Brazil, India, Mexico, the Republic of Korea and Taiwan are all examples of countries having intellectual property regimes aimed primarily at promoting (rather than restricting) competition in their domestic markets for prescription drugs in order to keep prices down. Apart from the social welfare rationale for this practice, there is a strong ethical dimension as well. In 1982 Indian Prime Minister Indira Ghandi argued that 'The idea of a better-ordered world is one in which medical discoveries will be free of patents and there will be no profiteering from life and death' (quoted in Braga 1990: 175). While this sort of public good argument has been associated with developing countries, it is hardly their exclusive preserve. Until recently, Italy had no patent protection on drugs, while Canada had compulsory licensing laws which forced competition on the pharmaceutical companies before patent protection expired.

Another argument against strong IPR regimes pertains to the issue of technology transfer. Patent owners may place onerous conditions on the use of new technology, or may simply refuse to license new technology at all in order to preserve their monopolistic position. In this way, instead of promoting innovation (the market failure argument for intellectual property protection), patents can actually slow the dissemination of new ideas, basic knowledge and technological advancement. This has been a longstanding area of concern for the importers of technology, especially for industrializing countries which have found their development objectives thwarted by the restrictive practices of foreign investors (Raghavan 1990: 133). Thus, as part of a strategy to promote their own technological development, many newly industrializing countries offered little patent protection to foreign companies, or used the threat of compulsory licensing as a tool to ensure that these companies put their intellectual property to good use.

A related argument refutes the claim that IPRs are necessary to promote research, and argues instead that they can inhibit research and the diffusion of knowledge, thus undermining the prospect of socially beneficial innovation. For instance, in the late 1970s inventors engaged in trying to develop personal computers openly shared and exchanged information on a regular basis. Once it became possible to commercialize these ideas and designs, this information-sharing gave way to secrecy, which led to costly duplication of research and other sub-optimal outcomes (Branscomb 1990: 52).

Another area of considerable concern, especially to South American and African countries, was the debate about the patentability of biological life. Traditionally biological processes and products have not been included in the domain of IPRs. However, as the global leader in the development of biotechnology, the USA (along with Japan and Switzerland) was keen to secure patent protection for processes and products involving genetic manipulation. This raised the spectre of foreign corporations raiding the forests and jungles of the poor nations in order to 'discover' and patent the genetic material of indigenous flora and fauna. Apart from any ethical considerations, 'biopiracy' would greatly undermine the national sovereignty over territory and resources.[2] Farmers in poor agricultural countries also feared that this would mean that they would be forced to pay royalties on the seeds of their plants and the offspring of their animals.

The TRIPs negotiations

Much of the academic literature depicts the TRIPs negotiations as a battle between 'developed' and 'developing' countries, the 'industrial countries' versus the 'Third World', the

'North' versus the 'South'. These dichotomies tend to gloss over some of the fundamental difficulties and issues at stake. To be sure, the most vociferous opponents of a strong and comprehensive TRIPs agreement were nations from Latin America, Africa and the Indian subcontinent. In that sense, it would be much more accurate to characterize the divide in the TRIPs negotiations as one which pitted OECD countries against the rest. However, as the negotiations proceeded, cracks and fissures emerged within both groups. Some newly industrializing countries (Mexico, South Korea, Singapore, Malaysia and Thailand) began to distance themselves from the G10 nations. This was due partly to unilateral pressure from the USA, but these countries also recognized that future foreign investment in their own high-technology sectors depended on improved levels of patent and copyright protection. But even among the OECD nations, as the negotiations moved from broad statements of principle to more specific concerns, sharp differences began to emerge.

The OECD nations were divided over issues pertaining to patents and copyright. In particular, the length of patent protection, especially for pharmaceutical drugs, was a long-standing issue that had often united rich and poor nations against the powerful drug companies in the USA and Western Europe. In the TRIPs negotiations, the USA and the EU were seeking the extension of protection on all patentable products and processes to a minimum of twenty years in all countries. By contrast, other OECD countries, together with developing countries, opposed this period, proposing instead that patents expire after fifteen years (twenty for drugs). Another patent issue that pitted the USA against the others concerned US discrimination against foreign patent seekers. US patents are awarded to the 'first-to-invent', whereas in the rest of the world, patent protection is granted on a 'first-to-file' basis. The effect of the 'first-to-invent' rule was to create a US patent system that discriminates against foreigners because US courts will not accept overseas evidence concerning the date of invention. In order to end this discrimination, all nations apart from the USA were seeking to negotiate an obligation that patents would be available without discrimination as to where the inventions were first made.

Another area of dispute that pitted the USA against most other countries related to copyright issues: neighbouring rights, rental rights, moral rights and parallel importation. Long before the Uruguay Round began, there was considerable ill feeling against the USA because of its longstanding refusal to accede to the Berne Convention and its withdrawal from the UCC (it rejoined in 1988). Similarly, during the TRIPs negotiations, there were points of fundamental disagreement between the USA and other countries on many aspects of copyright.

One area of conflict pertained to *neighbouring rights*, which refers to the right of producers, performers and broadcasting organizations to initiate action against pirates. These rights were strongly supported by Japan, the EU, Switzerland, the Nordic countries and Australia, but not the USA. There was disagreement as well with respect to *rental rights*, a copyright owner's right to collect extra royalties to cover the likelihood that his/her computer program, film or CD would be illegally copied. In essence, the USA wanted the recognition of a form of rental rights that would effectively prohibit the commercial rental of copyright material such as CDs. This was opposed by Japan, Australia and other countries which allowed consumers to tape rented music recordings for their own personal use. The issue of *moral rights* also divided the USA from others. Unlike other forms of intellectual property protection, moral rights do not involve issues of financial compensation, and relate instead to the creator's right to preserve the integrity of his/her original work. The USA opposed moral rights on the ground that they were not an economic right and therefore had no place in the TRIPs agreement.

Table 12.1 Illustrative TRIPs cases in the WTO

Year/date of settlement	*Complainant*	*Defendant and issue*	*Outcome*
18/08/2000	EU	Canada – Pricing of pharmaceuticals and patent protection against generic drugs	Canada required to amend patent legislation to offer greater protection for named brand drugs
19/07/2001	USA	Brazil – Parallel importation and compulsory licensing of AIDS drugs	WTO case withdrawn
26/03/2001	USA	Greece and European Communities – Enforcement of intellectual property rights for motion pictures and television programmes	Legislation developed that provides for the closure of television stations that broadcast pirated material
07/02/2001	Brazil	USA – Brazil detected several discriminatory elements in the US Patents Code	Brazil requested consultations in Geneva. No further action as of July 2003
11/12/1998	USA	Sweden – Measures affecting the enforcement of intellectual property rights	WTO case withdrawn. Sweden developed new legislation granting judicial authorities greater powers to investigate suspected TRIPs infringements
07/03/1997	USA	Pakistan – Patent protection for pharmaceutical and agricultural chemical products	WTO case withdrawn after Pakistan agreed to amend legislation

Source: World Trade Organization, Index of Disputes Issues. Available HTTP: <http://www.wto.org/english/tratop_e/dispu_e/dispu_subjects_index_e.htm#bkmk137> (accessed 30 July 2003).

The TRIPs agreement

As the previous section shows, no country supported the radical US proposals on intellectual property protection. For that reason, it is all the more astonishing that such a comprehensive TRIPs agreement was eventually concluded. The key aspects of the final agreement include the extension of basic GATT norms and principles. This meant that all WTO members had to:

- afford the same level of intellectual property protection to foreigners as accorded to nationals (national treatment);
- accord the same legal protections to all other WTO members on a non-discriminatory basis (most favoured nation);
- notify the TRIPs Council of their domestic laws and regulations concerning intellectual property; and
- respond to requests for information from the Council and other members (transparency).

The TRIPs agreement also establishes minimum standards of protection and requires all WTO members to establish mechanisms for the domestic enforcement of IPRs. Finally, the WTO's dispute settlement mechanisms apply to disputes over trade-related aspects of intellectual property. (See also Table 12.1.) Trebilcock and Howse (1995: 270) contend that this constitutes 'a largely unprecedented degree of control by an international regime over domestic civil and administrative procedures'.

There can be little doubt that the emerging WTO regime for intellectual property protection has been weighted heavily in favour of US interests. Issues of concern to other OECD countries (moral rights, rental rights, neighbouring rights and parallel importation) were either resolved largely in favour of the USA, or were held over for future negotiations. Only a few concessions were granted to developing countries, and these related mostly to timelines for implementation. For instance, developing countries were given five years to comply with the TRIPs agreement (extended to ten years in the case of patents for pharmaceuticals). Plants and animals were excluded from patentability, largely due to the EU's opposition. But the patentability of plant *varieties* was affirmed and the patentability of life continues to be a contentious issue. Finally, least developed countries were exempted entirely from the TRIPs agreement.

In the end, the TRIPs negotiations proved to be less contentious than some of the other difficult areas of the Uruguay Round such as trade in services, subsidies and agriculture. There are a few reasons why this 'new' issue was more easily concluded. First there was the potential in multilateral trade negotiations for issue 'linkages' that were not possible in the WIPO. During the Uruguay Round, countries which otherwise had very little economic or political leverage could make their cooperation in one area of negotiations dependent on progress in another. For instance, the developing countries were able to secure some of their trade objectives in contentious areas such as textiles and agriculture in return for their acquiescence to the TRIPs agreement (Hoekman and Kostecki 1995: 153). The same was true for countries like Australia and Canada which supported TRIPs partly as a trade-off for securing US and EU agreement to reduce the use of domestic and export subsidies in agricultural products. In that sense, one positive outcome from the inclusion of IPRs in the Uruguay Round was that it became more difficult for the USA and the EU to wriggle out of making commitments in regard to the liberalization trade in areas such as textiles and agriculture.

In addition to the linkages factor, many industrialising countries were moving towards a less hostile and more welcoming view of foreign investment. Whether this was due to an ideological shift among governing elites is open to debate, but there were certainly strong pressures on these governments to liberalize their investment and trade restrictions in the global competition to attract foreign investment (Stopford and Strange 1992). In this context, domestic pressure for intellectual property protection tended to come from two different sources.

First there were foreign-owned companies whose profitability was being undermined by inadequate IPRs; their influence increased as governments began to place more value on foreign investment. The other source of pressure came from exporters who feared retaliation from the USA as punishment for their 'inadequate' intellectual property laws. In particular, export interests in Brazil, Mexico, South Korea, Singapore and Taiwan lobbied their governments to strengthen their intellectual property laws (Gadbaw and Richards 1988: 16).

Finally, most countries were of the view that in the face of the continuing threat of further 'Section 301' actions by the USA, it was preferable to have a multilateral regime for IPRs. Developing countries in particular expected that participating in the TRIPs regime would protect them from future acts of aggressive unilateralism by the USA (Correa 2000: 11).

Case study: TRIPs, developing countries and access to pharmaceutical drugs

Like the GATT, which had been of great benefit to the exporters of manufactured goods, the TRIPs agreement will bestow great benefits on the exporters of intellectual property. But in the same way that the GATT has been less able to promote the interests of agricultural exporters and developing countries, it is likely the TRIPs agreement will be less accommodating of the needs of developing countries, which are net importers of intellectual property (Dhanjee and Chazournes 1990). In the immediate future, developing countries attempting to comply with the TRIPs agreement are likely to encounter many adjustment problems. While there may well be long-term benefits in terms of enhanced investment and export opportunities, in the short term many nations will be significantly worse off. It is not a case of governments, firms and consumers now being forced to pay the *market* price for drugs, food, books and technology. Rather, they will now be forced to pay the *monopoly* price. In particular, developing countries will be much worse off as wealth is transferred from their consumers to 'capital-exporters, technology-leaders and service-providers' (Nayyar 1997). This is a striking asymmetry or, in the words of prominent trade economist Jagdish Bhagwati (1994: 112), a zero-sum game 'with the majority of developing countries losing and many developed countries gaining, according to most impartial observers among the economists'.

In addition, many countries are bound to encounter high costs and great difficulties in developing their legal and administrative systems to the point that they meet their new obligations. As Ostry (1997: 190) notes: 'Compliance with these extremely detailed obligations will be very demanding for countries with legal systems or traditions that differ significantly from the American model.'

An area of particular concern is the impact of TRIPs on public health, and especially access to prescription drugs in developing countries. Prior to TRIPs, many developing countries established regulatory regimes aimed at ensuring affordability and equitable access to medicines. This was typically achieved through price control mechanisms, public subsidies and/or the promotion of generic competition. India's intellectual property legislation, prior to TRIPs, provides a good example of the latter: its prohibition of patents on prescription drugs resulted in not only the development of a strong domestic pharmaceutical industry, but more importantly from a public health and social welfare perspective, significantly lower prices for drugs. However, as developing countries like India move to implement their TRIPs obligations, the introduction of patents will have a detrimental impact on both access and affordability of drugs, while reaping profits for US and EU-based pharmaceutical companies (Pharma).

On the face of it, the TRIPs agreement provides a number of safeguards and exemptions to promote public policy goals such as access to life-saving drugs (Cullett 2003: 145–148). For instance, Article 8 of the agreement acknowledges the right of governments to adopt measures necessary to protect public health, including measures to override patents. But Legrain (2002: 260) notes that Pharma and the US Administration have adopted 'heavy handed intimidation whenever governments have tried to make use of this flexibility'. Brazil, Thailand and the Dominican Republic have all been subject to such bullying tactics, but the most notorious example of this kind of intimidation occurred in 2001 when thirty-nine drug companies challenged South African legislation that was aimed at reducing the cost of drug treatments for HIV/AIDS.

Throughout Sub-Saharan Africa, the HIV/AIDS epidemic has reached plague proportions, and the high cost of anti-retroviral drugs means that effective treatment is beyond the means of all but a tiny minority. Pharma argued that the South African legislation, which would allow parallel importation and compulsory licensing of anti-retroviral drugs, constituted a breach of its TRIPs obligations. A transnational campaign, spearheaded by Oxfam, Médecins Sans Frontières and a number of other non-governmental organizations, health activists and consumer rights groups, eventually forced the drug companies to drop their legal action.

Growing concern about the impact of TRIPs on access to essential medicines led developing countries to adopt a common position at the Doha Ministerial Meeting that launched a new round of WTO negotiations in November 2001. At Doha, WTO members agreed that 'the TRIPs Agreement does not and should not prevent Members from taking measures to promote public health' and affirmed the 'right to protect public health, and in particular, to promote access to medicines for all'.[3] Ironically, just weeks before the Doha meeting, fears of bio-terrorism prompted Washington to threaten to bypass Bayer's patent for the anthrax vaccine Cipro.

So, was US support for the Doha Declaration on TRIPs and Public Health motivated by a new appreciation of the importance of compulsory licensing of drugs to deal with public health crises? Probably not. US support for the declaration was motivated primarily by the need to ensure a successful commencement of the new round of WTO negotiations, and it claims to have 'fended off' attacks on TRIPs at Doha by weakening the language of the declaration (Legrain 2002: 262). More importantly, the declaration remains subject to interpretation by WTO members, and a number of key issues, including the circumstances in which compulsory licensing can be allowed, remain unresolved (Abbott 2002).

Conclusion

In summary, theoretical justifications for IPRs are strongly interest driven and certainly open to debate and contestation. Far from being a strictly individual and instrumental activity, the creation of intellectual property is almost always a highly social act. As Trebilcock and Howse (1995: 249) observe:

> Society provides the context in which creative activity takes place – few inventions or works of art or literature spring fully grown from the inventor's head. They usually depend on education within society, and build on the work of many others.

This understanding of intellectual property is common among many indigenous cultures that view intellectual 'property' as belonging to the community, not to an individual. In this sense, the notion of intellectual property being a 'private right' is problematic. Moreover, the economic rationale for IPRs remains underdeveloped and their inclusion in the Uruguay Round, and the establishment of the TRIPs agreement, represented a significant triumph for powerful corporations from rich countries. And unlike the GATT regime, the norms of reciprocity, mutual advantage and safeguards were pretty much absent from the TRIPs negotiations. Indeed, with respect to IPRs, it was much more a case of 'Just Do It'.

Notes

1   On 1 January 1995, when the TRIPs agreement came into formal legal existence, the Paris Convention had 134 members, the Berne Convention had 114 members and the Rome Convention had only 48 member nations.
2   The Biodiversity Convention, concluded at the Rio Environmental Summit in 1992, affirmed the sovereign right of nations to determine the terms and conditions of access to their own biological resources.
3   Ministerial Conference, Fourth Session, Doha, 9–14 November 2001, WT/MIN(01)/DEC/2, 20 November 2001. This statement can be accessed at the WTO's website at www.wto.org.

Bibliography

Abbott, F.M. (2002) 'The Doha Declaration on the TRIPs agreement and public health: lighting a dark corner at the WTO', *Journal of International Economic Law* 5: 469–505.

Benko, R.P. (1987) *Protecting Intellectual Property Rights*, Washington, DC: The American Enterprise Institute for Public Policy Research.

Bhagwati, J. (1994) 'Commentary', in S.M. Collins and B.P. Bosworth (eds), *The New GATT: implications for the United States*, Washington, DC: Brookings Institution.

Braga, C.A.P. (1990) 'The North-South debate on intellectual property rights', in M.G. Smith (ed.), *Global Rivalry and Intellectual Property: developing Canadian strategies*, Toronto: Institute for Research on Public Policy.

Branscomb, A.W. (1990) 'Computer software: protecting the crown jewels of the information economy', in F.W. Rushing and C. Ganz Brown (eds), *Intellectual Property Rights in Science, Technology and Economic Performance: international comparisons*, Boulder, CO: Westview.

Correa, C.M. (2000) *Intellectual Property Rights, the WTO and Developing Countries: the TRIPs agreement and policy options*, London: Zed Books/Third World Network.

Croome, J. (1995) *Reshaping the World Trading System: a history of the Uruguay Round*, Geneva: World Trade Organization.

Cullett, P. (2003) 'Patents and medicines: the relationship between TRIPs and the human right to health', *International Affairs* 79: 139–160.

Deardorff, A.V. (1990) 'Should patent protection be extended to all developing countries?', *World Economy* 13: 497–508.

Dhanjee, R. and de Chazournes, L. (1990) 'Trade-Related Aspects of Intellectual Property Rights (TRIPs): objectives, approaches and basic principles of the GATT and of intellectual property conventions', *Journal of World Trade* 24: 5–15.

Drahos, P. (1995) 'Global property rights in Information: the story of TRIPs at the GATT', *Prometheus* 13: 6–19.

Gadbaw, M.R. and Richards, T.J. (eds) (1998) *Intellectual Property Rights: global consensus, global conflict?* Boulder, CO: Westview.

Grossman, G.M. and Helpman, E. (1991) *Innovation and Growth in the Global Economy*, Cambridge, MA: MIT Press.

Hoekman, B. and Kostecki, M. (1995) *The Political Economy of the World Trading System: from GATT to WTO*, Oxford: Oxford University Press.

Legrain, P. (2002) *Open World: the truth about globalization*, London: Abacus.

Maskus, K.E. (1990) 'Economic analysis of intellectual property rights: domestic and international dimensions', in M.G. Smith (ed.), *Global Rivalry and Intellectual Property: developing Canadian strategies*, Toronto: Institute for Research on Public Policy.

Mody, A. (1990) 'New international environment for intellectual property rights', in F.W. Rushing and C. Ganz Brown (eds), *Intellectual Property Rights in Science, Technology and Economic Performance: international comparisons*, Boulder, CO: Westview.

Nayyar, D. (1997) 'Globalization: the game, the players and the rules', in S.D. Gupta (ed.), *The Political Economy of Globalization*, Boston: Kluwer Academic.

Ostry, S. (1997) *The Post-Cold War Trading System: who's on first?* Chicago: University of Chicago Press.

Raghavan, C. (1990) *Recolonization: GATT, the Uruguay Round & the Third World*, London: Zed Books.

Ringo, F.S. (1994) 'The Trade-Related Aspects of Intellectual Property Rights agreement in the GATT and legal implications for sub-Sahara Africa: prospective policy issues for the World Trade Organization', *Journal of World Trade* 28: 121–139.

Ruggie, J.G. (1983) 'International regimes, transactions, and change: embedded liberalism in the postwar economic order', in S.D. Krasner (ed.), *International Regimes*, Ithaca, NY: Cornell University Press.

Sell, S.K. (1999) 'Multinational corporations as agents of change: the globalization of intellectual property rights', in C.A. Cutler, V. Haufler and T. Porter (eds), *Private Authority and International Affairs*, Albany, NY: SUNY Press.

Stopford, J. and Strange, S. with Henley, J.S. (1992) *Rival States, Rival Firms: competition for World market shares*, Cambridge: Cambridge University Press.

Trebilcock, M.J. and Howse, R. (1995) *The Regulation of International Trade*, London: Routledge.

Key readings

Beier, F.K. and Schricker, G. (eds) (1989) *GATT or WIPO? New Ways in the International Protection of Intellectual Property*, Munich: Max Planck Institute for Foreign and International Patent, Copyright and Competition Law.

Capling, A. (1996) 'The conundrum of intellectual property rights: domestic interests, international commitments and the Australian music industry', *Australian Journal of Political Science* 31: 301–320.

Drahos, P. and Braithwaite, J. (2002) *Information Feudalism*, London: Earthscan.

Sell, S. (1995) 'Intellectual property protection and antitrust in the developing world: crisis, coercion and choice', *International Organization* 49: 315–349.

Stewart, G.R., Tawfik, M.J. and Irish, M. (eds) (1994) *International Trade and Intellectual Property*, Boulder, CO: Westview.

Stewart, T. (ed.) (1993) *The Uruguay Round: a negotiating history*, Deventer and Boston: Kluwer Law and Taxation Publishers.

Watal, J. (2001) *Intellectual Property Rights in the WTO and Developing Countries*, Boston: Kluwer Academic.

Useful websites

www.ictsd.org (International Centre for Trade and Sustainable Development).
www.msf.org (Médecins Sans Frontières).
www.oxfam.org.uk (Oxfam).
www.wto.org (World Trade Organization).

13 Linking competition policy and trade

Chad Damro

Summary

This chapter explores the international overlap between competition policy and trade. The central theme of the chapter is that, due to increasing linkages with trade policy, effective enforcement of competition disciplines requires international cooperation. The chapter investigates bilateral and multilateral efforts of competition regulators to create an international regime for cooperation in competition policy. These efforts emphasize the need for procedural and substantive convergence in national competition policies.

Since the promulgation of the first competition policy – the US Sherman Antitrust Act of 1890 – national competition policies have proliferated with the development of domestic, free-market economies.[1] Today's competition policies include an array of regulatory instruments designed to ensure that firms have opportunities to compete in various markets.[2] These instruments broadly include policies to manage mergers, cartels, monopolies and other forms of business activity that could reduce competition in domestic markets.

Trade and competition policies are undeniably interlinked because the implementation of a national competition policy can limit foreign firms' access to and opportunities in that domestic market and, thus, create significant obstacles to trade. At the same time, as business activity internationalizes, national competition policies must ensure that the activities of trading firms and those engaging in foreign direct investment (FDI) do not undermine fair competition in domestic markets. Therefore, national competition policies and trade policies increasingly intersect and create new political dynamics in business–government relations.

While many national competition policies share fundamental similarities, significant legal differences exist because countries develop their respective competition laws to address the unique characteristics and needs of their domestic markets. These differences can lead to the implementation of national competition policies on internationally oriented business activity in a way that is inconsistent with the economic interests of other states. Such inconsistent implementation of competition policies increases the likelihood that regulatory decisions in competition policy – such as the determination to approve or prohibit a merger – will diverge. Divergences in regulatory decisions in competition policy can lead to very real political disputes that threaten the international economy with destabilizing bilateral trade wars. This reality of internationalizing business activity reveals an urgent need for increased international cooperation to prevent trade disputes arising from divergences in the implementation of competition policy. As the European Commissioner for Competition forcefully stated, 'The globalization of the economy has made it imperative to improve global governance in competition matters' (Monti 2002: 3).

The international community has begun investigating possible ways to increase global governance in competition matters. National competition regulators play an important role in advancing this cooperative agenda because of their shared interest in avoiding divergent competition decisions. By reducing the likelihood of divergent competition decisions, regulators reduce the likelihood that individual competition cases will become politicized. In this manner, the competition regulators pursue dispute prevention in favour of relying on dispute resolution by politicians.

Despite previous and ongoing multilateral discussions on how to enhance dispute prevention, the current international regime in this policy area is characterized by a number of bilateral agreements, primarily between industrialized economies. Nevertheless, the debate over the possible multilateralism of competition policy has recently taken on great significance, as seen in the creation of the International Competition Network in 1999, and the inclusion of competition policy on the agenda of the World Trade Organization's Doha Round of trade negotiations in 2001. Both of these developments reflect an international desire to address the increasing linkages between trade and competition policies as well as the need for procedural and substantive convergence in the implementation of competition policies.

This chapter investigates the current international regime governing competition policy. The central theme of the chapter is that effective enforcement of competition disciplines requires international cooperation. The next section explores the increasing overlap between international competition and trade policy and identifies three ways in which these two policy areas are interlinked. The chapter then analyses current bilateral and multilateral efforts to increase international cooperation in competition policy. While international cooperation is primarily based on bilateral measures, important multilateral initiatives are emerging that may increase convergence in this policy area. The chapter concludes with a summary of the findings and a discussion of the future direction of the debate on international cooperation in competition policy.

Linking competition policy and trade

Competition policy has not always been a matter of highest concern for negotiators intent on creating a liberal trading system. However, competition and trade policies have become remarkably interlinked as trade and investment have increased over the last two decades. The growing linkages between these two policies have contributed significantly to calls for enhanced bilateral and multilateral cooperation in competition policy.

As markets internationalize through increasing trade and investment, national competition policies must increasingly address business activity that simultaneously affects multiple markets and is subject to different national competition and trade laws. Because competition laws are increasingly being applied to this internationally oriented business activity, they are linked and must be reconciled with the priorities of trade policy. In other words, the trade negotiator must ask whether a given competition policy could be impeding trade. The linkages between these two policies can be categorized as three separate types of anticompetitive actions that impede trade (ICPAC 2000: 203–208). Each type of action impedes trade by limiting firms' access to and competitive opportunities in foreign markets.

The first linkage between competition and trade policies results from the actions of firms. Domestic competition laws prohibit a variety of anti-competitive business activities – such as monopolistic and oligopolistic behaviour – that limit or prevent other firms from entering or competing in the domestic market. This type of business activity can dampen overall economic growth by reducing the incentives for such firms to innovate; without viable competitors, they feel little or no pressure to develop new products and services. Ultimately, domestic consumers are harmed because such anti-competitive business activity tends to increase prices and limit consumer choices. Trade and competition policies intersect when such anti-competitive business activity limits the access of *foreign* firms to a given market. For example, monopolistic practices by a single firm can impede trade by limiting the access of foreign firms to its domestic market. Oligopolistic practices (such as cartel agreements to divide a domestic or international market), which may include multiple firms operating in multiple markets, can similarly impede trade by limiting the access of other firms to those markets. In both cases, the business activity in question may require approval by multiple national competition regulators, which necessitates international cooperation in competition policy if divergent decisions are to be avoided.

The second linkage between competition and trade policies results from the actions of governments. The actions of governments can often enhance competitive opportunities for domestic firms while, at the same time, disadvantaging foreign firms. For example, governments may grant formal exemptions to their competition laws, develop policies designed to promote 'national champions', and/or implement their domestic competition policy in a strategic manner that benefits domestic firms. Each of these actions can advantage domestic firms by limiting the market access and reducing the opportunities for foreign firms to compete in that domestic market. Such government actions create obstacles for foreign firms intent on trading in that market and can run counter to international trade rules. When such government actions do run counter to international trade rules, the need for international cooperation in competition policy is equally evident if divergent decisions are to be avoided.

The third linkage between competition and trade policies results from a combination of the actions of firms and governments. Firms may engage in anti-competitive practices (in domestic and/or international markets) that are tolerated by their domestic government. Indeed, governments may even allow or encourage behaviour that has anti-competitive effects and limits market access for foreign firms. For example, governments may enact limitations on FDI and licensing or allow exclusive dealing contracts and other exclusionary practices (ICPAC 2000: 204). Regardless of the intent behind such behaviour, domestic firms may benefit. When domestic firms do take advantage of such government actions – regardless of the firm's intent – their behaviour can disadvantage foreign firms. In these cases, it is often not clear whether governments or firms should be held responsible under international trade rules and, once again, the need for international cooperation in competition policy is evident if divergent decisions are to be avoided.

The main point of the preceding discussion is that the intersection between trade and competition policy is extremely complicated because of the numerous private and public actors involved and the various ways in which the implementation of domestic competition policy can limit market access and the contestability of markets for foreign trading firms. Table 13.1 simplifies this complexity.

Governments previously resolved international disputes arising from disagreements over the issues outlined in Table 13.1 by imposing domestic laws extraterritorially, which often precipitated protective countermeasures from other governments and increased the likelihood of trade wars.[3]

Table 13.1 Linkages between competition policies and trade

Source of linkage	Type of action	Anti-competitive effects
Firms	Anti-competitive activity (e.g. monopolistic and oligopolistic behaviour)	Reduces domestic competition and limits market access
Governments	Competition exemptions, state actions that promote national champions, strategic implementation of competition policy	Possibly reduces domestic competition and definitely limits market access
Firms and governments	Firms benefiting from their own state's actions to the disadvantage of foreign firms	Possibly reduces domestic competition and definitely limits market access

Extraterritoriality occurs when one country attempts to apply its laws within the jurisdiction of another country. In competition law, the formalization of this type of behaviour can be traced to a US Supreme Court decision in 1962, in which the court decided that an anti-competitive activity was not outside the jurisdictional reach of the USA just because some of the activity in question occurred in other countries.[4] Rather, US regulators had the right to apply the Sherman Act if they could show that an anti-competitive activity had an effect on the domestic or foreign commerce of the USA. This so-called 'effects doctrine' alarmed other countries because it implied that the US could implement its rules on businesses located outside its borders. For a sovereign country, such extraterritorial interference in domestic affairs is often unacceptable and likely to trigger retaliation.

Despite the controversial nature of this decision, similar legal doctrines have emerged from the courts of other proponents of competition policy. For example, the EU developed an 'implementation doctrine' in 1988.[5] Under this legal doctrine, foreign firms would be subject to EU competition law if they implement anti-competitive agreements (regardless of where the agreement was entered into) by selling to EU purchasers (Devuyst 2001: 131). In addition, in 1999, the European Court of Justice's Court of First Instance allowed for the establishment of a test for EU jurisdiction similar to the effects doctrine.[6]

Not surprisingly, and regardless of the jurisdiction, the extraterritorial exercise of domestic laws tends to enflame domestic political sensibilities in foreign jurisdictions because it indicates foreign interference in domestic affairs.[7] This perception of foreign intervention in domestic competition affairs was, and remains, especially sensitive because it potentially infringes upon the priorities of trade policy.

Such an international system of politicized dispute resolution was particularly untenable in the face of increasing economic interdependence. Without a change, the traditional tit-for-tat system of international competition relations via extraterritoriality would increase the likelihood of competition-related trade wars that could destabilize the international trading system. The need to pursue some form of international governance in this policy area had become clear for most governments: the system of dispute resolution would have to be replaced with a system of dispute prevention.

International cooperation in competition policy

Today's regime for international cooperation in competition policy relies heavily on a network of bilateral agreements. These agreements between two governments take a variety of forms and address a variety of elements of competition policy. The vigorous approach taken by the EU and USA in signing such agreements reflects their respective, well-established, domestic experiences in enforcing competition laws. Indeed, the international governance regime in competition policy currently resembles a 'hub-and-spoke system' with the EU and USA serving as the hubs from which multiple spoke-like bilateral agreements radiate (Devuyst 2000).

This section notes some of the most important bilateral competition agreements and addresses efforts at enhancing multilateral governance in competition policy. Both bilateral and multilateral approaches address the increasing international linkages between trade and competition policies and the need for procedural and substantive convergence in the implementation of national competition policies. Procedural convergence refers to the evolution of similar procedures among different national competition authorities. Substantive convergence refers to the adoption of common rules and understandings about the nature and scope of anti-trust.

Such procedures include measures for collecting, evaluating and sharing information in individual competition cases. Substantive convergence can occur when national competition regulators increasingly reach similar, or 'consistent', final decisions in individual competition cases. Competition regulators seek procedural and substantive convergence in order to reduce the likelihood that they will reach politicizing divergent decisions.

The bilateral basis of cooperation in competition policy

The hub-and-spoke system of international governance in competition policy reflects the active role of the EU and USA in advancing bilateral cooperation in this policy area.[8] The EU and USA have initiated a number of bilateral competition agreements with each other and with other free-market economies. These agreements are designed to prevent disputes that may arise from divergent decisions in individual competition cases. While Table 13.2 is not intended as an exhaustive list, it suggests the determination of the EU and USA to sign numerous bilateral competition agreements and to incorporate competition disciplines in other formal trade agreements.[9] Taken together, the agreements listed below address a number of potential obstacles to trade and market access that can emerge from the implementation of domestic competition policies.

These formal agreements are notable because of the limited number of countries involved – the signatories are primarily industrialized and transition economies, not developing economies. Under this regime, disputes over trade–competition issues were traditionally dealt with on a bilateral basis. The resolution of such disputes was often based on a political tit-for-tat that threatened the stability of the international economy.

The bilateral agreements are also notable for the extent to which they promote procedural and substantive convergence in national competition policies. For example, the three EU–US agreements provide a framework within which competition authorities can exchange information and coordinate their respective investigations in order to avoid divergent decisions. The implementation of this cooperative framework required the development of new procedures for sharing non-confidential information. This cooperative

Table 13.2 Various EU and US competition agreements

Signatories	Year	Type of agreement
EU and USA	1991	Bilateral Competition Agreement
	1998	Positive Comity Agreement
	1999	Administrative Arrangements on Attendance
USA and:		
Germany	1976	Agreement Relating to Mutual Cooperation Regarding Restrictive Practices
Australia	1982	Agreement Relating to Cooperation on Antitrust Matters
Canada	1984	Memorandum of Understanding with Respect to National Antitrust Laws
Israel, Japan, Brazil	1999	Memorandum of Understanding
Australia	1999	International Antitrust Enforcement Assistance Act Agreement
EU and:		
Switzerland	1972	Bilateral Free Trade Agreement
Iceland, Liechtenstein, Norway	1994	European Free Trade Agreement
Turkey	1995	Customs Union Agreement
Hungary, Poland, Romania, Bulgaria, Slovakia, Czech Republic, Latvia, Lithuania, Estonia, Slovenia, Malta, Cyprus	Various	Europe Agreements (for accession to EU)
Canada	1998	Bilateral Competition Agreements

framework also increases the likelihood of substantive convergence via consistent final decisions in individual competition cases.

The multilateral basis of cooperation in competition policy

While the current hub-and-spoke system provides a bilateral basis for international governance in competition policy, as an increasing number of states develop their own domestic competition policies, the regime is increasingly taking on a multilateral dimension. As ICPAC reports,

> Today, more than 80 countries have [competition] laws, approximately 60 per cent of which were introduced in the 1990s. ... Another 20 or more countries are in the process of drafting laws. Moreover, those countries with competition laws accounted for nearly 80 per cent of world output and 86 per cent of world trade.
>
> (2000: 33)

This proliferation of domestic competition policies has increased the need for international governance in order to reduce the likelihood of divergent decisions among these growing numbers of competition regulators.

In addition to the many bilateral agreements, multilateral competition initiatives serve as complementary options for increasing international cooperation in competition policy (OECD 1999: 18). Previous efforts by international organizations have contributed significantly to creating avenues for cooperation between various national competition regulators. Such efforts include the work of the United Nations Conference on Trade and Development (UNCTAD) and the Organization for Economic Cooperation and Development (OECD). For example, international cooperation in this policy area began largely under a series of non-binding OECD Recommendations on Restrictive Business Practices Affecting International Trade signed in 1967, 1973, 1979, 1986 and 1995.[10] These non-binding recommendations were initiated by OECD members who realized that they would face increasingly similar competition problems as the global economy liberalized (OECD 1998: 7). In general, the recommendations encouraged informal contacts, mostly for the purposes of consultation and information sharing on specific competition cases.[11]

Because the OECD recommendations only provided for non-binding and voluntary cooperation, throughout most of the 1990s, countries with developed competition policies discussed the possibility of multilateralizing competition rules in other forums. During this dialogue, a fundamental transatlantic disagreement emerged regarding whether competition policy should be subsumed within the framework of the World Trade Organization (WTO). While the EU pushed for inclusion of competition policy on the WTO agenda, the USA steadfastly refused such a move.

Former US Assistant Attorney-General for Antitrust Joel I. Klein articulated the US opposition when he argued that beginning competition negotiations in the WTO would be premature because of the limited experience the USA, EU and other members had with international competition policy. Moreover, reaching an international consensus on what common rules might be most appropriate would be difficult to achieve because many other WTO members had only recently established national competition policies. As Klein argued,

> a trade-focused forum like the WTO is ... not the right place to develop such a consensus. Roughly half of the WTO's 135 members do not even have antitrust laws, and most of the members that do have them have only a very few years of very limited enforcement experience.
>
> (1999: 5)

Furthermore, and, according to Klein, probably most important, the inclusion of competition policy in the WTO would increase the likelihood of politicizing competition issues. As Klein argued,

---

Box 13.1 *Case study of the international competition policy network*

Instead of a formal international organization, the International Competition Network (ICN) functions as a new-style venue through which a variety of competition authorities can regularly discuss issues related to the multilateralization of competition policy. These discussions are designed to prevent international disputes that may arise from the incompatible application of different national competition laws.

After lengthy negotiations over the precise nature of this venue, which included significant contributions from the International Bar Association, competition authorities from over fifty developed and developing countries ultimately agreed to launch the ICN on 25 October 2001, in New York City. The inaugural conference of the ICN was held in September 2002, in Naples, Italy.

The founding members of the ICN decided to establish a voluntary, 'virtual' organization. It is not intended to be a new international organization of competition policy nor an alternative to membership in other relevant international organizations. Rather, the members of the ICN are national and multinational competition agencies. From this membership, the network draws a steering group that is responsible for developing a work plan to be carried out by working groups focusing on five areas: mergers, advocacy, fund raising, membership and capacity building, and implementation of competition policies. The five working groups of the ICN seek advice and contributions from 'non-governmental advisers', which include various private sector and non-governmental actors and organizations concerned with the application of competition laws.

In operational terms, the ICN makes clear that it will not exercise any rule-making function. When members reach consensus agreement on recommendations arising from various projects on international competition policy, the individual national competition regulators must decide whether and how to implement the recommendations. They can implement the recommendations through unilateral, bilateral or multilateral arrangements. Thus, the network defers to the discretion of various domestic competition authorities and allows them to decide whether or not to submit, if necessary, such recommendations for political approval.

The ICN does not have a permanent secretariat. Because the ICN lacks a permanent infrastructure, it relies on funding and other forms of support from participating authorities and facilitators.

The hosts of the next annual ICN conferences are scheduled to be Korea in 2004, Germany in 2005 and South Africa in 2006.[12]

extending the WTO dispute settlement mechanism to antitrust enforcement would necessarily involve the WTO in second-guessing prosecutorial decision making in complex evidentiary contexts – a task in which the WTO has no experience and for which it is not suited ... at this point in time, WTO antitrust rules would be useless, pernicious, or both, and would serve only to politicize the long-term future of international antitrust enforcement, including through the intrusion of trade disputes disguised as antitrust problems.

(1999: 5)

Despite this US resistance, it soon became clear that some type of internationally oriented initiative on competition policy would be useful to address the increasing levels of cross-border business activity and the number of states developing competition policies. An important effort emerged when Klein and Attorney-General Janet Reno established, in November 1997, the International Competition Policy Advisory Committee (ICPAC) of experts to investigate the new international competition landscape 'with a fresh perspective' (Klein 1999: 4). ICPAC was mandated to focus on three topics with international implications: multi-jurisdictional merger review, enforcement cooperation between US competition officials and their counterparts around the world (particularly in anti-cartel prosecution efforts), and the interface of trade and competition issues (ICPAC 2000: 34).[13]

After two years of discussions and extensive public hearings – including participation by competition authorities from outside the USA – ICPAC presented a lengthy and widely disseminated report. The report identified numerous policy recommendations to increase international cooperation in competition policy. A noteworthy policy recommendation was to create a new 'Global Competition Initiative'. ICPAC suggested that the membership of this initiative should include government officials, private firms, non-governmental organizations and others, with the intent of exchanging ideas and facilitating common solutions to international competition issues. Following ICPAC's final report, momentum for what became known as a Global Competition Forum (GCF) grew rapidly. Ultimately, the GCF concept was launched as the International Competition Network (ICN).[14] The ICN is the most recent and experimental effort at multilateral cooperation in competition policy (see Box 13.1).

Unlike the WTO, the ICN is designed to focus on competition matters exclusively. Trade issues do not appear prominently on its work agenda. Rather, the ICN develops recommendations intended to promote procedural and substantive convergence in the competition policies of its members. Such international convergence is hoped to reduce the likelihood of divergent decisions in individual competition cases, which, in turn, will reduce the likelihood of competition-related disputes that could destabilize the international trading system.

In addition to the advent of the ICN, the ultimate inclusion of competition issues on the WTO's Doha agenda provided a significant impetus for increasing international governance in competition policy. Despite earlier reluctance to discuss the inclusion of competition issues in WTO negotiations, the USA finally agreed to include linkages between trade and competition in the Doha Ministerial Declaration of 2001. Nevertheless, the Doha Declaration reflects the US position of allowing only limited discussion of competition issues within the WTO. Thus, the Doha Declaration represents a small first step. It addresses the international linkages between competition policy and trade policy by emphasizing the need to assist developing countries in creating functional competition policies and the need for

Table 13.3   Competition policy in the Doha Declaration

Article in Doha Declaration	Substance
Article XXIII	Recognizes need for multilateral efforts on linkage between trade and development
Article XXIV	Recognizes needs of developing and least developed countries for technical assistance and capacity building
	Promises to work through relevant intergovernmental organizations and regional and bilateral channels to achieve this goal
Article XXV	Agrees to negotiate core principles related to trade and competition policies, including:
	• Transparency, non-discrimination and procedural fairness, and provisions on hardcore cartels
	• Modalities for voluntary cooperation
	• Support for institutional capacity building in developing countries

international agreement on general competition principles. Table 13.3 outlines the WTO's approach to competition policy as envisioned in relevant articles of the Doha Declaration.

Following the Doha Declaration, trade negotiators have begun focusing on the much more difficult task of drafting a precise trade agreement that can be acceptable at the conclusion of this round of trade talks. In relation to competition policy, these talks target the provision of technical assistance to developing countries, many of which are promulgating competition laws for the first time (Article XXIV). The negotiators are also formulating core principles that can guide the trade and competition policies of all WTO members.

Due to the significant differences in national competition laws and institutions across this membership, such a task is more difficult than it might initially appear. For example, consider the principle of 'procedural fairness' (Article XXV), which may include the right of firms and other parties involved in a competition case to appeal a final decision. The perceived and actual availability of a right to appeal varies across national competition policies, even among member states with well-established competition laws. This variation reflects different national approaches to the review of administrative and judicial decisions in competition and other policy areas. Such laws, which may run counter to even the most general understanding of procedural fairness, are not easily changed because they are fundamental components of national judicial systems.

Conclusions

Competition policies and trade are becoming increasingly interlinked as business activity becomes more international in nature. As markets internationalize, national competition policies must increasingly address business activity that simultaneously affects multiple markets and is subject to different national competition and trade laws. Therefore, when competition laws are applied to this business activity, they must be reconciled with the priorities of trade policy. The linkages between these two policy areas are particularly evident in three types of behaviour – that of firms, governments and a combination of firms and governments. Each of these types of behaviour can run counter to international trade rules when they limit market access for foreign firms. International cooperation is required to address the potential contradiction between these two policy areas and to ensure effective enforcement of competition disciplines.

Domestic competition regulators play a significant role in developing and determining the contours of international cooperation in competition policy. In order to reduce the likelihood of divergent decisions in individual competition cases, national regulators have sought to develop an international competition regime that promotes dispute prevention over a reliance on political dispute resolution. In short, the regulators prefer that divergent decisions not occur in the first place. The regime displays two notable characteristics: it has important bilateral and multilateral components and frequently emphasizes procedural and substantive convergence.

Bilaterally, international cooperation in competition policy is conducted through an extensive system of agreements in which the EU and USA play prominent roles as hubs. While these bilateral agreements primarily exist between industrialized and transition economies, other complementary, multilateral efforts are broadening the number of countries joining the international debate over competition policy. Two recent examples are the establishment of the ICN and the addition of competition matters to the agenda of the WTO's Doha Round. The ICN is a new-style 'virtual' organization that promotes convergence among the competition policies of its member regulators. The WTO is more binding in its decisions, but its consideration of competition policy is largely limited to assisting developing countries and formulating core principles that can guide the trade and competition policies of its members.

The international competition regime emphasizes procedural and substantive convergence as a way to reduce the likelihood of divergent decisions in individual competition cases, which, in turn, reduces the likelihood that competition-related trade disputes will threaten the stability of the international economy. Nevertheless, the extent of convergence is limited by significant differences in national competition laws. Changes to these domestic competition laws typically require political approval, which can easily be stymied by the idiosyncrasies of domestic politics and the unique needs of domestic markets. It is around issues such as the optimal level of convergence that the debate over future international cooperation in trade–competition issues is currently taking place.

This debate will also have to address the best ways to encourage convergence of national competition policies. While Doha working groups pursue their daunting task of negotiating a new WTO agreement, other forums, such as the ICN, may prove more important venues for meeting the challenges of international governance in competition policy. For example, the ICN's explicit purpose is the promotion of procedural and substantive convergence as a means to reduce the likelihood of divergent competition decisions. The Doha Declaration envisions no similar efforts at increasing convergence. In addition, the ICN defers to the discretion of national competition regulators and allows them to decide whether and to what extent they will adopt recommendations agreed by its members. Such changes are particularly likely in areas under the discretionary authority of the regulators (i.e. those that do not require formal political approval for agreement and implementation). Because the ICN membership is comprised primarily of competition authorities – as opposed to trade diplomats in the WTO – it may be easier for regulators to agree to changes that will improve coordination and enhance international governance in competition policy. Such an outcome should not alarm observers and practitioners of competition policy. Indeed, for many WTO members who are now developing competition policies for the first time, the discretionary and flexible approach offered through the ICN may be the most viable option for preventing disputes that arise from the linkages between competition policy and trade.

Notes

1 Competition policy is known as 'antitrust' policy in the USA. While competition policy can be distinguished as a broader label – including matters traditionally outside US antitrust, such as 'state aids' – this chapter uses the terms interchangeably.
2 Without a competition policy, the free-market model would be subject to monopolistic, oligopolistic and other anti-competitive activity that would dramatically limit the ability of competitors to contest and/or enter the marketplace and, ultimately, reduce consumer welfare. Under such circumstances, the benefits and vibrancy of the free-market model would be seriously undermined.
3 Such countermeasures include so-called 'blocking' and 'clawback' statutes. For example, see Devuyst (2000), Griffin (1998), Price (1995) and Ham (1993).
4 See *Continental Ore Co.* v. *Union Carbide & Carbon Corp.*, 370 US 690, 704 (1962).
5 See the European Court of Justice's decision on the very important Wood Pulp case – *A. Ahlström Osakeyhtiö* v. *Commission*, Cases 89/85, 104/85, 114/85, 116–17/85 and 125–29/85, [1988] ECR, 4 Common Market Report (CCH), paragraph 14,491 (September 27, 1988). See also Lange and Byron Sandage (1989).
6 See Judgment of the Court of First Instance (Fifth Chamber, Extended Composition) in the so-called Gencor case – Case T-102/96, 25 March 1999, para. 90.
7 For more on the contemporary and historical tensions arising from the extraterritorial implementation of competition policy, see Evans (2002), Damro (2001), Devuyst (2001) and Griffin (1999, 1998).
8 For more on transatlantic competition relations, see Damro (2004) and Devuyst (2001).
9 Not all of these agreements are 'bilateral' in the sense that they were signed between two parties. For example, the European Free Trade Agreement (EFTA) was signed between the EU and three different EFTA countries.
10 For a discussion of international cooperation on restrictive business practices beginning in 1927, see Ham (1993: 572–573).
11 The record of the OECD recommendations does provide early empirical evidence of international cooperation in competition policy. Under the 1979 OECD Recommendation, Ham notes that from 1980 to 1985, OECD members notified each other 587 times that they were investigating individual competition cases that could be of interest to other national competition authorities. In particular, the USA notified 361 (almost two-thirds of total) cases to other OECD members. During the same period, the European Commission notified 57, Germany notified 40, Canada notified 39 and Sweden notified 25 (Ham 1993: 574).
12 For more on the ICN, see www.internationalcompetitionnetwork.org.
13 ICPAC's final report includes a broader list of topics than that originally mandated. For a summary, see ICPAC (2000: 34).
14 The GCF and ICN should not be confused with the OECD's Global Forum on Competition. In October 2001, the OECD organized its first Global Forum on Competition in Paris. This group is one of eight 'Global Forums' created by the OECD to increase contacts with non-OECD members.

Bibliography

Damro, C. (2001) 'Building an international identity: the EU and extraterritorial competition policy', *Journal of European Public Policy* 8: 208–226.

Damro, C. (2004) 'A sole of discretion: competition relations in the Transatlantic marketplace', in M. Egan (ed.), *Creating a Transatlantic Marketplace: government policies and business strategies*, Manchester: Manchester University Press.

Devuyst, Y. (2000) 'Toward a multilateral competition policy regime?', *Global Governance* 6: 319–338.

Devuyst, Y. (2001) 'Transatlantic competition relations', in M.A. Pollack and G.C. Shaffer (eds), *Transatlantic Governance in the Global Economy*, Lanham, MD: Rowman & Littlefield.

Evans, D.S. (2002) 'The new trustbusters: Brussels and Washington may part ways', *Foreign Affairs* 81: 14–20.

Griffin, J.P. (1998) 'Foreign governmental reactions to US assertions of extraterritorial jurisdiction', *European Competition Law Review* 19: 64–73.

Griffin, J.P. (1999) 'Extraterritoriality in US and EU antitrust enforcement', *Antitrust Law Journal* 67: 159–199.

Ham, A.D. (1993) 'International cooperation in the anti-trust field and in particular the agreement between the United States of America and the Commission of the European Communities', *Common Market Law Review* 30: 39–62.

ICPAC (2000) *Final Report*, Washington, DC: US Government Printing Office.

Klein, J.I. (1999) 'A reality check on antitrust rules in the World Trade Organization, and a practical way forward on international antitrust', OECD Conference on Trade and Competition, Paris, 29–30 June.

Lange, D. and Byron Sandage, J. (1989) 'The wood pulp decision and its implications for the scope of EC competition law', *Common Market Law Review* 2: 137–165.

Monti, M. (2002) 'A global competition policy?', Speech at the European Competition Day, Copenhagen, Denmark, September 17.

OECD (1998) 'The nature, history and potential benefits of positive comity', DAFFE/CLP/WP3(98)3, Paris: OECD.

OECD (1999) *Trade and Competition Policies: exploring the ways forward*, Paris: OECD.

Price, R.E. (1995) 'Foreign blocking statutes and the GATT: state sovereignty and the enforcement of US economic laws abroad', *George Washington Journal of International Law and Economics* 28: 315–343.

Key readings

Evenett, S.J., Lehmann, A. and Steil, B. (eds) (2000) *Antitrust Goes Global: what future for Transatlantic cooperation?*, Washington, DC: Brookings Institution.

Fox, E.M. (2001) 'Antitrust law on a global scale: races up, down, and sideways', in D.C. Esty and D. Geradin (eds), *Regulatory Competition and Economic Integration: comparative perspectives*, Oxford: Oxford University Press.

Graham, E.M. and Richardson, J.D. (eds) (1997) *Competition Policies for the Global Economy*, Washington, DC: Institute for International Economics.

Organization for Economic Cooperation and Development (1999) 'Consistencies and inconsistencies between trade and competition policies', COM/TD/DAFFE/CLP(98)25/FINAL, Paris: OECD.

Organization for Economic Cooperation and Development (2000) 'International options to improve the coherence between trade and competition policies', COM/TD/DAFFE/CLP(99)102/FINAL, Paris: OECD.

Waverman, L., Comanor, W.S. and Goto, A. (eds) (1997) *Competition Policy in the Global Economy: modalities for cooperation*, New York: Routledge.

Useful websites

www.globalcompetitionforum.org (International Bar Association, Global Competition Forum).
www.internationalcompetitionnetwork.org (International Competition Network).
www.usdoj.gov/atr/icpac/icpac.htm (International Competition Policy Advisory Committee).
www.oecd.org (Organization for Economic Cooperation and Development).
www.unctad.org (United Nations Conference on Trade and Development).
www.wto.org (World Trade Organization).

14 Investment issues in the WTO

Bijit Bora[1]

Summary

One of the most contentious issues facing the trading system is the extent to which multilateral rules should cover the entry and operations of foreign affiliates of multinational corporations. The purpose of this chapter is to present some of the many issues and parameters confronting investment negotiators in Geneva. It is illustrative and meant to be informative. If there is a message, it is that investment issues are not new to the trading system. History matters. Hence, what is on the table in the Doha Development Agenda reflects an incremental step from the treatment of foreign investment arising from the Uruguay Round. It is not a binary choice: yes, investment in the WTO; or no investment in the WTO. Rather, the challenges confronting negotiators are the extent to which rules governing investment in the WTO should be deepened and the architecture of an efficient framework with which to deal with investment issues.

An important part of the context of negotiations is the pattern and composition of FDI flows. Figure 14.1 indicates the most important aspect of FDI trends, which is the massive growth in flows in a short period of time. In 1985 total FDI inflows were less than $60 billion. In the year 2000 the flows were estimated to be $1.4 trillion. The rapid expansion is a reflection of the changing business practices of firms. Spurred on by a combination of technological advances, deregulation and privatisation firms are seeking international markets and more efficient platforms for production. The increase in FDI flows has not been widespread. Developed countries as a group have historically accounted for the majority of FDI flows (Figure 14.1). Developing countries as a group, correspondingly, account for a fairly small share. Even then, this share is accounted for predominantly by countries in East Asia and Latin America (Figure 14.2). The principal developing country recipients of FDI inflows are Argentina, Brazil, China, Hong Kong (China) and countries in South-East Asia.

FDI and development

The economics of development and the role that FDI can play in the development process should be at the centre of any debate on FDI policy. In this regard, the growth in the literature on FDI in the past fifteen years has been enormous (Bora 2002). Most of it supports the transition of developing country governments towards a more open and receptive policy

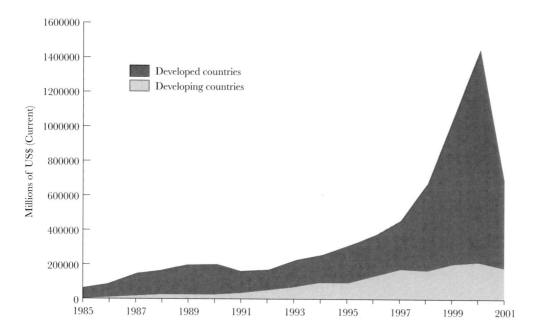

Figure 14.1: World FDI inflows, 1985–2001
Source: UNCTAD.

framework for FDI. It emphasises the assets possessed by multinational corporations and their ability to contribute to the economic growth and development of a host country.[2]

The literature also highlights the fact that there are also possible negative effects from opening up to FDI (Moran 1998; UNCTAD 1999). This is not surprising and in no way should be discounted. Any economic policy will have positive welfare effects, which require associated adjustment. FDI is not necessarily a prerequisite to economic growth in developing nations. The South Korean economy achieved one of the world's highest growth rates between the early 1960s and the late 1990s without receiving significant amounts of FDI. Since the Asian financial crisis of 1997, that picture has changed somewhat, i.e. South Korea is now receiving much more such investment than during the period stretching from roughly the 1960s to the late 1990s. But this does not belie the main point: South Korea for a sustained period of time grew at rapid rates without receiving much FDI.

Having said this, however, it must also be noted that some developing countries have received large amounts of FDI *and* have experienced high growth rates. Such countries have included Hong Kong, Singapore and Ireland, places that today that are no longer in the 'developing' category but arguably were when they began first to attract FDI and to grow rapidly (Ireland might not even then have been considered a developing country but in fact was, on a per capita income basis, at the very low end of the scale of what are now the European Union nations). But such countries also include ones that are, by almost any measure or definition, still of 'developing nation' status. There are a number of examples; a short list of these would include China, Costa Rica, the Dominican Republic and Mauritius.

Thus, although to attract large amounts of FDI certainly is not necessary if a country is to achieve rapid growth, it would appear that FDI can none the less be a positive agent

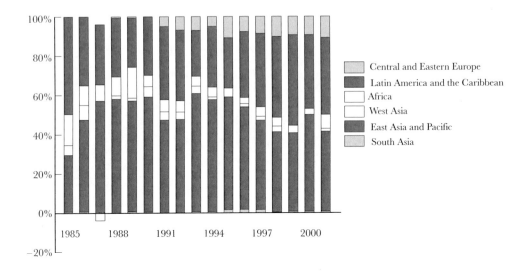

Figure 14.2: Composition of FDI inflows into developing countries, 1985–2001
Source: UNCTAD.

contributing to that growth. At least this has been the case in some developing nations but, apparently, not in others. What factors differentiate those countries with a positive experience with respect to FDI and development and those countries where the experience seems not to be so positive?

This question is not wholly answered in the research literature, but one important finding is that FDI in developing countries would seem to be positively associated with growth if and only if the country in question met a certain threshold with respect to human capital, measured in mean years of schooling completed by the population (Borzenstine *et al.* 1998). In other words, those countries where the population tended to be poorly educated tended to be ones in which FDI did not seem positively to affect growth, whereas a better result tended to be observed in those countries where the population was better educated.[3] A well-educated workforce might also be a prerequisite simply in order to attract FDI; operations of multinational companies most often require relatively highly skilled workers, and where such workers are not available, multinational firms usually will not locate their operations (Moran 1998).

Beyond education, what are the characteristics of countries that are successful in attracting FDI, and successful in making the investment work to serve the interests of the country itself? The list of factors that foreign investors seek in a country in which to locate major operations includes: political stability, a strong commitment to the rule of law (including well-functioning legal systems), growth in the domestic market, credible commitment to investor protection (i.e. that the property of foreign investors is not seized arbitrarily, and if, for a public purpose and under due process of law, property must be taken, prompt and adequate compensation is offered by public authorities). What may surprise some policy makers is that low-wage labour does not rank particularly highly on such investor 'wish-lists'; availability of skills, even if premium wages must be paid, ranks more highly, as suggested above. Surprisingly, perhaps, tax incentives to investors do not rank particularly highly either, although it is clearly true that if an investor must make a decision between two alternative locations, each of which is about as attractive in terms of the factors listed above, then the location with the best tax treatment will often be the one chosen by the investor. In other words, tax matters only if other criteria are met. Investors clearly prefer tax regimes where rates of tax are low on an across-the-board basis to those where rates are high, but special deals are cut with investors.

A question that needs then to be answered in the context of WTO negotiations is whether WTO rules might enable countries better to achieve those conditions under which FDI would seem to thrive, including whether or not there might be disciplines to limit the use of tax and other investment incentives meant to lure FDI to specific localities.

An equally heated and contentious issue as the link between FDI and economic growth is the ability of governments to intervene and affect the direction and level of benefits arising from the operation of foreign affiliates. The economic literature on FDI and growth emphasises the intrinsic differences between foreign and domestic firms, whereas the literature on foreign policy highlights the question of whether or not such differences warrant intervention. Instruments such as local content schemes, foreign exchange balancing and export restrictions and/or export performance requirements thus have been argued as instruments that can increase welfare and contribute positively to the development process. Both theory and empirical evidence, however, would seem to conclude the contrary (Moran 1998, 2002), or at least with respect to certain measures. At any rate, an issue raised at Cancún was whether there should be modification or deepening of the existing Agreement on Trade-Related Investment Measures. This issue is addressed in more depth in the following section.

Developments in investment rule making

A parallel issue that should be considered is developments in investment rule making. One rationale for considering investment at the multilateral level is to avoid the plethora of bilateral and regional instruments. This 'efficiency' argument has been made strongly for regional trade agreements and applies to investment issues.

There are two broad sets of investment rule-making initiatives pertinent to the WTO discussions on investment: Bilateral Investment Treaties (BITs) and plurilateral arrangements either specifically dedicated to investment, or regional trade agreements which incorporate investment provisions. Let us consider each in turn.

There is no specific or formal definition of a BIT other than it is investment related. The defining feature of BITs is that they typically revolve around the protection of investment. Prior to the Second World War such provisions were found in Friendship, Commerce and Navigation Treaties which were initiated by a few countries in the late nineteenth century. These treaties, however, were broad in coverage and included a number of issues such as trade and maritime transport. The modern version of the BIT evolved after the war with some BITs dedicated specifically to the protection of investment.

One interesting aspect of BITs is their inclusion of dispute settlement provisions. Such provisions and the enforcement of awards play a critical role in ensuring the effectiveness of BITs. Clearly, differences exist between the strength of such provisions across BITs. Nevertheless, what is important in the context of this chapter is that there is a history of investment protection and dispute settlement, including investor to state disputes. These developments play an important role in determining the extent to which similar provisions are necessary in the context of a multilateral trading system.

The second set of rule making is the high-profile dispute resolution mechanisms for investors contained in the North American Free Trade Agreement (NAFTA). This mechanism, contained in Chapter 11, was a significant step at the international level and also at the domestic level for Mexico. Previously Mexico, along with other Latin American countries, had been a strong supporter of the Calvo doctrine. This meant that foreign investors had no recourse to their home courts. It also meant that the host-country government had supreme control of foreign investment issues.

Table 14.1   Mandatory performance requirements prohibited by selected agreements

Prohibited performance requirement	*Sampling of agreements prohibiting*
Export performance requirements	NAFTA
	Canada–Barbados BIT
	Canada–Philippines BIT
	Canada–Trinidad and Tobago BIT
	Canada–Venezuela BIT
	US–Trinidad and Tobago BIT
	US–Bolivia BIT
Restrictions on sales of goods or services in the territory where they are produced or provided	NAFTA
	US–Bolivia BIT
Requirements to supply goods produced or services provided to a specific region or the world market exclusively from a given territory	US–Trinidad and Tobago BIT
Requirements to act as the exclusive supplier of goods produced or services provided	NAFTA
Requirements to transfer technology, production processes or other proprietary knowledge	NAFTA
	Canada–Barbados BIT
	Canada–Philippines BIT
	Canada–Trinidad and Tobago BIT
	Canada–Venezuela BIT
	US–Trinidad and Tobago BIT
	US–Bolivia BIT
Research & development requirements	US–Trinidad and Tobago BIT
	US–Bolivia BIT

Source: WTO (2001).

One of the consequences of the NAFTA dispute settlement mechanism has been the elevated concern that in certain circumstances an international agreement could override the sovereign ability of a government to regulate in the social interest (Graham 2000). This concern was the motivation for the coordinated public effort against the Multilateral Agreement on Investment (MAI) negotiations which began under the auspices of the Organization for Economic Cooperation and Development (OECD). Anxiety over the possibility of extending the NAFTA dispute settlement mechanism to a broader group of countries resulted in a backlash against investment rule making. Ultimately, the MAI effort failed in 1998.

Some BITs and free trade agreements also address the issue of performance requirements. Table 14.1 lists selected performance requirements and corresponding agreements that ban their use. The important point to note from this table, despite its selectivity, is that the list of performance requirements in some ways goes beyond what is contained in the WTO Agreement on Trade-Related Investment Measures.

Despite the failure of the MAI, the exposure of investment issues to a broader community and the accumulation of human capital on the issue by various negotiators have resulted in a situation where an increasing number of countries are positive about investment in the multilateral trading system. The precise architecture for such rules, however, remains to be determined. In the end, if investment is to be in the WTO it will first need to augment the current provisions on investment, to be discussed in the next section. And, second, it will borrow from the experience of various countries with BITs and also from lessons learned from the NAFTA dispute settlement mechanism.

Investment issues in the Uruguay Round

An important element of the debate on investment in the WTO is the extent to which the Uruguay Round agreements cover investment issues. Koulen (2001) makes the point that despite the absence of a separate legal instrument on foreign investment, investment issues are either directly or indirectly taken up in a number of agreements. He identifies the following agreements: the plurilateral Agreement on Government Procurement (AGP), the General Agreement on Trade in Services (GATS), the Agreement on Trade-Related Aspects of Intellectual Property Rights (TRIPs), the Agreement on Trade-Related Investment Measures (TRIMs) and the Agreement on Subsidies and Countervailing Measures (ASCM).

Instead of going through each agreement this section is structured around three themes: market access, incentives and performance requirements. It is important to note the implications of these agreements and also the fact that key issues in investment policy such as investor protection are not part of the covered agreements.

Market access

Market access, or the liberalisation of entry into a market, differs between foreign investment and trade in goods. For trade in goods this implies zero tariffs and the absence of non-tariff measures at customs borders. For investment this means more favourable treatment with respect to the entry and treatment of foreign persons and enterprises, or to the protection of certain property rights of foreign persons (Koulen 2001).

Such treatment is provided in the AGP and the GATS. The standard provided in these agreements, and, indeed, in other agreements such as BITs and NAFTA, is national treatment for foreign investors. This means providing treatment to foreign investors which is no less favourable than that provided to domestic investors. A corresponding principle is the most-favoured-nation principle, which prohibits discrimination between investors from different countries.

The AGP provides that there be no discrimination against foreign suppliers and, also, no discrimination against locally established suppliers on the basis of their degree of foreign affiliation or ownership.[4] The GATS treats foreign investment in the service sector as a mode of supply. This is done by defining the commercial presence of a foreign supply as

> any type of business or professional establishment, including through (i) the constitu-
> tion, acquisition or maintenance of a juridical person or (ii) the creation or
> maintenance of a branch or a representative office, within the territory of a Member
> for the purpose of supplying a service.[5]

Another mode of supply is through the presence of 'natural persons'. Koulen (2001) argues that this is closely related to the commercial presence mode since it includes the temporary entry of business visitors and intra-company transfers of managerial and other key personnel.

A word of caution or clarification: while the GATS and the AGP have elements of market access for foreign investors, their architecture differs substantially from that proposed in the MAI or from Chapter 11 of NAFTA. One of the key differences, with respect to the GATS, is that there is no general obligation. Members apply the standards of treatment through specific commitments. These commitments apply only to the listed sectors and the reservations and exceptions expressed by members. Figure 14.3 provides a graphic exposition of the commitments made by members under commercial presence (Mode 3).[6] The height of each bar indicates the number of total commitments. The upper part of the bar reflects partial commitments, while the lower part reflects full commitments. The figure shows that a relatively lower level of commitments has been made in commercial presence.

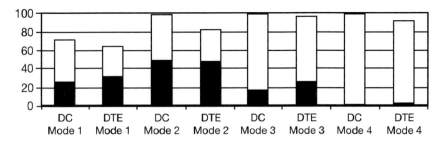

The upper part of each bar represents partial commitments,
the lower part full commitments

DC = Developed countries, DTE = Developing and transition economies

Figure 14.3: GATS commitments by mode of delivery (per cent of total commitments)
Source: WTO.

One final note with respect to market access concerns the role of the TRIPs agreement. While the agreement itself does not provide a standard of market access it does provide for a standard of intellectual property rights protection. One element of the determinants of FDI flows is the extent to which a firm-specific asset can be protected from either expropriation or dissipation (Maskus 2002). If intellectual property rights protection is of a sufficient standard it could induce FDI flows.

Incentives

The establishment of a system of remedies to challenge the use of subsidies in the Uruguay Round agreements was a major achievement. However, the jurisdiction of the WTO agreements over investment incentives is not very clear. The first and foremost reason for this ambiguity is that the WTO deals with trade in goods and services, not explicitly foreign investment. Therefore, if there is a link, it must be through the relationship between investment and trade in goods and services. For goods trade the prevailing agreement is likely to be the ASCM for industrial products and the Agreement on Agriculture (AoA) for agricultural products. For services trade it is the GATS.

The ASCM is a very broad agreement and contains a number of specific steps that are used to determine whether or not a measure comes under its jurisdiction. For example, a three-part definition is used to determine whether the measure is indeed a subsidy. These is a clear financial contribution that must be provided by a government or any public body within the territory of a member that confers a benefit. A second condition is that the measure must then be specific to an enterprise, or group of enterprises.

Most measures that can be classified as investment incentives would fall within the jurisdiction of the ASCM. The extent, which can be subject to discipline, depends upon a number of additional factors. First, there is a category of prohibited subsides. This includes specific trade-related subsidies, such as direct export subsidies and subsidies that are contingent on exporting. Second, the burden of proof under the agreement rests with the complaining party. Since the ASCM covers industrial goods the complaining member must show that it has suffered adverse effects. This means that its domestic industry has suffered either injury from imports sourced from the country offering the incentive, or serious prejudice arising from export displacement in either the market of the country offering the incentive or a third market. Finally, there is nullification and impairment of benefits from improved market access that is undercut by subsidisation.

The AoA provides special provision for agricultural products. These provisions for the most part insulate subsidies to industries that produce agricultural products from the disciplines contained in the agreement. However, after the implementation period of the agreement, which was 1 January 2003, the ASCM will apply to subsidies for agricultural products.

Therefore, for the types of measures that can be classified as investment incentives it would appear that the WTO agreements appear to have broad, although as yet untested, disciplines. The policy question is the degree to which the precise nature of these disciplines will evolve over future dispute cases. Or, as in the case of TRIMs, as will be shown below, precise guidance over the disciplines as a negotiated outcome.

Performance requirements

The fact that there is a separate text called an 'Agreement' on TRIMs as part of the WTO agreements is a paradox. In essence, all the TRIMs agreement does is clarify the application of GATT 94 Articles III(4) on national treatment and XI(1) on quantitative restrictions.[7] It does not even define a trade-related investment measure. Instead the approach taken was to include an illustrative list of measures, which were agreed to be inconsistent with the two key paragraphs of the GATT (III.4 and XI.1).[8] This list covers TRIMs which are mandatory or enforceable under domestic law or under administrative rulings and measures for which compliance is necessary to obtain an advantage. The list includes local content schemes, foreign exchange and trade balancing, and export restrictions. There is no text specifically addressing issues related to granting national treatment to investors.

The agreement allowed any members access to an extended transition period for bringing policies that they may have into compliance with it, if and only if these policies were notified within ninety days of the commencement of the agreement. Twenty-six members, all developing countries, notified a variety of policies (Bora 2001). The economic characteristics of these countries varied considerably. The overwhelming policy adopted by them was local content schemes. The second most frequent one was foreign exchange balancing. There was some variance in the approach used by these countries in the application of these policies. The most frequent industry where the policies were in existence was the automotive industry, although some members applied local content schemes in a general fashion across all industries. The second most prominent industry was agriculture.

Therefore, in the context of notification it would seem that the agreement worked relatively well, as approximately only 20 per cent of the WTO membership were adopting policies that contravened the agreement. However, there is an issue given that none of the countries were developed countries, and only one least developed country notified. Furthermore, some developing countries argue that the notification period was too short; hence they were unable to enjoy the benefit of the transition period for such policies.

Given that any member can initiate proceedings of a dispute against any other member it makes little sense simply to add up the number of disputes. Using that approach one would find that sixteen requests for consultation were initiated, with two proceeding to an actual dispute panel. The problem is that one WTO member may find itself defending one particular policy against a number of other members. This was the case in the notifications against Indonesia, when Japan, the EU and the USA each filed notifications citing the same policy. Similarly, Japan and the EU filed notifications against Canada. Perhaps the highest profile case was India having to defend its use of local content schemes. Once the double counting is considered, only eight countries (five developing and three developed) had to defend their policies.

One interesting aspect of the notifications for dispute is that in each case the complaint listed other policies in addition to those that were claimed to be inconsistent with the TRIMs agreement. This is an important point in that it reflects on the types of policies in the context of general industrial policy objectives as opposed to an isolated or targeted policy intervention. The most common agreement to be cited in conjunction with TRIMs is the ASCM. In fact, Article 3 appears to be quite specifically correlated with the TRIMs agreement. The TRIPS agreement was listed in one case. This, however, is due to the sector specificity of some of the complaints. In the two cases where the TRIMs is applied in the agriculture sector the AoA is also alleged to be violated. In the context of the GATT the two articles referred to directly in the TRIMs agreement – III and XI – are cited. In one case, Canada and the EU and Japan, Article XXIV, which relates to the multilateral consistency of regional agreements, is cited. The general conclusion that one can draw from the operation of the TRIMs agreement is that it is typically implemented with policies related to the ASCM, rather than as a standalone agreement.

Three of the notifications, against Canada, India and Indonesia, could not be resolved outside the dispute settlement mechanisms and had to proceed to panel reports. In all three cases the complaining country was a developed country. The decision in each case went against the defending party requiring it to bring its laws into conformity with the TRIMs agreement.

In general, the experience with the TRIMs agreement is that it has been able to achieve its modest goals, which are to discipline a small number of, although quite popular, instruments. Of these, the most significant is the emphatic closure on the use of local content schemes and trade balancing requirements. The twin questions of whether (and how) to expand the disciplines on TRIMs, and whether to amend or contract the illustrative list, now need to be addressed.

The Doha mandate

The Doha Ministerial Declaration mandated the Working Group on the Relationship Between Trade and Investment to focus on clarifying the following issues: scope and definition; transparency; non-discrimination; modalities for pre-establishment commitments based on a GATS-type, positive list approach; development provisions; exceptions and balance of payments; consultations and the settlement of disputes between members. In addition, the Working Group also continued work on the relationship with other WTO agreements and International Investment Agreements and also on the issue of FDI and the transfer of technology. Each of the seven issues identified in paragraph 22 are now considered in turn.[9]

Scope and definition

There are two main approaches to defining investment – an intrinsically narrow approach, such as an enterprise-based or transaction-based definition, and a broad, asset-based approach, with different options for including or excluding various categories of investment. The USA for the most part has championed the broader approach. A number of developing countries, however, if they supported further work on investment proposed a narrower approach, e.g. that the coverage of any future WTO agreement be limited to FDI (but see the subsection on balance of payments below).

In addition to the difficulty of defining investment, there is the added difficulty of defining what exactly an 'investor' is for the purposes of implementing an investment agreement. This is an important issue because implicitly any agreement involves the rights and obligations of investors, as opposed to governments. For example, if a future agreement were to guarantee national treatment to investors and/or their investments, it would be of paramount importance to define precisely what entities qualified for this treatment.

Transparency

In describing the objectives of a multilateral investment framework, ministers at Doha began with the concept of securing a 'transparent' framework for foreign investment. There was general agreement that the focus of discussion should not be on the benefits of transparency, but rather on the nature and depth of transparency provisions and on the scope of their application in a possible WTO agreement on investment. It is clear that transparency involves providing information on rules and regulations; but whether transparency extends to the way rules and regulations are administered is not an issue on which there is consensus.

Some possible transparency obligations are:

- Publication and notification requirements
- Enquiry points
- Prior notification and comment
- Administrative and judicial procedures
- Investor and home-country obligations

At this point in time, the positions of individual WTO members on what transparency-related obligations should be contained in any future investment agreement are not fully clear. Even so, it is probable that members are not in consensus on this set of issues.

Development provisions

The main areas where developing countries are seeking flexibility in any WTO agreement on investment are in regulating the entry of foreign investment (through general screening, selective restrictions and conditions on entry) and in using policies to enhance the contribution that foreign investment made to their economic and social development needs and objectives (through performance requirements, investment incentives and preferences for domestic investors). There is no consensus on exactly what approach is best from a development perspective. Rather, views range from it being desirable that there be widespread scope for government intervention or, alternatively, that there be strong obligations on governments not to use such intervention on a selective basis. Nevertheless, various broad options have been identified during the period after the Doha ministerial. These are: (a) that the development objectives of an agreement on investment be included in the preamble of the agreement; (b) that the scope of an agreement be clearly delineated, e.g. that it be made explicit whether the agreement applied to FDI only or to all forms of investment, and whether it covered the pre- as well as the post-establishment phase of investment; (c) that the agreement should allow at least some exemptions from obligations; (d) that member countries be allowed some flexibility in undertaking specific commitments; (e) that any agreement allow longer transition periods for implementation for poor countries than for richer countries; and (f) that some means should be provided for technical assistance and capacity building for poorer countries. Furthermore, it should be recognised that the seven issues listed for 'clarification' in paragraph 22 did not exhaust the scope for development provisions; rather, it was expected that further discussion would reveal whether certain items should be excluded from the list, and whether new items (such as performance requirements) should be added.

Non-discrimination

The principle of non-discrimination is at the core of most international commercial treaties, although its application is typically subject to carefully defined conditions. These conditions might allow governments to give preferential treatment to domestic products, producers and investors, or to certain of their commercial partners but not to others, or to pursue domestic policy objectives that could not be realised without practising some degree of discriminatory treatment. The scope for the application of non-discrimination can also be limited by the definition of 'investment' in an agreement, i.e. by the range of assets to which non-discriminatory standards applied.

An important distinction can be drawn between the application of non-discrimination – and national treatment in particular – at the pre-establishment and post-establishment phases of investment. Similarly, MFN and national treatment also differ. An argument can also equally be applied to the application of the national treatment standards. National treatment, like MFN treatment, could also be extended to all stages of investment – its entry, its operation after establishment and its liquidation. In doing so, however, it will be important to take into account the need (or at least preference) on the part of some developing countries to have some flexibility to discriminate between domestic and foreign investors.

In the context of the discussion of non-discriminatory standards at both the pre- and post-establishment phases, it is important to note, once again, that scope of application depends crucially on the definition of the term 'investment', as well as on the exceptions allowed and the specific commitments made under the agreement's provisions by individual members.

Modalities for pre-establishment commitments based on a GATS-type positive list approach

The GATS approach to scheduling market access commitments has been put forth as a model of development-friendly multilateral rules. Discipline is achieved through the binding of policy, but at a pace that is consistent with the needs of each member. At the same time, there are also valid criticisms about the degree of liberalisation that could be realised through such an approach. Bindings have policy value in the sense that they are credible commitments of policy, but under the GATS approach, different countries can put forth significantly different bindings. Moreover, it has been argued that, under the GATS approach, the degree of effective liberalisation has been limited to the status quo; to date countries have been unwilling to bind themselves to any commitment that does not already exist under current law and policy.[10]

Exceptions and balance-of-payments safeguards

Another element for consideration is ways in which general, security and regional integration exceptions as well as balance-of-payments safeguards might be incorporated in a prospective WTO investment agreement. An issue of great importance to some developing countries is balance-of-payments safeguards, since it touches directly on concerns about short-term capital flows and exposure to financial volatility. Indeed, such concerns are at the heart of why these countries seek that any such agreement be limited to cover FDI only. However, it is also noted that foreign direct investors do engage in short-term financial transactions, and thus it is argued that even an investment agreement that is limited to FDI must contain some balance-of-payments safeguard, perhaps one similar to that already contained in the GATT (which in turn is meant to be consistent with IMF rules regarding balance of payments).

Consultation and the settlement of disputes between members

Although there are different models for settling investment-related disputes (e.g. NAFTA Chapter 11, which allows for private parties in some circumstances to initiate dispute settlement procedures under so-called investor-to-state provisions) there is a widely shared view that the existing WTO dispute settlement mechanism should apply to any future investment agreement – just as it applied to all other WTO agreements. Moreover, there seems to be a widely shared view that the WTO would not include investor-to-state dispute settlement procedures such as are found in the NAFTA. Even so, there is no doubt that the application of the existing WTO dispute settlement system to investment obligations and disciplines would raise a number of issues that would require further examination and clarification, such as: the scope for non-violation actions; extending cross-retaliation and cross-compensation to the investment area; the interaction of investment rules with other substantive rules in existing WTO agreements; and the relationship with other dispute settlement systems in existing international investment agreements.

Conclusions

Much of the concern about a possible framework for FDI is the possibility that it may shift the balance of rights and obligations of firms operating in a national jurisdiction. Such a concern is warranted and we would not quarrel with that. The focus of this chapter, however, is on the issue of whether or not good investment policy requires a multilateral system of binding and enforceable rights and obligations. The chapter takes as a starting point the ongoing debate on the link between FDI and development, noting in particular that FDI can make significant contributions to development but, at the same time, is not strictly necessary for development to occur.

Two matters can be identified that bear on whether a constructive negotiation is now likely to ensue. The first is that there does exist a group of members who are steadfastly opposed to investment issues in the WTO under any circumstances. Estimates of the number of members in this camp diverge. One estimate is that it is limited to India and certain of the ASEAN countries. Another estimate suggests that it is a majority of developing countries. Since the exact numbers are not known – many countries have maintained a stance of deliberate ambiguity – it is difficult to examine the probability that the 'Indian position' (i.e. do nothing on the investment front) is likely to carry the day.

The second matter, which compounds the first, is that there is genuine concern on the part of a number of developing countries that, even if they were to support investment negotiations publicly, they do not have the power or capacity to negotiate an agreement that is in their interests. Thus, these countries might be classed as ones that believe that, although an agreement in their interests is indeed feasible, none the less the actual outcome of a negotiation could very well be an agreement that is antithetical to their interests.

The existence of these two groups of developing nations must be taken into account when viewing the broader context of the negotiations. How these groups 'play their cards' in the Doha Round will bear greatly on the nature and extent of any negotiation on investment. The most divisive but key issue in the upcoming round of negotiations, for example, is not investment, but agriculture. *Demandeurs* for agricultural reform could very well be willing to use investment negotiations as a 'bargaining chip' to affect the outcome in agriculture, regardless of whether or not they fundamentally support inclusion of an investment agreement in the negotiations. Thus, developing countries in the second of the two groups, and perhaps even in the first, might be quite willing for extensive negotiations on investment to proceed, if this would induce the EU to reduce its resistance to reform of its agricultural policy. Investment could prove to be a bargaining chip with respect to other issues as well, e.g. access to essential medicines. In the end, whether an investment agreement is to be negotiated in the WTO might thus itself be a matter for negotiation.

Notes

1 The views expressed in this chapter are personal and should not be interpreted as reflecting the views of the WTO or its member states.
2 These assets include additional capital, advanced technology, managerial expertise and linkages to international markets.
3 However, Carkovic and Levine (2002) dispute this result. The disparity between their results and those of Borzenstine *et al.* does not at this time seem to be resolved.
4 The agreement also has a provision against the use of offsets, which for the most part is parallel to the issue of performance requirements.
5 Article XXVIII(d) of the GATS.
6 Modes 1 and 2 are cross-border supply and the movement of a consumer to a supplying country, while mode 4 is the temporary movement of labour.
7 The TRIMs agreement is a rather modest attempt at disciplining policies that are targeted at foreign enterprises and which came about through conflicting positions on the extent to which investment issues should be covered by the WTO. Many developing countries resisted the extent to which market access for foreign firms would be covered, and as a result the negotiations focused on policies that applied to the operations of foreign firms. Even then, negotiations proved difficult, as there was no consensus as to whether or not a specific policy instrument was indeed trade distorting. Furthermore, some developing countries took the position that they should have access to policy instruments that could be used to offset any perceived negative effects associated with the operations of transnational corporations.
8 There was nothing to suggest that the list was exhaustive of all the measures that could be considered to be inconsistent.
9 This section draws heavily from the Annual Report of the Working Group on Trade and Investment. See also Ferrarini (2003) for an overview of all the proposals.
10 Indeed, a frequently heard complaint about GATS is that national commitments under GATS often are less than the *de facto* status quo. In other words, the extent of *de facto* liberalisation actually exceeds that achieved *de jure* under GATS. Defenders of the GATS approach counter that, while the latter might be true, GATS is an unfinished work that will, with time, achieve a net liberalisation. Whether this proves true, of course, only time will tell.

Bibliography

Bora, B. (2001) 'The Agreement on Trade Related Investment Measures: 1995–2001', Mimeo, UNCTAD.

Bora, B. (ed.) (2002) *Foreign Direct Investment: research issues*, London: Routledge.

Borzenstine, E., de Gregorio, J. and Lee, J.W. (1998) 'How does foreign investment affect growth?', *Journal of International Economics* 45: 115–135.

Carkovic, M. and Levine, R. (2002) 'Does foreign direct investment accelerate economic growth?', Paper prepared for World Bank Conference 'Financial Globalization: A Blessing or a Curse?', Washington, DC, May 30–31. Available HTTP:
http://legacy.csom.umn.edu/WWWPages/FACULTY/ RLevine/FDI.pdf> (accessed 25 July 2003).

Ferrarini, B. (2003) 'Multilateral framework for investment?', in. S. Evenett and State Secretariat of Economic Affairs (Switzerland) (eds), *The Singapore Issues and the World Trading System: the road to Cancun and beyond*, Berne: World Trade Institute.

Graham, E.M. (2000) *Fighting the Wrong Enemy*, Washington, DC: Institute for International Economics.

Koulen, M. (2001) 'Foreign investment in the WTO', in E.C. Nieuwenhuys and M.M.T.A. Brus (eds), *Multilateral Regulation of Investment*, The Hague: Kluwer Law International.

Maskus, K. (2002), 'FDI and intellectual property', in B. Bora (ed.), *Foreign Direct Investment: research issues*, London: Routledge.

Moran, T. (1998) *Foreign Direct Investment and Development*, Washington, DC: Institute for International Economics.

Moran, T. (2002) 'The relationship between trade, foreign direct investment, and development: new evidence, strategies and tactics under the Doha Development Agenda', Mimeo, presented at the Asian Development Bank.

UNCTAD (1999) *World Investment Report: FDI and the challenge of development*, Geneva: UNCTAD.

WTO (1996) *Annual Report: special topic foreign direct investment and trade*, Geneva: WTO.

WTO (2001) 'Trade Related Investment Measures and Other Performance Requirements, part 1', Joint UNCTAD and WTO Study, G/C/W/307.

WTO (2002) 'Trade Related Investment Measures and Other Performance Requirements, part II', Joint UNCTAD and WTO Study, G/C/W/307.

Key readings

Bora, B. (ed.) (2002) *Foreign Direct Investment: research issues*, London: Routledge.

Ferrarini, B. (2003) 'Multilateral framework for investment?', in. S. Evenett and State Secretariat of Economic Affairs (Switzerland) (eds), *The Singapore Issues and the World Trading System: the road to Cancun and beyond*, Berne: World Trade Institute.

Graham, E.M. (2000) *Fighting the Wrong Enemy*, Washington, DC: Institute for International Economics.

WTO (2001) 'Trade Related Investment Measures and Other Performance Requirements, part 1', Joint UNCTAD and WTO Study, G/C/W/307.

WTO (2002) 'Trade Related Investment Measures and Other Performance Requirements, part II', Joint UNCTAD and WTO Study, G/C/W/307.

Useful websites

www.unctad.org (United Nations Conference on Trade and Development).

www.wto.org/english/tratop_e/invest_e/invest_e.htm (Working Group on Investment, World Trade Organization).

15 Trade and the environment

Duncan Brack

Summary

The story of the trade and environment debate within and around the WTO is one of growing salience in the minds of negotiators and civil society, a continued failure to make any substantial progress in rewriting WTO rules, but significant changes in the way in which existing rules have been interpreted to deal with environmental concerns. This chapter examines the ways in which the expansion of trade may sometimes conflict with and sometimes support environmental regulation; highlights the main areas of trade–environment tensions – over product standards, processes and production methods, and trade measures in multilateral environment agreements – and considers the politics behind the debate.

Since trade and environmental policies both affect the use of natural resources, it is hardly surprising that the two should interact. In theory, the objectives of trade liberalization and environmental protection should be entirely compatible. Both have as their aim the optimization of efficiency in the use of resources, whether from the perspective of maximizing the gains from the comparative advantages of nations, through trade, or of ensuring that economic development becomes environmentally sustainable. As international trade regulation impinges on increasingly broad areas of public policy – including agriculture, investment, services, intellectual property and health standards – and as environmental agreements increasingly cover wider and wider areas of economic activity – such as the Kyoto Protocol on climate change or the Cartagena Protocol on trade in GM products – it is to be expected that the two areas of international policy should increasingly interact.

Both sets of international regulations pay at least lip-service to the other. The agreement establishing the WTO recognizes that trade should be conducted 'while allowing for the optimal use of the world's resources in accordance with the objective of sustainable development, seeking both to protect and preserve the environment and to enhance the means for doing so'.[1] Agenda 21, the programme for action aimed at achieving sustainable development in the twenty-first century signed at the 1992 UN Conference on Environment and Development (UNCED), the 'Earth Summit' in Rio, states that: 'An open, multilateral trading system, supported by the adoption of sound environmental policies, would have a positive impact on the environment and contribute to sustainable development.'[2] Several of the more recent multilateral environmental agreements (MEAs), out of the 250 plus that now exist, borrow language from the GATT in describing their approach to trade restrictions.

Box 15.1 WTO Doha Declaration

6. We strongly reaffirm our commitment to the objective of sustainable development, as stated in the Preamble to the Marrakech Agreement. We are convinced that the aims of upholding and safeguarding an open and non-discriminatory multilateral trading system, and acting for the protection of the environment and the promotion of sustainable development can and must be mutually supportive. We take note of the efforts by Members to conduct national environmental assessments of trade policies on a voluntary basis. We recognize that under WTO rules no country should be prevented from taking measures for the protection of human, animal or plant life or health, or of the environment at the levels it considers appropriate, subject to the requirement that they are not applied in a manner which would constitute a means of arbitrary or unjustifiable discrimination between countries where the same conditions prevail, or a disguised restriction on international trade, and are otherwise in accordance with the provisions of the WTO Agreements. We welcome the WTO's continued cooperation with UNEP and other inter-governmental environmental organizations. We encourage efforts to promote cooperation between the WTO and relevant international environmental and developmental organizations, especially in the lead-up to the World Summit on Sustainable Development to be held in Johannesburg, South Africa, in September 2002.

Trade and Environment

31. With a view to enhancing the mutual supportiveness of trade and environment, we agree to negotiations, without prejudging their outcome, on:

(i)   The relationship between existing WTO rules and specific trade obligations set out in multilateral environmental agreements (MEAs). The negotiations shall be limited in scope to the applicability of such existing WTO rules as among parties to the MEA in question. The negotiations shall not prejudice the WTO rights of any Member that is not a party to the MEA in question;

(ii) Procedures for regular information exchange between MEA Secretariats and the relevant WTO committees, and the criteria for the granting of observer status;

(iii) The reduction or, as appropriate, elimination of tariff and non-tariff barriers to environmental goods and services.

We note that fisheries subsidies form part of the negotiations provided for in paragraph 28.

32. We instruct the Committee on Trade and Environment, in pursuing work on all items on its agenda within its current terms of reference, to give particular attention to:

(i)   The effect of environmental measures on market access, especially in relation to developing countries, in particular the least-developed among them, and those situations in which the elimination or reduction of trade restrictions and distortions would benefit trade, the environment and development;

(ii) The relevant provisions of the Agreement on Trade-Related Aspects of Intellectual Property Rights; and

(iii) Labelling requirements for environmental purposes.

Work on these issues should include the identification of any need to clarify relevant WTO rules. The Committee shall report to the Fifth Session of the Ministerial Conference, and make recommendations, where appropriate, with respect to future action, including the desirability of negotiations. The outcome of this work as well as the negotiations carried out under paragraph 31(i) and (ii) shall be compatible with the open and non-discriminatory nature of the multilateral trading system, shall not add to or diminish the rights and obligations of Members under existing WTO agreements, in particular the Agreement on the Application of Sanitary and Phytosanitary Measures, nor alter the balance of these rights and obligations, and will take into account the needs of developing and least-developed countries.

33. We recognize the importance of technical assistance and capacity building in the field of trade and environment to developing countries, in particular the least-developed among them. We also encourage that expertise and experience be shared with Members wishing to perform environmental reviews at the national level. A report shall be prepared on these activities for the Fifth Session.

WTO, Ministerial Declaration, 14 November 2001, www.wto.org

More recently, the Doha Declaration, agreed at the fourth WTO ministerial meeting in November 2001, reaffirmed the organization's commitment to the objective of sustainable development: 'We are convinced that the aims of upholding and safeguarding an open and non-discriminatory multilateral trading system, and acting for the protection of the environment and the promotion of sustainable development can and must be mutually supportive.'[3] More importantly, the agenda for the next round of trade negotiations which was agreed at Doha contained, for the first time in a trade round, a series of commitments to discussions and possible negotiations on major trade and environment issues. (See Box 15.1.)

So the trade and environment debate has steadily moved inwards from the fringes of the WTO agenda. Because of its nature it also overlaps with many of the other topics of discussion, such as agriculture, subsidies, or investment. But that does not mean to say that much progress has actually been made in terms of reaching a resolution of the tensions inherent in the trade–environment relationship. The rest of this chapter examines the key issues within that relationship; and before that, a look at why tensions may exist in the first place.

The environmental impact of trade and investment

Trade impacts both positively and negatively on the environment. The *net* impact in any given case of an increase in trade volumes will depend on the aggregate outcome of a number of effects:

- *Scale effects* In general, trade and investment liberalization accelerates economic growth. Positive scale effects then result from a reduction in poverty-driven environmental degradation, and from the increased attention countries tend to pay to environmental quality and regulation as income rises (though it is possible that by the time this 'turning point' is reached, the environmental resource base may have suffered irreversible degradation). Emissions of many global pollutants such as greenhouse gases, however, tend to grow as income rises, displaying negative scale effects, i.e. without any turning point. This is at base a result of market failures, such as ill-defined property rights (no one 'owns' the atmosphere), and a failure to incorporate environmental externalities (such as the costs of climate change).

- The *structural effects* of shifts in the structures of economies, which are accelerated by openness to trade, tend to be positive for the environment. Typically economies develop from primary resource extraction through processing to manufacturing and then to services, and each step tends to lead to a reduction in pollution output and resource depletion, though the correct pricing of environmental externalities is again an important factor.

- *Technology effects* arise from greater access to new technologies (again promoted by trade and investment liberalization), which in general tend to produce less pollution and use fewer resources than their predecessors.

- *Product effects* – changes in the mixes of goods produced and consumed, shifts in production methods (such as outsourcing component manufacture among different countries), and associated energy, transport and other environmental implications – can be positive or negative for the environment, once again largely depending on the extent to which prices and decisions reflect environmental costs.

- The *distribution effects* of shifts in production and consumption between countries (and sometimes within countries), which are promoted and accelerated by trade and investment liberalization, may be an important determinant of environmental impact. It is often argued that business may respond to higher environmental standards – which are assumed to lead to higher business costs and lower profits – through migration, of investment flows if not of industrial plant itself, to countries with less stringent regulatory regimes, where the cost of production is lower. In fact this is a complex area with a dearth of empirical evidence (Zarsky 1999). Most research indicates that environmental standards play no significant part in investment location decisions, largely because the costs associated with them are relatively low; many other factors, including political stability, the potential of domestic markets, quality of infrastructure, labour costs and ease of repatriation of profits are more important. While true in general, however, some specific industry sectors may be more significantly affected by environmental policy. In particular, policies designed to mitigate climate change are bound to require increases in the cost of carbon-intensive energy sources, with a major impact on energy-intensive industries such as iron and steel, or aluminium, where energy consumption may account for up to 15–20 per cent of total costs. Furthermore, as with any measure where the benefits are diffuse and widespread but the costs are concentrated, political lobbies *against* action may often prove stronger than lobbies *for*. Industry lobbyists, and political decision makers, often end up behaving as though they believe that environmental regulation does invariably raise costs. Thus competitiveness concerns are likely to remain an important part of the debate.

It is impossible to be precise about the net environmental outcome of these impacts of trade and investment growth, though key sectors can be identified where the liberalization process is more likely to have net positive environmental outcomes. In general these are industries in which subsidies for environmentally damaging production processes, which would be reduced or removed under liberalized trade and investment regimes, are widespread: agriculture, fossil fuels and fisheries (the inclusion of agriculture and fisheries in the Doha Round is therefore of potential environmental significance). Other benefits can flow from liberalization, particularly in the freight transport and environmental goods and services sectors.

Overall, however, given the widespread failure so far (with a few notable exceptions) of policies to halt or reverse environmental impacts, it is difficult to be optimistic about the future. It seems likely that any positive technology and structural effects of trade and investment liberalization will be swamped by the large negative scale effects from the expansion of economic activity, and smaller aggregate negative distribution effects. It should be noted, however, that the situation is not necessarily improved if the liberalization process is slowed down or halted: negative scale effects are reduced in magnitude, but so are the positive technology and structural effects. The key question in each case is the effectiveness of *environmental policy frameworks*, which have the potential, if they are adequately constructed and enforced, to offset, or even in some cases reverse, the negative environmental impacts. In general, it seems likely that environmental policies will be more strongly implemented and enforced under conditions of strong economic growth, though even then it is difficult to believe that they can reverse the overall process of environmental degradation worldwide.

The final impact of trade and investment liberalization on the environment is expressed through the *regulatory effects* of the legal and policy impacts of trade and investment policies: do these make environmental regulation easier or harder to implement? This is the key question underlying most of the trade–environment debate within the WTO, and is the subject of the remainder of this chapter.

The multilateral trading system and environmental policy

As described elsewhere in this book, the central aim of the multilateral trading system – the set of agreements overseen by the WTO – is to liberalize trade between WTO members. WTO members are not permitted to discriminate between other WTO members' traded products, or between domestic and international production.

Article XX of the GATT, however (and similar provisions in the other WTO agreements) permits, under particular circumstances, unilateral trade restrictions for various reasons, including the pursuit of environmental protection. Paragraph (b) of Article XX creates an exception for measures 'necessary to protect human, animal or plant life or health', and paragraph (g) for measures 'relating to the conservation of exhaustible natural resources if such measures are made effective in conjunction with restrictions on domestic production or consumption'; such measures must also satisfy the headnote (or 'chapeau') of Article XX, the requirement that the measures must not be applied 'in a manner which would constitute a means of arbitrary or unjustifiable discrimination between countries where the same conditions prevail, or a disguised restriction on international trade'. One or both of these two paragraphs, XX(b) and XX(g), have been cited in a series of trade–environment dispute cases coming before the WTO's disputes body. Given the fact that several key terms in the text of the GATT and other agreements – such as 'like product' in GATT Articles I and III – are not defined, the findings of panels and the Appellate Body in these dispute cases have in practice determined how the multilateral trading system treats trade-related environmental measures, and will continue to do so in the absence of any agreement to modify the WTO system to meet environmental objectives.

As noted above, the WTO itself contains a reference to sustainable development in the preamble of the agreement establishing the body. Initially regarded as little more than a symbolic acknowledgement of the issue, it has been accorded considerably greater significance since the WTO Appellate Body cited it as an acceptable justification for particular trade measures in the 1998 shrimp–turtle dispute, which involved a US embargo on imports of shrimp from South-East Asian nations which did not require the fitting of turtle-excluder devices to their trawlers (designed to avoid incidental catches of endangered sea turtles).[4]

The heart of the multilateral trading system is the principle of non-discrimination between 'like products'. Although in most instances this would appear to cause no problem for environmental regulation, there are in fact three main areas where conflicts may arise: over internationally determined product standards; where processes, rather than products, cause the environmental damage; and in the enforcement of MEAs.

Product standards

Although the GATT in general frowns on trade restrictions, the existence of Article XX suggests that countries should be able to ban or restrict the import of products which will harm their own environments, as long as the standards applied are non-discriminatory between countries and between domestic and foreign production. As the GATT secretariat expressed it in 1992, 'GATT rules place essentially no constraints on a country's right to protect its own environment against damage from either domestic production or the consumption of domestically produced or imported products' (GATT 1992: 23).

The Uruguay Round, however, saw a significant extension of the two main WTO agreements governing the application of potentially trade-restrictive measures in the fields of standards. Technical standards, including packaging and labelling requirements, are covered by the Agreement on Technical Barriers to Trade (TBT Agreement), and human, animal and plant health standards by the Agreement on the Application of Sanitary and Phytosanitary Measures (SPS Agreement). Both aim to encourage the international harmonization of product standards and to avoid their use as disguised protectionism. Where possible, internationally agreed standards, such as those agreed by the International Organization for Standardization (ISO) or the Codex Alimentarius Commission, are to be used.

Under paragraph 2.2 of the TBT Agreement, technical regulations 'shall not be more trade-restrictive than necessary to fulfil a legitimate objective'. This is defined as including environmental protection, and environmental grounds have indeed become more widely cited as an objective and rationale for applying trade-restrictive regulations including, most notably, measures aimed at controlling air pollution and hazardous chemicals (GATT 1992: 32). However, there is almost no experience with the way in which the WTO dispute settlement system might interpret the phrases 'not be more trade-restrictive than necessary' and 'unnecessary obstacle to international trade' in the TBT Agreement, particularly where non-international standards (e.g. standards more rigorous than those agreed by ISO) are involved.[5]

The SPS Agreement allows WTO members to take protective measures in the face of a threat from one of a number of specific causes (such as disease-causing organisms) as long as certain conditions are met, including the requirement that the measure is based on a risk assessment. This was a key point in the 1998 beef hormones dispute, in which the USA argued that an EU ban on imports of beef from cattle treated with growth hormones was WTO-incompatible. The Appellate Body found that the ban could be justified as long as the EU provided convincing scientific evidence of the danger to human health; when the European Commission failed to supply this within the set period, the WTO authorized the USA to levy tariffs on specific categories of EU exports.

This was not, however, an argument about discrimination, as the EU also bans its own producers from using the hormones in question. Effectively the Uruguay Round agreements have taken the WTO beyond the simple issue of trade discrimination into a new realm of global standard setting. In turn this focuses attention on the standard-setting bodies themselves – both their composition (they are typically dominated by industry experts) and their modes of operating. It also raises the question of how appropriate standards can be set in the absence of complete scientific knowledge, and how the WTO would treat trade measures justified by the precautionary principle, familiar to environmental policy makers, which argues for preventive action without full scientific certainty, particularly in instances where the costs of actions are low and the risks of inaction high.

The SPS Agreement itself contains only a rather weak version of the precautionary principle, and the Appellate Body in the beef hormones dispute was not convinced that it had yet been accepted as a principle of general international law. However, the Cartagena Protocol on biosafety, agreed in January 2000, contains a distinctly stronger version of a precautionary approach to the movement of genetically modified products; this may reinforce the status of the principle in WTO disputes. This issue has been raised once again by the US decision, in May 2003, to challenge the EU's *de facto* moratorium on approval of genetically modified organisms (GMOs) pending the adoption of rules ensuring labelling and traceability of GMOs and GMO-derived products; the USA claimed this was inconsistent with obligations under the SPS, TBT and Agriculture Agreements, as well as the GATT itself. The highly charged and politically controversial issue of the acceptability of GM products, featuring very different views between the USA and EU (governments and public alike), brought the threat of a possible new trade war to the fore at the WTO Ministerial meeting in Cancùn in September 2003, and seems likely to overshadow the post-Cancùn period.

Process and production methods

The problem with trade restrictions based on environmental regulations derived from process and production *methods* (PPMs), as opposed to *product* standards, stems from the meaning of the GATT term 'like product'. This has become one of the most difficult issues in the trade–environment arena. Originally incorporated into the GATT in order to prevent discrimination on the grounds of national origin, GATT and WTO dispute panels have in general interpreted the term more broadly to prevent discrimination in cases where *process* methods, rather than *product* characteristics, have been the distinguishing characteristic of the product and the justification for trade measures. In the well-known US–Mexico tuna–dolphin dispute in 1991, for example, the dispute panel ruled that the trade restriction in question (the US import ban on Mexican tuna caught with dolphin-unfriendly nets) was in breach of the GATT because it discriminated against a product on the basis of the way in which it was produced, not on the basis of its own characteristics – that is, it discriminated against a 'like product'.

In 1994, another GATT panel, ruling on an EU–US dispute over car imports, slightly relaxed the definition, considering that vehicles of different fuel efficiency standards could be considered *not* to be like products. However, it placed strict boundaries on this conclusion, arguing that Article III of the GATT referred only to a 'product as a product, from its introduction into the market to its final consumption' (GATT 1994: para. 5.52). Factors relating to the manufacture of the product before its introduction into the market were, therefore, still irrelevant. In 1996 another panel found that chemically identical imported and domestic gasoline were like products regardless of the environmental standards of the producers.

This series of disputes has led to a widely held view that the GATT automatically rules out any discrimination in trade based on the way in which products are manufactured, caught or harvested. In turn this has aroused much concern among the environmental policy community, where policies designed to regulate PPMs (such as controlling emissions from manufacturing processes, or promoting sustainable production) are seen as increasingly important. This has resulted in a longlasting – but somewhat sterile – debate. It should be noted, however, that contrary to this widespread belief, nowhere does the GATT explicitly rule out process-based trade discrimination; indeed, in some areas it is clearly permitted (Charnovitz 2002). Both the Agreement on Subsidies and Countervailing Measures and the Agreement on Trade-Related Aspects of Intellectual Property Rights (the TRIPs Agreement) regulate some aspects of *how* goods are produced, allowing importing countries to discriminate against products if they are produced using excessive subsidy or misappropriated intellectual property. GATT's Article XX(e) allows countries to discriminate against products produced using prison labour.

In any case, more recent disputes have led to very different conclusions about how the dispute settlement system may deal with trade restrictions deriving from PPMs. In the shrimp–turtle case, for example, the US embargo on imports of shrimp from nations which did not require the fitting of turtle-excluder devices to their trawlers, a measure which US fishing fleets were required to undertake, clearly embodied discrimination on the basis of the way in which the shrimp were caught (a PPM). The Appellate Body, however, considered that this discrimination between like products could be justified under Article XX(g) of the GATT. In the end, the measure failed, among other reasons because the USA had applied the embargo against all shrimp exports from a country unless it could demonstrate that it took sea turtle protection measures comparable with those of the USA. If the exporting country in question could not do so, *all* its shrimp exports to the USA were banned even if individual consignments were caught in turtle-friendly ways, e.g. by trawlers which *were* fitted with turtle-excluder devices. The US process of country-by-country 'certification' thus failed to satisfy the conditions set out in the headnote to Article XX, and was one of a number of elements that did constitute, the Appellate Body decided, 'arbitrary or unjustifiable discrimination'.

In the light of this finding, the USA amended its regulations in various ways, including permitting the import of shrimp harvested by particular commercial vessels using devices comparable in effectiveness with those required by the USA. In the second WTO dispute on the case, in 2001, the dispute panel and Appellate Body ruled that the new measures *were* compatible with the GATT, having satisfied the requirements of the headnote, and the measure remains in force today (Howse 2002).

This dispute case helps to illustrate the fact that there are different ways in which PPM-based trade measures may be applied.[6] Almost all of the relevant dispute cases to date have involved fairly crude trade measures involving discrimination against all exports from particular countries, or particular producers, on the basis of the processes permitted, or not permitted, in that country or by that producer. The shrimp–turtle case demonstrates that a carefully targeted measure, designed to exclude particular products on the basis of the way in which the *individual products* are produced (not on which country or which company they come from), could well be found to be GATT compatible.

This is, however, a complex debate. Where the environmental damage caused by the PPM is confined to the locality of the process, PPM-based environmental trade measures are not easy to justify. Different parts of the world vary widely in their ability to assimilate pollution, depending on factors such as climate, population density, existing levels of pollution and risk preferences. Environmental regulations suited to industrialized nations, with high population densities and environments which have been subject to pollution for the past 200 years, may be wholly inappropriate for newly industrializing countries with much lower population densities and inherited pollution levels – and yet trade measures based on PPMs could in effect seek to impose the higher standards regardless. Carried to its logical extreme, enforcing similarity of PPMs could deny the very basis of comparative advantage, which rests on the proposition that countries possess different cost structures for the production of various goods. It is hardly surprising that many developing countries view the motives of those wishing to introduce the PPM issue to the debate as protectionist.

Where the environmental damage is transboundary or global, however, the argument is different, since the impact of the PPM is not confined to the country of origin. PPM-based measures are, furthermore, becoming increasingly important in strategies for environmental sustainability. Particularly where the use of energy is involved (as it is in virtually every manufacturing and processing activity), the pollution caused stems from the process and not the product. Attempts to reduce energy use in order to mitigate climate change – through, for example, energy or carbon taxes – may well be applied to processes. Life-cycle approaches, and eco-labelling schemes based on them, have similarly focused attention on the way in which products are manufactured, grown or harvested, as well on product characteristics themselves; indeed, the whole point of eco-labelling schemes is to provide information on differences in characteristics between like products.

The Appellate Body in the shrimp–turtle case did not – unsurprisingly – produce any general guidance on the circumstances in which PPM-based trade measures might be acceptable in the future. But its arguments were reinforced by its conclusions in the 2001 asbestos case, where a Canadian challenge to a French prohibition on the use of building materials containing asbestos was upheld. Canada had argued that building materials containing asbestos and those not containing it should be treated as like products, but the Appellate Body concluded that even where two products are deemed to be 'like' under the terms of GATT Article III, they could still be treated differently in regulation, as long as this did not lead to systematic discrimination against imports. As long as the relevant regulation was even-handed between imports and domestic products, and focused on appropriate goals (in the asbestos case, on the health impacts), then it should be WTO compliant.

These two cases together could well signal the settlement of the PPM issue in the trade and environment debate – as the well-known academic commentator John Jackson has argued, in the light of the shrimp–turtle case, 'the product-process distinction will probably not survive and perhaps *should* not survive' (2000: 222). This is a good example of where the argument has moved forward entirely through dispute settlement rather than political negotiations; indeed, the issue does not feature at all on the Doha Round's agenda. Whether this is a firm and lasting conclusion, and what the implications are for the design of PPM-based trade measures, remains to be worked out, probably through further disputes.

MEAs

As Principle 12 of the Rio Declaration states, international agreement is clearly preferable to unilateral action in tackling transboundary or global environmental problems. Well over 250 MEAs now exist, with memberships varying from a relatively small group to over 180 countries – which means effectively the whole world. Almost thirty of these MEAs incorporate trade measures, restraints on the trade in particular substances or products, either between parties to the treaty and/or between parties and non-parties. A wide variety of measures have been used, including reporting requirements on trade flows, labelling or other identification requirements, requirements for movement documents (such as permits or licences, or systems of prior notification and consent), and export and/or import bans, with varying degrees of specificity (Brack and Gray 2003; OECD 1999).

There are three broad sets of reasons why trade restrictions have been incorporated in MEAs (Charnovitz 1998):

1   To provide a means of monitoring and controlling trade in products where the uncontrolled trade would lead to or contribute to environmental damage. This may extend to a complete exclusion of particular products from international trade.
2   To provide a means of complying with the MEA's requirements.
3   To provide a means of enforcing the MEA, by forbidding trade with non-parties or non-complying parties.

The Montreal Protocol, for example, contains examples of all three types. Considering the first category, a system of import and export licences was introduced in 1997, through the Montreal Amendment, primarily in order to control illegal trade. In the second category, countries have used a variety of policies (such as taxes and quotas) to limit imports and exports, in order to fulfil their obligations to control the consumption of chlorofluorocarbons (CFCs) and other controlled substances; since consumption is defined as 'production + imports − exports', control of trade is essential. And in the third category, the protocol requires parties to ban imports of ozone-depleting substances from non-parties, and potentially from non-complying parties, as an enforcement measure. On the face of it, this last type of trade measure in particular would appear to conflict with the GATT, since it discriminates between the same product imported from different countries on the basis of their membership of the protocol. It is widely accepted, however, that the inclusion of this measure in the Montreal Protocol has contributed significantly to its success in attracting signatories (Brack 1996).

This topic has become one of the main items of debate within the trade–environment agenda in recent years, and was a particularly important topic in discussions in the WTO's Committee on Trade and Environment in its first two years of existence, during the run-up to the Singapore WTO Conference in 1996. Members put forward proposals designed variously to define under what conditions trade measures taken pursuant to an MEA could be considered to be 'necessary' according to the terms of GATT's Article XX, or to establish a degree of WTO oversight on the negotiation and operation of trade provisions in future MEAs. The EU pressed for an amendment to the GATT itself to create a presumption of compatibility with MEAs, but no consensus was reached about the need for modifications to trade rules. Other options include waivers for MEA trade measures from the provisions of the multilateral trading system, or a WTO 'understanding' or full-blown agreement on MEAs. Like every other item on the Committee on Trade and

Environment's agenda, however, the discussions never resulted in a firm conclusion, and the debates are now being largely repeated, with a few variations, under paragraph 31(i) of the Doha Round agenda.

It is worth noting, however, that no complaint has yet arisen within the GATT or WTO with respect to trade measures taken in pursuit of an MEA, and this may continue to be the case; in instances such as the Montreal Protocol, where the trade provisions were mainly designed to encourage countries to accede, this has been so successful that there are virtually no non-parties left against whom trade measures could be taken in any case. On the other hand, the threat of a conflict with WTO rules has been raised in almost all recent MEA negotiations, generally by those opposed to the principle of the MEA and/or its effective enforcement, and there have been various attempts to write 'savings clauses' into them, ensuring that they remain subordinate to WTO disciplines.[7] The lack of clarity on the issue, and the uncertainty about the outcome of any WTO dispute, has thus led many to call for some kind of resolution. The entry into force of the Cartagena Protocol in September 2003 will add another dimension to the US–EU dispute over trade in GM products, and may provide the first testing ground for an MEA–WTO clash.

The latest stage of the shrimp–turtle dispute contains a potentially important development of WTO jurisprudence in this area. In the second shrimp–turtle case, in June 2001 the dispute panel found that the USA was entitled to maintain its embargo (having adjusted its original regulations in various ways; see above), even though it was a unilaterally applied measure, as long as it was engaged in 'serious good-faith efforts to negotiate an international agreement, taking into account the situations of the other negotiating countries' (WTO 2001: para. 5.73). It did not accept Malaysia's contention that the agreement had to be concluded *before* a trade restriction could be enforced. In addition, the panel believed that the US trade measures would 'be accepted under Article XX if they were allowed under an international agreement', but in the absence of such agreement, such measures are 'more to be seen, for the purposes of Article XX, as the possibility to adopt a *provisional* measure allowed for emergency reasons than as a definitive "right" to take a permanent measure'.

The Appellate Body came to a somewhat different conclusion, arguing that there was no absolute requirement that countries had to offer to engage in multilateral negotiations before they were allowed to apply trade measures (Howse 2002). In the first shrimp–turtle case, it was the fact that the USA had negotiated an agreement with Caribbean nations but had not tried to do so (at least initially) with South-East Asian shrimp-exporting countries that had led to the conclusion of 'arbitrary and unjustifiable treatment' – underlining the WTO dislike of discrimination between WTO members. So while unilateral trade measures may well be permissible, depending on how they are designed, trade measures taken in the context of a multilateral agreement ought to be even more justifiable under the WTO.

Although it is always dangerous to extrapolate too widely from particular disputes, it may well be that, as with the PPMs argument, this conclusion has taken the heat out of the WTO–MEA debate. However, there are still open questions over various aspects of the issue, particularly over the design of so-called 'non-specific' trade measures, those which may be applied in order to implement an MEA but which are not specifically described or required in the treaty itself (the second category identified above). These may be of particular importance in the implementation of the Kyoto Protocol on climate change (e.g. in the use of carbon or energy taxes, and how these are applied to imported products), which, because of its economic impact, could lead to more controversies and, potentially, WTO disputes (Brack *et al.* 2000).

Conclusion: the environment beyond Doha

The initial injection of trade and environment issues onto the GATT/WTO agenda was largely due to developments in the environment world. The UN Conference on the Human Environment in Stockholm in 1972 helped drive the establishment of the GATT's group on environmental measures and international trade. This EMIT group remained inactive, however, until the run-up to the Earth Summit in Rio twenty years later, when it finally started to meet on a regular basis, and in due course was transformed into the Committee on Trade and Environment (CTE), set up when the WTO was established in 1995. At the same time the tuna–dolphin dispute helped turn the topic into a high-profile political issue, taken up by many NGOs around the world (and not only, it should be noted, by those hostile to globalization in general, and the WTO in particular).

Although the CTE was established with a mandate to 'identify the relationship between trade measures and environmental measures, in order to promote sustainable development [and] to make appropriate recommendations on whether any modifications of the provisions of the multilateral trading system are required' (WTO 1994b) it has never managed to reach any conclusions on any such modifications. In one sense this is not particularly surprising. WTO trade rounds tend to make progress through agreement on a broad package of measures, inevitably involving national trade-offs – and there has never been enough scope within the CTE's agenda for such trade-offs to be reached in isolation. Discussions within the CTE have undoubtedly contributed towards a greater understanding of the issues, but there is not much else one can say for its deliberations.

The inclusion of the trade and environment paragraphs in the Doha Round agenda was almost entirely due to the insistence of the EU, supported only by a few other developed country allies.[8] The USA, prone to see any development of multilateral rules as a potential inhibition on its predilection for unilateral trade measures, largely stayed clear of the debate. Under the Bush Administration, both environmental policy and support for international institutions in general appear to have been heavily downplayed, so it seems highly unlikely that the USA will express much interest in seeing these debates advance. Indeed, it may adopt an increasingly hostile position, as evidenced by its challenge to the EU's regulations on GM products (see above).[9] Matters are also complicated by the greater degree of scepticism European populations – and, usually, their governments – often display over matters such as food safety (e.g. over GM products, or hormone-treated beef) compared with the US public and government, who seem more likely to accept business-promoted new technological developments.

Developing countries as a whole also tend to be hostile to the trade–environment proposals of Northern countries, fearing that new environmentally directed trade restrictions will discriminate disproportionately against their exports, and potentially lead on to other new bases for trade barriers, such as labour or animal welfare standards. Discussions within the CTE on the Doha agenda have not proceeded with any great degree of rapidity or likelihood of consensus – though in that sense they are no different from discussions on most of the other topics on the Doha agenda – and in practice the trade and environment discussion was entirely sidelined at Cancùn as attention focused on the much higher profile issues such as agriculture or services. It should also be remembered that the Doha agenda focuses only on a few trade and environment issues, and avoids the more controversial ones, such as the PPMs debate.

It is now commonplace to observe that much of the problem stems from a failure of 'policy coherence' of national governments to integrate their environmental and trade objectives. A stark example of this is provided by the tendency of developing country trade negotiators firmly to oppose any new trade-related environmental measures, while at the same time their counterparts in environment ministries argue for stricter trade restrictions in certain MEAs than the developed world wants.[10] (This is not to say that developed countries handle the relationship any better – most of them do not.) To a certain extent this is a problem with environmental policy as a whole (e.g. in respect of its integration, or lack of it, into agriculture, or economic, policy), and is likely to remain so as long as most governments afford higher priority to economic and trade issues than they do to environmental ones.

In practice, such movement as there has been on the trade and environment agenda has derived almost entirely from two sources. First, the evolving way in which the WTO's dispute settlement system has interpreted the WTO agreements in trade–environment cases, which, as can be seen from the discussion above, has led to quite different conclusions in more recent cases than would have been predicted by most observers in the early 1990s. Second, from the way in which more recent MEAs have incorporated steadily more sophisticated trade measures, and tried themselves to address their relationships with the WTO.

In the absence of any political agreement on modification of WTO rules, this seems likely to be the pattern of future developments. A political crisis can never, however, be ruled out – a serious clash between the USA and EU over GM products, or a challenge to an MEA under the WTO, are the most likely candidates. Crises have the benefit of focusing attention and political will on the issue – and it may well be that without such a development, the relationship between trade liberalization and environmental protection will remain as a set of unresolved tensions on the international agenda.

Notes

1   Marrakech Agreement Establishing the World Trade Organization, preamble, para. 2.
2   United Nations Conference on Environment and Development, Agenda 21, Chapter Two, Section B.
3   WTO Ministerial Declaration, 14 November 2001, para. 6.
4   This line of argument may widen the future potential for process-based trade restrictions (see further below) beyond what was generally thought the WTO would allow, which is probably why it generated almost as much criticism from the complainants in the case as from the defendant.
5   The 2001 sardines dispute between the EU and Peru over labelling of fish products resulted in a finding that the EU Regulation diverged unjustifiably from the relevant international (Codex Alimentarius) standard, but it did not rule on any wider issue.
6   Charnovitz divides PPMs into three types: ones based on a government policy standard, on a producer characteristic or on a 'how produced' standard.
7   The Cartagena Protocol contains both such a phrase and another sentence explaining that the protocol is not subordinate to any other agreement, thus entirely avoiding resolving the issue.
8   The EU's commitment to environmental priorities is always somewhat undermined, however, by its attachment to existing and environmentally damaging subsidies for agriculture and fisheries.
9   The USA's increasing tendency to adopt a bilateral approach in trade policy was illustrated in June 2003 by the threat made by Senator Chuck Grassley (Chairman of the Senate Finance Committee) to Egypt, which had decided against joining the US challenge to the EU. Grassley said that while he was supportive of a possible US–Egypt Free Trade Agreement, 'one of the criteria that ought to be used to determine with whom the United States negotiates future FTAs is whether a country shares the same vision of the global trading system as does the United States. I certainly would like to be able to include Egypt in that camp.' 'US announces panel on EU GMO moratorium, as Grassley warns Egypt', *Inside US Trade* 20 June 2003: 1.

10 The Basel Convention on hazardous waste, and the Cartagena Protocol on GM products, are both good examples – instances of where countries lacking strong domestic regulatory capacity effectively co-opt trade policy (allowing them to control imports) to serve the same purpose.

Bibliography

Brack, D. (1996) *International Trade and the Montreal Protocol*, London: RIIA/Earthscan.

Brack, D. and Gray, K. (2003) *Multilateral Environmental Agreements and the WTO*, London: Royal Institute of International Affairs and International Institute for Sustainable Development.

Brack, D., Grubb, M. and Windram, C. (2000) *International Trade and Climate Change Policies*, London: RIIA/Earthscan.

Charnovitz, S. (1998) 'The role of trade measures in treaties', in A. Fijalkowski and J. Cameron (eds), *Trade and the Environment: bridging the gap*, London: Cameron.

Charnovitz, S. (2002) 'The law of environmental "PPMs" in the WTO: debunking the myth of illegality', *Yale Journal of International Law* 27: 59–102.

GATT (1992) *International Trade 1990–91*, Geneva: GATT Secretariat.

GATT (1994) 'US: taxes on automobiles: report of the panel', Geneva: GATT Secretariat.

Howse, R.L. (2002) 'The Appellate Body Rulings in the Shrimp/Turtle Case: a new legal baseline for the trade and enviromental debate', Symposium on Trade, Sustainability and Global Governance, *Columbia Journal of Environmental Law* 29(2): 491–521.

Jackson, J.H. (2000) 'The limits of international trade: workers' protection, the environment and other human rights', *Proceedings of the 94th Meeting of the American Society of International Law*.

OECD (1999) *Trade Measures in Multilateral Environmental Agreements*, Paris: OECD.

United Nations Conference on Environment and Development, '*Agenda 21*', Rio de Janeiro, June 3–14.

World Trade Online (2003) 'US announces panel on EU GMO moratorium, as Grassley warns Egypt', *Inside US Trade* 20 June: 1.

WTO (1994a) 'Marrakech Agreement Establishing the World Trade Organization', Geneva: WTO.

WTO (1994b), 'Decision on Trade and the Environment', 14 April. Available HTTP: <http://www.wto.org/english/tratop_e/envir_e/issu5_e.htm> (accessed 22 July 2003).

WTO (2001) 'United States – Import prohibition of certain shrimp and shrimp products', recourse to Article 21.5 of the DSU by Malaysia, report of the panel, 15 June 2001 (WT/DS58/RW).

Wynter, M. (2001) 'International trade and environmental protection: domestic PPM regulations and WTO jurisprudence', Unpublished thesis, Australian National University.

Zarsky, L. (1999) 'Havens, halos and spaghetti: untangling the evidence about FDI and the environment', Paper for OECD Conference on FDI and the Environment, January 1999.

Key readings

Bail, C., Falkner, R. and Marquard, H. (eds) (2002) *The Cartagena Protocol on Biosafety: reconciling trade in biotechnology with environment and development?*, London: RIIA/Earthscan.

Brack, D. (ed.) (1998) *Trade and Environment: conflict or compatibility?*, London: RIIA/Earthscan.

Cameron, J., Demaret, P. and Geradin, D. (eds) (1994) *Trade and Environment: the search for balance*, London: Cameron May.

Esty, D. (1994) *Greening the GATT: trade, environment and the future*, Washington, DC: Institute for International Economics.

International Centre for Trade and Sustainable Development: Bridges, journal (print) and Bridges weekly trade news digest (electronic): www.ictsd.org.

International Institute for Trade and Sustainable Development/UN Environment Programme (2000) *Environment and Trade: a handbook*, Winnipeg: IISD.

Konz, P. (ed.) (2000) *Trade, Environment and Sustainable Development: views from sub-Saharan Africa and Latin America – a reader*, United Nations University/International Centre for Trade and Sustainable Development.

Mann, H. and Porter, S. (2003) *The State of Trade and Environment Law: implications for Doha and beyond*, Winnipeg: IISD.

Sampson, G.P. (2000) *Trade, Environment and the WTO: the Post-Seattle agenda*, Washington, DC: Overseas Development Council.

Sampson, G.P. and Bradnee Chambers, W. (eds) (2002) *Trade, Environment and the Millennium*, 2nd edn, Tokyo: UN University Press.

United Nations Environment Programme (UNEP) Economics and Trade Programme. Available HTTP <www.unep.ch/etu/etp/index.htm> (accessed 22 July 2003).

Ward, H. and Brack, D. (eds) (1999) *Trade, Investment and the Environment*, London: RIIA/Earthscan.

Useful website

www.riia.org/sustainabledevelopment (Royal Institute of International Affairs).

16 Trade and human rights

The issue of minimum labour standards

Gijsbert van Liemt[1]

Summary

Discussions on trade and labour standards revolve around three questions: (1) How essential is universal respect for minimum international labour standards? (2) Should outside pressure or encouragement be used to help promote respect for these standards? (3) What is the role that international institutions can or should play in this? Conditionality (the use of trade sanctions to enforce labour standards) – and multilateral conditionality in particular – has for a long time dominated the debate. To a large extent it still does. But there is now a broad consensus that minimum labour standards should be respected universally; that outside help can be useful; and that the International Labour Organization (ILO) has a prime role to play in this.

Few trade issues are as controversial as the link to labour standards. Proponents of such a linkage argue that the international exchange of goods cannot and should not disregard the conditions under which these goods are being produced, and that the international community has a legitimate role in the promotion of minimum labour standards such as the freedom of workers to bargain collectively and the freedom of children not to be exploited. They are not suggesting a global minimum wage (as many critics claim they do), but argue that when workers are unable to bargain for the best wages and working conditions possible, this could be interpreted as 'social dumping'. Also, when workers in exporting countries are seen to be enjoying certain basic rights, it is easier to convince workers in import-competing industries of the benefits of lower trade barriers.

Critics oppose the link with labour standards because it complicates already highly complex trade negotiations. They question whether there exists a set of universally agreed minimum labour standards as these are culture specific. Insisting on their universality might lead to poor countries adopting inappropriate labour practices and may be irreconcilable with the principles of state sovereignty and non-interference in domestic affairs. Proponents of such a link would be more concerned about a loss of their own privileged position and a refusal to adapt to new realities, than by genuine feelings of solidarity. They point to the tuna–dolphin ruling to illustrate that actions taken against countries with different domestic policies are not compatible with WTO–GATT regulations.[2]

Conditionality (making market access conditional on respect for minimum labour standards), a key feature of most discussions on trade and labour standards, is responsible for much of the controversy. 'Northern' trade unions and workers' rights activists see the possibility to restrict market access as a necessary measure of last resort for ensuring that exporters respect certain basic labour standards. These exporters, operating in market segments where competition is fierce and margins thin, strongly oppose this threat of trade sanctions. So controversial is conditionality that it overshadows most other elements of the trade–labour debate, including that of the universality of 'core' labour standards. Privately, exporters may agree that these are universal rights, but their opposition to trade conditionality and their scepticism about the (lack of) fairness with which it might be applied leads them to disagree in public.

This chapter discusses the role of labour standards in the global economy; trade conditionality, its most controversial dimension; and some recent initiatives that have raised the attention given to minimum labour standards. It is organized as follows. The next section argues that solidarity is at the root of the international concerns about working conditions and labour standards in poor, exporting countries. Economic arguments also play a role; to deny workers certain basic rights could constitute an unfair trade advantage (third section). But the magnitude of that advantage may be hard to establish, as the fourth section argues. The discussion on trade and labour standards centres on a select group of 'core' or 'basic' minimum labour standards. The fifth section asks whether these standards are universally accepted as such. Conditionality is at the heart of the discussion (sixth section). It is highly controversial. The fairness of the system is placed in doubt. Insistence on respect for minimum labour standards can be seen as interference with the sovereignty of the state. The example of the Generalized System of Preferences (GSP) and the one on China's MFN status illustrate the point.

Trade sanctions are the prime source of leverage. But sanctions are not without costs. What are they meant to achieve; and do they achieve what they are meant to? The threat of sanctions may be the true source of leverage as the seventh section points out. The example of trade sanctions and child labour in Bangladesh illustrates the point. A multilateral arrangement might be able to accommodate some of the drawbacks usually associated with the trade–labour link. There is, however, little enthusiasm to do so in the International Labour Organization (ILO) or the World Trade Organization (WTO), the two organizations most frequently mentioned in this respect (the eighth section). The last section argues that the absence of a multilateral trade–labour link should not distract from the fact that the last decade has seen a proliferation of initiatives to give more attention to labour standards in international economic integration. Respect for minimum labour standards is a condition for membership of the EU and for trade preferences allotted by the USA and the EU. It is an essential component of the codes of conduct adopted by internationally operating companies and of the UN's 'Global Compact'. And it has become an obligation for all ILO members, including those that have not ratified the corresponding conventions.

Globalization and labour

The internationalization of production and investment affects labour in several ways. It opens up new job opportunities. It also threatens jobs in import-competing industries. And it accelerates the speed of structural change, and thus the need for rapid adjustment.

Globalization also affects labour standards, which are set through legislation or collective agreement. Labour, the immobile production factor and the nation-state (which generates regulation) are widely seen as having to compete to attract internationally mobile capital and technology. Labour standards thus suffer from regulatory competition (Klevorick 1996). Also, workers' bargaining power is under threat as capital has acquired the option of exit and labour has not.

The pressure on labour legislation and labour's weakened bargaining power are pretty much universal features. But their potential effects on labour standards are particularly serious in the developing countries where, on the whole, labour protection is at a lower level than in the more developed economies. In certain developing countries (but not necessarily in those that trade the most), labour standards are particularly low.

Workers in low-income countries tend to receive low wages. Also, when wages are low, people need to work long hours in order to make ends meet. Safety and health conditions are usually inferior to those in rich, industrialized countries. History has shown that as economies develop, wages go up, working hours come down and safety and health considerations receive more attention. However, low wages and poor working conditions need not necessarily, or not exclusively, be the result of a country's low level of development. On the whole, wages reflect the general level of productivity. But they may be kept *artificially* low when the labour movement is suppressed or controlled. Collective bargaining may not be permitted, legislation may be inadequate and existing laws may not be enforced.

International solidarity can play two roles in raising labour standards. Where poor working conditions are simply the result of a low level of development, greater capital flows and increased market access in importing countries can help economic and social development in exporting countries. Where, on the other hand, these conditions are also caused by inadequate legislation, a weak enforcement of the law, the absence of democratic controls, or of workers being unable to bargain for the best wages and working conditions possible, complementary actions – such as linking respect for labour standards to market access – can make a difference. As a rule, these actions aim at strengthening the position of domestic pressure groups in what is essentially a domestic bargaining process.

Solidarity or unfair trade advantage?

Solidarity is not the only argument for a trade–labour link. There is also an economic argument. Exporters would have an unfair advantage when workers are denied certain basic rights such as the right to bargain for the best wages and working conditions possible under the circumstances.

The solidarity or moral argument emphasizes that core workers' rights are human rights. It is morally wrong to exploit or to repress trade unions. Whether this also provides exporters with a competitive advantage is of secondary importance. The moral argument is fairly straightforward (although the underlying presumption that core labour standards are universal is not accepted by all – see below). The moral argument considers labour standards in the exporting country as a whole.

The economic argument in contrast focuses on the (manufactured) export sector. The distinction is important because the most blatant cases of exploitation are not generally found in manufacturing industries, which produce for export. The worst offences are usually found in plantations and mines, construction industries and small service firms working entirely for the domestic market. Serious violations of labour standards also occur in export industries, 'but this often indicates that conditions are even worse in other sectors' (Edgren 1979: 525).

The economic argument must take account of several variables including long- and short-term effects, and the interests of individual firms compared with those of society as a whole. For instance, when children receive a lower wage than adults at the same level of productivity do, their use may give the firm that employs them a competitive advantage. But it is a moot point whether society as a whole benefits from letting children spend their formative years in low-productivity jobs instead of educating them for subsequent employment in high-productivity jobs. Similarly, the effects on competitiveness of trade union action must distinguish labour surplus from full-employment economies. It must also consider whether legislation helps non-union members (through, for example, the legal extension of collective agreements to non-union establishments) or discriminates against them (the 'closed shop').

The economic case for a trade–labour link

The validity of the economic argument critically depends on two factors: what are the effects of non-respect for basic workers' rights on labour costs, and how important are the latter for a country's or a sector's competitiveness? The second factor (the role of labour costs in competitiveness) is part of a larger and well-researched debate that need not be repeated here. The first question is relevant for the current debate: does the absence of the freedom to bargain collectively, the use of child and forced labour, or discrimination in employment and remuneration provide exporters with a competitive advantage, and if so by how much?[3]

These questions are of critical importance for the outcome of the debate on the trade–labour link. Yet they have been the subject of comparatively little research. The use of forced labour might well constitute a competitive advantage; and discrimination in employment a disadvantage. With child labour, once account is taken of differences in levels of productivity, the outcome is likely to be less clear cut. Also, children are more docile, but whether this is an advantage or disadvantage must be seen in the light of the nature of the products they make and how these are produced.

Freedom of association has basically two effects as the OECD (1996) argues. On the one hand, unions raise costs when they protect the rights of their members to the detriment of non-members and the unemployed. The 1996 OECD study found strong empirical evidence that forming a union introduces a distortion between union and non-union workers in terms of a wage (and fringe benefits) premium. On the other hand, the study noted that in the absence of free bargaining rights, wages might be maintained at artificially low levels compared with what market forces would justify. On the whole, the study found that, on the basis of 'sparse and incomplete data' core labour standards did not play a significant role in shaping trade performance.

Is the concept of minimum international labour standards a universal concept?

The discussion of trade and labour standards centres on a group of core or 'basic' minimum standards: freedom of association, the right to bargain collectively, freedom from forced labour and from child exploitation, and non-discrimination in employment and pay. The question whether these are universally accepted basic labour standards is of great relevance to the discussion of the trade–labour link. Most would agree that they are. It is the rationale for the existence and the actions of the International Labour Organization (ILO). However, several countries outside the OECD area take a different view. They see the insistence on these standards as a new form of imperialism, a way to impose 'Western' values or 'Northern standards' on countries and people with a different cultural background and at a lower level of development.

The ILO is the UN organization concerned with social development. The ILO's main means of action is the promotion of labour legislation through the adoption of international conventions, and to ensure that these are complied with. Member states voluntarily submit themselves to international scrutiny: they are free to ratify (or not) each convention. But once they do so they become subject to a supervisory procedure. This supervision takes place through regular reporting. There is also a complaint procedure. The ILO supervisory bodies do not impose sanctions but their conclusions are sometimes regarded as political or moral sanctions ('mobilization of shame').

The ILO argues that its conventions are designed to be of universal application. They have been adopted in a forum in which virtually all countries participate. The principles contained in each convention are universal; flexibility of provisions ensures that they can be applied progressively with due regard to the stage of social and economic development of the country concerned (Valticos 1994). Those who question the view that core labour standards are universal argue that many ILO conventions were adopted before their country was independent and became a member of the ILO. They point at the divergence in ratifications by region. West European nations have ratified far more ILO conventions than developing Asian countries.

Solidarity and sovereignty

International action can help reinforce the efforts of domestic actors to improve domestic labour standards. Exchanges of experiences and information provide these local actors with better tools to pursue their actions. The mobilization of international public opinion can help indirectly as it places pressure on governments to pay more attention to the demands of domestic pressure groups. Consumer pressure has led to a large number of companies adopting codes of conduct (van Liemt 2000). Social labels attached to hand-made carpets guarantee that these have been made without child labour. Such initiatives provide consumers with more (socially responsible) choice and place pressure on producers to improve working conditions.

Coercive action (conditionality) takes this international solidarity one step beyond the voluntary actions described above. When governments show little sensitivity to domestic and international actions of a voluntary nature, or when effective domestic actions are virtually impossible due to the repressive nature of the regime, coercion has been suggested as a measure of last resort.

Conditionality can be expressed in positive and in negative terms. In the former case, a party that fulfils certain conditions or complies with certain minimum requirements is rewarded with a more favourable treatment. In the latter case, a party that does not fulfil certain conditions or fails to comply with certain requirements is 'sanctioned' through the reduction or the elimination of a favourable treatment. The target countries resent economic sanctions because they see them as interference in their domestic affairs. Positive measures are less controversial.

Conditionality runs counter to the spirit and the principles of the GATT–WTO. The MFN (Most Favoured Nation) principle provides that international trade should be conducted on a non-discriminatory basis. But importing countries can apply conditionality under their GSP and in their relations with non-GATT–WTO members. The following two examples illustrate some of the controversy surrounding trade conditionality.

Labour standards conditionality in the GSP

The GSP allows duty-free access for a selected number of products from developing countries. Many OECD countries operate such a programme. But the steady worldwide reduction in tariff barriers has diluted the significance of the preferences offered.

The USA was the first to have a labour clause attached to its GSP. This clause was introduced in 1984. It states that in extending preferences the President should not designate or maintain the designation of any country as a beneficiary if 'it has not taken or is not taking steps to afford internationally recognised worker rights to workers in the country'. Concerned individuals and organizations can petition for action against trading partners that seek to get ahead in international trade through the systematic repression of basic rights of workers (Harvey 1996). The EU amended its GSP in 1995 to include a 'special incentive clause' (in addition to a withdrawal clause comparable with the US GSP labour clause). The incentive clause offers additional benefits to countries that commit themselves to implement ILO conventions on freedom of association, the right to collective bargaining and the elimination of child labour.[4] The government of the country concerned must formally request these additional preferences. The incentive regime is seen as complex and few countries have invoked it to obtain additional preferences (Rosas 2001: 213)

The GSP procedure is not uncontroversial. In the USA, much of the controversy is rooted in the different expectations held by GSP officials and workers' rights advocates. The former generally believe that the workers' rights provisions have provided leverage to get beneficiary developing countries to initiate changes 'to the best degree possible, given other trade and foreign policy concerns'. The latter, however, would have liked country practice cases more vigorously pursued and sanctions more frequently exercised (Harvey 1996). A major point of discord centres on the discretion left to the Administration in the interpretation of the words 'taking steps' to meet international standards, which are open to interpretation. The Administration has been accused of having accepted, for certain friendly or strategically located countries, undertakings of a vague and general nature as evidence that appropriate steps were being taken.

Needless to say that what OECD-based trade unions and NGOs see as international solidarity is perceived in a totally different light by the governments of the countries, which are the potential target of such sanctions. They consider such actions as interference in their domestic affairs and an attack on the sovereignty of the state; the insistence of Western governments on the universality of certain basic workers' rights resembles a 'new type of imperialism'. In fact, moral questions are invoked by both sides, with one side insisting that the international community has the obligation to insist on respect for these rights, and the other arguing that it is morally wrong for one country to attempt to shape the institutions of other societies.

US trade conditionality, China's MFN status and 'constructive engagement'

Small and weak economies stand the greatest chance of becoming the target of sanctions. Large, powerful economies are less easily pushed. The discussions in the USA on the renewal of China's MFN status illustrate the point.

Until China became a party to the GATT–WTO in 2001, every year US Congress had to renew the authorization to provide MFN status to China (and other countries which are not parties to the GATT–WTO). This renewal had been routine since 1980 when it had been extended for the first time (Steiner and Alston 1996). After 1989, however, Congress felt that this could only be done if China was taking steps to improve the domestic human rights situation. The Chinese government strongly objected to this type of pressure. It argued that the USA would suffer more than China if its trading privileges were revoked. It mobilized US exporters and would-be exporters to press this point in Washington. It placed (or threatened to place) orders with non-US companies, which might otherwise have gone to US companies. And it released several prominent prisoners.

However, this annual ritual became increasingly strenuous as China's economic and political power increased and its assertiveness in the international arena grew. Then, in May 1994, President Clinton announced that he would renew China's MFN trading status *without* reference to its human rights record. Clinton said:

> China has an atomic arsenal and a vote and a veto in the UN Security Council. It is a major factor in Asian and global security. We share important interests, such as in a nuclear-free Korean peninsula and in sustaining the global environment. China is also the world's fastest growing economy. Over $ 8bn US exports last year supported more than 150,000 American jobs.
>
> (Martin 1994)

In addition to this essentially pragmatic decision he raised the fundamental issue of constructive engagement: 'Will we do more to advance the cause of human rights if China is isolated, or if our nations are engaged in a growing web of political and economic co-operation and contacts?' (ibid.)

Sanctions and the threat of sanctions

OECD-based activists have argued that to halt violations of labour standards, trade sanctions should be considered as a measure of last resort. Governments of potential target countries are, understandably, against the use of sanctions. NGOs in these countries are divided on the issue, aware that what is intended as an act of solidarity could well have significant negative effects on employment. 'Sending' country companies question the effectiveness of sanctions. They feel that their governments underestimate the damage sanctions do to commercial relations.[5]

Governments that would be applying the sanctions have to find a balance between principles and interests. They cannot afford to take a narrowly focused position, as many NGOs do. They must consider the impact on the commercial and bilateral relationship. Interstate relations are not just concerned about human rights and workers' rights. They cover a whole range of issues, from landing rights for the domestic airline to access to government procurement contracts, not to mention trade and investment promotion. On the whole, states are keen to develop good contacts with other states because both parties expect to benefit from such good relations.

Sanctions are meant to send a signal. Governments have imposed sanctions for a number of reasons: to protect workers' and human rights, to halt nuclear proliferation, to promote political stability, to settle expropriation claims, and to combat international terrorism, among others. Whether and how effective sanctions are as a policy instrument is the subject of much discussion.

In fact, the *threat* of sanctions may be the true source of leverage. Governments concerned about their international image do not want their labour standards situation to be criticized in public. Several countries reformed their labour code following the announcement by the US GSP Subcommittee that a GSP review would be initiated. It is important to note that such threats can have both desired and undesired effects as the example of US trade sanctions and child labour in Bangladesh showed.[6]

US trade sanctions and child labour in Bangladesh

Spurred by US-based NGOs, in 1992, US Senator Tom Harkin introduced the *Child Labour Deterrence Act* that would ban the importation into the USA of products from industries which use child labour. This caused alarm in Bangladesh, which, in 1991–1992, depended for over 60 per cent of its export earnings on garment exports, much of it to the USA. Immediately, the Bangladesh Garment Manufacturers and Exporters Association (BGMEA) urged its members to dismiss all child workers. Within a few months, BGMEA could report that there were virtually no children left in the industry. Around 20,000 children had been dismissed. The threat of sanctions had clearly been successful.

There were, however, other dimensions to the problem. The children who had been dismissed (most of them girls) were too old to go back to school. There were no suitable alternative jobs available. Their families needed the money. In Muslim Bangladesh, the garment sector is one of the few occupations in which females have been able to move out of the home and into the workforce. These women brought their daughters so that they could ensure that the girls were not mistreated and that their virtue was protected. The girls only performed light work; but long working hours was a problem.

With no clear alternative, the children staged a demonstration demanding that they be given their jobs back. It was then that local, US and international organizations (such as the ILO and UNICEF) representing different viewpoints – retention of child garment workers, removal of child workers, and those advocating a wider solution – met with the BGMEA to find a way to mitigate the effects of the dismissals on the children. After long negotiations it was agreed that the BGMEA would delay the deadline for the dismissals of the children in favour of their gradual removal tied to the availability of educational facilities. No new children would be hired. UNICEF would fund the schooling of the youngest.

Trade and labour standards at the multilateral level

Should the GATT–WTO operate a labour conditionality scheme? Should the GATT–WTO establish a working group on trade and labour standards? Should it do research on the issue? Should it work more closely with the ILO? These questions have been the subject of intense, and sometimes emotional and acrimonious, debate at the WTO and other international forums, and in academic journals. Some even blamed the trade–labour issue for the failure of the Seattle ministerial. After many years of intense discussions and negotiations it can be said that the answer to the above questions is negative. There is no trade–labour link at the GATT–WTO; nor is one foreseen in the near future. But this simple fact hides some interesting developments that we will examine below.

Autonomous procedures such as the GSP conditionality are comparatively easy to establish. They are popular with NGOs because they allow them a good deal of leverage. But these procedures have been criticized for being vulnerable to trade-offs against strategic interests. They also lack the moral authority of multilateral procedures. The interests of smaller countries would seem to get a fairer hearing in a multilateral than a bilateral setting.

Most agree that the moral force that results from an agreement reached amongst all, or at least a large majority of, nations is superior to a unilaterally imposed arrangement. That is why those in favour of a trade and labour link have continued to try and place the issue on the multilateral agenda. A multilateral agreement should guarantee that procedures and objectives are seen as fair by all involved. It would apply to all participating countries (contrary to the GSP conditionality, which applies only to 'beneficiary countries'). The

GATT–WTO and the ILO are most frequently mentioned in this respect. The two organizations have a dispute settlement procedure (in the GATT–WTO) and an elaborate supervisory procedure (in the ILO).

Nevertheless, there is much controversy over the possible involvement of these two organizations in some kind of labour conditionality scheme. Also, they are ill-equipped for operating such a scheme. The GATT–WTO's mandate is to work towards the elimination of trade barriers; labour conditionality would add a trade barrier. Similarly, the ILO's mandate is to promote respect for labour standards and not to apply sanctions to countries that do not respect them. The ILO claims no authority in the trade field. Similarly, the WTO does not pretend to have any authority in the labour field. More generally, the GATT–WTO does not want to take account of production conditions: 'like' products should be treated alike. The tuna–dolphin ruling illustrates the point. The panel stated that each country should have the right to determine its own regulations regarding the production process of traded goods and that the presence or absence of these regulations could not justify trade restrictions by other contracting parties.

Developing country governments have successfully kept minimum labour standards off the WTO agenda. Trade conditionality is not the right way to promote respect for these standards. Trade negotiations are sufficiently complicated as they are. Why, such governments ask, add a potential new trade barrier, particularly one that clearly targets us?

The intense debate has thus not led to a WTO trade–labour link but it did give much attention to the need for a social 'level playing field'. It is now widely recognized that a set of minimum international labour standards should be respected. The status, functions and potential of the ILO received a boost. At the 1996 WTO ministerial in Singapore, WTO members declared: 'we renew our commitment to the observance of internationally recognised core labour standards. The International Labour Organization (ILO) is the competent body to set and deal with these standards, and we affirm our support for its work in promoting them' (para. 4 of the Singapore Ministerial Declaration). At the fourth ministerial in Doha, WTO members reaffirmed their declaration at Singapore. The USA, Germany and other OECD countries have together made available tens of millions of US dollars to support the ILO's technical cooperation activities under its programme to eliminate child labour (IPEC) and those resulting from its 1998 declaration (see below).

The renewed attention given to minimum labour standards is also notable in the codes of conduct that many companies and industries have adopted. The UN's 'Global Compact', an initiative of Secretary-General Kofi Annan, invites internationally operating companies to commit themselves voluntarily to a set of nine principles relating to human rights, the protection of the environment and labour rights (these include freedom of association and collective bargaining; abolition of forced and child labour; and freedom from discrimination).

International and supranational organizations now demand respect for labour standards as a condition for membership. New EU members must subscribe to the entire body of EU law (the *Acquis Communautaire*) including all regulations concerning social policy. The Republic of Korea was asked to commit to labour law changes when it joined the OECD in 1996 (Charnovitz 2002: 23). Since 1998, the ILO has insisted that all its member governments – regardless of whether they have ratified the underlying conventions – comply with a set of obligations listed in its *Declaration on Fundamental Principles and Rights at Work*. According to the declaration, governments 'have an obligation, arising from the very fact of membership in the Organization, to respect, to promote and to realise' the principles concerning these fundamental rights.[7] WTO members are also members of the ILO.

In bilateral and regional agreements, labour conditionality continues to be a feature. In addition to the GSP (to which we referred earlier) it can be found in the trade and cooperation agreements that OECD governments sign with third countries. Following the NAFTA labour side agreement (*The North American Agreement on Labour Cooperation*– see van Liemt 1994) labour clauses have been added to the trade agreements that the USA has signed with a number of countries. The EU routinely adds a human rights clause to its trade and cooperation agreements with third countries (Rosas 2001).

Conclusion

Trade conditionality has long dominated the debate on the social dimension of globalization. To an extent it still does. Multilateral conditionality continues to be controversial. There is no trade–labour link in the WTO and none is foreseen in the future. But attitudes have changed. The intense debate of the past decade has led to a better understanding of the issues involved. There is broad agreement that respect for minimum labour standards is essential in an integrating world economy. The ILO's mandate is now more appreciated; support (including financial support) for its activities has increased.

Notes

1   I am grateful to Pitou van Dijck, Brian Hocking, Steven McGuire, Dean Spinanger and Steve Woolcock for their comments on an earlier version of this chapter.
2   In 1988, the USA tightened the embargo on tuna fish caught by using methods causing a high rate of dolphin mortality. Mexico objected to this attempt to limit the importation of goods *not because of their characteristics as products, but because of the way they were being produced*. It took the matter to the GATT, which ruled in Mexico's favour.
3   A related question is whether withholding market access is used for protectionist purposes. For this to be the case it is necessary not just that respect for core standards raises unit import prices, but also that the export economy or economies concerned are responsible for a sufficiently large proportion of the imports of the commodity in question in the importing economies (Hansson 1993).
4   The 1999 US–Cambodia Textile Agreement also includes an incentive clause. It offers a possible 18 per cent annual increase in Cambodia's export entitlements to the USA provided the government of Cambodia supports 'The implementation of a program to improve working conditions in the textiles and apparel sector, including internationally recognized core labor standards, through the application of Cambodian labor law' (Article 10B, US–Cambodia Textile Agreement).
5   Commercial relationships cannot just be turned on and off. Business relations take a long time to mature: 'Who wants to deal with an unreliable supplier, especially when the supplier is not the only game in town?' (National Association of Manufacturers 1997).
6   Based on Taher *et al* (n.d.).
7   These fundamental principles are: freedom of association and the right to bargain collectively; the elimination of all forms of forced or compulsory labour; the abolition of child labour; the elimination of discrimination in employment and occupation.

Bibliography

Bhagwati, J. and Hudec, R. (eds) (1996) *Fair Trade and Harmonization: prerequisites for free trade?*, Cambridge, MA: MIT Press.

Charnovitz, S. (2002) *Trade Law and Global Governance*, London: Cameron May.

Edgren, G. (1979) 'Fair labour standards and trade liberalization', *International Labour Review* 118 (September–October): 523–535.

Hansson, G. (1993) *Social Clauses and International Trade*, London: Croom Helm.

Harvey, P. (1996) 'US GSP labor rights conditionality: "aggressive unilateralism" or a forerunner to a multilateral social clause?', Paper presented at the Conference 'Labour and International Economy' organized by the International Institute for Labour Studies, Geneva, 14–15 March.

Klevorick, A. (1996) 'Reflections on the race to the bottom', in J. Bhagwati and R. Hudec (eds), *Fair Trade and Harmonization: prerequisites for free trade?*, Cambridge, MA: MIT Press.

Langille, B.A. (1997) 'Eight ways to think about International labour Standards', *Journal of World Trade* 31: 27–53.

Van Liemt, G. (1994) 'The Multilateral Social Clause in 1994', ICDA Discussion paper; ICDA, Brussels.

Van Liemt, G. (2000) 'Codes of conduct and international subcontracting: a "private" road towards ensuring minimum labour standards in export industries', in R. Blanpain (ed.), *Multinational Enterprises and the Social Challenges of the 21st Century*, The Hague: Kluwer Law International.

Martin, J. (1994) 'Mr. Clinton eats humble pie in Asia', *Financial Times* 28–29 May: 3.

National Association of Manufacturers (1997) *A Catalogue of New US Unilateral Economic Sanctions for Foreign Policy Purposes 1993–96*, Washington, DC: NAM Trade and Technology Department.

OECD (1996) *Trade, Employment and Labour Standards: a study of core workers' rights and international trade*, Paris: OECD.

Rosas, A. (2001) 'Human rights in the external trade policy of the European Union', in Institut René Cassin de Strassbourg, *World Trade and the Protection of Human Rights: human rights in face of global economic exchanges*, Brussels: Bruylant.

Steiner, H.J. and Alston, P. (1996) *International Human Rights in Context: law, politics and morals*, Oxford: Clarendon Press.

Taher, M.A., Rahman, W. and Gunn, S. (no date) 'Child labour and the trade debate: new initiatives by Bangladesh', Mimeo.

Valticos, N. (1994) 'The Asian states and international labour conventions', in R. St Macdonald (ed.), *Essays in Honour of Wang Tieya*, Boston: Kluwer Academic.

Key readings

Bhagwati, J. and Hudec, R. (eds) (1996) *Fair Trade and Harmonization: prerequisites for free trade?* Cambridge, MA: MIT Press.

Charnovitz, S. (2002) *Trade Law and Global Governance*, London: Cameron May.

Hansson, G. (1993) *Social Clauses and International Trade*, London: Croom Helm.

Van Liemt, G. (1989) 'Minimum labour standards and international trade: would a social clause work?', *International Labour Review* 128: 4.

OECD (1996) *Trade, Employment and Labour Standards: a study of core workers' rights and international trade*, Paris: OECD.

Steiner, H.J. and Alston, P. (1996) *International Human Rights in Context: law, politics and morals*, Oxford: Clarendon Press.

Useful websites

www.ictsd.org (International Centre for Trade and Sustainable Development).
www.ilo.org (International Labour Organization).
www.laborrights.org (International Labour Rights Fund).
www.oxfam.org (Oxfam).
www.twnside.org.sg (Third World Network).

17 Trading food

The politics of genetically modified organisms

Robert Falkner

Summary

Genetically modified organisms (GMOs) and genetically modified (GM) food are at the centre of a new global trade conflict. Within less than a decade since the first GM crops were commercially planted, North American and European governments have become locked into a World Trade Organization (WTO) dispute; powerful economic interests are pitted against consumer and environmental organisations; and North–South tensions have emerged over the use of agri-biotechnology. At the centre of this conflict is the European Union's (EU's) 1998 *de facto* moratorium on GMO authorisations, as well as the growing spread of GMO regulations worldwide, which have created new barriers for agricultural trade. The global GMO dispute is but the latest, and potentially most complex, case of conflict between environmental regulations and international trade rules.

This chapter reviews the debate on trade in GMOs and maps the major conflict lines that have emerged in recent years. It argues that the GMO dispute does not easily fit into conventional debates on the use of non-tariff trade barriers, which are often portrayed as a disguised form of protectionism. Instead, the global opposition against agricultural biotechnology is driven primarily by environmental and ethical concerns that reflect differences in societal values and attitudes towards risk. The WTO's dispute settlement body faces a serious challenge in attempting to adjudicate GMO trade conflicts in the first such legal challenge brought by the USA against the EU.

What is at stake in the GMO conflict?

Modern biotechnology, often also referred to as genetic engineering, represents a revolutionary technological advance in agricultural production. Whereas traditional forms of plant and animal development rely on selective breeding to improve quality, modern biotechnology allows the direct manipulation of genetic material in plants and animals, through inserting, removing or altering genes. This new form of biotechnology provides a vast new range of opportunities for genetic change across the boundaries of species and allows a more rapid and targeted form of modification. The nature and relative novelty of this technology have given rise to an international debate over the desirability and safety of genetic engineering in agriculture and food production.

In common with other health and environment-related trade disputes, the GMO conflict is characterised by a complex mix of actors and interests as well as a high degree of politicisation. Its complexity stems from the fact that it involves not only competing commercial interests but also a wide range of consumer and environmental concerns. In a sense, the conflict transcends the conventional free trade–protectionism divide in trade policy that the GATT/WTO system has so successfully managed to overcome in successive trade rounds since the Second World War. Considerable commercial interests are, of course, at stake. But the concerns expressed by anti-GM campaigners and regulatory authorities cannot be summed up with reference to protectionist interests alone; they express, first and foremost, a set of social and cultural values that are at odds with the trade interests of biotechnology firms and commodity exporters.

Furthermore, the GMO conflict raises some fundamental questions about the relationship between WTO trade rules, on the one hand, and environmental regulations and multilateral agreements, on the other (see Brack's chapter in this volume). It goes to the heart of the debate on the extent to which greater harmonisation of trade rules can be allowed to infringe on the sovereignty of WTO member states. In the post-Seattle environment of trade politics, the GMO conflict may well become a critical test case for the international community's ability to deepen further the WTO's system of trade rules, while simultaneously trying to strengthen its legitimacy.

Commercial interests

The commercial interests at stake in the GMO dispute are considerable, and are bound to increase as agricultural biotechnology is being applied to an ever-growing range of crops. The commercial use of genetic engineering began in the early 1990s, when biotechnology firms introduced the first genetically modified crops, after years of laboratory development and field trials. New crop varieties such as soybeans and maize caught on rapidly, particularly in North America, leading to one of the fastest take-up rates in the history of agricultural innovation. Within only six years, between 1996 and 2002, the area of GM crop production has grown thirty-five-fold, from 1.7 million to 58.7 million hectares globally. The USA has been the dominant player in agri-biotechnology from the beginning, in terms of both research expenditure and commercial planting, accounting for 66 per cent of the global production area in 2002. It is followed by Argentina, Canada and China, with 23, 6 and 4 per cent of the global GM crop area respectively (James 2003).

The situation in North America contrasts sharply with that of Europe. Although European firms have actively participated in the biotechnology revolution of the 1970s and 1980s, their attempts to introduce GM crops and foods stalled in the late 1990s, when the EU imposed a temporary ban on new approvals for GM products. As a consequence, European agriculture has been largely unaffected by the agri-biotechnological revolution, except for small-scale field trials of GM crops. The European biotechnology industry, as well as Commission officials, have repeatedly warned that further delays in the commercialisation of GM crops would hold back the development of Europe's industrial and scientific base in biotechnology. Some of these fears have been underpinned by recent research suggesting that plant biotechnology research has fallen in the EU by 76 per cent since 1998, the year that the EU moratorium came into force (Lheureux *et al.* 2003).

The divergent paths of biotechnological development and regulatory approval have had a direct impact on the transatlantic trade relationship. While the USA has become a major exporter of GM crops, the EU has increasingly adopted the perspective of a GMO-importing country. US farmers complain that the EU moratorium has led to an estimated loss of $300 million of corn sales to Europe. And with new GM crop varieties expected to enter the US market in the near future – Monsanto is set to introduce a GM variety of wheat – Washington is concerned that US agricultural producers will be locked out of lucrative markets in the future. This fear is amplified by what US officials describe as the European GMO ban's spillover effect in the developing world that remains largely unde-cided about biotechnology. Zambia's and Zimbabwe's refusal to accept US food aid in 2002 was thus interpreted in US trade policy circles as an outgrowth of a global anti-GMO sentiment that originates in Europe (*Financial Times* 2003).

Environmental and health concerns

Much of the opposition to agri-biotechnology, in Europe and worldwide, reflects concerns over the ecological and human health impact of the release of GMOs into the environ-ment, as well as ethical implications of genetic engineering more generally. Critics of the technology point out that despite decades of research, too little is known about the poten-tial long-term effects of GMOs on ecosystems and the human body, and that therefore caution should guide policy makers in their decision. The spectrum of critical opinions expressed, however, is vast, ranging from radical voices who reject genetic engineering per se on ethical grounds to reformist environmentalists who advocate a case-by-case assess-ment of the risks involved in agri-biotechnological production.

With regard to the environmental effects of GMOs, scientists have raised, *inter alia*, the following concerns:

- that genes from plants that are genetically modified to be herbicide resistant could be transferred to other crops or weeds, thereby spreading herbicide resistance with unde-sirable results;
- that farmers would use greater amounts of herbicides without fear of crop damage in cases where GM crops possess herbicide resistance;
- that insect-resistant crops would have a detrimental effect on non-target insect popula-tions, and by implication bird populations that feed on insects; and
- that insect-resistant crops might lead to resistance by target insects to the toxins contained in the GM crops.

Human health concerns over the introduction of GM ingredients into the food chain centre on:

- toxins contained in GM crops that pose a threat to humans;
- proteins introduced through genetic engineering that may cause allergenicity; and
- antibiotic marker genes routinely used in the genetic engineering of crops, which may be transferred to the human body causing resistance to commonly prescribed antibi-otics.

The need for precaution

As in many other environmental areas, the scientific community is far from united in its assessment of the environmental and health risks involved in agri-biotechnology. Many years of research and field trials have so far failed to produce a conclusive answer as to whether or not the new technology is safe. In fact, a summary evaluation of biotechnology is unlikely to be feasible; only a case-by-case assessment of individual GMOs and the specific natural environment which they are released into can provide appropriate answers. The situation is further complicated by the long-term perspective that certain ecological risk assessments demand. For example, the impact that a new GM crop might have on the biological diversity of a given ecosystem may only materialise many years, even decades, later, thus making it impossible to ascertain the safety of the GM crop here and now.

In the view of critics of agri-biotechnology, the lack of a scientific consensus, combined with the potentially long-term risks of GMOs, necessitates the application of the precautionary principle in regulatory decision making. According to this principle, which has emerged as a guiding norm in international environmental law and diplomacy (Birnie and Boyle 2002: 115–121), precautionary action is to be taken

> in situations of potentially serious or irreversible threats to health or the environment, where there is a need to act to reduce potential hazards *before* there is strong proof of harm, taking into account the likely costs and benefits of action and inaction.
>
> (Harremoës *et al.* 2002: 4)

In other words, the principle of 'better safe than sorry' applies wherever serious risks exist under conditions of scientific uncertainty.

By legitimising precautionary action, including trade-restrictive measures, on the basis of *suspected*, not proven, environmental harm, the precautionary principle poses a serious challenge to the WTO's system of trade rules. What makes sense in an environmental context – where policy makers seek to prevent future ecological damage against the background of uncertain scientific knowledge – threatens to undermine the WTO's demands for certainty and transparency in trade relations. The issue is not that the WTO categorically rejects precaution as such; in fact, precautionary action is permissible under the Agreement on the Application of Sanitary and Phytosanitary Measures (SPS) and the Agreement on Technical Barriers to Trade (TBT). But the WTO puts the burden of proof on the party taking a trade measure, requiring, in the case of SPS rules, that it is based on risk assessment and is of a provisional nature (Cameron 1999). It is these rules, among others, that the EU finds itself accused of having violated in imposing a precautionary ban on GMOs.

The widening transatlantic gulf

The EU's moratorium on GMOs

The transatlantic dispute is firmly centred on the EU's GMO regulations that have had the effect of an agricultural trade barrier. Responding to growing concerns over environmental and health risks associated with GMO releases into the environment, the EU imposed a *de facto* moratorium on GM crop authorisations in October 1998, despite having initially approved several GMOs for commercial planting since 1991. The ban is not based on a legislative measure that explicitly declares GMOs unsafe. Instead, the EU's GMO approval process came to a halt because of objections raised by several member states demanding that GMO traceability and labelling rules be agreed before the passing of new GMO approvals (European Commission 2002).

The European Commission has repeatedly tried to restart the authorisation process by proposing new regulations that would satisfy the sceptical member states. A new directive

(2001/18/EC) revising the EU's ten-year-old GMO regulations entered into force in October 2002, and new rules on traceability and labelling were adopted in July 2003. While the European Commission insists these new rules will restore public confidence in biotechnological products, France and Italy, with the support of Austria, Belgium, Denmark, Greece and Luxembourg, have so far refused to lift the ban, citing widespread consumer pressure and scientific concerns over food safety.

From the beginning of the EU's moratorium, the USA challenged the scientific grounds on which it was imposed and accused the EU of back-door protectionism. US farm exporters claim that they have suffered an annual loss of $300 million in agricultural sales to the European market, and that the EU's hostility to agri-biotechnology is spreading to other markets worldwide. Against the background of an expanding use of biotechnology in US agriculture and increasing frustration with the EU's lack of willingness to reform its GMO rules, the US Administration took the step of formally launching a WTO case against the EU's GMO ban. It requested formal consultations with the EU in May 2003, and following the failure of negotiations initiated the creation of a disputes panel in August 2003.

The legal challenge at the WTO represents a significant escalation of the five-year-old transatlantic GMO conflict and risks dragging the WTO into a highly politicised area. Concerns about a public backlash may have prevented US trade officials from bringing the case in the past, but US concerns over the intractability of the EU's regulatory process and the growing use of regulatory trade barriers by the EU in a number of environment and health-related areas finally triggered the decision to seek a legal ruling. The US Administration has since further raised the stakes in the dispute, accusing the Europeans of harming the interests of poor farmers in developing countries who would be deprived of the benefits of agri-biotechnology should the European anti-GM attitude spread worldwide (*Guardian* 2003).

US policy makers have repeatedly emphasised that the GMO challenge reflects a growing concern in North America with European environmental legislation that goes beyond the narrow question of GMOs. A report by the National Foreign Trade Council, published in May 2003, lists complaints by US farm exporters about EU trade barriers in areas ranging from beef to poultry and wine (National Foreign Trade Council 2003). Fears that the EU is abusing its regulatory powers to disrupt international trade have recently focused on the EU Chemicals White Paper, which proposes to introduce a registration and testing system for approximately 30,000 chemical substances. The US Administration blames the tide of new non-tariff trade measures on the EU's use of the precautionary principle, which according to US trade officials leads to a politicisation of the regulatory process and allows scientifically unfounded concerns to trump international trade obligations.

Regulatory differences

To understand why the two sides became entangled in such a polarised and highly charged trade conflict over GM regulations, it is important briefly to outline the major transatlantic differences with regard to regulating agricultural biotechnology (Young 2001; Vogel 2001). At first sight, governments on both sides of the Atlantic appear keen to promote biotechnology as a leading industrial sector for the twenty-first century. The European Commission has identified biotechnology as essential to its vision of the knowledge-based European economy that it seeks to promote. But in ensuring the safety of research and commercial application of biotechnology in agriculture, the regulatory authorities on both sides of the Atlantic have followed markedly different models and principles, reflecting to some extent different levels of public awareness and concern regarding the risks involved in agri-biotechnology.

Regulation in the EU has been driven primarily by health and environmental safety concerns. The first EU Directives on contained use and on release of GMOs into the environment (90/219/EEC and 90/220/EEC) laid down rules for GMO authorisation that are based on the key principle of prior approval. According to this principle, applicants seeking approval for the contained use, deliberate release or marketing of GM products must submit technical information and detailed risk assessment to the relevant national authority, which decides on a case-by-case basis and communicates the decision to the EU. Should another EU member state object to the approval given by any national authority, a decision is taken at Community level, after the European Commission's scientific advisory bodies have considered the scientific case. The 2002 revision of 1990 Directives strengthened these rules by introducing, *inter alia*, principles for risk assessment; mandatory post-market monitoring requirements; mandatory information to the public; and labelling and traceability requirements.

In the USA, the regulation of agricultural biotechnology is shared between three federal agencies: the Animal and Plant Health Inspection Service (APHIS) of the Department of Agriculture, which deals with movement and release of GMOs into the environment; the Environmental Protection Agency (EPA), which covers GM crops containing genes that are considered as pesticides (e.g. *Bacillus thuringiensis* – Bt); and the Food and Drugs Administration (FDA), which is concerned with human health aspects of most GM foods. Until 1993, prior approval for release into the environment was mandatory for all GM crop varieties, similar to the EU's regulatory system. In 1993, however, APHIS decided that six GM crops (maize, cotton, soybeans, potatoes, tomatoes and tobacco) had been found to be safe and could thus be released into the environment under a notification system, which was extended in 1997 to all GM plants not listed as noxious weeds. As a consequence, nearly 90 per cent of current field trials in the USA now follow the notification, rather than permit, procedure.

The FDA's approach to regulating GM foods also signalled a more pro-biotechnology stance. The FDA declared in 1992 that it considered most GM products as equivalent to other food products produced by conventional means, and that review requirements for GM foods would only apply in special circumstances. Likewise, the FDA does not require the mandatory labelling of GM ingredients in food products, unless specific health concerns, such as those related to the allergenicity of GM products, exist. Although the agency embarked on a series of public consultations in 1999 and strengthened public information requirements, responding in part to growing concerns about the safety of GM foods, it has so far stopped short of significantly changing its regulatory approval process.

Thus, during the 1990s US authorities had reached the conclusion that most GM crop varieties were safe for agricultural production and human consumption. At around the same time, however, European authorities became more and more concerned about the environmental and health risks involved in genetic engineering, and in October 1998 stopped authorising new GMO releases into the environment. This is in line with the divergent paths of the development of public awareness of, and concern over, agri-biotechnology. Whereas throughout the 1990s, US consumers showed little concern about GM food ingredients and environmental campaign groups largely ignored the issue of genetic engineering, Europe saw a gradual erosion of the public's trust in food safety standards in the aftermath of a series of food scares (e.g. Mad Cow disease), and European NGOs such as Greenpeace helped raise public awareness of GM safety issues in widely publicised acts of public protest and civil disobedience.

Rising North–South tensions over agri-biotechnology

Although the media spotlight has been firmly on the US–EU dispute, more and more developing countries are being drawn into the controversy over biotechnology as the use of GM crops spreads worldwide. So far, only a small number of developing countries are growing GM crops on a commercial scale. Argentina accounts for 23 per cent of the global GM area, followed by China (4 per cent) and South Africa (0.5 per cent) (James 2003). Most of the crops grown are non-staple crops (soybeans, cotton, maize) for commercial reasons, e.g. for export as animal feed. A number of other countries are considering, or have recently decided, to grow GM crops, most notably Brazil and India.

Advocates of the new technology point out that genetic engineering may hold the key to ensuring food security particularly in the poorest nations. The prime benefit of GM crops to developing countries lies in the promise of an increase in agricultural productivity, which in turn may help to alleviate food shortages and malnutrition and contribute to a country's overall economic development. This is the case with GM crops that promise greater resistance to diseases and pests (e.g. Bt cotton and Bt maize). Genetic engineering can also increase the nutritional value of crops by enriching them with minerals and vitamins. For example, rice can be produced with higher beta-carotene levels ('Golden Rice') that would help fight Vitamin A deficiencies, a common source of malnutrition especially among poor children (Nuffield Council on Bioethics 2003).

At the same time, critics warn that agricultural biotechnology poses particularly high ecological risks to biodiversity-rich countries and may be ill-suited to address the needs of the predominantly small-scale farmers in the developing world. To some extent, developing countries' concerns about the safety of GM crops mirror those of Northern societies: for example, with respect to the creation of 'superweeds' and human health problems such as allergeneity. A specifically Southern concern over the safety of GM crops has arisen in those countries that possess exceptional levels of biological diversity and are centres of origin of modern crops. Countries such as Mexico have expressed the fear that GM crops may threaten the great variety of indigenous crops on which a highly diversified agricultural system is based. Other fears concern the dependence on multinational biotech and seed companies that would result from the wide-scale introduction of GM crops, and a general fear of becoming the testing ground for what some perceive as an 'untested' technology from the North.

Developing countries also face a capacity problem, in terms of both benefiting from biotechnology and safeguarding against its risks. With regard to access to biotechnological advances, many developing countries have been constrained in two important ways: they often lack the necessary financial resources and technical know-how to develop suitable GM crops themselves; and the multinational corporations at the forefront of the biotechnological revolution have so far concentrated their R&D efforts on crops grown for Northern markets, often ignoring the specific needs of developing countries. Some charitable institutions, such as the US-based Rockefeller Foundation, have sought to bridge the gap in public and private funding for biotechnological research, but a much larger effort is required for the technology to become more widely available in the developing world.

Moreover, developing countries have found it difficult to develop not only a scientific and commercial base for biotechnology, but also a regulatory framework that would guard them from potential risks resulting from the new technology. Although biosafety regulations have been introduced during the 1990s in a number of countries from India to Brazil, most countries' regulatory frameworks either have not been implemented or lack the resources to make them effective. Increasingly, as the biotechnological revolution proceeds, developing countries face a dual capacity gap – scientific and regulatory – that slows down the adoption and control of biotechnological innovation.

It should therefore not come as a surprise that the technological paths in the developing worlds vary greatly. A few countries, most notably Argentina and China, have embraced the new technology and developed a strong stake in promoting GM crops as part of their national agricultural strategy. Others, such as India and Brazil, have sought to build up their scientific expertise in agricultural biotechnology but remain divided over whether to allow the full-scale commercial introduction of GM crops. At the other end of the spectrum, countries such as Ethiopia and Zambia have taken the view that the new technology promises more harm than benefit to their agricultural systems, and have actively opposed the introduction of GM crops into their ecosystems, including in the form of food aid.

The policy dilemmas faced by many developing countries are further accentuated in those that are agricultural exporters. With Europe having banned most GM imports and North America actively promoting the technology abroad, commodity-exporting countries are having to balance the gains from genetic engineering with the potential loss of export markets. The increasing use of GM labelling and traceability requirements has further alerted developing countries to the commercial risks involved in introducing GM crops. Most developing countries find it impossible, or at least too costly, to segregate GM from non-GM crops, and thus face the prospect of losing market share in those developed countries that have strict GM regulations and thresholds in place (Nielsen and Anderson 2001).

Brazil's experience is symptomatic of the policy dilemmas faced by developing countries seeking to balance the risks and benefits of biotechnology. Having invested in indigenous biotech capacity for many years, and having authorised the commercial planting of Monsanto's Roundup Ready soya in 1998, Brazilian authorities were forced to halt the sale of GM soya in June 1999, following a court decision in response to NGO complaints that no comprehensive environmental impact assessment had been carried out. Demand from Europe for non-GM soya has since resulted in Brazilian farmers expanding their global market share. But this niche market has now come under threat because of the widespread illegal use of Monsanto's GM soya variety in Brazil's southern regions, imported mainly from neighbouring Argentina where farmers have embraced the GM crop. Market observers reported in 2002 that over half of the soybean crop in the state of Rio Grande Do Sul, the country's third-ranking soya state, may be of the GM variety. Thus, Brazil may soon find that it will not be able to choose a non-GM future for its agricultural sector, irrespective of the government's decision on the safety and commercial benefits of the new technology (Falkner 2002).

The domestic debate in Brazil and elsewhere in the developing world has been characterised by sharp divisions between supporters and opponents of biotechnology. Most developing countries have taken a cautious approach, viewing the new technology with considerable scepticism. Apart from a mere handful of countries, the developing world has so far approached the biotechnology debate from the perspective of GMO-importing nations, calling for international support and safeguards to protect their environmental and socio-economic interests. It is this defensive, reactive, approach that explains why developing countries are among the most outspoken supporters of GMO trade restrictions, quite in contrast to their traditional hostility to environmentally motivated trade measures.

GMOs on the international agenda: The Cartagena Protocol on Biosafety and the WTO

The biosafety negotiations

Developing countries were among the first to call for an international treaty dealing with the safety of trade in GMOs.[1] In the late 1980s and early 1990s, the risks involved in the release of GMOs, rather than their contained use in research, became the focus of international efforts to establish a regulatory framework. This emerging issue of 'biosafety' gained in political salience when it was debated at the 1992 United Nations Conference on Environment and Development (UNCED) and during the negotiations on the Convention on Biological Diversity (CBD). Although the UNCED participants could not agree on any specific regulatory mechanism for ensuring biosafety, they nevertheless included in Agenda 21 and the CBD a mandate to consider the need for a separate international biosafety treaty.

The failure to establish a biosafety framework at the Rio 'Earth Summit' revealed a significant difference in perspective between developed and developing countries. Whereas the former wanted to concentrate on biodiversity conservation and remained unconvinced of the need for a biosafety treaty, the latter urged the international community to address the development needs of poorer nations and pushed for a binding international biosafety instrument. It took three years before a mandate for biosafety talks was eventually agreed in 1995. The G77 group, which had emerged as a united negotiation group on this issue, had succeeded in pushing for a biosafety protocol to the CBD, which was eventually agreed in January 2000, after almost four years of increasingly contentious negotiations.

The choice of the negotiation forum was to have a significant impact on the international process. Framing biosafety as a predominantly environmental issue left the negotiations in the hands of environment and health ministers. In the early phase of the biosafety talks, up until 1997/1998, trade concerns were relatively marginal, not least since GM crops only began to enter agricultural trade in the second half of the 1990s. By the time agricultural exporters and trade ministers began to highlight the trade implications of a future biosafety protocol, the scene was already set for an international treaty that was concerned, first and foremost, with the conservation and sustainable use of biological diversity, and that was designed as an essentially precautionary instrument.

The negotiations on the Cartagena Protocol lasted from 1996 to 2000. What started as a relatively unnoticed set of meetings of scientific and regulatory experts soon developed into a highly politicised and public negotiation. By the time of the 1999 conference in Cartagena, Colombia, which was meant to adopt the protocol, the growing rift between GMO-exporting nations on the one hand, and the European Union and a large coalition of developing countries on the other, came to dominate the biosafety talks. US-led opposition to the draft agreement eventually led to the collapse of the Cartagena meeting in February 1999, but the negotiations resumed shortly thereafter and were concluded successfully in January 2000, with both sides making concessions but leaving some areas of contention unresolved.

The protocol's key regulatory mechanism is that of advance informed agreement (AIA), which requires GMO exporters to provide detailed information on the organism in question and to seek the importing nation's prior approval before any transboundary movement takes place. Importing nations are to carry out risk assessments before reaching a decision, and in doing so can invoke the precautionary principle (Cartagena Protocol on Biosafety, Articles 7–10). A simplified procedure applies to agricultural commodity shipments, which may need to be identified as containing GM material, a provision that is to be specified by the parties to the agreement within two years of entering into force (Article 11).

The relationship between the Cartagena Protocol and the WTO

One of the thorniest issues in the negotiations was the relationship between the protocol and the WTO's trade rules. The US-led group of GMO-exporting nations had insisted during the negotiations that the Cartagena Protocol should not weaken, or even annul, existing obligations under the WTO. In contrast, the EU and the Like-Minded Group of developing countries sought to insert language that shielded the protocol's trade provisions from future legal challenges under WTO jurisdiction. This 'relationship' question could not be resolved in the end, and an ambiguous preambulary text stressing the 'mutual support-iveness' of the protocol and other international agreements was agreed at the last minute that left the issue open to interpretation.

In the view of the USA, which has not signed up to the Cartagena Protocol nor the CBD, the agreement does not in any way change existing trade obligations in the areas of agricultural trade and food safety (Safrin 2002). Having unsuccessfully tried to open discussions at the WTO on clarifying biotechnology-related trade disciplines – a move that was blocked by the EU in the run-up to the 1999 Seattle WTO ministerial meeting – the US Administration has now chosen to seek clarification of the issues through the WTO's dispute settlement procedure. By challenging the EU's *de facto* moratorium on GMO authorisations, and by threatening to extend the case to the EU's new labelling and traceability rules, the USA has opened the door to a landmark ruling on the trade–environment relationship, the outcome of which most trade experts see as being in the balance.

In its justification for bringing the case, the USA alleges that the EU's moratorium constitutes an illegal trade barrier that lacks scientific evidence and is applied in a non-transparent manner. US Trade Representative Robert Zoellick cited, *inter alia*, the Agreement on the Application of Sanitary and Phytosanitary Measures (SPS) in support of the US case. According to SPS rules, trade measures to protect human, animal or plant health require risk assessment based on scientific evidence, leaving the burden of proof with the importing nation. Precautionary action in the absence of scientific certainty is only permissible as a provisional measure. The party imposing trade restrictions is required to produce scientific evidence, in the absence of which the trade measure has to cease (Charnovitz 1999).

The crux in this dispute is that the environmental and health risks associated with genetic engineering remain contested within the scientific community, and both sides of the conflict are able to point to some scientific evidence backing their claims. Even if a scientific consensus on the safety of GMOs were to emerge, which in itself is highly unlikely, fundamental questions would remain as to how we should treat long-term risks to humans and the environment that current scientific tests are unable to ascertain. The difficulty, indeed the infeasibility, of delegating these matters to the scientific community raises important questions: first, how should we interpret the meaning of the precautionary approach as contained in the WTO (esp. the SPS Agreement) and the Cartagena Protocol, and can these two legal contexts be reconciled? Second, who should we entrust with adjudicating the merits of any restrictive measure taken against trade in GMOs based on the precautionary principle, under conditions of scientific uncertainty? Both these questions suggest that neither a scientific nor a legalistic solution can be expected to resolve the conflict. Finally, it remains to be seen whether consumers in Europe and elsewhere would embrace GM food even if a solution can be found.

Conclusion

While trade experts remain divided over the prospects for the WTO challenge brought by the USA against the EU's GMO ban, it seems certain that it will have a profound impact on the trade–environment relationship. As this will be the first legal case involving agricultural biotechnology and rules on food safety, the WTO dispute settlement body will enter new, politically sensitive, territory in adjudicating on this case. In a sense, the global dispute over agricultural biotechnology has become the new *cause célèbre* for environmental campaign groups and others critical of the WTO's trade liberalisation agenda. The often extreme politicisation of the global GMO debate has certainly not helped the search for a compromise between trade imperatives and environmental demands. Given the political and commercial stakes involved in the dispute, it is questionable whether such a compromise can indeed be found within the parameters of the WTO's dispute settlement mechanism.

Note

1   The following account of the international negotiations on the Cartagena Protocol on Biosafety is based on Falkner (2000) and Bail *et al.* (2002).

Bibliography

Bail, C., Falkner, R. and Marquard, H. (2002) *The Cartagena Protocol on Biosafety: reconciling trade in biotechnology with environment and development?*, London: RIIA/Earthscan.

Birnie, P. and Boyle, A. (2002) *International Law and the Environment*, 2nd edn, Oxford: Oxford University Press.

Brack, D., Falkner, R. and Goll, J. (2003) The Next Trade War? GM products, the Cartagena Protocol and the WTO, RIIA Briefing Paper No. 8, London: RSSA.

Cameron, J. (1999) 'The precautionary principle', in G.P. Sampson and W.B. Chambers (eds), *Trade, Environment and the Millennium*, Tokyo: United Nations University Press.

Cartagena Protocol on Biosafety to the Convention on Biological Diversity. Available HTTP: <http://www.biodiv.org/doc/legal/cartagena-protocol-en.pdf> (accessed 5 July 2003).

Charnovitz, S. (1999) 'Improving the agreement on Sanitary and Phytosanitary Standards', in G.P. Sampson and W.B. Chambers (eds), *Trade, Environment and the Millennium*, Tokyo: United Nations University Press.

European Commission (2002) 'Questions and answers on the regulation of GMOs in the EU', Memo/02/160, 15 October, Brussels. Available HTTP: <http://europa.eu.int> (accessed 5 June 2003).

Falkner, R. (2000) 'Regulating biotech trade: the Cartagena Protocol on Biosafety', *International Affairs* 76: 299–313.

Falkner, R. (2002) 'Gene wars go South', *The World Today* 58: 17–18.

Financial Times (2003) 'Sowing discord: after Iraq, the US and Europe head for a showdown over genetically modified crops', *Financial Times* 14 May.

Guardian (2003) 'Bush attack on Europe's GM barrier', *Guardian* 24 June.

Harremoës, P., Gee, D., MacGarvin, M., Stirling, A., Keys, J., Wynne, B. and Vaz, S.G. (eds) (2002) The Precautionary Principle in the 20th Century: late lessons on early warnings, London: Earthscan.

James, C. (2003) 'Preview: Global status of commercialized transgenic crops: 2002', ISAAA Briefs No. 27, Ithaca, NY: ISAAA.

Lheureux, K. *et al.* (2003) *Review of GMOs under Research and Development and in the Pipeline in Europe*, Brussels: European Commission Joint Research Centre.

National Foreign Trade Council (2003) Looking Behind the Curtain: the growth of trade barriers that ignore sound science, Washington, DC: National Foreign Trade Council. Available HTTP: <http://www.nftc.org> (accessed 31 July 2003).

Nielsen, C.P. and Anderson, K. (2001) 'Global market effects of alternative European responses to genetically modified organisms' *Weltwirtschaftliches Archiv* 137: 320–346.

Nuffield Council on Bioethics (2003) 'The use of genetically modified crops in developing countries', Discussion paper.

Safrin, S. (2002) 'The relationship with other agreements: much ado about a savings clause', in C. Bail, R. Falkner and H. Marquard (eds), *The Cartagena Protocol on Biosafety: reconciling trade in biotechnology with environment and development?*, London: RIIA/Earthscan.

Vogel, D. (2001) 'Ships passing in the night: GMOs and the contemporary politics of risk regulation in Europe', EUI Working Papers, No. 2001/16, European University Institute.

Young, A.R. (2001) 'Trading up or trading blows? US politics and transatlantic trade in genetically modified food', EUI Working Papers, No. 2001/30, European University Institute.

Key readings

Birnie, P. and Boyle, A. (2002) *International Law and the Environment*, 2nd edn, Oxford: Oxford University Press.

Cameron, J. (1999) 'The precautionary principle', in G.P. Sampson and W.B. Chambers (eds) *Trade, Environment and the Millennium*, Tokyo: United Nations University Press.

Falkner, R. (2000) 'Regulating biotech trade: the Cartagena Protocol on Biosafety', *International Affairs*, 76: 299–313.

Useful websites

www.biodiv.org/doc/legal/cartagena-protocol-en.pdf (Cartagena Protocol on Biosafety).
www.nftc.org (National Foreign Trade Council of the United States).
www.useu.be/Categories/Biotech/Index.htm (United States Mission to the EU, Dossier on biotechnology).
http://gmoinfo.jrc.it (EU Commission, Biotechnology and GMO's website).
http://pewagbiotech.org (Pew Initiative on Food and Biotechnology).

Part IV

Actors and processes

Key part issues

- Why and how have domestic trade policy processes adapted to the changing character of the trade agenda?
- How has the role of business in trade policy changed in the light of the transformation of the global economy?
- What are the key features of the EU as a trade policy actor? Why is it suggested that it occupies a unique place in the world political economy?
- What are the major characteristics of the US trade policy process? Do the consequences of 11 September 2001 present serious problems for the multilateral trade regime?

In the previous part, we have seen how the trade agenda has expanded to embrace a range of new issues. In doing so, trade policy now penetrates far deeper into national societies and touches on matters of intense political interest – such as the issue of food safety, for example. Not surprisingly, this has increased the cast of actors involved in trade policy, and also the way in which it is formulated. The aim of the final part of the book is to explore how the traditional actors in trade politics, principally governments, are adapting to these developments and the role of non-state actors. Obviously, relevant material on this theme will be found in earlier parts – Shaw and van der Westhuizen's chapter on Africa and Scholte's chapter on the WTO and civil society, for example.

It has become commonplace to conceive of the state as an actor that is steadily losing political ground to other actors such as firms, non-governmental agencies or supranational bodies like the WTO. These new actors are by no means eclipsing the state; no other form of political or economic organisation rivals it in terms of public legitimacy or in the capacity to coerce compliance from civil societies. Rather, the picture is one of governments – still the primary actors in international trade – increasingly finding that other voices can have an important influence in the conduct of international trade politics. But as Hocking's chapter demonstrates, the nature of trade policy making has adapted to the forces of change examined in this book. The argument in this chapter is that governments are now confronted by an environment where the consensus underpinning the desirability of free trade is being eroded. Consequently, the older 'club' model of policy making is having to be reformulated to embrace new actors and interests.

The significant presence of business in trade issues links this chapter to McGuire's. Firms have always played an important role in development of trade policies. As McGuire's chapter explains, *the state–firm relationship continues to be one of mutual dependence. The state needs the employ-ment, technology and investment that firms bring, while firms themselves recognise that government has a key role to play in the provision of public goods underpinning competitiveness. However, the patterns of relationships between both firms and governments and between firms themselves are highly complex.*

The final two chapters focus on the trade policy processes in two of the most influential global players: the United States (US) and the European Union (EU). In his chapter, Smith analyses the emergence of the EU as a trade actor and the character of the policy framework. As he points out, the behaviour of the EU in this policy area bears some similarities to the ways in which national governments behave, but there are also important differences. One of the more general themes that emerges here, as in other chapters, is the significance of relationships between public and private actors. Pigman compares the record of the Clinton Administration with that of George W. Bush. Having set out the key features of the US trade policy processes – such as the relationship between the White House and Congress – varying analytical approaches are reviewed. Whilst noting the considerable element of continuity between the two Administrations, Pigman concludes that the most serious challenge to the trade agenda is to be found in the impact of the events post 11 September 2001 and the potential impact of concerns with 'Homeland Security' on Washington's commitment to multilateral free trade.

18 Beyond Seattle: Adapting the Trade Policy process

Brian Hocking

Summary

As Part III of this book clearly demonstrates, the trade agenda has changed in highly significant ways over the last three decades or so. Moving trade issues 'behind the border' impacts more immediately on the interests and concerns of domestic constituencies, producing a growing sense of disquiet with the pro-trade liberalisation agenda and a demand for greater consultation on the shaping of national trade policies. Consequently, *international* trade diplomacy is now accompanied by enhanced processes of *domestic* diplomacy. This chapter reviews the transition from a closed 'club' model of trade policy making to a more open and inclusive 'multistakeholder' model, and notes the issues that the latter present for governments, business and civil society.

Following the experience of the Seattle World Trade Organization ministerial in December 1999, there is a growing recognition that trade policy processes need to be adapted to an environment in which the pro-trade liberalisation consensus is crumbling. No longer can trade issues be dealt with as a brand of technocratic politics insulated from the mainstream of political dialogue, a game for an elite operating behind closed doors, removed from prying eyes and the glare of publicity. Trade politics is being reconfigured and, with it, the modalities through which governments define their interests and articulate them both to their negotiating partners and to critical interests at home.

To a considerable degree, as Scholte's chapter in this book demonstrates, the focus of discussion has turned on the World Trade Organization (WTO) and the legitimacy and transparency of its operations – particularly in terms of the dispute settlement process. Here, issues of access for civil society groups and the effects that such access might have on the negotiating processes within the WTO have become the object of intense debate (Garten 1997; Esty 1998; Marceau and Pedersen 1999). But these issues, significant as they are, cannot be isolated from the ways in which national trade policy making are structured (Evans 2003). Indeed, they are inseparably linked in an environment where globalisation dictates that policy arenas are intertwined, thus necessitating that processes aimed at enhancing democratisation of policy making develop a multifaceted approach spanning national and international policy milieux. Hence the transparency–legitimacy debate directed towards international institutions such as the WTO is shadowed at the domestic level by intensive discussions as to how the processes of national trade policy making might best be adapted to the demands of the new environment.

It is with this dimension of the trade policy processes that the chapter is concerned. It tracks the arguments as to how trade diplomats might best respond to the challenges represented by the growing impact of pressures from disaffected domestic constituencies and non-governmental organisations (NGOs), and the emergence of more open 'multistakeholder' models of consultation in place of the older, closed 'club' model, for long a feature of trade diplomacy.

The changing diplomatic environment

The experience of Seattle, together with that of the failed Multilateral Agreement on Investment (MAI) negotiations, has prompted a recognition that the environment in which trade diplomacy is taking place has altered in significant ways. It is not the case, of course, that observers agree on what is significant. Whilst to some, these events represent a triumph for the forces of civil society and the expertise of NGOs in marshalling the powers of the Internet in the pursuit of their goals, to others they reflect much deeper changes in the trade policy milieu and systemic failures at both the national and the multilateral levels, specifically in the operation of the WTO itself. These changes can be presented in terms of the *what, how* and *who* of trade diplomacy.

In terms of *what* trade diplomacy is about, the implications of the changes in the trade agenda are well understood. As noted elsewhere in this book, trade negotiations have moved from concerns with protection at the border, as represented by the focus of earlier GATT negotiating rounds on tariffs, to much more complex issues that have changed the nature of trade negotiations and the configuration of forces that lie behind them. The emergence of 'new' issues such as financial services, telecoms and intellectual property has not simply demanded the cultivation of new strategies and techniques in trade negotiations, but has changed their context as closer international economic integration directs attention behind national borders. This is even more marked in the case of the 'trade and' issues such as the environment, labour policy and taxation. With the growing interaction between international and domestic issues, actors and policy arenas, the trade environment has become more complex and more politicised as trade issues rub against various aspects of domestic politics, ultimately posing challenges to the independence and autonomy of national and subnational jurisdictions.

Changes in the *how* of trade diplomacy have been presented by Dymond and Hart in terms of the emergence of what they refer to as a 'post-modern' trade policy environment marked by the transition from the negative prescription of the GATT to that of the positive rule making epitomised in the dispute settlement system of the WTO (Dymond and Hart 2000). They and many others note that the character of negotiation in the trade arena is conditioned by this development because, whereas in the context of negative prescription there was a natural inclination towards negotiation, agreements based on positive rule making tend towards litigation as the roots of conflict are to be found in differing domestic regulations rather than trade barriers. Not only is this brand of regulatory diplomacy far more sensitive in terms of its impact on domestic constituencies and their interests, the economic gains deriving from such negotiations are far more difficult to demonstrate (ibid.: 34). Keohane and Nye have portrayed these and associated developments in the trade environment as accompanying the demise of the 'club' model of multilateral cooperation in which trade negotiations were insulated from domestic politics and other issues on the political agenda – such as the environment – and lack of transparency was a key element in the negotiation process and outcomes (Keohane and Nye 2000).

Inevitably, these developments are reflected in the *who* of trade policy and diplomacy, that is to say, the range of players involved. Here, the pattern of trade diplomacy reflects changes to be found in other policy areas. Traditionally, the number of government departments involved in trade negotiations was small – most commonly departments of trade and finance – but since the start of the Uruguay Round, it has grown markedly. The expanded agenda of trade negotiations has brought with it a new cast of bureaucratic actors just as it has in other areas of economic diplomacy. To this layer of change has been added another, however, as non-state actors have increasingly sought to open up the closed processes of trade policy making against the background outlined above. Technocratic and diplomatically negotiated solutions to trade problems are regarded as illegitimate by civil society organisations (CSOs) – and, increasingly, significant sectors of the public at large – which demand instead a more inclusive and transparent approach to trade policy. The growing claims of NGOs for greater transparency in the trade agenda and involvement in WTO processes have served to add a significant new dimension to the diplomatic milieu, one that has been designated a 'complex' and 'new' multilateralism as multilateral economic institutions expand their patterns of interaction beyond governments and embrace a range of civil society actors (O'Brien *et al.* 2000).

But it is not only at the multilateral level that this pattern of change is occurring. Indeed, the distinction between bilateral and multilateral diplomacy, rather than representing the triumph of the former over the latter, is becoming less marked as both governmental and non-governmental actors pursue their policy goals in a variety of national and international policy milieux, often simultaneously. Thus both the processes and machinery of national diplomacy have become far more diffuse, not simply in a bureaucratic sense as the conduct of international policy moves outside the territory inhabited by the professional diplomat to include officials from line ministries, but also in terms of the involvement of CSOs. This reflects a diminished capacity on the part of all actors, not simply national governments, to achieve their objectives in the face of pressures associated with globalisation. Increasingly, what contemporary diplomacy demands is the creation and management of coalitions of public and private sector actors (Hocking 1999). Given the fact that trade policy, for the reasons noted above, now enmeshes domestic and international constituencies to a far greater degree than ever before, it provides a highly developed example of these more general trends to be found in the management of public policy domains. And it is against this background that the growing concern with processes of consultation on trade issues at the national level is occurring.

The logic of trade consultation

As we shall see later, consultation on trade policy is not a new phenomenon but is one that, as Winham notes in his review of the Tokyo Round, is particularly important in trade negotiations. Ensuring that narrow, sectional interests do not triumph over broader policy goals places a premium on the need for 'control', or the management of significant domestic constituencies having an interest in the outcomes of negotiations (Winham 1986: 346). Events since the late 1970s have simply served to reinforce this imperative through the emergence of three forms of 'deficit' which have grown more marked and underpin the development of diplomacy, both in the trade sphere and in the more general context.

The first of these is a 'legitimacy deficit' reflecting a decreased level of trust in the institutions of government. As Ostry has noted, accompanying changes in the nature of the trade agenda there is a more general decline in public confidence in the institutions of representative democracy, mirrored in aspirations towards modes of participatory democracy (Ostry 2002a). Haynal sees this development as having a particular significance in the realm of diplomacy that represents a form of mediating institution between people and policy arenas. What he terms the growth of 'disintermediation', namely a rejection of such institutions in all areas of society, poses particular challenges to those charged with the conduct of international policy (Haynal 2002). The involvement of a broader cross-section of societal interests as represented in CSOs, particularly the NGOs, is thus a logical strategy for dealing with this alienation.

Not surprisingly, in the wake of the experiences of the abortive MAI negotiations in 1998 and the 1999 Seattle WTO ministerial, policy makers have made much of the need to consult domestic constituencies if support for trade liberalisation is to be sustained and anti-globalisation forces resisted. Thus the Canadian Department of Foreign Affairs and International Trade (DFAIT) is clear in its objectives regarding consultative procedures:

> By mobilizing popular opinion and keeping people fully informed of the issues and the direction of trade negotiations, transparency and engagement combine to establish the legitimacy, consistency and the durability of policy decisions and outcomes.
>
> (DFAIT 2003)

Very similar sentiments have been voiced in the USA and the EU. In evaluating the US system of trade consultation, Huenemann suggests that its biggest weakness is its failure to engage the public in a discussion on the aims of trade policy (Huenemann 2001). In Brussels, the Seattle experience led Commissioner Pascal Lamy to introduce a DG Trade–Civil Society Dialogue designed to 'develop a confident working relationship among all stakeholders interested in trade policy, to ensure that all contributions to EU trade policy can be heard'.[1] The underlying goal is, as Ostry suggests, for government to engage in capacity building within civil society if the anti-globalization backlash is to be contained (Ostry 2002b: 4).

The second deficit that underpins the growing interest in consultation relates to knowledge. In the trade sphere, negotiators have long recognised that advice from the business community is an essential component in the framing of trade policy. Hence, for example, the advisory structures put in place by Cordell Hull following the enactment of the US Trade Reciprocity Act of 1934 (Aaronson 2001: 27). But in the face of growing resource constraints, the knowledge capacity of government has, relatively, diminished just as the demands imposed on it have grown. Against this background, NGOs have a window of opportunity to fill this gap by capitalising on their own knowledge and expertise. From a US perspective, Aaronson has suggested that one of the key functions that consultative processes in trade policy perform is to establish a 'common language' regarding the nature and objectives of trade agreements (ibid.: 12).

Looked at from the CSO perspective, there is a resource deficit of a third kind – namely, that of access. Whereas the point is often made that the growing role of NGOs in world politics is underpinned by the diminishing obstacles on non-state actors operating at a global level and that there are advantages inherent in the 'non-sovereign' qualities of such actors, it is still the case that access to key diplomatic networks is dominated by governments and the sovereignty-related rules governing the international system. Despite some movement at the WTO towards greater NGO access, it still remains the case that its inter-governmental qualities place a premium on opportunities provided by modes of consultation at the national level. In short, the conduct of many areas of contemporary diplomacy, including that relating to international trade policy, involves the trading of resources between different species of actor, each possessing resources that the others need (Cooper and Hocking 2000). Consequently, diplomacy is becoming more of a networking mode of activity and less hierarchical in both its structures and processes as its demands favour the establishment of coalitions of diverse actors to manage complex policy agendas and the communications revolution facilitates the creation and maintenance of horizontal networks.

The costs of the legitimacy and knowledge deficits, however, extend beyond the management of the domestic political arena. Indeed, trade negotiations provide clear illustrations of Putnam's image of 'two level games', whereby negotiators operate simultaneously in two linked diplomatic environments – the international and the domestic (Evans *et al.* 1993). Success in the one is intimately linked to developments in the other. Much of the contemporary analysis of trade negotiations focuses on this linkage – as Winham's study of the Tokyo Round exemplifies: 'An important requirement of diplomacy today is for internal control over domestic politics in order to conduct negotiations abroad', he writes (1986: 344). The Uruguay Round subsequently reinforced Winham's observation that the political and constitutional structures of states had become far more significant in determining the outcomes of trade negotiations.

Put simply, the costs of failure at the domestic level are now more marked than in the past. But there are two sides of the trade policy coin to be considered here. On the one hand, the desire to achieve 'internal control' (however difficult this might be to achieve in practice) is based on the recognition that there are dangers in domestic incoherence in trade policy that can erode a government's credibility as a negotiating partner. In the US context, for example, commentaries on the weaknesses of current trade policy note that the USA is perceived as lacking coherence in reconciling the promotion of trade liberalisation on the one side and environmental and social values on the other (Aaronson 2001: 11). The consequence may be that other governments are reluctant to engage in trade negotiations where they believe that there is a significant likelihood of domestic opposition to them and inadequate consultative structures in place to counter it. In this sense, each government, potentially, has an interest in how other governments structure their consultation processes and the degree of success they achieve in operating them.

A logical corollary of this is that governments wish to ensure, to the extent they can, that there is a level playing field in consultative systems. Dissatisfied NGOs in a country lacking adequate processes may seek to compensate for domestic influence by developing coalitions with NGOs elsewhere and, in effect, use the consultative processes in other countries to affect outcomes in trade negotiations.

But if process is a determinant of policy, the reverse side of the coin, namely that policy helps to determine process, is equally true. In the context of Latin America, several countries have found it necessary to develop or review consultative processes in the light of regional trade initiatives such as NAFTA and Mercosur (INTAL-ITD-STA 2002). Similarly, as we shall see later, Canada developed its trade consultation processes during the Canada–US free trade negotiations in the 1980s, recognising that the implications of a major shift in trade strategy demanded that domestic support be cultivated.

Table 18.1 Models of trade consultation

Model	Participants	Aims	Characteristics
Club model			
Internal bureaucratic consultation	Foreign/trade ministries. Sectoral ministries, depending on issue	Policy coordination in face of increasingly complex trade agenda	Closed bureaucratic system. May be marked by 'turf' conflicts. Tendency to assume legitimacy of free trade goals
Adaptive club model			
Business-focused consultation	As above with addition of business representation	Advice focused. To add private sector resources, particularly knowledge, to trade policy processes	'Controlled' openness operating within established rules. Debates on relative gains from specific trade policies but not designed to question free trade goals
Multistakeholder model			
Mixed-mode consultation	Variable, but key feature is addition of civil society representatives to process	Consensus-focused; to enhance consensus in favour of free trade in face of growing public opposition	Linked to broader patterns of public diplomacy. May produce conflict and 'crisis of expectations' amongst governmental and non-governmental participants. Designed to cope with questioning of the objectives and legitimacy of goals of free trade. May lead to withdrawal by some participants

Models of trade consultation

Despite a growing interchange between trade policy practitioners in different national settings, models of trade consultation are not always exportable commodities since they will be conditioned by constitutional, political and social realities in each country. At the constitutional level, one of the major determinants is the distribution of power in territorial terms. Federal systems have become increasingly sensitive to the changing demands of the trade agenda and this is reflected in a growing awareness on the part of subnational jurisdictions as to the impact of trade agreements on their interests and, consequently, a desire to develop a voice in national policy formation. The reverse side of this coin is that the more centralised a political system, the less pressure is likely to exist for subnational involvement.

Political culture constitutes another determinant in terms of the prevailing relationship between government, the business community and civil society. Where these relationships are weak or skewed in a particular direction, then the consultative processes are likely to be weak or to favour particular constituencies. Linked to this are the patterns of bureaucratic politics that develop around consultative processes in given areas of public policy. Different configurations of officials not only develop links with interest groups through such processes, but also develop vested interests in protecting specific modes of consultation. Alongside these factors are to be found the character of the national economy and the types of trade policies to which this gives rise. Against such a background, forms of trade consultation will vary widely. In the case of the Tokyo Round, Winham found that the USA, Japan, Canada and the European Community (as it then was) demonstrated differing patterns of emphasis on controlling their 'domestic' environments. In the case of the USA, the primary focus was on economic interest groups, in Canada and the EC internal governments (the provinces and the member states respectively), and in Japan, the bureaucracy (Winham 1986: 347).

It is, therefore, dangerous to identify oversimplified models and, even more so, trends with general applicability. Nevertheless, past and present experience suggests that three basic models of trade consultation can be identified. These are summarised in Table 18.1.

The first model, according most closely to Keohane and Nye's 'club' model of trade policy making, is focused on bureaucratic adaptation in the face of the changing trade agenda. The key dimension is the recognition that the interaction of trade issues and, for example, environmental and social issues, has increased the demand for interagency coordination. At one level, of course, there is nothing particularly remarkable in this, for one of the main themes in the development of contemporary diplomacy is the growing involvement of sectoral ministries in the conduct of international policy. This has led to a growing diffusion in diplomacy that is mirrored in the trade sphere. Yet, at the same time, some bureaucratic systems (such as Australia and Canada) have also experienced the concentration of trade policy making through the merging of the international trade function with the foreign ministry. The more complex the trade agenda has become, the greater the quest for coordination.

During the 1970s and the 1980s, the requirements of horizontal coordination on trade issues within the Canadian federal bureaucracy were reinforced by the need to accommodate the pressures for vertical coordination in the form of growing provincial demands for consultation on the negotiating agenda (Winham 1986: 339–340). Whereas the Canadian system has evolved towards an open system, the case of Argentina is one where executive-branch coordination has been undertaken within a more 'top-down' process (Bouzas and

Avogadro 2002). In an environment 'often marred by functional overlaps, inter-agency competition and the withholding of information', the demands posed by the Mercosur and FTAA negotiations in the 1990s required more effective coordination within the bureaucracy. Despite attempts to reinforce this in 2000 through the creation of the Inter-Ministerial Foreign Trade Commission under the chairmanship of the President, this has not assumed its intended role as the key coordinating agency for trade policy making (Bouzas and Avogadro 2002).

Alongside the demand for more effective bureaucratic coordination, there has emerged an 'adaptive club' model. This term has been used to reflect, on the one hand, the recognition that trade diplomacy demands greater outreach to the constituencies most affected by it, whilst still operating by rules ensuring that modes of consultation remain relatively closed. In the case of Brazil – as with other countries in the region – the FTAA negotiations encouraged the creation of a new coordinating secretariat at the bureaucratic level (Secretaria Nacional da ALCA – SENALCA), which was expanded to include business and labour representatives. However, the scope of the discussions, as well as the agenda and limits of the debates, are clearly defined by the forum's government coordinators – that is, representatives of the foreign ministry (da Motta Veiga 2002).

Apart from the general need to ensure the acceptance of negotiating outcomes at the domestic level, this model of trade consultation reflects the imperatives of the knowledge deficit noted above and the fact that business has become a necessary partner in dealing with an increasingly complex agenda (Garten 1997). Thus the logic of the model is one of overlaying private sector advice mechanisms onto the policy process. One of the best developed systems of this kind is that created in the USA in 1974, which included, amongst other bodies, thirty-three Industry Sectoral Advisory Committees intended to establish fair representation of key interests in trade negotiations (Huenemann 2002). As the demands for consultation developed during the 1980s and 1990s in terms of state-level pressures for involvement, so the system has been adapted and expanded. As with the club model, the purpose of consultation is not to question the overall goals of trade policy, but to engender support for the goals set by policy makers and to enhance support where that policy may be moving in new directions (as with the Brazilian and Argentinian cases).

The third layer of consultation, however, as represented in the 'multistakeholder' model, is very different in this respect. Responding to the developments in the milieu of trade politics discussed earlier, the aim is to counter growing opposition to the goals of free trade from a variety of civil society organisations. Although, therefore, it might be seen as sharing the goal of providing 'advice' to policy makers, this advice has at its core a consensus-building rationale. Hence the development of systems – as in Canada and the EU – which are intended to engage a variety of stakeholders alongside the more traditional business constituencies which are the focus of the second model.

As we have seen, political systems with little tradition of involvement of civil society either in policy making generally or trade policy more specifically – as appears to be the case in Latin American countries, for example – are hardly likely to be to the fore in terms of this development. Adding another set of stakeholders – especially NGOs whose attitudes to the goals of trade liberalisation are at best ambivalent – presents dilemmas for all the parties involved in the consultative processes. Differing interests and approaches to these processes are likely to produce, as we shall see later, what are often conflicting and incompatible expectations regarding their objectives.

It needs to be stressed that these modes of consultation not only vary with the political and economic contexts in which they are located, but also may not be sequential. In some cases, such as Sweden, the development of a civil society dialogue in the trade policy area in preparation for the Doha negotiations was coterminous with a review of the political and bureaucratic processes (a State Secretary Working Group and a Preparatory Group comprising civil servants from relevant departments). Alongside this, a civil society dialogue in the form of an advisory Reference Group was established, meeting on a monthly basis. As with the EU Trade–Civil Society Dialogue in Brussels, the Reference Group operates on the basis of the presentation of position papers regarding Sweden's views on particular topics on the trade agenda. Membership embraces business coalitions, trade unions as well as individual NGOs and NGO networks (Ahnlid 2002: 6–7).

However, there are problems in transforming the older, adaptive club model to the new multistakeholder model which need to be resolved – or at least managed – if the goals of consolidating a broader approach to legitimising trade policy are to be achieved. To summarise, these can be identified in terms of 'institutional tension' created by attempts to graft newer onto older modes of consultation; a 'crisis of expectations' which results from a mismatch of goals and ambitions on the part of the participants in the various processes; and a more general legitimacy debate which is part of the broader debate about the nature of democratic processes in the face of globalisation.

The institutional tensions are to be found in the attempts to redefine the role of older business-based consultative mechanisms. As we have seen, these brought together policy makers and business people in a closed environment with rules and procedures that ensured the older ethos of the club model was sustained, albeit with a wider cast of players. Moreover, it ensured that consultation was focused on participants in broad agreement on the goals of trade policy, if not on specific issues. But business is now confronted by an expanded membership that embraces the NGO community. This, according to some observers, is causing business to 'retreat' from trade policy, a view shared by Dymond and Dawson who attribute, at least in part, a reluctance by business to engage in a trade policy dialogue to its sense of alienation from a process with which it is no longer comfortable and whose value it regards as diminished by a growing emphasis on civil society (2002: 29–30).

Stairs has added considerable substance to this feature of trade consultation in his analysis of the elaborate consultative processes surrounding the WTO Seattle summit in December 1999. Apart from membership of the eighty-four-strong official delegation (including parliamentarians, provincial representatives, business and labour representatives and NGOs), sixty-five private Canadian organisations were registered through the WTO (Stairs 2000: 22–33). He found there to be considerable disquiet amongst the business representatives at the behaviour of the NGOs and the substance of their interventions, both at home and during the Seattle meeting (ibid.).

Much of this disquiet, of course, is related to the second factor identified above, namely a crisis of expectations concerning the objectives of consultations, the means through which they are achieved and the likely outcomes. And, equally obviously, this phenomenon is part of the stresses that are more generally manifest in the conduct of international policy making and diplomacy as NGOs, the business community and officials from government find themselves rubbing shoulders with increasing frequency. It is hardly surprising that in the case of trade policy, as elsewhere, differing operational styles, organisational characteristics and, simply, a lack of familiarity between differing categories of participants, condition the workings of consultative processes.

This has been the case with the EU DG Trade–Civil Society Dialogue in which, as one commentator has noted, factors such as these 'make it difficult for the creation of consultation spaces where the actors feel comfortable and, sometimes, frustrations and misunderstandings arise' (Muguruza 2002: 13). In both Brussels and Canada, expectations veer between those groups adopting a cynical approach, viewing dialogue as a sham, intended to legitimise official policy, and those which regard it, despite its defects, as a useful means of airing – and even resolving – problems. But a common response from NGOs is that trade dialogues are treated by officials more as briefing sessions than genuine attempts to seek a broader input into the formulation of policy. Whilst it is likely to be the case that this is precisely how some trade officials view the exercise, even those who do not, recognise that 'opening up' the trade policy processes poses very real problems, some relating to confidentiality, others to decisions as to how consultative processes should be structured.

Even more fundamentally, though, expectations reflect assumptions as to what might and should be achieved in this area of public policy. We have already noted that there is a mismatch in broad approaches to the trade agenda. As Stairs notes in the Canadian context and Muguruza in the European, there is an inherent inclination amongst the NGO community to pursue the trade dialogue at a much deeper level than the business community desires. After all, the fundamental concerns of civil society groups are with the principles on which globalisation rests, and the 'trade and' issues represented by, for example, the environmental agenda. Stairs notes that during the Seattle process, the tendency of the NGOs was to add issues to the negotiating agenda thereby complicating the task of trade officials, whereas, historically, the role of business has been to strengthen their hand by providing valuable advice and information and links to business interests in other jurisdictions (Stairs 2000).

Underpinning these issues are the deeper ones relating to the legitimacy of specific consultative processes as governments seek to respond to domestic and international pressures associated with globalisation. Clearly, there are several facets to the problem. If the older business-based systems posed questions of legitimacy specified in terms of a nexus between economic interests and the trade bureaucracy, then these are no less evident in the multistakeholder model. The well-rehearsed question directed to CSOs regarding the validity of their oft-proclaimed credentials as spokespersons for society is as telling in this sector of the policy agenda as it is elsewhere. But as Dymond and Dawson note, there is a further problem relating to the legitimacy and democratic credentials of processes that are highly bureaucratised (2002: 23). Partly, this relates to the lack of officials' political authority to respond to the often highly politicised demands made by NGOs. Stairs suggests that this is one of the great weaknesses of the Canadian system and serves to elevate expectations to a level which officials are unable to satisfy (2000: 37). It is even more marked in the case of the EU, given the highly fragmented milieu in which trade policy emerges. But beyond this, there are concerns that those responsible for maintaining and developing the consultative processes may well have a vested interest in its expansion which has more to do with furthering careers than the desire to enhance the democratic qualities of the environment in which trade policy is framed (Dymond and Dawson 2002) .

Conclusion: towards new rules of engagement

The growing trend, certainly in developed countries, towards the expansion and redefinition of trade consultative processes is another facet of the concern with transparency and access which has become an essential part of the debate on globalisation and global governance – not least in the WTO. In fact, the nature of the political processes and interests around which the international debate turns requires that the national dimension be taken into account since, as both the Seattle summit and the 2003 Cancùn summit clearly demonstrate, there is a close link between the activities of CSOs in an international context and at the national level. Moreover, establishing accountability and transparency in trade policy outside the borders of the state is linked inevitably to their development inside national boundaries. However, the latter appears to have received less attention than the former. As we have seen, the reasons for growing interest within national bureaucracies in developing a dialogue on trade issues with publics and CSOs reflect fundamental changes in the character of the trade agenda, a weakening of the consensus favourable to trade liberalisation and a recognition that this can only be re-established by an opening up of what has hitherto been a closed process.

Hence national processes, and multilevel processes in the case of the EU, have sought to tackle this growing problem by transforming closed systems into a multistakeholder model intended to embrace the expanding range of constituencies with an interest in the trade agenda. But it is not a problem-free process. Earlier models of consultation – the adaptive club model – rested on a high degree of consensus between the key participants, namely business and trade officials, as to the aims and worth of the exercise. Expanding the forms of consultation poses very real problems in terms of tensions induced by differing goals and assumptions as to the objectives to be achieved.

One consequence is a clash of expectations regarding what can be realistically achieved through what are essentially bureaucratic processes, especially where some of the participants are seeking to redefine the political agenda in ways to which bureaucratic interlocutors are unable to respond. What appears to be happening is that 'rules of engagement' between the key sets of actors – government, business and CSOs – are gradually being shaped, based on shared interests in trading resources – knowledge, conferral of legitimacy and access to key diplomatic forums – which each possess to differing degrees. Not surprisingly, these rules are tenuous and fuzzy. But the success of much contemporary diplomacy, not just in the trade arena, demands that they be developed.

Note

1 See DG Trade–Civil Society Dialogue website:
   <http://trade-info.cec.eu.int/civil_soc/intro1.php> (accessed 20 July 2003).

Bibliography

Aaronson, S. (2001) *Redefining the terms of trade policymaking*, Washington, DC: National Policy Association.

Ahnlid, A. (2002) 'The consultative process with civil society in the formulation of Sweden's positions on trade policy within the EU', Working paper prepared for the Inter-American Development Bank Regional Policy Dialogue Trade and Integration Network, Washington, DC, 17–18 September.

Bouzas, R. and Avogadro, E. (2002) 'Trade policy-making and the private sector: a memorandum on Argentina', in INTAL-ITD-STA (Inter-American Development Bank), *The Trade Policy-Making Process. Level one of the two level game: country studies in the Western Hemisphere*, Occasional Paper 13, Buenos Aires

Cooper, A. and Hocking, B. (2000) 'Governments, non-governmental organisations and the re-calibration of diplomacy', *Global Society* 14: 361–376.

Da Motta Veiga, P. (2002) 'Trade policy-making in Brazil: transition paths', in INTAL-ITD-STA, (Inter-American Development Bank), *The Trade Policy-Making Process. Level One of the Two Level Game: country studies in the Western Hemisphere*, Occasional Paper 13, Buenos Aires.

Dymond, W.A. and Dawson, L.R. (2002) 'The consultative process in the formulation of Canadian trade policy', in INTAL-ITD-STA (Inter-American Development Bank), *The Trade Policy-Making Process. Level One of the Two Level Game: country studies in the Western Hemisphere*, Occasional Paper 13, Buenos Aires.

Dymond, W.A. and Hart, M.M. (2000) 'Post-modern trade policy: reflections on the challenges to multilateral trade negotiations after Seattle', *Journal of World Trade* 34: 21–38.

Esty, D. (1998) 'Non-governmental organizations at the World Trade Organization: cooperation, competition or exclusion', *Journal of International Economic Law* 1: 83–122.

Evans, P. (2003) 'Is trade policy democratic? And should it be?', in N. Bayne and S. Woolcock (eds), *The New Economic Diplomacy: decision-making and negotiation in international economic relations*, Aldershot: Ashgate, 147–162.

Evans, P., Jacobson, H. and Putnam, R. (eds) (1993) *Double-Edged Diplomacy: international bargaining and domestic politics*, Berkeley, CA: University of California Press.

Garten, J.E. (1997) 'Business and foreign policy', *Foreign Affairs* 76: 67–79.

Haynal, G. (2002) 'DOA: diplomacy on the ascendant in the age of disintermediation', Paper presented at a conference on The Future of Diplomacy, Munk Centre for International Studies, University of Toronto, 22 April.

Hocking, B. (1999) 'Catalytic diplomacy: beyond "newness" and "decline"', in J. Melissen (ed.), *Innovation in Diplomatic Practice*, London: Macmillan.

Huenemann, J.E. (2002) 'On the trade policy-making process in the United States', in INTAL-ITD-STA (Inter-American Development Bank), *The Trade Policy-Making Process. Level One of the Two Level Game: country studies in the Western Hemisphere*, Occasional Paper 13, Buenos Aires.

INTAL-ITD-STA (Inter-American Development Bank) (2002) *The Trade Policy-Making Process. Level One of the Two Level Game: country studies in the Western Hemisphere*, Occasional Paper 13, Buenos Aires, 2002. Available HTTP:
<http://www.iadb.org/intal/pub> (accessed 14 May 2003).

Keohane, R. and Nye, J. (2000) 'The club model of multilateral cooperation and the WTO: problems of democratic legitimacy', Paper presented at a conference on Efficiency, Equity and Legitimacy: the multilateral trading system at the Millennium, Kennedy School of Government, Harvard University, 1–2 June.

Marceau, G. and Pedersen, P. (1999) 'Is the WTO open and transparent? A discussion of the relationship of the WTO with non-governmental organisations and civil society's claims for more transparency and public participation', *Journal of World Trade* 33: 5–49.

Muguruza, M.I. (2002) 'Civil society and trade diplomacy in the "global age". The European case: trade policy dialogue between civil society and the European Commission', Document for the Fourth Meeting of the Trade and Integration Network, Inter-American Development Bank, Washington, DC, 17–18 September.

O'Brien, R., Goetz, M., Scholte, J.A. and Williams, M. (2000) *Contesting Global Governance: multilateral economic institutions and global social movements*, Cambridge: Cambridge University Press.

Ostry, S. (2002a) 'Trade negotiations and civil society: the trade policy-making process at the national level', Paper presented at the Fourth Meeting of the Trade and Integration Network, Inter-American Development Bank, Washington, DC, 17–18 September.

Ostry, S. (2002b) 'Preface', in INTAL-ITD-STA (Inter-American Development Bank), *The Trade Policy-Making Process. Level One of the Two Level Game: country studies in the Western Hemisphere*, Occasional Paper 13, Buenos Aires, iv.

Stairs, D. (2000) 'Foreign policy consultations in a globalizing world: the case of Canada, the WTO, and the shenanigans in Seattle, policy matters', Institute for Research on Public Policy, Montreal, 1.

Winham, G. (1986) *International Trade and the Tokyo Round Negotiation*, Princeton, NJ: Princeton University Press.

Key readings

Dymond, W.A. and Hart, M.M. (2000) 'Post-modern trade policy: reflections on the challenges to multilateral trade negotiations after Seattle', *Journal of World Trade* 34: 21–38.

Evans, P. (2003) 'Is trade policy democratic? And should it be?', in N. Bayne and S. Woolcock (eds), *The new economic diplomacy: decision-making and negotiation in international economic relations*, Aldershot: Ashgate.

Evans, P., Jacobson, H. and Putnam, R. (eds) (1993) *Double-Edged Diplomacy: international bargaining and domestic politics*, Berkeley, CA: University of California Press.

INTAL-ITD-STA (Inter-American Development Bank) (2002) *The Trade Policy-Making Process. Level One of the Two Level Game: country studies in the Western Hemisphere*, Occasional Paper 13, Buenos Aires. Available HTTP: <http://www.iadb.org/intal/pub> (accessed 14 May 2003).

Marceau, G. and Pedersen, P. (1999) 'Is the WTO open and transparent? A discussion of the relationship of the WTO with non-governmental organisations and civil society's claims for more transparency and public participation', *Journal of World Trade* 33: 5–49.

Useful websites

www.dfait-maeci.gc.ca/tna-nac/consult-en.asp (Canadian Department of Foreign Affairs and International Trade).

www.trade-info.cec.eu.int/civil_soc/intro1.php (Civil Society Dialogue of the European Commission).

www.ustr.gov (Office of the United States Trade Representative).

19 Firms and governments in international trade[1]

Steven McGuire

Summary

This chapter examines both the role of firms in the trade-policy-making process and the issues that confront corporate and political actors. It considers how firms try to translate policy preferences into state action – and factors that condition success. This is done by examining how trade policy making has changed since the creation of the GATT in 1947. The chapter also shows how the content of trade policy has changed from an emphasis on tariffs to a more complex agenda that embraces regulatory issues and industrial policies.

This chapter seeks to understand the interaction of firms and states in the development and conduct of international trade policy by examining both the processes of this inter-action and the type of policy issues that are addressed. The steady, if geographically uneven, internationalisation of business has been accompanied by an evolution in the content and conduct of firm–state relations. Firms now confront government with a bewildering array of policy demands, many of which would not strike someone as having much at all to do with trade politics. What is distinctive about these policies is the degree to which they centre on domestic arrangements of states rather than on external economic policies. Modern trade politics is as much about what goes on inside states as between them. Trade policy now is a bundle of industrial and regulatory policies and this has brought firms and states into new types of interaction over new issues. In contrast to earlier decades where there was a clearer distinction between the outside world of trade and the inside realm of the domestic economy, industrial policy questions are now inextricably bound up in trade issues.

Since firms' competitive prospects in the international economy can be shaped by state policies, international trade matters are less and less about 'trade' as conventionally defined. Rather they are about the complex interplay between corporate strategies and policy preferences and government regulatory regimes. Thus, it is misleading to say that firms simply demand an ever more deregulated marketplace. In many ways the international economy is more, not less, regulated than ever as more areas of business activity are coming under national or supranational scrutiny. Intellectual property protection, health and safety standards, to say nothing of competition policies, were not on the trade agenda thirty years ago – now they are.

Perspectives on firm–government relations

That firms have preferences on commercial matters is neither new nor controversial; the international political economy, management and the public policy literature provide important insights into firm activity on particular issues. Much of international political economy (IPE) work on multinationals explored the extent to which firms allegedly exploited a state's need for the economic benefits that firms bring (Rugman and Verbeke 1998: 117). While this critical view of the MNE concentrated on firms' relations with developing states, the critique was also applied to the developed world. A more nuanced view of the firm draws attention to the interdependency that exists between firms and states. This view arises from the observation that firms are not borderless entities which lead a nomadic existence in search of the lowest tax rates, the most lax labour standards or the most liberal pollution regulations. Instead, the 'home base' of a firm can provide key competitive ingredients in the form of education systems, tax incentives for research and other policies (Porter 1998: 126–128). Moreover, as Rugman and Brain (2003) show, the sales of most multinationals display a clear bias towards the home region, reflecting the benefits brought by familiarity with the competitive environment.

Firms have always been political actors and their control over resources always gave them input into government policy. However, some scholars argue that the international system is now characterised by a multiplicity of actors, where states are only one source of power. The ideological ascendancy of economic liberalism has seen states come under pressure to offload a variety of governmental functions onto private or quasi-private actors in the belief that markets are inherently better at providing goods and services than the state. Moreover, rapid technological change, particularly in information technologies, has led to charges that governments will always be 'behind the curve' in developing regulation: far better to let the private sector lead (Lawton and McGuire 2003a). This has led to work examining the rise of private regulatory regimes in areas such as Internet domain names and securities regulation (Hall and Biersteker 2002). But this focus on the supposed efficacy of market-based solutions has also led to concerns that business is too influential in the shaping of economic policies.

The anti-globalisation movement routinely directs much of its anger towards the privileged place that business is said to have in economic policy making: 'Activists always target the people who have the power … so if the power moves from government to industry to transnational corporations, so the swivel will move on to these people' (Vidal in Klein 2000: 342–343). Increasing criticism is directed towards the alleged dominance of business interests in important policy making such as WTO ministerial meetings, IMF annual meetings, or gatherings of the 'great and the good' at places like the World Economic Forum in Davos. Hertz, for example, argues that:

> Propelled by government policies of privatisation, deregulation and trade liberalisation, a power shift has taken place. … Business is in the driving seat, corporations determine the rules of the game, and governments have become the referees, enforcing rules laid down by others.
>
> (Hertz 2002: 8–9)

The perception not merely that business does have good access to policy makers, but that political discourse now more or less accepts the primacy of capitalism, is central to Marxist-informed analyses of the international economy. Gill, for example, speaks of the

'new constitutionalism' as the legal counterpart to the market civilisation that now dominates economic governance – and in doing so enshrines the privileged place of firms in
public policy debates (2003: 131–135). The agents of this dominant free-market perspective are a global elite comprised of leaders of multinational companies, aided by
sympathetic policy makers in national governments and international institutions like the
IMF or WTO. But organisation is not the key advantage this elite possesses. The crucial
point made by Gramscian analysts is that the entrenchment of business interests is not
merely a structural phenomenon, but is underpinned by a normative dominance:
'Capitalist commercialisation shapes outlooks, identities, time-horizons and conceptions of
social space' (Gill 2003: 120).

The Gramscian view of the firm and its relationship to political institutions has been
subject to the criticism that it exaggerates the coherence of the transnational elite and, in
doing so, overestimates firms' impact on public policy decisions. As Amoore argues, neo-
Gramscian analyses reify the firm; it is considered outside the society that constitutes it and
no attention is paid to its internal workings (2000). In doing so, neo-Gramscians conceive of
firms as utterly indistinguishable from each other – and all wanting the same thing from
policy makers. This robs the theory of the ability to explain particular policy outcomes. It is
also misleading to think that firm–government relations are characterised by either an
extreme degree of collusion or confrontation. Rather, it is often the case that the relationship is cooperative, with firms and governments working well together to address policy
problems. Spar (2001) notes that firms often want government regulation: the rule of law
remains the best guarantee that they can conduct their business safely.

Processes of firm–government relations

Business does not always get its way, nor is it even able to articulate a consistent set of
policy preferences. Rather business engages with governments across a range of trade
policy issues in a process that is at once complex and evolving. Braithwaite and Drahos
(2000) have developed a useful framework for understanding how firms get their policy
preferences translated into rules. First, there is an identification of a problem: what,
exactly, do firms want a new rule for? Second, firms need to mobilise fellow firms to their
cause. In Braithwaite and Draho's terminology, the firms enrol organisational power in
support of their policy preference. Building an industry or sectoral coalition helps blunt
any charge that a firm is looking for special treatment; far better to portray the issue as
one that confronts the entire industry – or economy. For example, the US pharmaceutical
industry was a motive force in the creation of the pan-industry Intellectual Property
Committee, which lobbied hard and successfully for the TRIPs Agreement (Capling in
this volume; Sell 2002, 2003). As Sell argues, the IPC successfully portrayed patent protection as an issue of competitiveness and fairness; the US economy was losing out to foreign
competitors who had no qualms about abusing patents, pirating products and otherwise
damaging the US economy. The third and final stage sees corporate lobbying activity
aimed at translating the preference into legislation. What makes firms influential at this
stage is expertise; firms naturally know more about the day-to-day competitive situation in
the market than do governments.

Firms – even the most effective political operators – do not always get their preferences
translated into policy. Interestingly, resources per se do not always translate into policy-
making success. Pfizer, the US pharmaceutical firm, was an active member of the
successful lobbying effort behind TRIPs, but was also in the much less successful coalition

pushing for tough, WTO-level investment rules through TRIMs (Sell 2003). But what governs success? Cohesiveness seems to be a key variable, as does the involvement of major firms. In the TRIPs example, the IPC developed into a strong and stable corporate lobby able to stay the course over a long period and comprising major multinationals. Other corporate lobby groups, such as the European Round Table, are likewise able to keep their members pulling in the same direction over the long time frames associated with legislative action. Another instructive example is in the area of anti-dumping. In their study of EU anti-dumping (AD) activity, Liu and Vandenbussche (2002) observe that AD petitions stand a much better chance of success where the petitioners comprise the dominant players in the European market.

Another factor in success is coherence: are firms all saying the same thing and can their preferences be translated into policy? Coherence is not always easy to get; as firms become more global – in both their own operations and their relationships with suppliers – it is not easy to determine the firms' interest in every situation. The EU–US dispute over Foreign Sales Corporations saw exactly this type of incoherence. As the US and European governments struggled to come to a deal concerning US tax treatment of export sales, firms were extensively consulted about the form of new policy. Yet firms were not always able to offer much help. EU firms with extensive investment in the USA did not mind the legislation as they could benefit. US firms without major export sales resented the attention paid to big multinationals like Boeing and were not prepared to spend time developing proposals (Hocking and McGuire 2002).

National to international markets: from Bretton Woods to the Uruguay Round

When international trade was truly about trade between countries, the firm–state relationship revolved around protection of the home market where the key policy issue was the tariff rate. Essentially, this was the model of late nineteenth- and early twentieth-century trade politics when trade, as opposed to investment, was the important feature of cross-border commerce. Firms were largely confined to their home markets, and, as a result, trade politics was about tariff protection. However, tariffs were to lose their centrality to trade politics; protectionism of the late 1920s was widely regarded as having caused the Great Depression and, indirectly, the Second World War as economic collapse spurred the rise of fascist parties in Europe and elsewhere. After 1945 politicians, with the ruinous consequences of the 1920s fresh in their minds, pressed for a liberalisation of international trade. The vehicle for this liberalisation, the General Agreement on Tariffs and Trade (GATT), enjoyed an astonishing track record of reducing tariffs. In a series of multilateral negotiations – rounds – held in the 1960s and 1970s, the average tariff in industrialised countries was cut dramatically. By the time the Tokyo Round negotiations concluded, tariffs had ceased to be much of a policy concern.

As firms became more engaged in the international system their trade policy preferences likewise shifted. In general, it was observed that firms came to advocate an open international trading system. A tariff-free system clearly benefits large exporters – it makes their products cheaper in export markets. It is important to underline that firms do not merely advocate the liberalising of foreign markets; export dependence pushes firms to advocate free trade as the policy for their home base as well. Why? These firms have to consider that foreign markets might only be freed up, or remain liberalised, if the same liberalisation applies to all countries, including the home base. Firms would have to worry that if their home market does not opt for liberalisation, foreign markets may be closed off in retaliation. Milner's work provides the best illustration of the shift in corporate trade preferences that flow from firm dependence on exports. She shows how in both the USA and France, industrial sectors typically associated with protectionism altered their behaviour over time. The process was not quick but, as a sector came to export more, it saw advantage in advocating free trade (Milner 1988).

Mechanisms of firm–government consultation over trade policy were also evolving during this period – most importantly in the USA. There was some disappointment over the results of the Kennedy Round of GATT talks and business came to blame inadequate consultative processes for this outcome. During the late 1960s and early 1970s, the USA saw its competitive position eroded in a variety of industries, and the perennial surplus on merchandise trade swung into deficit. As more and more US firms found themselves in ever more fierce competition with foreign firms, they complained that trade negotiators had let them down by opening the US market without addressing the unfair trade practices of foreign governments. Congress responded by refusing to approve key elements of the Kennedy Round agreements; it also succeeded in getting direct private sector involvement in the trade policy process via the creation of Industry and Sector Advisory Committees (ISACs). USTR was obliged to consult regularly with company officials as part of any trade negotiation. At one level, this involvement provided negotiators with valuable expertise about technical issues, but close private sector participation in the process fed criticisms that US policy was beholden to narrow, sectoral interests.

Towards post-modern trade

By the end of the Uruguay Round tariffs – at least in industrial goods – had ceased to be much of a concern for firms. However, other government instruments that affect exports remain in place in the form of a myriad of non-tariff barriers (NTBs). These include policies such as government procurement regulations that favour domestic firms over foreign ones, or national standards that disadvantage importers. These matters were placed on the international agenda by the USA, which by the 1970s was seeing its dominance of the international economy eroded by Japan and the European Community. Moreover, the economic strains induced by the 1973 oil crisis provided many countries with an excuse to erect a variety of trade barriers, a process known as the 'new protectionism'.

The type of firm involved in trade policy also began to change by the 1980s, with important implications for trade politics. As Hart observes, liberalisation from 1947 to 1973 was successful because export-oriented manufacturing firms got what they wanted – lower tariff barriers – without trade policy becoming entangled in domestic economies (2002: 432). States were free to organise their economies as they wished, so the international trading system did not impinge on domestic arrangements such as regulatory regimes or welfare states. But this changed in the 1980s, largely at the behest of multinationals. The growth of service industries, such as banking and telecommunications, as well as the emergence of sectors where intellectual property, rather than goods, was the key competitive component, changed the trade policy landscape. The demands that these firms made, such as better protection for intellectual property or access to foreign markets for services, call for a different policy response as they raise questions about a state's domestic system of economic governance.

Dymond and Hart (2000) refer to a 'post-modern' trade policy that has been ushered in under the WTO. Trade liberalisation for forty years under the GATT was 'negative' in the sense that governments essentially denied themselves the ability to protect national firms from international competition via raising tariffs, as well as the ability to discriminate between domestic and foreign firms operating in the home market. Tariffs were 'bound': once lowered they could not be raised again. The principle of national treatment meant that foreign firms, once established in an economy, had to be treated as well as any domestic firm. Negative trade policy is relatively painless for states; it requires merely that they stop doing something. The WTO agreements signed in Marrakech, however, were different. In a swathe of areas, trade policy was transformed into positive rule making, or post-modern trade policy (Dymond and Hart 2000: 22). Dymond and Hart note that the Marrakech Agreement's preamble affirms that the WTO *raison d'être* is market liberalisation, to be accomplished via the adoption by members of market-oriented policies. This changes the nature of international trade governance; whereas GATT merely required that states stop doing something, the WTO requires that nations actively adopt new policies to facilitate trade liberalisation.

With the domestic arrangements of states now fair game for trade disputes, how a firm makes its product is as much an interest of rival firms as the price it charges. This woolly – yet widespread – perception that rival firms benefit from government support shapes firms' policy preferences in favour of a complex mix of deregulation, state intervention and outright protectionism. The US imposition of steel safeguards in 2001 illustrates this complex policy blend. In response to demands from the well-organised and politically astute domestic steel industry, the Bush Administration imposed protectionist tariffs and quotas on a swathe of steel products from around the world. Industry representatives argued that protection was warranted because foreign firms refused to play by the rules; they dumped steel onto US markets and in some cases could afford to do so because of government subsidies. However, accompanying the safeguard was a prominent debate about government support for restructuring in the US industry. Further, the Bush Administration pledged to negotiate an international agreement on steel production, designed to limit global production and so stabilise prices (Lawton and McGuire 2003a).

Aside from simple use of traditional trade protection instruments, governments around the globe remain interested in using trade in combination with industrial or technology policies. The policy package is designed to enhance the competitive position of domestic firms by providing them with intangible assets needed for international competition and relatively open markets to exploit this asset. Thus, the traditional division between trade policies and industrial and technology policies is eroding quickly. The same can be said about a number of other policy areas, particularly taxation, competition and health and safety regulations. Ostry suggested that we might come to a situation of almost absurd dimensions where virtually all areas of national economic policy come to have a trade dimension (Ostry 1997: 119). We are not there yet (and may never get there) but there is a growing realisation that domestic economies are more deeply affected by trade issues than ever. The expanding and increasingly complex trade agenda can be grasped by examining: first, the rise of regulation as a trade issue; and second, the linkage between trade and technology policies.

The politicisation of regulatory regimes

A key aspect of firm–state trade relations is the extent to which trade negotiations are focusing on the conflicts between differing methods or conceptions of regulation. Again, this is a function of the interpenetration of domestic and international political economies. As firms move abroad, they are confronted with new types of regulation, as well as different conceptions about the role of regulation. Compliance with various types of regulations represents a transaction cost or an opportunity to arbitrage; firms have an incentive to minimise these costs whenever possible and exploit arbitrage opportunities (Hart 2002). Firms may view regulation as another type of NTB where the intent is to protect a home market from imports via arbitrary bureaucracy. Alternatively, different forms of regulation can be exploited by firms. Bringing national forms of regulation onto the international trade agenda may from a firm's perspective be quite sensible, but international regulation strikes at the very heart of state autonomy and sovereignty. As Mattoo and Subramanian note (1998: 303), securing compliance with multilateral trade rules, while preserving the ability of states to pursue domestic political objectives, is a central issue for the WTO. Broadly, globalisation has resulted in a creeping multilateralisation of regulatory issues. But multilateralisation is itself fraught with difficulties, not least of which concerns how to make different regulatory regimes compatible. A contest of sorts is developing in the Doha Round negotiations. The EU's negotiating position in the Doha Round presents one side of this contest. The EU advocates a stronger role for the WTO in a range of trade-related areas such as competition policy, labour standards and environmental protection. As Sally notes in this volume, the mechanism to achieve these aims is to turn the WTO into a Geneva-based version of the European Commission, complete with a strong preference for regulatory harmonisation and a dislike for regulatory competition.

One mechanism for reconciling firm demands for lower transaction costs and state prerogatives in policy making is to use mutual recognition agreements (MRAs). Mutual recognition is the process whereby states agree that, if a product or service satisfies regulatory authorities in one state, it satisfies them for all other parties to the MRA. This mode of international regulation is a feature of the EU's single market, but has been applied to European–American trade relations through negotiations for a series of transatlantic MRAs. MNEs were heavily involved in the initiative to lower transatlantic regulatory barriers and this reflects business's view that regulations represent costs that should, where possible, be limited. The Transatlantic Business Dialogue (TABD) was created as a vehicle for MNE interest in the talks and the deep involvement of private sector actors in the process is a signal characteristic. One TABD official justified the early and extensive MNE involvement on the grounds that business decided that, rather than wait for the inevitable regulatory squabbles, it could help solve problems before they arose by 'attempting to set the regulatory agenda' (Cowles 1997: 3–4).

Mutual recognition can go some way to reducing firms' concerns about the costs of complying with multiple regulatory regimes. For a pharmaceutical firm, for example, the ability to certify a drug only once, not two, three or ten times, has obvious appeal. But it is not clear whether the MRA approach can have wide applicability. Arguably, the MRA process works in the EU–US context because the two regulatory regimes are already highly compatible; what disagreements there are occur at the margins. But would an MRA work between two states where one, for example, has an extensive intellectual property regime while in the other it is virtually non-existent? It is worth noting that the EU has, or is negotiating, MRAs with only six states (Japan, the USA, Canada, Australia, New Zealand, Switzerland), all of which are advanced industrialised states (WTO 2000: 37). This is a challenge for trade politics: how do you go about devising a system that is suitable for a myriad of legal systems, cultures and economic policies?

Such difficulties would bedevil efforts to develop supranational regulatory regimes as well. However, that has not stopped some observers from arguing that increased supranational regulation is the best option for both firms and states in the globalised economy.

Proponents of this view argue that as firm operations become ever more global, issue-areas like competition policy essentially 'leave the reach' of national regulators. This is because an increasing number of industries are truly global; that is, the competitive position of the firm cannot be sustained in one market alone, but depends on its performance in several markets. This may be due to high fixed costs for R&D (commercial aircraft, pharmaceuticals) or production (automobiles, oil and gas), which cannot be recouped in a national (or regional) market alone (Porter 1998: 53). This dependence on numerous markets can provide firms with an incentive to argue for the creation of supranational regimes as the simplest means of reducing the costs associated with contesting a global market. However, it is not clear that firms are clamouring for increased supranationalism. Supranational regulation will be most welcomed by firms if it accords closely with their preferred, national style of regulation. Rugman (2003) has argued that firms are much less globalised than commonly thought: most have a clearly identifiable home base that takes most of their sales and provides them with the most comfortable, familiar regulatory environment. In short, a 'whose standard?' problem could confound any effort to agree a supranational framework.[2]

Firms can and do exploit host countries' needs for investment and their resources – and do so by exploiting different forms of regulation. Firms play off one state against another in a competition to offer the firm the most attractive package of inducements. These inducements can include very liberal labour regulations, public subsidies in the form of tax breaks or relaxed planning permission. Yet, even these incentives may not keep a firm rooted to the locality; another jurisdiction can tempt it away with a still more lucrative package. Thus the incipient threat of relocation keeps wages low and maintains a regulatory environment that is MNE-friendly. Moreover, some critics charge that MNEs maintain control over their technology and so do not transfer know-how to the host state's economy. These latter criticisms are increasingly seen as misplaced, even in developing states that were regarded as the most vulnerable to MNE exploitation.

The criticism that firms in developing states are at the mercy of foreign multinationals is eroding in the face of work that shows a much more complex political process. Firms in developing countries are just as able as their OECD counterparts to enter the national policy process in an effort to gain competitive advantage (Guillen 2000). Firms in developing states may welcome foreign investment and liberalised trade in circumstances where they can benefit. Goldstein (2002) shows how Brazil's successful aircraft maker – Embraer – combined protectionist policies with engagement with foreign suppliers. Kaplinsky (1993) notes how some developing country multinationals grew by exploiting the international quota systems in industries like textiles. Low labour costs are not the only or most important locational factor for many firms. In a post-Fordist world of flexible specialisation, proximity to markets may be even more important. Kaplinsky (1993) also notes that several emerging economies have developed significant domestic industries based on linkages with regional markets like the EU or NAFTA. Rugman (2003) similarly notes how regionalisation is allowing developing states an opportunity to develop via preferential access to major Triad markets.

The trade policy–industrial policy link

In many states industrial and trade policies can be about propping up declining industries such as steel or shipbuilding. Governments would pour billions of dollars into sectors in a vain attempt to save them from falling victim to international competitive pressures. In this guise, industrial policy is a backward-looking, defensive response to changing international economic conditions. Competitiveness policy, in contrast, is underpinned by a faith in new technology. As such, it attempts to develop and encourage sunrise industries such as semi-conductors, aerospace and biotechnology as well as service industries like banking.

Thus, technology has become an important element in any discussion of international commercial relations. The notion that technologically advanced (or knowledge-based) sectors are better for the national economy has become popular and politicians feel that their state must develop indigenous high-technology sectors as a motor for economic growth. High-technology manufacturing is considered less prone to competition from low-wage economies due to the enormous expense of research, development and production. They are also thought to offer spillover benefits to the domestic economy. Many political leaders would agree that a state can best improve its standard of living by developing what Porter has termed 'structurally attractive industries' (1998: 36). Thus, state policies in recent years have moved towards a complex mix of deregulatory policies as well as more interventionist ones. These 'innovation' or 'competitiveness' policies seek to accommodate a firm's need for an open, dynamic market with its need for a public infrastructure capable of supporting the firm's innovative activities.

Scope for trade conflict

In an industry where the first-mover advantages of pioneer firms may be durable, government interventions in support for local firms, such as tax incentives or research and development funding, may be vital in ensuring that domestic firms win out over foreign rivals. Trade is seen as a zero-sum contest between economies where a gain for one implies a loss for another. Governments are tempted – or are urged by firms – to develop industrial policies that will allow these firms to vanquish the international competition. Foreign states cease to become trading 'partners' and become trading 'competitors'.[3] Strategic trade theory, developed in the early 1980s to analyse competition in imperfectly competitive markets, appeared to offer politicians and business leaders an intellectually defensible case for greater government intervention on behalf of firms. Imperfectly competitive markets offer the promise of economic rents accruing to the firm (and its state) that succeeds in gaining a first-mover advantage in a sector. To the extent that innovation policies are designed to bolster the competitiveness of domestic firms at the expense of foreign rivals, they can produce trade conflict. Japan's post-war success has been ascribed to the sophisticated use of industrial policy first to establish Japanese firms in various sectors and then move them into commanding positions in international market shares for medium- and high-technology goods. Much of the trade friction between the USA and Japan during the 1980s grew out of US perceptions that Japan had targeted sections of US industry, notably semiconductors, automobiles and supercomputers.

Generally however, the prognostications of widespread trade conflict in high-technology sectors have proved wide of the mark. Trade wars, at least among developed states, tend to occur in primary industries, agriculture and some medium-technology industries. Busch (1999) examines several of the most important commercial rivalries in high technology – civil aircraft, high-definition television, robotics and semiconductors – seeking to explain this variability in trade rivalry and disputes: trade wars do not occur as often as one might predict and, when they arise, they do so in unexpected sectors. He does so by explicitly linking the likelihood of states risking trade war with the ability of their domestic economies to capture the benefits of subsidy programmes. States will only adopt industrial policies if policy makers actually believe that their firms would be able to capitalise on the spillovers generated. Busch also develops a second variable. Governments are more willing to implement strategic trade policies if the benefits flow disproportionately to domestic firms. These kinds of trade and industrial policies are designed to benefit domestic firms, but if the externalities cannot be contained within the domestic economy – that is, they cannot be fully internalised – then the state has little reason to support these sectors. Indeed, if externalities flow easily across borders then policy makers have an incentive to free-ride on the strategic trade and industrial policies of others.

Scope for trade cooperation

Although they can provoke trade conflict, knowledge-based sectors simultaneously provide a basis for firm cooperation, rather than rivalry. Technology complicates life for the firm as the increasing complexity of production overwhelms the firm's organisational capacity. In this circumstance, the firm cannot remain a master of all aspects of its product; increasing specialisation requires a greater reliance on expert subcontractors and suppliers. Thus modern technology exhibits a tendency to generate interdependencies among firms and for the firm itself to become less a hierarchy than a network of interacting units. The civil aircraft industry provides a good example of this phenomenon (see also Box 19.1): firms like Boeing and Embraer are the hub of a complex and interdependent web of supplier firms. A similar development is seen in the computer industry where products are the result of cooperation among a network of firms even if the product is branded as one company's work. In their detailed study of the flat-panel display industry, Murtha *et al.* (2001) illustrate how the most successful firms were ones most willing to enter into cooperative agreements, to share technologies and demonstrate a high capacity for organisational learning. The few successful US firms in the industry were not the ones lobbying Washington for trade action against Japanese competitors; instead they were concluding agreements with Japanese partners, sending technical staff to Japan for training and providing expertise and finance for the development of new products.

Box 19.1 How trade conflicts arise from industrial policies

Brazil and Canada were embroiled in what became one of the longest running and most bitter trade disputes in recent years. Both countries deliberately targeted aerospace as a key economic sector and encouraged two firms, Bombardier (Canada) and Embraer (Brazil). The firms competed in the fiercely competitive regional aircraft market and both accused the other of using WTO-illegal government subsidies. In a series of WTO decisions, both Canada and Brazil were found guilty of illegally supporting the firms – and told to stop. Yet, neither country abandoned the field and charges of unfair support continue to be exchanged. Embraer was Brazil's most successful multinational and Bombardier is similarly a 'Canadian' success story in a country whose economy is dominated by US multinationals. Both countries feared that appearing to give in on the dispute would damage both their aerospace firms and the wider economy.

(Abdelal *et al.* 2003; Goldstein and McGuire 2004)

This increased technological sophistication and the pressures on the firm that it implies have led to the development of corporate relationships characterised by interdependence among firms: international strategic alliances (ISAs). These alliances represent an important development in the international political economy and are concentrated in high-technology industries like biotechnology, aerospace, advanced materials and electronics as well as in service sectors like law and airlines. Alliances are cooperative arrangements between two or more firms. Each firm brings a specific asset – technology, production skills and market access – into the arrangement. What distinguishes them from other types of firm cooperation is their global scope. Partners are selected on the basis of their contribution to the global strategy of the firm.

If firms wish to participate in technologically based ISAs, then they have to have something to offer, some competitive asset which makes them valuable to prospective partners. This, in turn, places pressure on the firm to invest more in research and development, either by drawing on its own resources or by a combination of these and public sector funding. Firms argue that, in the absence of an effective national research base, their opportunities in the international trading system will be compromised. This implies state support for R&D through a variety of sources such as universities, government research laboratories or a variety of subsidy programmes designed to encourage the development of firm-specific technological advantages that can be transformed into greater market share.

The political problem that arises from innovation policies is that economic and technological pressures produce a conflicting set of incentives for policy makers – and firms. On the one hand, seizing the technological high ground via a nationally based innovation policy can be very attractive as it would provide those home firms with significant competitive advantages. The counter argument is that international business relies more and more on networks of firms and is underpinned by an essential interdependency. This situation requires an open market for technological cooperation among firms. Trade policy outcomes should preserve the ability of firms to tap foreign markets. Discriminatory innovation policies threaten this access and should be avoided.

Conclusion

Trade politics is no longer about goods that arrive at a country's dock and are sold to its consumers. The growth of international business has brought about a new type of trade politics where firms are concerned with the domestic arrangements of states and this produces a variety of conflicting pressures on policy makers. This arose partly as service industries outgrew their national boundaries and became global players, but also reflects the broader trend towards complex networks of firms as a key organisational form. The role of technology is also important. On the one hand, incentives for economic openness flow from the advantages to be gained from welcoming foreign direct investment and in seeing domestic firms tap foreign markets in search of new technologies to enhance their competitiveness. However, the possibilities of seeing domestic firms capture first-mover advantages and dominating key industries (whatever they might be) can prove irresistible for politicians and business leaders. Thus, it is simplistic to view contemporary firm–government relations as a simple effort to deregulate the international economy. Rather a complex process of deregulation, regulation and selective government intervention is evident.

Firms are influential in this process – and will remain so as long as governments require their technical expertise and value the economic benefits capitalism brings. Yet, at the level

of specific policy outcomes, what is striking is the complexity of process and the varia
of outcomes. Firms do not always agree with each other on policy and do not relate
government in either a uniformly hostile or collusive fashion. Firms understand that trad
rules, like domestic regulation, can offer competitive advantage or present an obstacle to
success. Therein lies their abiding interest in trade policy making.

Notes

1   The author is grateful to George Frynas, Brian Hocking, Georgine Kryda, Thomas Lawton, Johan Lindeque, Amrita Narlikar and Chris Nicoll, all of whom offered comments on earlier versions of this chapter.
2   This may explain the attraction of regional trade agreements for firms. It is easier to gain agreement among states that already have high degrees of interaction – and there are fewer players to accommodate.
3   Academics bitterly debate the efficacy of competitiveness policies. The key issue here is that politicians and business groups often believe the policies to be effective.

Bibliography

Abdelal, R., Alfaro, L. and Laschinger, B. (2003) 'Bombardier: Canada versus Brazil at the WTO', Harvard Business School case study, 9 703 022.

Amoore, L. (2000) 'International political economy and the "contested firm" ', *New Political Economy* 5: 183–204.

Braithwaite, J. and Drahos, P. (2000) *Global Business Regulation*, Cambridge: Cambridge University Press.

Busch, M.L. (1999) *Trade Warriors: states, firms, and strategic-trade policy in high-technology competition*, Cambridge: Cambridge University Press.

Cowles, M.G. (1997) ' "A Conference Report", The limits of liberalisation: regulatory cooperation and the new Transatlantic Agenda', American Institute for Contemporary German Studies, Baltimore: The Johns Hopkins University Press.

Dunning, J. (1993) *The Globalization of Business*, London: Routledge.

Dymond, W. and Hart, M. (2000) 'Post-modern trade policy: reflections on the challenges to multilateral trade negotiations after Seattle', *Journal of World Trade* 34: 21–38.

Gill, S. (2003) *Power and Resistance in the New World Order*, Basingstoke: Palgrave.

Goldstein, A. (2002) 'The political economy of high-tech industries in developing countries: aerospace in Brazil, Indonesia and South Africa', *Cambridge Journal of Economics* 26: 521–538.

Goldstein, A. and McGuire, S. (2004) 'The political economy of strategic trade policy and the Brazil–Canada export subsidies saga', *The World Economy* (forthcoming).

Guillen, M. (2000) 'Business groups in emerging economies: a resource-based view', *Academy of Management Journal* 43: 362–380.

Hall, R.B. and Biersteker, T. (eds) (2002) *The Emergence of Private Authority in Global Governance*, Cambridge: Cambridge University Press.

Hart, M. (2002) *A Trading Nation: Canadian trade policy from colonialization to globalization*, Vancouver: UBC Press.

Hertz, N. (2002) *The Silent Takeover: global capitalism and the death of democracy*, London: Arrow.

Hocking, B. and McGuire, S. (2002) 'Government–business strategies in EU–US economic relations: the lessons of the Foreign Sales Corporation issue', *Journal of Common Market Studies* 40: 449–470.

Kaplinsky, R. (1993) 'TNCs in the Third World: stability or discontinuity?', in L. Eden and E. Potter (eds), *Multinationals in the Global Political Economy*, New York: St Martin's Press, 108–121.

Klein, N. (2000) *No Logo*, London: Flamingo Books.

Lawton, T. and McGuire, S. (2003a) 'Governing the electronic market space: appraising the apparent global consensus for e-commerce self-regulation', *Management International Review* 42: 51–71.

(2003b) 'Constraining choice: the World Trade Organisation and US
··· presented at the Academy of International Business annual meeting,

'2002) 'European Union anti-dumping cases against China', *Journal*

··· A. (1998) 'Regulatory autonomy and multilateral disciplines: the
··· resolution', *Journal of International Economic Law* 1: 303–322.
··· *Resisting Protectionism: global industries and the politics of international trade*, Princeton, NJ:
··· ·on University Press.

··· urtha, T., Lenway, S. and Hart, J. (2001) *Managing New Industry Creation*, Stanford, CA: Stanford
University Press.

Ostry, S. (1997) *The Post-Cold War Trading System: who's on first?*, Chicago: University of Chicago Press.

Porter, M. (1998) *The Competitive Advantage of Nations*, Basingstoke: Macmillan.

Rugman, A. (2003) 'The demise of the WTO and the rise of regional trade agreements', Paper
presented at the Academy of International Business annual meeting, Monterey, California.

Rugman, A. and Brain, C. (2003) 'Multinational enterprises are regional, not global', *Multinational
Business Review* 11: 3–12.

Rugman, A. and Verbeke, A. (1998) 'Multinational enterprises and public policy', *Journal of International Business Studies* 29: 115–136.

Sell, S. (2002) 'Intellectual property rights', in D. Held and A. McGrew (eds), *Governing Globalization*,
Cambridge: Polity Press.

Sell, S. (2003) *Private Power, Public Law*, Cambridge: Cambridge University Press.

Spar, D. (2001) *Pirates, Prophets and Pioneers: business and politics along the technological frontier*, London:
Random House.

Vogel, D. (1997) *Barriers or Benefits: regulation in Transatlantic trade*, Washington, DC: Brookings Institution.

WTO (2000) *Trade Policy Review of the European Union 2000*, Geneva: WTO.

Key readings

Braithwaite, J. and Drahos, P. (2000) *Global Business Regulation*, Cambridge: Cambridge University
Press.

Busch, M.L. (1999) *Trade Warriors. States, Firms, and Strategic-Trade Policy in High-Technology Competition*,
Cambridge: Cambridge University Press.

Dymond, W. and Hart, M. (2000) 'Post-modern trade policy: reflections on the challenges to multilateral trade negotiations after Seattle', *Journal of World Trade* 34: 21–38.

Gill, S. (2003) *Power and Resistance in the New World Order*, Basingstoke: Palgrave.

Guillen, M. (2000) 'Business groups in emerging economies: a resource-based view', *Academy of
Management Journal* 43: 362–380.

Hall, R.B. and Biersteker, T. (eds) (2002) *The Emergence of Private Authority in Global Governance*,
Cambridge: Cambridge University Press.

Useful websites

www.iie.com (Institute for International Economics).
www.iccwbo.org (International Chamber of Commerce).

20 The European Union as a trade policy actor

Michael Smith

Summary

This chapter deals with the emergence of the European Union as a major actor in global trade politics. It focuses on three key areas: first, the EU policy framework and the policy environment; second, the EU's powers and processes of trade policy making; third, the EU's relationship to the changing trade policy agenda and the broader multilateral order. It concludes with an evaluation of key trends and future prospects for the EU as a trade policy actor.

Introduction

The European Union (EU) is the world's largest single trading entity, accounting for over 20 per cent of total world trade. Although historically its strengths have been based on exchange of manufactures and industrial goods, increasingly the EU's international economic presence reflects its leading role in the international service economy, which by some estimates accounts for 60 per cent of its international activity. In 2001 the EU achieved merchandise exports of US$875 billion and imports of just over US$900 billion (WTO 2001, Table I.6). This put its share of total world merchandise trade just behind that of the USA; but the EU is also the world's leading exporter of services, as shown by Figure 20.1, and a predominant source of and target for foreign direct investment (FDI), as indicated in Figure 20.2.

This general picture, though, conceals significant variation among different trading relationships. Whilst the EU's relationship with the USA – its predominant external trading link – is approximately in balance year on year, it runs consistent deficits with Japan and (especially) with China. The EU's strength in industrial products and services contrasts with its weakness in commodities and semi-manufactured products. And although there are areas of considerable strength in high-technology exports, there are also crucial weaknesses, for example in some key areas of information technology equipment. Perhaps most importantly, a view of the EU based on trade between the EU and the rest of the world misses out what has historically been the most dynamic element of its trading activity: trade between its member states themselves, or so-called 'intra-trade'; in many areas of trade the member states find each other at least as interesting as the outside world. This tension between the development of internal commerce and the demands of international trade is, of course, experienced by many countries in the global economy.

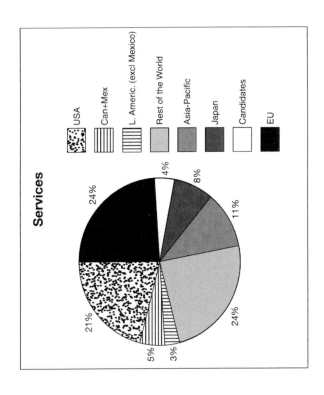

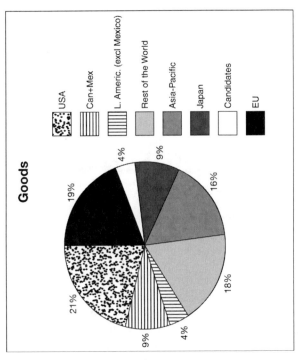

Figure 20.1: Trade in goods and services, 2000

Source: http://europa.eu.int/comm/trade/issues/bilateral/data.htm.

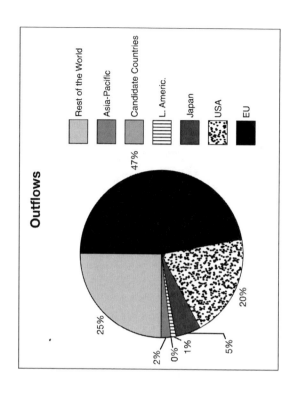

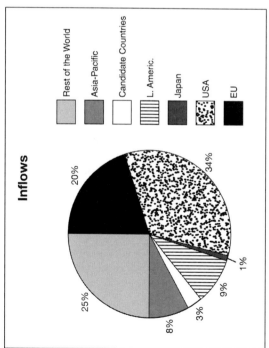

Figure 20.2: Foreign direct investment flows, 2000

Source: http://europa.eu.int/comm/trade/issues/bilateral/data.htm.

But the EU is not a 'country' in the normal sense of the word. It is an entity which in many respects mimics the actions and performance of states and national governments, but which in some crucial aspects is different. In the global arena, this raises questions about the capacity for action, influence and leadership of the EU; in the EU itself, it raises questions about the process of trade policy making and about the tensions between EU and other levels of economic action.[1]

This chapter centres on these questions about trade policy making and international role. It does so by focusing on three key areas: first, the EU policy framework and the policy environment in the EU, highlighting the characteristics of the EU as a potential actor in trade politics; second, the EU's powers and processes of policy making; third, the EU's relationship to the changing trade policy agenda and the broader multilateral order. It concludes with an evaluation of key trends and future prospects for the EU as a trade policy actor.

The policy environment

Compared with other actors under examination in this part of the book, the EU is distinctive; indeed, it is often argued that it is *sui generis* in the world political economy. This argument is based on a number of features, perhaps the most important and distinctive of which is, as noted above, that the EU is not a state with a national government. The EU represents the fruits of a process which began in the 1950s with the establishment of the European Coal and Steel Community (ECSC), the European Economic Community (the EEC) and the European Atomic Energy Community (Euratom); this has reached new levels of activity and influence since the late 1990s, with a majority of EU member states proceeding to establish Economic and Monetary Union, centring on a common currency, the euro, and the prospect of a major enlargement taking in an initial ten new member states from Central and Eastern Europe and the Mediterranean during 2004.[2]

Even this brief sketch indicates the exceptional nature of the institutional framework established in the EU, and its distinct characteristics as a trade policy actor (Dent 1997; Piening 1997). A conventional way of portraying the EU is as an organisation centred on three 'pillars' of activity, each with its distinctive decision-making processes: the first 'pillar' is that of the original European (Economic) Community, the second that of Common Foreign and Security Policy, and the third that of Justice and Home Affairs. For our purposes, the key areas of the framework are those in the 'first pillar' of the EC. From the outset, European integration had an external dimension: indeed, it could not help but do so, since the establishment of decision-making bodies in key economic areas entangled the Communities immediately in the development of the world political economy. In many ways, the earliest of the Communities' common policies was the Common Commercial Policy, based on Article 113 of the EEC Treaty (now Article 133 of the consolidated treaties). Once this was in place, it was inevitable that there would be a call for trade negotiations and trade agreements – and also that there would be trade disputes as the Community's policies developed. As a result, the EEC was a trade policy actor from the moment of its establishment.

The responsibility for handling trade relations between the Community and the outside world was given to the European Commission, which still retains this leading role. This executive agency thus has some of the institutional attributes of a 'government' for trade policy purposes, but as we shall see later these attributes are not unchallenged. In fact, the EC in trade policy terms is a curious hybrid: the Commission has the responsibility for conducting negotiations and administering trade policy instruments, but the member states retain important areas of influence and representation. Thus, in the WTO, the Commission now formally represents the Community, but each of the fifteen member states is also a member. Such hybrid forms also exist in other trade-related bodies such as the Organization for Economic Cooperation and Development (OECD).

Although the EU, through the EC, is thus heavily involved in the trade policy arena, the influence of its institutions does not stop there. The EC has developed a complex and sophisticated economic policy system in a number of areas central to the world political economy – for example, in agriculture, industrial and technology policies and in the area of economic development assistance. Not only this, but through the programme to complete the Single European Market (SEM) during the early 1990s, it developed a major capacity in regulatory policy and standards setting. The advent of EMU has created a further dimension to EC institutional capacities in the area of monetary and macroeconomic policy, although it remains to be seen how far this will extend into fiscal policy, for example. This pattern of dense and firmly based institutional growth surrounds EU trade policies with important institutional assets, whose management and deployment is bound to influence the broader trade policy arena (Tsoukalis 1997).

From what has been said already, it can be seen that the institutional framework is not the only feature bearing on the EU's trade politics. Equally important in many ways, and linked to the working of the institutions, are the relations between the member states themselves, which can encompass deep differences in trade 'culture', between protectionism and free trade, for example. Also, as the Community grew, it was clear that its 'centre of gravity' shifted, essentially towards the south and the Mediterranean, whilst the 'triangle' of France, West Germany and the UK remained the core. The addition of Austria, Finland and Sweden in 1995 shifted the balance again, to the north, whilst further enlargement in the Mediterranean and particularly Eastern Europe during the early 2000s will represent an even more significant movement.

A key feature of the EU as an actor in trade politics is thus the relationship between its member states on two levels: first, the links between the core of major states; and second, the balance between this core and the shifting focus of the EU as a whole. When this is added to the balance between the EU's institutions – especially the Commission – and the member states in general, we can begin to see some of the layers of trade policy formation. A further layer is added by the fact that the EU, as well as being the largest single market in the world, is heavily penetrated by external influences. The process of globalisation has found some of its most potent expressions in the EU, through a continuing intensification of mergers and acquisitions and through the influence of increasing investment by US and other multinational firms. In some areas, this penetration has extended to such a level that it is difficult to identify exactly what is a 'European' and what is a 'foreign' company, with consequences for trade politics which will be examined later in this chapter (Strange 1998). The Single Market Programme, though a major step forward in market integration, thus only accentuated a trend which had been evident from the foundation of the EEC in the 1950s, towards the intensification of foreign investment and the formation of corporate links between the Community/Union and the global political economy.

One consequence of this penetration of the EU and the single market has been growing salience for the politics of regulation and market access, as opposed to traditional trade politics. Given the multilayered linkages between multilateral institutions, the EU's institutions, national governments within and outside the EU and a host of private corporate actors, it has become apparent that the 'inside' and 'outside' of the EU are intimately connected if not indistinguishable (Hocking and Smith 1997). The single market can thus be used as a weapon or a source of influence at the same time as it forms a powerful attraction for non-EU actors in the world political economy. There is a tension here between two images of the EU: on the one hand, the EU and its market as a 'magnet', attracting exchange and investment; on the other hand, the EU as a (potential) 'fortress', dedicated to preserving the advantages of those inside the walls and committed to the framework.

The tension between 'magnet' and 'fortress' in the EU's trade politics is given greater weight by the fact that the EU is expanding. There has never been a time since its establishment when the EC/EU has not been negotiating with applicants for membership, admitting new members or coping with the consequences of their admission. As time has gone on the EU has 'internalised' a growing part of the world economy, not only through the growth of trade between its existing members but also through the incorporation of new members. Each such expansion has consequences not only for the EU itself but also for the pattern of trade in the global arena, for accompanying issues of investment or of regulation, and for the effectiveness of institutions at the regional or at the global level.

Finally, we must note another feature of the EU as a trade policy actor, which arises directly out of its roots as a 'trading state' and its predominant concern with the stability and growth of the world political economy. To put it simply, the EC and the EU have a basic tendency to seek stability and predictability in the world arena, and have bent considerable efforts towards the encouragement of these qualities. As a result, there has emerged a complex system of 'environmental management' in which the Community/Union has developed a network of agreements with both its near neighbours and those further afield. This has been described as a 'pyramid of privilege', constructed around partnership and cooperation agreements, preferential trade agreements and association agreements (the last often with potential future members). A question that inevitably arises is whether this web of agreements can be effectively managed and adapted to changing circumstances.

What are we to make of this complexity, and of the general picture described in this section? It is clear that the EU is more than simply an expression of the regionalisation of processes of production or exchange, and that it has considerable impact as a trade policy actor in its own right. The EU has a hard 'shell' of institutions and practices, which give it a distinctive presence and impact. Some have gone so far as to describe the EU as a 'trade superpower', or as one of the key components in a world of competing blocs (Turner 1998). But these images are at odds with the complex and multilayered processes we have described here, which raise important problems of access, management and institutional capacity. In the next section, we explore some of the issues in trade policy making to which these features give rise.

Powers, participants and pressures: processes of policy making

The first issue to address in assessing the EU's trade-policy-making processes, and one which has been at the centre of EU trade politics since the beginning, is that of competence and legitimacy (Meunier 2003). As already noted, the EU – and particularly its 'first pillar', the EC – has a strong and well-rooted institutional existence. For our purposes, the key issue is that of what might be described as the 'division of powers' in trade policy, which arises from the workings primarily of Article 133. This article has often been said to give the EC exclusive competence in the conduct of trade negotiations and the making of trade agreements (Macleod *et al.* 1996; Smith 1997). Two qualifications became clear during the later 1990s, however. First, the 'Community method' of decision making means that although the EC may be given competence (and the Commission given the responsibility of negotiating or otherwise applying that competence), there is in fact a division of powers. For trade negotiations such as those carried out in the Uruguay Round or the Doha Development Round, the Council of Ministers, representing the member states, acts on a proposal from the Commission to produce 'negotiating directives'; these guide the Commission in the negotiations, but can be revised especially during extended negotiations. In other areas, such as the use of anti-dumping legislation, the Commission may have the power to impose provisional measures, but this must then be validated by the Council. In addition, when it comes to certain trade agreements, the European Parliament (EP) has the power of assent over the final outcome. The result is a constant if muted tension between the institutions, particularly when the Commission seeks to expand its freedom of action in trade matters. This in turn is given new dimensions by the changing nature of world trade, which means that the issue of competence can be raised almost continuously, for example by the growth of trade in services. Not least, this means that unexpected parts of the Commission itself, such as the Competition Directorate-General, or DG Agriculture, can often become key parts of the trade-policy-making community in the EU.

The Uruguay Round, by dealing explicitly with such issues as services and intellectual property, gave new focus to the problem. In EU terms, the agreements themselves created a political problem: although the Commission acting for the Community had negotiated the agreements, was it competent to operate them? The net result of the argument was that on the 'new' issues, the Commission had in each case to act jointly with the member states (Macleod *et al.* 1996). Although the Commission asked again for an extension of competence in the negotiations for the Amsterdam Treaty of 1997, the final text contained only a provision that issues of competence in the 'new' areas should be agreed between the Council and the Commission on an ad hoc basis (requiring a unanimous vote in the Council). The issue was not essentially resolved until the Nice Treaty of 2000, which established a new baseline for the exercise of trade-policy-making powers by the Commission, by including most areas of services but excluding a number of sensitive sectors and still reserving certain rights of national action to member states (Galloway 2001; Meunier and Nicolaidis 2000; Young 2002). Even this, however, did not do away with the 'division of powers' noted above.

Such a tension over matters of competence expresses in part a second key issue: the differing philosophies and preferences of EU member states when it comes to matters of international trade. We noted earlier the tension in the EU between 'free-traders' and 'protectionists', which often (but not always) corresponds to a North–South tension. In the original Community of six members, the French and the Italians were in general more protectionist and interventionist than the Germans and the Dutch, for example; this in turn reflected national positions on key internal policies such as the Common Agricultural Policy, which fed through into external commercial policy. As the Community and then the Union have grown, the balance has shifted several times, leading to fluctuations in trade policies. The enlargement of the EU in 2004 will provide yet further diversification of influences, especially those emanating from the countries of the former Soviet Bloc.

The effects of this fluctuating balance are to be seen both at the broad strategic level and in the operation of specific trade policies within the EU. Strategically, the EU's entry into broad global trade arrangements is almost invariably accompanied by hard bargaining within the EU, in which the more protectionist elements attempt to preserve its 'trade defences'; thus in the final stages of the Uruguay Round negotiations, the French and others were able to extract commitments to strengthen surveillance and unfair trade measures as part of the price for their agreement (Paeman and Bensch 1995), whilst in the Doha Development Round there has already been evidence of tensions over traditional issues such as agriculture. At the level of operational policy, some of the more striking examples are provided by the EU's anti-dumping measures. For example, in 1997, the Commission (responding to pressure from mainly French cotton producers) imposed provisional anti-dumping duties on imports of unbleached cotton. This move evoked the opposition both of cotton processors in the EU and of the more 'free trade'-orientated member states. As a result, the provisional duties were not confirmed by the Council of Ministers. But during late 1997 and 1998, again under pressure from the French and Eurocoton (the producer body), the Commission not only reopened the anti-dumping investigation, but also reimposed provisional duties (Allen and Smith 1998). The story continued in this way for some time, reflecting the pressures both of public and of private interests.

As these examples indicate, there are a number of important participants and influences present in the EU's trade policy community. From the outset, there have been organisations in Brussels and elsewhere designed to promote the interests of producers or consumers in relation to trade policies; for a long time, perhaps inevitably, these organisations represented predominantly producer interests, but during the 1990s and after they experienced a number of important transformations. The cast of characters on the trade policy stage now includes trade union interests, consumer lobbies, a wide range of non-governmental organisations with interests in such areas as human rights, and a range of local and regional agencies from within member states. As a result, the management of trade policies has become less technocratic and more subject to pressures for accountability and short-term responsiveness (Smith and Woolcock 1999; Smith 2001). Arguably, this has increased the

Table 20.1   Instruments and audiences in EU trade policy making

'Internal' instruments and audiences	*'External' instruments and audiences*
Instruments	**Instruments**
Tariffs (CET)	WTO dispute settlement
Quotas (at EU level)	Association Agreements
Voluntary Export Restraints	Partnership and Cooperation Agreements
Anti-Dumping and Anti-Subsidy Measures	Inter-Regional Arrangements
Generalised System of Preferences	Free Trade Areas (EEA, bilateral)
Audiences	**Audiences**
European Commission (various DGs)	Key trading partners
Council of the EU	World Trade Organization
European Parliament	Other Commercial Policy institutions
Member states	Regional trading arrangements
Producers and consumers	Importers and investors

constraints on the trade policy makers, and thus the possibility of inconsistency and reactiveness on their part. It can be seen that this brings us back again to issues of legitimacy and authority in EU trade politics, and also that it links processes in the EU with those for example in the USA, where politicisation of trade policy is a long-established fact of life.

Table 20.1 summarises the range of instruments, participants and pressures described in this section. Although it makes an apparently clear-cut distinction between 'internal' and 'external' mechanisms and participants, it should be clear from the discussion so far that there are in fact very close links between these two areas; it can again be seen that analysis of the EU as a trade policy actor inevitably focuses on the interconnections between a number of levels and arenas. In the next section, the focus will be on the way in which the EU forms and pursues relationships within the global trade arena.

The EU and the global trade arena

Article 113 of the European Community Treaty, signed in 1957, committed the EEC as it was then not only to internal coordination of trade policies but also to an active role in the liberalisation of world trade. Integral to the bargains that set up the Community (and indeed to the establishment of the ECSC before it) was recognition of the external forces to which it would become subject, and the global constraints imposed by institutions and other actors. Indeed, the EEC as a customs union could only be set up explicitly under the provisions of Article XXIV of the GATT, and – less formally – with the acquiescence of the USA as the dominant economic power. The playing out of these external forces has been a constant theme in the trade politics of the EC and then the EU, and can be seen in terms of the major external relationships in which the EU is embroiled.

The predominant feature of the EU's external environment is the relationships with other industrial countries and groupings. In particular, the relationship with the USA embodies the largest flows of goods, services and capital in the global economy. At the same time, the links between the EU and its near neighbours in Europe have been consistent and intimate, to the extent that a number of the former members of the European Free Trade Area (EFTA) are now members of the EU itself, and even the remaining members of that body and the European Economic Area constitute one of the EU's largest external relationships. Links with Japan are less intense than those with the USA, but have generated a considerable number of trade disputes as well as efforts to collaborate. The links between the EU and other industrial groupings thus embody what has often been called the 'management of interdependence': those involved in the relationships need each other and profit from each other, but the very intensity of the links between them creates a vital need for active management of the inevitable disputes and tensions (Dent 1997).

Another key focus for EU trade politics is what some have termed the 'near abroad': those countries in Central and Eastern Europe, the former Soviet Union and the Mediterranean which proliferated during the 1990s as the result of the end of the Cold War (Piening 1997). During the height of the Cold War, in a way the trade politics of many of these links was repressed, with the US–Soviet confrontation and the predominance of security or ideological concerns acting as a kind of insulation. The post-Cold-War era saw an eruption of trade politics, as those in the 'near abroad' sought new patterns of exchange and the EU sought to stabilise or manage the consequences of this disruption. Here, we can see the true power of the EU's 'magnet' role; many of the countries concerned not only wanted to develop new trade and investment links with the EU and its members, they also wanted to become members. As a result, the EU spent much of the 1990s and early 2000s searching for ways of managing these demands; at one level, by reaching new trade and cooperation arrangements, and at another level by preparing for a new and far-reaching enlargement process (Smith 2000; K. Smith 1999). The difficulty from the EU's perspective was that these two things are inextricably linked, and that what might be seen as technical economic provisions are heavy with political symbolism. In particular, the relationships with Central and Eastern European Countries (the CEEC) moved through a number of hard-fought bargaining stages: first, the attempt to construct new trade and cooperation agreements, then the 'Europe Agreements' which embodied closer cooperation and eventually preparations for membership, and finally, the pre-accession and accession stages, in which an initial ten new members would be admitted during 2004. Not only has this posed an immense negotiating challenge for all of those involved; it also implies a major redirection and rebalancing of the EU's external trade patterns and of many of its internal policies such as the CAP, with consequent effects on a number of 'great outsiders' such as the USA. In a different way, and certainly not with the prospect of membership, the EU moved during the 1990s to create a broader framework for its trading relationships with Mediterranean countries, through what had become known as the Barcelona process (after the agreements reached between the EU and its Mediterranean partners in 1995 and after).

Whereas the relationships between the EU and its industrial rivals illustrate the 'management of interdependence', it is clear that relations with the 'near abroad' embody considerable asymmetries and patterns of dependency. The trade politics of these relationships is thus distinct, although in themselves they are differentiated between 'pre-members', possible members and those who will never be members. The last are in some ways more like the countries of the African, Caribbean and Pacific grouping, who have relations with the EU largely through the Lomé Conventions of 1975–2000 and now the Cotonou Convention; here, the emphasis is on economic restructuring and technical assistance as well as on specific provisions for market access for sensitive commodities (Holland 2002; Lister 1997). Although it is in many respects odd to link developing countries in the 'South' with countries in the 'near abroad' such as Russia or the Ukraine, the point here is that when we move into these areas we are dealing more with the trade politics of dependency than with that of interdependence and interpenetration, and thus the issues for the EU are different. This is not to say that these problems are disconnected from each other, however: one of the first effects of the ending of the Cold War and the redirection of EU interest towards the East was a fear in ACP (African, Caribbean and Pacific) countries that they would lose out, and there has been a continual balancing act for the EU in reassuring both sets of partners that their interests will be safeguarded. It must also not be forgotten that a number of developing countries have important sponsors in the EU itself – not least those such as France, the UK, Spain and Portugal whose former colonies have an obvious claim for their attention.

Each of these sets of relations has to be seen not only as a discrete source of trade policy issues but also as embedded in a global system. As has been pointed out many times in this book, the processes of globalisation and regionalisation have posed challenges to all of those involved in trade politics; we have already noted that the EC and the EU are inseparable from the development of the broader world trading system. Whereas with industrial partners we are concerned with the politics of interdependence and interpenetration, and in the case of developing countries we confront the politics of dependency, in the case of the global system we are presented with what might be termed the politics of compatibility. The central question here is, to what extent are the EU's trade policies and practices compatible with the multilateral system or with the activities of other regional groupings?

This is not simply an abstract issue. The EEC originally was set up within the GATT system, but it has created a number of important frictions with multilateral trade rules as it has developed and grown (Woolcock 1993). Indeed, even before the Treaty of Rome in 1957, the ECSC had caused frictions with US steel producers who claimed that it set up an illegal cartel and thus traded unfairly. During the 1960s, the development of the CAP in particular created important tensions with the USA, whilst the successive enlargements of the EU have created a demand for compensation as more and more countries are surrounded by the customs union and the Common External Tariff. The programme to complete the single market during the late 1980s and early 1990s also raised important issues for the multilateral system, since many of the areas in which the single market had most effect (for example, regulatory policy, trade in services) were precisely those most at issue in the Uruguay Round (Woolcock and Hodges 1996). Quite apart from these broad issues, there have been many instances of complaints against specific EU trade measures (most of them from the USA), ranging from the treatment of banana imports to the apparent subsidisation of large civil aircraft. The EU has an important interest in defending itself against these complaints, and specific EU producer groups have even more intense feelings; but at the same time, the EU profits immensely from the maintenance of the multilateral system, and is inexorably committed to its strengthening (see below). The result is another series of essentially political issues.

The EU also has important interests in developing relationships with other regional groupings, and has pursued a consistent policy of promoting and maintaining such relationships (including those for example with Mediterranean countries mentioned above). Indeed, it could be argued that links with such groupings as Mercosur (the Southern Common Market) in Latin America and ASEAN (the Association of South-East Asian Nations) are important not only in terms of EU trade policy interests, but also and much more broadly in terms of competition among the leading trading entities within the global arena. During the mid-1990s, the Commission in particular developed a wide-ranging strategy of forming links with regions in which the EU's profile had historically been underdeveloped. This led for example to the establishment of the Asia–Europe Meeting (ASEM), between the EU and ten Asia–Pacific partners, which met for the first time in March 1996 and thereafter every two years. ASEM was explicitly linked by the EU not only with the promotion of inter-regional trade and investment, but also with some broader security issues and with the assertion of an EU presence in a region previously dominated by the USA and Japan (Dent 1997; Smith 1998). Although not so fully developed (beyond the inter-regional contacts noted above), the EU's links with South American and African countries were also given new attention during the early 2000s.

Issue-linkages

It has been apparent throughout the preceding discussion that a key problem for the management of EU trade policy is the handling of issue-linkages: both those that occur as a fact of international life and those that are designed into the EU's policies and institutions. In this section, the focus is on three types of issue-linkage which have profound implications for trade politics in the EU: first, the internal/external linkage; second, linkages between policy sectors; finally, the question 'who are EU?' in trade policy (Strange 1998).

In the first case, it is clear that many issues in EU trade politics cannot be neatly consigned to the 'internal' or 'external' box. A number of challenging policy issues in the 'new' trade politics embody both internal/external linkages and inter-sectoral linkages, and demand complex processes of management and regulation (Young 2002). In the area of more conventional trade politics, the EU has been confronted by the complexities of relationships between importers and exporters, producers and consumers, in areas as diverse as the trade in handbags, mountain bikes, bananas and semiconductors (Allen and Smith 1998). Likewise, the Commission has had to deal with major cross-sectoral linkages in the context of negotiations as large scale as those of the Uruguay Round or the 'Europe Agreements' and as intimate as those on teddy-bears from China or the liquor tax in Japan. In all of these areas, the EU has been engaged in dealings not only with other governments but also with international institutions and with private corporations, trade associations and pressure groups.

The upshot of these complex interactions in EU trade politics is a European version of the question posed by Robert Reich 'Who is US?', given the increasing evidence that territory and tangible assets matter less in international exchange and competition than knowledge and intangible resources (Reich 1991). For the EU, the question in a sense has always been there, given the in-built tensions between institutions, and between institutions and member states. But the 1990s and 2000s have exposed it even more sharply, as the implications of increasing interpenetration and the impact of globalisation have made themselves felt. Susan Strange has rephrased Reich's question as 'Who are EU?' in exploring the ways in which firms have responded to the pressures and opportunities of the global marketplace (Strange 1998). In this marketplace, it is increasingly difficult to identify the 'European' as opposed (say) to the 'American' or 'Japanese' interest in specific policy areas.

We are left with an image of the major issues in EU trade politics which is complex and challenging. At one level, it clearly validates the focus of this book on multilevel and multilayered trade politics processes; but then, the EEC and the EU have embodied those qualities since the 1950s. At another level, it validates the proposition that the growth of interdependence and interpenetration exacerbate the 'who is us?' issue; the EU has always experienced this challenge, in the context of a shifting internal balance as well as a changing membership, and moreover it has long experience of the intersection between the public and the private in the management of trade policy, both in its internal market and in the world arena. EU trade politics is characterised above all by an emphasis on process, rather than on results, a feature which can make it difficult for those with other presuppositions to accommodate the European style. They are also characterised by an underlying tension, sharper in the 2000s than before, between technocratic styles of trade policy making and broader questions of accountability.

Conclusion

The implications of the discussion in this chapter can be seen in terms of the roles the EU plays in a number of key areas of global trade politics. Put briefly, there are implications and subsequent questions in relation to:

- *Strategic coherence and credibility*: the ability to make and pursue coherent policies, to adapt them to changing circumstances and to convince negotiating partners of the EU's intentions. How well does the EU match up to these requirements, on the evidence presented here and in light of the tensions between technocratic and politicised styles of policy making?

- *Processes of bilateral management*: the ability to maintain effective relations with a variety of partners, to handle crises that occur within these relationships and to balance different sets of relations off against each other. Does the evidence here demonstrate that the EU can manage its bilateral relations effectively, particularly with respect to its key trading partners?
- *Inter-regional and inter-system cooperation*: the effort to create and sustain relationships with regional partners in Asia–Pacific, Latin America and elsewhere, and to provide consistent institutional resources for these relationships. The EU has placed a lot of emphasis on these efforts, but how efficient and effective have they been?
- *Multilateral rule making*: the pursuit of global governance through the WTO and related bodies, and the capacity to act authoritatively and consistently in global arenas. To what extent has the EU been able to develop a leadership role in these global multilateral activities?
- *Private management of trade policy issues*: the capacity to represent and to form relationships with private actors, and to provide the types of regulatory and other resources that are becoming increasingly the core of 'network management' in the global economy. Does the EU succeed in effectively balancing these private management issues with its broader strategic roles?

All are central to an evaluation of EU trade policy, and the role of the EU as a trade policy actor, in the late 1990s. The key questions, inevitably, remain unresolved. It is easy on the basis of the argument here to imagine an EU in the year 2010 with perhaps twenty-seven members and with a stable single currency, which could use these assets to play a predominant role in world trade and investment, including all of the above areas. After all, the advantages of scale, of regulatory capacity and of financial management would be significant if not crucial. The discussion in this chapter does not rule out such an outcome. What it does do, though, is to indicate two things: first, that exploiting the potential of major enlargement and EMU is likely to be very hard work and to absorb a good deal of the energy of the EU and its member states; second, that the concomitant increases in the internal complexity of the EU and its trade politics will not allow a simple linear relationship on the lines of 'more means better'. For trade politics in particular, the chapter has indicated a number of features and issues which simultaneously bestow enormous influence and potential on the EU and limit the extent to which that influence and potential can easily be deployed. The EU may be a 'trade superpower', but it will continue from time to time and from issue to issue to display its feet of clay.

Notes

1 For other treatments dealing with these questions, see the list of key readings at the end of this chapter.
2 As of the writing of this chapter, three of the EU's fifteen member states had abstained from EMU: Denmark, Sweden and the United Kingdom. The Danes held a referendum in 2001 which rejected euro membership, and the Swedes were due to hold a referendum in late 2003. The UK government, whilst committed to a referendum, had still not determined a date.

Bibliography

Allen, D. and Smith, M. (1998) 'External policy developments', in G. Edwards and G. Wiessala (eds), *The European Union, 1997: annual review of activities*, Oxford: Blackwell.

Bretherton, C. and Vogler, J. (1999) *The EU as a Global Actor*, London: Routledge.

de Burca, G. and Scott, J. (eds) (2001) *The EU and the WTO: legal and constitutional issues*, Oxford: Hart.

Dent, C.M. (1997) *The European Economy: the global context*, London: Routledge.

Galloway, D. (2001) *The Treaty of Nice and Beyond*, London: Sheffield Academic Press/Continuum.

Hocking, B. and Smith, M. (1997) *Beyond Foreign Economic Policy: the United States, the Single European Market and the changing World economy*, London: Cassell/Pinter.

Holland, M. (2002) *The European Union and the Third World*, London: Palgrave.

Lister, M. (1997) *The European Union and the South*, London: Routledge.

Macleod, I., Hendry, I.D. and Hyatt, S. (1996)*The External Relations of the European Communities*, Oxford: Oxford University Press.

Meunier, S. (2003) 'Political legitimacy and European Union trade policy', *Comparative European Politics* 1: 67–90.

Meunier, S. and Nicolaidis, K. (2000) 'EU trade policy: the "exclusive" versus shared competence debate', in M.G. Cowles and M. Smith (eds), *The State of the European Union: risks, reform, resistance and revival*, Oxford: Oxford University Press.

Paeman, H. and Bensch, A. (1995) *The European Union in the Uruguay Round*, Leuven: Leuven University Press.

Piening, C.(1997) *Global Europe: the European Union in World affairs*, Boulder, CO: Lynne Rienner.

Reich, R. (1991) *The Work of Nations: preparing ourselves for twenty-first century capitalism*, New York: Knopf.

Smith, A. (2000) *The Return to Europe: the reintegration of Eastern Europe into the European economy*, London: Macmillan.

Smith, K. (1999) *The Making of European Union Foreign Policy: the case of Eastern Europe*, Basingstoke: Macmillan.

Smith, M. (1994) 'The European Union, foreign economic policy and the changing World arena', *Journal of European Public Policy* 1: 283–302.

Smith, M. (1997) 'The commission and external relations', in G. Edwards and D. Spence (eds), *The European Commission*, 2nd edn, London: Cartermill.

Smith, M. (1998) 'The European Union and the Asia-Pacific', in A. McGrew and C. Brook (eds), *Asia-Pacific in the New World Order*, London: Routledge/The Open University.

Smith, M. (1999) 'Negotiating globalisation: the foreign economic policy of the European Union', in R. Stubbs and G. Underhill (eds), *Political Economy and the Changing Global Order*, 2nd edn, Oxford: Oxford University Press.

Smith, M. (2001) 'The European Union's commercial policy: between coherence and fragmentation', *Journal of European Public Policy* 8: 787–802.

Smith, M. and Woolcock, S. (1999) 'European commercial policy in the new Millennium: a leadership role for the European Union?', *European Foreign Affairs Review* 4: 439–462.

Strange, S. (1998) 'Who are EU? Ambiguities in the concept of competitiveness', *Journal of Common Market Studies* 36: 101–114.

Tsoukalis, L. (1997)*The New European Economy Revisited*, Oxford: Oxford University Press.

Turner, M. (1998) 'Unified trade policy gives EU superpower status', *European Voice* 26 February–4 March: 13.

Woolcock, S. (1993) 'The European *acquis* and multilateral trade rules: are they compatible?', *Journal of Common Market Studies* 31: 539–558.

Woolcock, S. and Hodges, M. (1996) 'EU policy in the Uruguay Round', in H. Wallace and W. Wallace (eds), *Policy-Making in the European Union*, Oxford: Oxford University Press.

WTO (2001) 'Leading exporters and importers in world merchandise trade (excluding intra-EU trade)'. Available HTTP:
  <http://www.wto.org/english/res_e/statis_e/its2002_e/section1_e/i06.xls> (accessed 31 July 2003).

Young, A. (2002) *Extending European Cooperation: the European Union and the 'new' international trade agenda*, Manchester: Manchester University Press.

Key readings

Meunier, S. (2003) 'Political legitimacy and European Union trade policy', *Comparative European Politics* 1: 67–90.

Paeman, H. and Bensch, A. (1995) *The European Union in the Uruguay Round*, Leuven: Leuven University Press.

Smith, M. (2001) 'The European Union's commercial policy: between coherence and fragmentation', *Journal of European Public Policy* 8: 787–802.

Woolcock, S. (1993) 'The European *acquis* and multilateral trade rules: are they compatible?', *Journal of Common Market Studies* 31: 539–558.

WTO (2001) 'Leading exporters and importers in world merchandise trade (excluding intra-EU trade)'. Available HTTP:
<http://www.wto.org/english/res_e/statis_e/its2002_e/section1_e/i06.xls> (accessed 31 July 2003).

Young, A. (2002) *Extending European Cooperation: the European Union and the 'new' international trade agenda*, Manchester: Manchester University Press.

21 Continuity and change in US trade policy, 1993–2003

Geoffrey Allen Pigman

Summary

US trade policy from 1993 to 2003 has shown greater continuity than change. The principal trade policy political dynamic remains Congress–Executive branch interaction. Members of Congress defend interests of particular firms and consumers, whilst the President integrates trade policy with broader foreign policy objectives. The Clinton Administration concluded the GATT Uruguay Round and promoted US exports to rapidly developing economies with large emerging middle classes. The George W. Bush Administration secured renewal of 'Fast Track' trade promotion authority and launched a new multilateral trade round.

As with most states, US trade policy is regulated by a combination of domestic legislation and international treaty commitments. Still the most important piece of domestic trade legislation is the oft-amended Franklin Roosevelt-era Reciprocal Trade Agreements Act of 1934 (RTAA). RTAA replaced the previous broadly protectionist US trade policy dating from the post-colonial era with the principle of mutual trade liberalization. Under RTAA the President was empowered to grant imports from another country access to the most favourable tariff schedule the USA had, in return for that country offering comparable import terms to US exports: the origin of most favoured nation (MFN) status. Although RTAA did not represent unilateral trade liberalization, it did open the door for US governments after the Second World War to make disproportionate trade concessions to trading partners to promote broader US global political and economic objectives (Destler 1992; Bhagwati 1988: 37–40).

The General Agreement on Tariffs and Trade (GATT), signed in 1947, enshrined the RTAA MFN principle: each GATT member was obliged to grant other members the most favourable tariff schedules it offered to any nation's imports. GATT originally only covered trade in manufactured goods but has been expanded to include non-tariff barriers to trade, intellectual property issues, agricultural trade and trade in services. Since coming into operation in 1995 the World Trade Organization (WTO) shows indications of expanding the GATT's purview further to include trade-related labour and environmental measures (Gilpin 2002).

Many US trade conflicts with the EU and Japan in particular have been over allegations that particular US domestic trade laws were not GATT-legal. This occurred frequently in the 1970s and 1980s over so-called Section 301 cases. Section 301 of the 1974 Trade Act created a mechanism for US businesses to seek relief against so-called 'unfair foreign trade practices' allowing for alleged unfair trade practices to be investigated and adjudicated within the Executive branch of the US government, and penalties to be imposed against the offending country without the offender having any neutral recourse. GATT members said this procedure violated basic GATT principles, but Washington claimed only to apply it in cases where there was no remedy procedure under GATT law (Destler 1992: 126–127). The problem eased once the stepped-up WTO trade dispute resolution procedure took effect in 1995.

US trade policy interests and structural change in the global economy

Throughout much of the twentieth century US interests in trade policy were as would be expected for a large, productive, industrialized but 'continental' economy: promotion of exports and access to cheap imports of industrial inputs and consumer goods, whilst at the same time protecting sensitive sectors against increased import penetration (Lake 1988: 33–49). For the first two-thirds of the century change was incremental, with trade as a percentage of national output remaining at a low level customary for a largely self-sufficient continental economy (Webb and Krasner 1989: 192). US exports were dominated by agricultural production, durable and consumer industrial manufactures such as aircraft and automobiles, military production, technology-intensive manufactures and increasing sales of services. Imports, traditionally dominated by agricultural products, commodities, industrial inputs and low-wage manufactures and consumer goods, have shifted towards finished industrial goods and manufactures, as inter-industry trade has grown worldwide, and higher technology manufactures, such as consumer electronics. These secular trends evolved despite cycles of economic growth, wars, interwar protection and subsequent institutionalization of international economic cooperation.

In the last third of the century, however, US trade policy interests changed because structural developments in the global economy affected US trade flows. Technological advances have accelerated, particularly in telecommunications, informatics and biotechnology. Services as a percentage of economic output have increased enormously relative to manufacturing and agriculture, spanning a range of activities from financial and legal services to consulting, entertainment, professional sports and construction services. The lowering of barriers to capital flows and cross-border ownership has facilitated the globalization and de-nationalization of large firms and mid-size enterprises, leading to a significant increase in intra-firm trade in many industrial and service sectors. Trade has become an appreciably larger percentage of US economic output, increasing the beneficiaries from trade and thereby prompting shifts in political support for pro-trade policies (Webb and Krasner 1989: 192).

As the US economy has become more dependent upon trade even whilst facing increased import competition, the core pro-trade liberalization political constituency has shifted. A left–right coalition of managers in heavy industries and traditional organized labour, the majority of whose members worked in those industries, has been replaced by a cross-party centre coalition of business leaders in high-technology and services industries, labour in exporting industries, and consumers seeking inexpensive imported consumer goods. This new economy/high-technology coalition is opposed by a nationalist right–labour left coalition of managers and workers in import-competing industries allied with Greens and other opponents of the prevailing neoliberal, transnational, capital-friendly version of globalization. Another result of the rapidly changing structure of the global economy is that the ambit of trade policy itself has been expanded progressively from agricultural and manufactured goods to include non-tariff barriers, government subsidies, intra-firm trade and trade in services. Other politically contested issues have since been rebranded 'trade' issues: cross-border sales of services, government subventions to business (e.g. tax abatements), environmental policies, labour policies, tax policies and cross-border investment policies (Drake and Nicolaidis 1992).

Key features of the contemporary US trade policy process

US trade policy gets made and implemented in a dynamic political process reflecting tension between two power poles, one grouped around the White House and the other grouped around Congress. Around the presidential pole are grouped the President's economic advisers, the Treasury and Commerce Departments. The pivotal Office of the US Trade Representative (USTR), although created by Congress, is in practice close to the White House as well. Beyond the simple desire of each pole to accumulate greater powers than the other, each has different objectives with respect to trade policy. Broadly speaking, the President wants to make trade policy in the nation's foreign policy interest and wants to be able to link trade policy objectives to broader foreign policy objectives, both political and economic. The President is responsible for integrating US foreign policy objectives, and how successful he is perceived to be in that project plays a significant role in his prospects for re-election.

Members of Congress tend to get re-elected by serving the direct interests of their constituents. Every Member of Congress and Senator must weigh the demands of firms in their district, which may be major exporters or in import-competing industries. Members of Congress are subject to increasing pressures from organizations representing a range of social interests affected by trade, such as labour, the environment and human rights. They must also take into account the often conflicting demands of individual constituents, all of whom are consumers and some of whom are employed in exporting or import-competing industries. The net effect of these 535 individual member calculations is to produce a Congress that since the Second World War has tended to be somewhat more protectionist than the White House, whilst none the less endorsing liberal trade. Congress tends to attach more strings to White-House-led trade liberalization projects to safeguard the interests of particular constituents (Destler 1992).

This divergence is reflected both in the legislation of trade policy and in the administration of existing trade law after its enactment. After trade legislation is passed by Congress and signed by the President, it is administered by several different government agencies including the Departments of Commerce, Agriculture, Treasury, State, Labor and Energy, as well as the USTR, the Export–Import Bank and the Overseas Private Investment Corporation. The most significant agency responsible for administering US trade law is the Commerce Department, particularly through its International Trade Administration (ITA). ITA performs a huge range of tasks, such as monitoring imports to make sure they are not being subsidized by their home government, which is GATT-illegal and would trigger a countervailing duty or CVD investigation. ITA enforces statutes against dumping, in order to ensure that imports are not being sold in the USA at prices below what they sell for in their home country. To calculate the economic impact of dumping and subsidies on competing US firms an independent technical agency created by Congress, the US International Trade Commission, assesses the monetary impact of dumping and subsidies. This allows ITA to impose anti-dumping and countervailing duties on imports when required. The Agriculture Department also plays a major role by overseeing all aspects of agricultural trade policy, which despite Marrakech is still subject to a very protectionist regime.

Perhaps the single most important trade policy organ is the Office of the US Trade Representative. The USTR was originally created by Congress in 1962 as a way to make trade policy more sympathetic to Congressional interests. Before this, Presidents received most of their trade policy advice from the State Department, which Congress regarded as taking a uniformly free trade stance that was geared to external US geopolitical objectives and was not sufficiently responsive to Congressional constituent demands. By requiring that the USTR be appointed by the President but must be confirmed by the Senate, Congressional leaders hoped to develop greater institutional access to the policy process prior to the arrival of proposed trade bills from the White House on Capitol Hill. What the USTR has evolved into, however, is a small, highly professional staff of skilled trade policy experts who advise the President, write trade legislation and oversee the implementation of a range of existing trade laws. They tend to take a perspective more in line with the traditional foreign-policy-oriented White House view of trade than that of more particularistic interests in Congress (Destler 1992: 18–21).

Trade treaties

The principal trade policy conflicts between the White House and Congress take place over trade treaties. Treaties are negotiated by the USTR with input from Members of Congress, from industry through Trade Policy Advisory Committees and from interest groups representing consumers, labour, environmental concerns and elements of civil society. After the President signs an international treaty, it must then be ratified by Congress. By the 1960s, as reduction of non-tariff barriers began to comprise an important part of the trade policy agenda, trade treaties became increasingly complex, lengthy documents. Like other legislation, trade treaties were subject to amendment at the committee, on the floor of the House and Senate, and in the conference committee to resolve differences between the House and Senate-passed versions. If a treaty was amended at any stage, even only slightly, it would have to go back to the other treaty signatory countries for their approval. This posed the risk of trade treaties becoming permanently enmeshed in revisions between other governments and Members of Congress.

The Nixon Administration sought, and received from Congress in the 1974 Trade Act, a provision that came to be known as 'Fast Track' under which once a trade treaty was submitted to Congress, Congress would have to vote after forty-five days with no amendments permitted. Not being inclined to give away its prerogatives freely, Congress has only ever granted Fast Track to Presidents for fixed periods of time, requiring the legislation to be renewed periodically. Periodic Fast Track renewal enables the political battle between the White House and Capitol Hill over trade policy priorities and prerogatives to be separated from debate over the merits of any particular trade treaty. The Congressional leadership also required the White House and USTR to agree to an informal 'mark-up' process for trade bills prior to their formal submission for passage. In this way problems with the treaty politically serious enough to endanger passage could be resolved, first between Congress and the White House, and then between the White House and the other parties to the treaty negotiation. Through this reordering of the political process for ratifying trade treaties, both sides got much of what they wanted, and every major trade treaty since 1974 has been passed under Fast Track.

Explaining US trade policy formulation

The major historical cleavage that has persisted in the USA, as in the UK and other states, has been the debate between unilateral and negotiated trade policy. Advocates of domestically legislated trade policies argue that domestic legislation gives the state maximum ability to act in its own interests and adjust policies as those interests change. Advocates of negotiated, or treaty-based, trade policies contend that making and receiving commitments through treaties is the best way to ensure that other states will act in ways that further the home state's interests; for example, by lowering trade barriers by a certain amount for a fixed period of time. In practice, the USA has employed both approaches simultaneously. The conflict between US treaty commitments and domestically legislated 'remedies' for US firms adversely affected by trade is the greatest source of conflict between the USA and its trading partners and often also between the White House and Capitol Hill.

Most theoretical explanations of the US trade policy process and speculation on future policy outcomes have tended to ascribe particular interests and motivations to the President and Congress. They then map their relative success in advancing their respective interests in each policy situation to policy outcomes. For example, Lake (1988: 66–74) contends that the representative element of government, in which he groups Congress and the constituent–responsive executive agencies such as the Commerce and Agriculture Departments, pursue narrow interests such as re-election and are easily 'captured' by the interests they are intended to serve. By contrast the foreign policy executive, which includes the President and executive agencies involved with making foreign policy, is responsible for defending US global interests. Hence the two elements' objectives will always diverge, with the foreign policy executive tending to favour more liberal trade and the representative element favouring more protection. The effectiveness of the bargaining process determines how well US interests in aggregate will be served by the resulting policy.

Viewing international system-based and socioeconomic explanations as insufficient to explain US trade policy, Goldstein argues that ideas, as mediated by institutional structures of the state, play a defining role in both the creation and administration of trade law. Since the Second World War, the dominant liberalization objective has been supported institutionally by the office of the President with the acquiescence of Congress. The success of sectoral interests seeking protection through the legislative process has depended on how well they have chosen institutional mechanisms appropriate for the respective historical moment. Successful supplicants have achieved three major types of protection: 'escape clause' protection for industries injured by trade liberalization (GATT Article XIX); 'fair trade' or a 'level playing field' for US goods through the anti-dumping and countervailing duty laws and Section 337 of the 1930 Trade Act unfair trade practices statutes; and Trade Adjustment Assistance, a socially redistributive form of aid to workers displaced by imports. Once enacted, legislation changing the balance between liberalism and other sociopolitical interests acquires an institutional legitimacy and permanence that may outlive the original impetus for its enactment, although its implementation will vary over time according to the shifting ideological balance in US trade politics (Goldstein 1988).

Destler (1992) argues that Congress is willing to allow the President to take the lead in making trade policy so long as the White House is sufficiently responsive to domestic demands to keep pressure on Congress from constituents from becoming too great. When the President is seen as unwilling or inattentive to trade politics, Congress is prepared to intervene on behalf of constituents, thereby reducing the President's discretionary authority over trade policy. Enactment of Fast Track is the classic model of the

President–Congress trade policy relationship. Passage of the Super 301 market-opening provisions of the 1988 Trade Act, which required the President to name a list of countries that maintained barriers to US exports and then engage in market-opening negotiations with the threat of mandatory retaliation in the event of non-compliance, was the response of Congress to its perception that the Reagan Administration was not sufficiently responsive to domestic pressures for more open export markets for US goods and services, primarily in Japan. Similarly Bergsten (2002) explains the Bush countervailing duties on steel imports in 2001 and passage of renewal of Fast Track (Trade Promotion Authority) in 2002 by arguing that the White House must make protectionist concessions to domestic interests to secure Congressional support for Trade Promotion Authority. According to Bergsten, historically the protection is usually modest and temporary, whilst the liberalization it permits is usually more institutionalized and durable.

Trade policy under Clinton: trade policy as growth strategy

The Clinton Administration responded to the post-Cold-War reintegration of a labour market of over 1 billion people into the neoliberal global economy by constructing a trade policy geared to opening new markets and expanding existing markets for US exports in industries that were creating jobs for the US workforce. The incoming Clinton team understood that economic and security policy were converging: US national security strategy would have to be recast in such a way as to place economic security and opportunities for US workers at its core (Clinton 1996; Berger 1993; Christopher 1993; Cox 1995). In contrast with the Cold War regime of export controls on sensitive technologies, defence was now as much about creating and maintaining jobs for Americans at home as about protecting the territory and resources of the USA and its citizens against attack.

In turn, guaranteeing jobs at home more than ever required a trade policy focused on assuring access to stable, growing markets for US goods, services, capital and knowledge on a global scale. Creation of well-paying jobs in industrial sectors in which the USA excelled, such as aerospace, telecommunications, food products, entertainment and automobiles, were all linked to exports, and export-related jobs paid better on average than other jobs (Clinton 1996). The ability of US-based firms and workers to benefit from a stable, growing global economy in turn required the maintenance of peace and political stability over as much of the world as possible. Key security objectives falling under this rubric included maintaining the trajectory of democratization, economic stabilization and transition to capitalism in Russia, denuclearization of the non-Russian post-Soviet states, and managing the relationship with China. The Administration's early decision to decouple its stance on the annual renewal of China's MFN status from the contentious dialogue on human rights was indicative of the significance of economic objectives in the Clinton security strategy.

Clinton's trade strategy focused on increasing cooperation between the federal government and US-based firms in creating opportunities for US firms and US workers in areas of the world, both geographical and sectoral, where they were likely to yield the greatest gain in terms of exports, profits and domestic employment. This approach represented a real shift towards different target states and different methods of creating opportunities. Spearheaded by Commerce Secretary and Clinton confidante Ronald Brown, it was geared towards competition without confrontation. Unlike existing mature markets such as Japan and the European Union, the new target states and sectors represented new and growing markets in which every competitor could gain something.

The main targets of the new policy were the 'Big Emerging Markets' (BEMs), a group of ten middle-tier industrializing countries with large populations whose demand for US products could be expected to grow significantly (Brown 1995; Cox 1995: 34–36). The list of BEMs, which possess a large, growing population and a growing economy with an expanding middle class of consumers, included Mexico, Brazil, Argentina, India, Indonesia, South Korea, China (including the 'Chinese economic area' of China, Hong Kong, Taiwan and Singapore), South Africa, Poland and Turkey. The list transcended Cold War era categorizations, grouping newly industrializing countries with other developing states and former socialist economies in transition (Garten 1997: xiii–xiv).

Russia and Ukraine fell into a second category of target states under the new strategy. A policy of combining promotion of democratization and promotion of US exports and investments would focus on geopolitically significant potential markets most held back by past political instability and which could hold the greatest potential for US-based firms as the market grew. US-sponsored democratization efforts, which received nearly 13 per cent of the Administration's 1994 international affairs budget, would seek to create state institutions and political conditions in which markets could take root and eventually flourish and to which US-based firms could export.

Beyond Clinton's export promotion strategy lay a commitment to continuing US support for negotiated trade liberalization. The Reagan Administration had begun to pursue bilateral and regional trade liberalization initiatives with like-minded states that wished to liberalize more rapidly at a time when the future success of GATT multilateral trade liberalization appeared uncertain (US–Israel Free Trade Agreement 1985, Canada–US Trade Agreement 1988). The Clinton Administration showed promptly and conclusively that the two objectives were mutually compatible and even reinforcing. In November 1993 Clinton secured passage in the House of Representatives of the North American Free Trade Agreement (NAFTA), which expanded the Canada–US free trade zone to Mexico, with a cross-party coalition that overcame vigorous opposition led by economic nationalist and erstwhile presidential candidate Ross Perot. Immediately afterwards Clinton chaired a summit of the Asia–Pacific Economic Cooperation (APEC) forum at which APEC ministers agreed an ambitious programme of reduction of trade barriers around the Pacific Rim. The Administration used NAFTA and APEC progress effectively to bring pressure on the European Union and other major negotiating parties in the Uruguay Round to make key concessions needed to conclude the agreement in December 1993 (Cox 1995: 29–31). Ratified by Congress under Fast Track in 1994, the Treaty of Marrakech entered into force on 1 January 1995.

The second Clinton term saw the first term's trade policy initiatives bear fruit: strong economic growth led by vigorous expansion of US exports, particularly to the BEMs; political stabilization and development of functioning markets in transition economies; and agricultural and services trade liberalization and the coming into operation of the World Trade Organization. Closer economic ties that the Administration had built with Mexico and the Pacific Rim nations through NAFTA and APEC facilitated a strong US role in limiting damage from the financial crises that those areas suffered in 1994 and 1997 respectively. A Transatlantic Business Dialogue promoted public–private cooperation in managing US–EU trade conflicts.

However, new Clinton trade policy initiatives encountered partisan opposition from a now Republican-majority Congress and strengthened policy opposition from the left–right constellation of powers opposing trade liberalization. The Administration's efforts to convince Congress to renew Fast Track, most of which had expired in 1994, failed by 1998.

This forced the Administration to delay conclusion of a bilateral free trade agreement with Chile and talks on the Free Trade Area of the Americas (FTAA) initiative, which was intended to expand NAFTA into a hemispheric free trade zone by 2005. Administration support for a Multilateral Agreement on Investment (MAI) under the auspices of the Organization for Economic Cooperation and Development (OECD) was also frustrated when the text of the agreement, which would have established a multilateral code governing cross-border investment flows, was leaked to the public in 1998. Opponents of the MAI accused OECD member governments of negotiating, in secret and without public input, an agreement that in effect would have universalized the most business-friendly regime in the OECD by allowing companies and shareholders to sue governments that maintained barriers to investment designed, for example, to safeguard labour rights and the environment (Chomsky 1998).

In retrospect, Clinton trade policy can be seen in two important respects to be the victim of its own success. In boom times like the 1990s, opposition came less from the economic nationalist elements of the anti-trade liberalization coalition, whom the Administration effectively defeated in the debates on NAFTA and joining the WTO. Rather, the apparent achievements of the Clinton global economic policy empowered civil society opponents of the neoliberal version of globalization to increase their public pressure for the economic gains being reaped by managers and shareholders of global firms to be translated into greater safeguards for workers, better protection of the environment, and more transparency and participation in the policy process. The achievements also engendered partisan resentment that manifested itself in an exceptionally virulent attack on a sitting President, culminating in use of the impeachment provision of the US Constitution as a parliamentary no-confidence measure in the Monica Lewinsky affair. Given their animosity towards Clinton, Republicans in Congress were more sympathetic to lobbying by industries and labour adversely affected by NAFTA. This expanded those industries' influence in Congress beyond their core of generally Democratic defenders.

Trade policy under Bush: mitigating the bust and security crisis

George W. Bush assumed the presidency in a very different economic and political climate from that of his predecessor. Economic uncertainty created by the bursting of the technology bubble combined with political uncertainty caused by the disputed election contributed to a recession already well underway before the 11 September 2001 attacks on the World Trade Center and Pentagon. The return of the Senate to Democratic control in early 2001 portended a challenging legislative environment for enacting economic policy.

None the less, despite (or perhaps because of) the 2001 attacks and subsequent war on the Taliban in Afghanistan, the administration of Bush the Younger by the end of 2002 boasted a string of substantial trade policy accomplishments, several of which had eluded the Clinton Administration (see Table 21.1): renewal of Fast Track; initiation of the WTO Doha Round; completion of free trade agreement negotiations with Chile and Singapore; initiation of FTA negotiations with Morocco, Australia and the regional trade associations of the Southern African Customs Union (SACU) and the Caribbean Community (CARICOM); and renewal of the GATT Generalized System of Preferences (GSP) under which the poorest developing countries receive tariff preferences for exports to the USA (USTR 2003).

Table 21.1   Major US trade policy accomplishments, 1993–2003

Bill Clinton	George W. Bush
Signed NAFTA	Renewal of Fast Track/Trade Promotion Authority
APEC trade liberalization agreement	Launch of WTO Doha Round
Signed GATT Uruguay Round creating WTO	Negotiated FTAs with Chile and Singapore
Big Emerging Markets export strategy	Initiated FTA negotiations with Morocco, Australia, SACU and CARICOM
Transatlantic Business Dialogue	Renewed GSP

Of these, Fast Track and the Doha Round were the most important. The Bush Administration was able to convince Congress to renew Fast Track, which has been renamed Trade Promotion Authority (TPA), in July 2002, enabling US negotiators to negotiate a broad accord in the Doha Round. Renewal of Fast Track was a prerequisite for passing any major trade agreements. Passage in the House of Representatives was by a razor-thin 215–212 vote margin comprised of the usual bipartisan pro-trade coalition drawn from the centre of both parties. Securing passage of TPA required concessions on issues such as labour and environment. The Trade Act of 2002 included health insurance and job training benefits for US workers displaced by foreign competition (Allen and Blustein 2002; Mitchell 2002).

The WTO Doha Round, officially titled the 'Doha Development Agenda', can be understood as the point where the 'bicycle theory' ran into the 'clash of globalizations'. Bhagwati described the process of trade liberalization as being like a bicycle: if it is not pedalled forward continuously, it falls over (Bhagwati 1988: 41). Proponents of trade liberalization since the Second World War have preferred to have a multilateral trade round either about to be started, underway or being signed, as a way of holding opposing forces at bay. Many trade policy experts believed that this pattern might change once the WTO was created in 1995. The Uruguay Round chartered a big programme of further trade liberalization negotiations in various sectors, such as financial services and agriculture, to be carried out under the institutional auspices of the WTO. It was thought that a bigger secretariat with greater powers would be able to make liberalization an ongoing process that would render multilateral rounds less crucial or unnecessary. But by the late 1990s this new process was not yielding as much fruit as hoped. The bicycle seemed to be coming to a halt, so the USA, the EU and other major players decided to seek a new multilateral round.

The clash of globalizations refers to what the Clinton Administration encountered in the protests against the 1999 WTO Ministerial Conference in Seattle. Only a small fraction of the protesters at the Seattle and subsequent meetings of multilateral institutions genuinely oppose globalization per se. Most represent civil society interests favouring a different, democratic, more transparent version of globalization, with a more labour-friendly, greener economic policy mix less closely aligned with the particular interests of managements and shareholders of global firms. The Seattle protests prevented the WTO from launching a new multilateral round in December 1999. The Bush Administration, led by US Trade Representative Robert Zoellick, responded to critics of neoliberal globalization by agreeing an agenda for a new round that would focus on making trade more of an engine for economic development (Bergsten 2002).

We can also understand the Doha development focus as a product of the real redistribution of power in trade negotiations brought about by the Uruguay Round and furthered by the entry of China and Taiwan into the WTO. The WTO decision-making mechanism of one-state one-vote, with supermajorities required, which has replaced the old GATT system of *de facto* consensus decision making, has meant that the traditional dominant actors, such as the USA, the EU and Japan, now must build winning coalitions that include powerful developing countries (Ford 2002). Support for trade issues important to the USA has become more contingent upon US backing for the trade–development agenda of the countries that Clinton dubbed 'Big Emerging Markets'. This can be a win–win agenda for the USA, because the fastest growing US export markets have been the BEMs. Convincing them to play by global trading rules has been the best protection for US producers against competition from so-called unfair foreign trade practices such as counterfeiting, prison labour, dumping and illegal subsidies.

To this end, the USA has made some major negotiating proposals in the Doha Round, including moving the industrialized countries to zero import tariffs on manufactured goods. This is more complex than it appears, because the USA and EU, for example, have very different 'shapes' to their MFN and non-MFN tariff schedules. Many tariffs on industrial goods are already so low that it is a smaller step than it sounds initially. The logic is that by giving their developing countries' exports of manufactures greater opportunities to compete in industrial country markets it would encourage them to move up the production chain (Zoellick 2003). Integrating environment and labour provisions is also a top priority because in response to domestic political pressure Congress has directed the Administration to adopt the 'Jordan' model in all future trade agreements (Polaski 2002).

Progress with bilateral or regional free trade agreements represents the ongoing success of the second track of trade liberalization and the continuation of its complementarity with multilateral liberalization (Bergsten 2002). An FTA negotiated by the Clinton Administration with Jordan in 2000 was ratified by Congress. Negotiations between Chile and the USA for an FTA were revived and completed, and a deal with Singapore had also been contemplated, so once it was clear that momentum existed to renew Fast Track it facilitated the negotiations for the Chile and Singapore FTAs. Similar talks have now begun with Australia, Morocco and regional trading associations CARICOM in the Caribbean Basin and SACU in Southern Africa (Becker 2003).

Like their predecessors, trade officials in the Bush Administration have already faced their share of trade disputes. In summer 2001 they imposed anti-dumping duties of up to 30 per cent on steel imports from virtually every major steel-exporting country, arousing the ire of US trading partners ranging from Japan and Korea to Russia and Brazil. Although the steel industry in the USA is no longer pivotal to US economic fortunes, steel interests are influential in pivotal states for Bush's 2004 electoral prospects, such as Pennsylvania and Michigan. Steel anti-dumping duties can be understood according to Bergsten's theory as a temporary protectionist concession by the Administration for subsequent renewal of Fast

Track or, following Destler, as easing constituent pressures on Members of Congress, thereby ensuring continued Congressional delegation of trade policy-making authority to the White House (Bergsten 2002; Destler 1992; Allen and Pearlstein 2002).

Two significant US–EU trade disputes that began in the late 1990s continued: an EU complaint that US 'Foreign Sales Corporations' conferred an unfair tax advantage on US firms, and a US complaint that an EU ban on imports of hormone-treated beef was GATT-illegal. Both sides were continuing measures to resolve the conflicts within the WTO dispute resolution framework rather than rejecting WTO disciplines, and despite the disagreements US–EU trade relations in early 2003 were on a good footing. Although the negative impact of the Anglo-American invasion of Iraq in March 2003 on US–European relations increased uncertainty about the future of the trading relationship, both sides acknowledged the structural importance of the degree of interdependence between the two economic areas. At a joint press conference with EU Trade Commissioner Pascal Lamy on 3 March 2003, US Trade Representative Zoellick said the USA and EU are 'joined at the hip economically', pointing out that bilateral US–EU trade amounts to $770 million per year, with bilateral FDI flows at $1.5 billion per year and 4 million people from each polity working in the other's economy (Zoellick and Lamy 2003).

Conclusion: looking ahead

The most serious challenge for the ongoing agenda of promoting job and export growth by stimulating global demand for US goods and services is the return of the security discourse to dominate foreign policy. This complex social–political process of redefining and redrawing boundaries has resulted in a shift from a post-Cold War dynamic of removing barriers to trade at borders to a 'Homeland Security' dynamic in which barriers are being restored or initiated, at least selectively. The Administration is having to revisit Cold War era trade issues such as border controls and export controls on military hardware and dual-use technologies. Export controls streamlined dramatically after the Cold War are likely to make a significant revival in the context of potential 'terrorist' states and various types of technologies. Cyber-warfare and cyber-terrorism are major items on the 'Homeland Security' agenda. The increased use of trade sanctions to discourage further proliferation of weapons of mass destruction is also likely. Strengthening of border controls poses a potentially large risk to cross-border trade. Lorry traffic crossing into the USA from Canada, which accounts for a huge portion of total US trade volume, has been disrupted massively since 11 September 2001, and projects are underway to screen cargoes of ships prior to unloading in US ports. All these actions can raise the cost of imports, impose delays and constitute real barriers to trade that could potentially be WTO-actionable. Over time, better technology will reduce disruption to trade flows from increased security screening. At the same time a technology race is likely to continue between the US government and groups seeking to smuggle banned items into US territory, disrupting trade flows regularly.

A greater systemic impact upon trade policy may be felt in the negative global reaction to the Bush foreign policy doctrine of unilateral pre-emptive intervention in sovereign states in the pursuit of US security objectives. Worldwide fears about the US commitment to multilateralism in global governance have been heightened by the Administration's view that a second United Nations Security Council resolution was not required to authorize the invasion of Iraq and removal of its government. This could make the US objective of obtaining concessions in the Doha Round difficult to achieve. Two US-led military conflicts in two years have distracted governments and negotiators from trade issues, even as fears of additional wars and heightened war risk premiums are slowing global economic growth, in turn depressing trade flows. Poor domestic economic performance also hampers trade liberalization objectives by increasing pressures on Congress for protection from industries adversely affected by imports.

Administration supporters argue that negative repercussions for trade resulting from the dominance of the security discourse should be mitigated by a heightened global perception of US power that should encourage other countries to make US-sought concessions. Bringing Russia into the WTO is seen as important to resuming what had been a burgeoning US–Russia security-driven alliance between September 2001 and the UN Iraq debates of February 2003. Conclusion of an agreement in the Doha Round by 2005 could stimulate the global economy. Both Bergsten and Destler would argue that the Administration has taken the requisite steps (at least thus far) to maximize the prospects for Congressional ratification of a Doha agreement. Bergsten sees the concessions made to Congress by the Bush Administration to secure passage of TPA as a major accomplishment that could be a big net winner in the Doha process. Goldstein, however, might identify the recent achievements of labour and environmental interests in advancing their social objectives against liberal trade orthodoxy as indicating a new incremental shift in the balance between liberal trade and other sociopolitical interests. Overall, the basic dynamic in making trade policy between the White House and Congress referred to by all the theorists has persisted despite structural change in the global economy and geopolitics, reinforcing the expectation for greater continuity than change in process and outcome.

Bibliography

Allen, M. and Blustein, P. (2002) 'President signs bill on trade authority', *Washington Post* 7 August: A6.

Allen, M. and Pearlstein, S. (2002) 'Bush settles on tariff for steel imports', *Washington Post* 5 March: A1.

Becker, E. (2003) 'US begins talks for trade pact with Central Americans', *New York Times* 8 January.

Berger, S. (1993) Remarks by National Security Adviser at press briefing, 14 December.

Bergsten, C.F. (2002) 'A renaissance for US trade policy?', *Foreign Affairs* 81 (November/December): 86–98.

Bhagwati, J. (1988) *Protectionism*, Cambridge, MA: MIT Press.

Brown, R.H. (1995) 'BEMs message from commerce secretary Ronald H. Brown', US Department of Commerce.

Chomsky, N. (1998) 'Domestic constituencies', *Z Magazine* May.

Christopher, W. (1993) 'World security requires strong economies', Testimony to Senate Foreign Relations Committee, 4 November.

Clinton, B. (1996) *Between Hope and History*, New York: Random House.

Cox, M. (1995) *US Foreign Policy Since the Cold War*, London: Royal Institute of International Affairs.

Destler, I.M. (1992) *American Trade Politics*, 2nd edn, Washington, DC: Institute for International Economics and the Twentieth Century Fund.

Drake, W.J. and Nicolaidis, K. (1992) 'Ideas, interests and institutionalization: "trade in services" and the Uruguay Round', *International Organization* 46: 37–100.

Ford, J. (2002) 'A social theory of trade regime change: GATT to WTO', *International Studies Review* 4: 115–138.

Garten, J.E. (1997) *The Big Ten*, New York: Basic Books.

Gilpin, R. (2002) 'The rise of American hegemony', in P.K. O'Brien and A. Clesse (eds), *Two Hegemonies*, Aldershot: Ashgate.

Goldstein, J. (1988) 'Ideas, institutions, and American trade policy', *International Organization* 42: 179–217; reprinted in J.A. Frieden and D.A. Lake (eds) (1995) *International Political Economy*, 3rd edn, London and New York: Routledge.

Lake, D.A. (1988) *Power, Protection and Free Trade*, Ithaca, NY: Cornell University Press.

Mitchell, A. (2002) 'Bush hails vote in House backing trade legislation', *New York Times* 27 July: A1.

Polaski, S. (2002) 'US trade policy after Fast Track: the coming choice on global trade and labour rights', Carnegie Endowment for International Peace, Issue Brief, 9 August.

Robinson, W. (1996) *Promoting Polyarchy*, Cambridge: Cambridge University Press.

USTR (2003) 'Ambitious trade agenda outlined in annual report submitted to Congress by Bush Administration', Press release, 3 March. Available HTTP: <http://www.ustr.gov/releases/2003/03/03-11.pdf> (accessed 6 June 2003).

Webb, M.C. and Krasner, S.D. (1989) 'Hegemonic stability theory: an empirical assessment', *Review of International Studies* 15: 183–198.

Zoellick, R.B. (2003) 'US Trade Representative Robert B. Zoellick press conference following the WTO informal ministerial meeting', Tokyo, 16 February. Available HTTP: <http://www.ustr.gov/releases/2003/02/2003-02-16-pc-tokyo.PDF> (accessed 28 July 2003).

Zoellick, R.B. and Lamy, P. (2003) US Trade Representative Robert B. Zoellick and EU Trade Commissioner Pascal Lamy press conference, Washington, 3 March. Available HTTP: <http://www.ustr.gov/releases/2003/03/2003-03-03-pc-lamyDC.PDF> (accessed 6 June 2003).

Key readings

Bergsten, C.F. (2002) 'A renaissance for US trade policy?', *Foreign Affairs* 81 (November/December): 86–98.

Bhagwati, J. (1988) *Protectionism*, Cambridge, MA: MIT Press.

Destler, I.M. (1992) *American Trade Politics*, 2nd edn, Washington, DC: Institute for International Economics and the Twentieth Century Fund.

Ford, J. (2002) 'A social theory of trade regime change: GATT to WTO', *International Studies Review* 4: 115–138.

Garten, J.E. (1997) *The Big Ten*, New York: Basic Books.

Goldstein, J. (1988) 'Ideas, institutions, and American trade policy', *International Organization* 42: 179–217; reprinted in J.A. Frieden and D.A. Lake (eds) (1995) *International Political Economy*, 3rd edn, London and New York: Routledge.

Lake, D.A. (1988) *Power, Protection and Free Trade*, Ithaca, NY: Cornell University Press.

Useful websites

www.ustr.gov (Office of the United States Trade Representative).
www.doc.gov (United States Department of Commerce).
www.usitc.gov (United States International Trade Commission).

Index